❖ THE WARS OF THE ROSES ❖

THE WARS OF
✣ THE ROSES ✣

MICHAEL HICKS

YALE UNIVERSITY PRESS
NEW HAVEN AND LONDON

For information about this and other Yale University Press publications, please contact:
U.S. Office: sales.press@yale.edu   www.yalebooks.com
Europe Office: sales @yaleup.co.uk   www.yaleup.co.uk

Set in Minion Pro by IDSUK (DataConnection) Ltd
Printed in Great Britain by TJ International Ltd, Padstow, Cornwall

Library of Congress Cataloging-in-Publication Data

Hicks, M. A.
   The Wars of the Roses / Michael Hicks.
      p. cm.
   Includes bibliographical references and index.
   ISBN 978-0-300-11423-2 (cl:alk. paper)
   1. Great Britain—History—Wars of the Roses, 1455–1485. 2. Great
Britain—History—Lancaster and York, 1399–1485. I. Title.
   DA250.H548 2010
   942.04—dc22

                                                              2010015475

A catalogue record for this book is available from the British Library.

10 9 8 7 6 5 4 3 2 1

Contents

ILLUSTRATIONS

Pedigrees

Map

PREFACE

Everyone has heard of the Wars of the Roses. However, they are no longer the standard part of school education that they were for W.C. Sellar and R.J. Yeatman, authors of *1066 and All That* (1930), and that they were for myself, whether encountered in history lessons or via the medium of Shakespeare's History Plays. All history of course offers political and psychological parallels and contrasts. Its study develops skills that are transferable to many other contexts. But why do these particular wars matter? A tale of internecine strife five centuries old sounds dead and redundant. Is this not exactly the sort of history that was dubbed irrelevant by a British prime minister trained as a modern historian, Gordon Brown? But all history, however distant and apparently forgotten, has a habit of becoming suddenly relevant and even topical. This has happened several times to the Wars of the Roses whilst I have been writing this book.

History must be studied at primary school, declared Ed Balls, then Secretary of State for Education, citing in particular the Romans and the Wars of the Roses. The peace dividend and knife-crime are themes that resonate in the fifteenth century. Just as I was writing about the fifteenth-century credit crunch, I found that I was living through one. My building-society interest and my shares have gone the way of the Welsh rents of Richard, Duke of York, Humphrey, Duke of Buckingham, and Warwick the Kingmaker. The *Great Slump* was a fifteenth-century credit crunch. Gordon Brown's aspirations for the premiership and then the machinations of his rivals in the spring of 2009 recall the ambitions of the dynastic rivals of the Wars of the Roses – not least those of York, Warwick the Kingmaker and Richard III, who, like today's contenders, convinced themselves (and sought to convince others) that their candidacies best served the public interest and commonweal. Suddenly the press, written, aural and televisual, was full of quotations about power politics taken from Shakespeare – from *Julius Caesar, Hamlet, Macbeth* and even *Richard III*. The leader of the Liberal Democrats denied any intention to be a Kingmaker. I have found so much in common between the MPs' expenses scandal of 2009–10 and fifteenth-century denunciations of the covetousness of contemporary councillors, not least the difficulty for the public in allowing any scope for the legitimate exercise of patronage and for proper remuneration of those in government. If Michael Martin was indeed the first Speaker of the House of Commons forced out of office since Sir John Trevor in 1695, so too was Thomas Thorpe in 1454. Just as I finish this book, finally, the quincentenary of the heir to both the rival roses, red and white, is splashed across my television screen. Henry VIII is celebrated in print, in a television series and in lavish exhibitions at Hampton Court and elsewhere, whilst the historian Clifford Davies intriguingly questions whether there was a 'Tudor Dynasty' at all. Inevitably these immediate parallels, contrasts and issues will recede from public consciousness, but others, in due course, will revive.

For five centuries all the English accepted the Tudor view of the Wars of Roses. William Shakespeare taught us that they were dynastic wars, fought between royal houses – the rival roses – for the Crown, and that the Wars were finally won in 1485 at the Battle of Bosworth by the first Tudor king, Henry VII. The Tudors declared them to be an unmitigated disaster, any repetition of which must be avoided at all costs, even at the price of tolerating tyranny. As their interpretation has faded and lost its force, we have been left with a conglomeration of confusing strife, one event after another and kaleidoscopic reversals of fortune, fought by a vast cast of characters who repeatedly changed their names, each with his (almost always his) distinct and short-term motives. The explosion in research since the Second World War that has been undertaken by academic historians, military historians, supporters of Richard III (Ricardians) and so many others has added enormously to our knowledge of people, events, sources and much else. We know vastly more about the various battles and about anything and anyone connected with Richard III. This book is enormously in all their debt. Yet all these endeavours have revealed little as to what the Wars were about or meant. Many textbooks on Late Medieval England have been written by the best academic historians and survey what happened, and yet they still do not explain the Wars. A noble exception is Professor Christine Carpenter, who sought to move beyond the short-term accounts of patronage and self-interest to the constitutional issues that were at stake.

This book is different. It seeks to make sense of it all. Inevitably it has to retell the story. It aims quite simply to explain why the Wars happened, why they kept recurring, and why they ceased. It focuses on the combination of problems that underlay all the Wars, which made it difficult for any king to rule effectively, and which no king could satisfactorily solve.

Chapters 1–4 set the scene: they set out what the Wars were, how they have been explained in the past, the political system of the time, and the massive *Crisis of 1450* that established Richard, Duke of York, as the leader of a popular programme of reform opposed to what was presented as the king's corrupt and incompetent councillors and household.

Chapters 5–9 trace the series of frictions and political experiments that erupted into the *First War* of 1459–61.

Chapters 10–13 treat the recurrences of the Wars: the Lancastrian failures of the 1460s, the *Second War* of 1469–71, and the *Third War*, from 1483.

Chapters 14 and 15 explain why the Wars ceased.

The Wars of the Roses are revealed as a distinct era of English history of real importance and well-worth studying.

For forty years I have been adding to my knowledge and understanding of the topic, taking on the discoveries and insights of many other historians, and this has undoubtedly changed, developed and refined my perspective. Constantly revisiting the same topics from different points of view has enriched my perception and, I hope, that of my readers. A full appreciation of the Wars of the Roses is a collaborative project involving many participants who certainly do not all agree – and who will not all agree on my version of events. It is not possible to credit all these contributors individually, but I hope that the bibliography will indicate what underlies this book and who has influenced me most. First of all there is my wife Cynthia, without whom the book could not have been written at all and to whom I dedicate it. Any defects are of course my own.

One area of potential confusion is the state system of northern Europe. Apart from England (including Wales and Ireland) and Scotland, then separate kingdoms, and France, there was a powerful state called Burgundy that no longer exists. Apart from the wine-producing province of Burgundy now in France, it included the modern Netherlands, Belgium and the provinces of Artois and Picardy in north-west France. This was the most industrialized area of northern Europe, the most urbanized – with the great towns of Antwerp, Bruges and Ghent – and thickly populated, and hence the most wealthy. Its rulers, the Valois and Habsburg dukes of Burgundy, the great dukes of the west, commanded impressive resources and carried considerable clout in international affairs. The Wars of the Roses coincided with the struggles of Burgundy and France.

All quotations from whatever language have been rendered into modern English and all places of publication are in London unless otherwise stated. Articles by Ralph Griffiths, Jack Lander, Tony Pollard, J.S. Roskell and Roger Virgoe, to whom I am particularly indebted, and by myself, are quoted wherever possible from their collected essays.

Michael Hicks
Winchester 2009

CHRONOLOGICAL TABLE OF PRINCIPAL EVENTS

1327–77		Reign of Edward III. Father of Lionel, Duke of Clarence, John of Gaunt, Duke of Lancaster, and Edmund, Duke of York, who were the ancestors of the two Houses of Lancaster and York
1399		Deposition of Richard II Revolution of 1399
1399–1461		Reign of the three Lancastrian kings Henry IV, Henry V and Henry VI
1399–1413		Reign of Henry IV
1413–22		Reign of Henry V
1415		Southampton Plot. Execution of Richard, Earl of Cambridge, father of Richard, Duke of York Battle of Agincourt. Henry defeats the French
1420		Treaty of Troyes Charles VI of France recognizes Henry V as his heir Henry V marries Katherine of France
1422–61		Reign of Henry VI, King of England and France
1444		Treaty of Tours with Charles VII of France. Start of five years of truces.
1445		Marriage of Henry VI and Margaret of Anjou
1447		Death of the king's uncle Humphrey, Duke of Gloucester, at Bury St Edmunds on the eve of his projected trial
1449		English attack on Fougères breaks truce French invasion of Normandy Impeachment and arrest of Duke of Suffolk
1450	 June	Exile and murder of Duke of Suffolk Rebellion of Jack Cade Loss of Normandy Edmund Beaufort, Duke of Somerset, defeated

		commander in France, returns to England and becomes Henry VI's prime favourite
	October	Return of Richard, Duke of York from Ireland
		Call for reform in Parliament
1451	June	Fall of Bordeaux and Gascony
1452	February–March	York's failed Dartford *coup d'état*
		York swears never to rebel again (take the way of fait)
1453		Reading Parliament crowns Henry VI's recovery
	17 July	Final defeat of English in France at Castillon
	August	Henry VI becomes insane
	13 October	Birth of Prince Edward of Lancaster
	November	Recall of York to royal council
		Charges of treason against Somerset, who is imprisoned in the Tower
1454	27 March	York's *First Protectorate*
1455	9 February	Henry VI recovers sanity: end of York's protectorate
	22 May	First Battle of St Albans: Yorkist victory. Deaths of Somerset and Northumberland
		Yorkists take control of government
	19 November	York's *Second Protectorate*
1456	25 February	Henry VI resumes control
		Richard, Earl of Warwick, becomes Captain of Calais
1456–60		Margaret of Anjou supposedly rules from the Midlands
1458	25 March	*Loveday at St Paul's*
1459–61		*The First War*
1459		Yorkist uprising
	23 September	Battle of Blore Heath. Yorkist victory
	13 October	Battle of Ludford. Yorkists flee abroad: York to Ireland, Salisbury and Warwick to Calais
		Coventry Parliament. Attainder of Yorkists
1460	26 June	Warwick invades Kent. He enters London
	10 July	Battle of Northampton. Yorkist victory: Henry VI captured
	October	York claims the throne
	November	*Accord*: York recognized as Henry VI's heir
	30 December	Battle of Wakefield: York, Salisbury and Rutland killed
1461	2–3 February	Battle of Mortimer's Cross
	17 February	Second Battle of St Albans, Warwick defeated
		Queen Margaret refused access to London
	4 March	Accession of Edward IV
	29 March	Battle of Towton: decisive Yorkist victory
1461–70		Edward IV's *First Reign*
1464	15 May	Battle of Hexham: destruction of Northumbrian Lancastrians
	September	Recognition of Elizabeth Wydeville as queen to Edward IV at Reading Abbey

1467		Dismissal of Archbishop Neville as chancellor
1469–71		*The Second War*
1469	11 July	Marriage of Warwick's daughter Isabel to George, Duke of Clarence
		Rebellion of Robin of Redesdale
	24 July	Battle of Edgecote: execution of Rivers, Pembroke and Devon
		Imprisonment of Edward IV by Warwick
	October	Release of Edward IV
	December	Reconciliation of Warwick and Clarence with Edward IV
1470	12 March	Lincolnshire Rebellion: battle of Empingham (Losecote Field)
	9 April	Warwick and Clarence flee to France
	22–25 July	Treaty of Angers: agreement of Warwick and Margaret of Anjou
	13 September	Warwick invades England: Edward IV flees to Low Countries
	6 October	Henry VI's *Second Reign:* his *Readeption*
1471	14 March	Return of Edward IV
	14 April	Battle of Barnet: death of Warwick
	4 May	Battle of Tewkesbury: death of Edward of Lancaster
	21 May	Death of Henry VI
1471–83		*Edward IV's Second Reign*
1478	February	Parliamentary trial and execution of Clarence
1482		Treaty of Arras between France and Burgundy
1483–		*The Third War*
1483	9 April	Death of Edward IV
	10 April	Accession of Edward V
	30 April	*First Coup* of Richard, Duke of Gloucester
	4 May	Gloucester becomes Lord Protector
	13 June	Gloucester's *Second Coup:* death of Hastings
	25–26 June	Deposition of Edward V: Gloucester becomes Richard III
	August	Probable death of the Princes in the Tower
	October	Buckingham's Rebellion
	25 December	English exiles vow allegiance to Henry Tudor at Rennes
1484	1 March	Richard III makes peace with Queen Elizabeth Wydeville
		Death of Richard's son Edward of Middleham
1485	7 August	Landing of Henry Tudor at Milford Haven
	22 August	Battle of Bosworth: death of Richard III and accession of Henry VII
1486	18 January	Marriage of Henry VII and Elizabeth of York
	April	Minor rebellions in Yorkshire and West Midlands
		Birth of Prince Arthur
1487		Coronation at Dublin of Lambert Simnel (who pretended to be Edward, Earl of Warwick) as Edward VI
	4 June	Landing of Simnel at Furness (Lancs.)

	16 June	Battle of Stoke: Tudor victory. Death of John, Earl of Lincoln
1489	28 April	Henry, Earl of Northumberland, killed by Yorkshire tax rebels
1491–7		Conspiracy of Perkin Warbeck
1495		De Facto Act
	3 July	Landing at Deal. Warbeck defeated
1496	22–24 September	Scottish invasion of Northumberland
1497	17 June 7 September 19 September	Cornish Rebellion defeated at Blackheath Warbeck lands near Land's End Warbeck deserts rebels at Taunton
1499	November	Execution of Warbeck and Edward, Earl of Warwick
1502		Death of Prince Arthur
1503		Death of Elizabeth of York
1506		Extradition of Edmund, Earl of Suffolk
1509		Death of Henry VII. Accession of Henry VIII Death of Margaret Beaufort Execution of Empson and Dudley
1509–47		Reign of Henry VIII
1513		Execution of Edmund, Earl of Suffolk
1521		Execution of Edward, Duke of Buckingham
1525		Death of Richard de la Pole (the White Rose of York) at Pavia
1539		Death of William de la Pole in the Tower
1541		Execution of Clarence's daughter Margaret, Countess of Salisbury

Pedigree 1 Kings of England 1377–1547

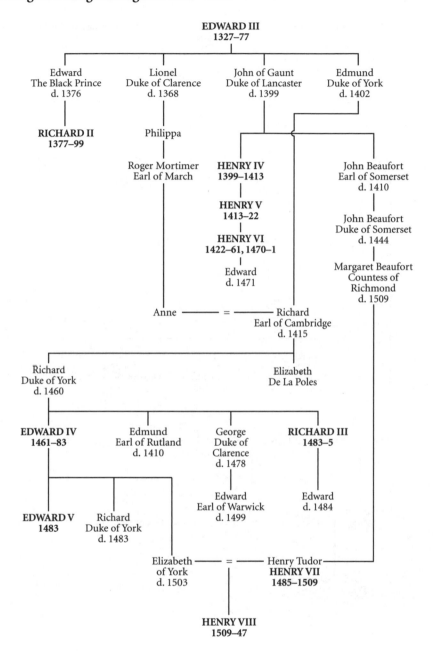

Pedigree 2 The House of Lancaster in the Early Fifteenth Century

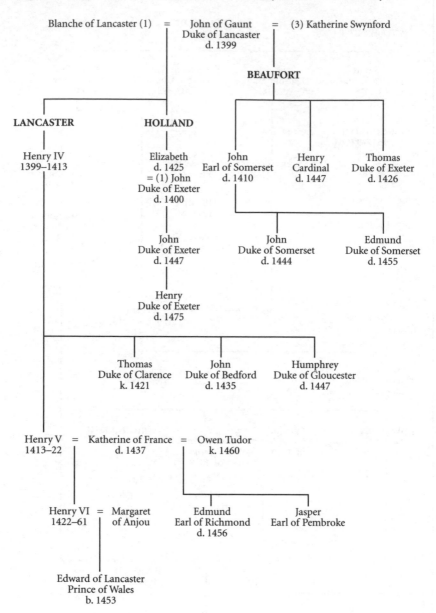

Blanche of Lancaster (1) = John of Gaunt = (3) Katherine Swynford
Duke of Lancaster
d. 1399

BEAUFORT

LANCASTER   **HOLLAND**

Henry IV   Elizabeth   John   Henry   Thomas
1399–1413   d. 1425   Earl of Somerset Cardinal   Duke of Exeter
                      = (1) John   d. 1410   d. 1447   d. 1426
                      Duke of Exeter
                      d. 1400

                      John   John   Edmund
                      Duke of Exeter   Duke of Somerset Duke of Somerset
                      d. 1447   d. 1444   d. 1455

                      Henry
                      Duke of Exeter
                      d. 1475

            Thomas   John   Humphrey
            Duke of Clarence Duke of Bedford   Duke of Gloucester
            k. 1421   d. 1435   d. 1447

Henry V = Katherine of France = Owen Tudor
1413–22   d. 1437   k. 1460

Henry VI = Margaret   Edmund   Jasper
1422–61   of Anjou   Earl of Richmond Earl of Pembroke
                         d. 1456

Edward of Lancaster
Prince of Wales
b. 1453

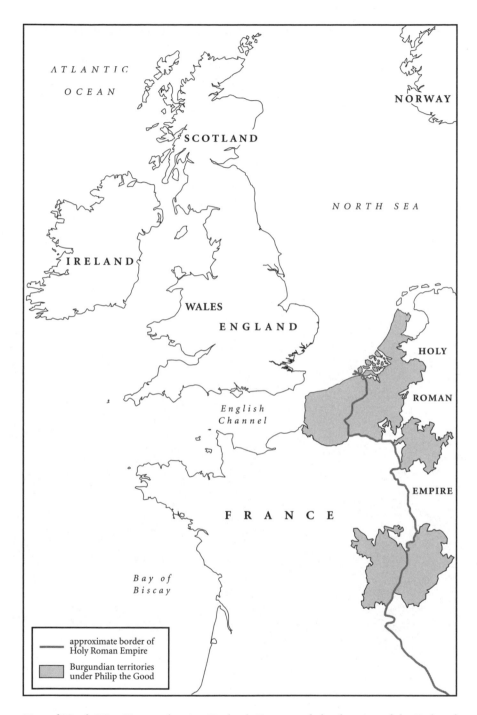

Map of North-West Europe showing England, France, and the domains of the Duke of Burgundy.

PART I

UNDERSTANDING THE WARS OF THE ROSES

CHAPTER 1

WHAT WERE THE
WARS OF THE ROSES?

This book explains the civil wars that beset England roughly between 1450 and 1509, known as the Wars of the Roses. The Wars of the Roses are actually the longest period of civil war in England's post-conquest history. They are much longer and also much more complex than either the Anarchy of King Stephen's reign (1135–54) or the English Civil War (1642–51) that are the principal parallels in English history.

There is a great deal to explain, for never before and never again after the Wars of the Roses was the government of England to be so insecure. There were three regional revolts, in 1450, 1489 and 1497; a host of private feuds, murders, ambushes, skirmishes and sieges; thirteen full-scale battles, including four in 1461, 1471, 1485 and 1487 that were decisive; at least ten *coups d'état* and attempted coups; fifteen invasions, including the four in 1460, 1470, 1471 and 1485 that succeeded; five usurpations, in 1461, 1470, 1471, 1483 and 1485; five kings – Henry VI, Edward IV, Edward V, Richard III and Henry VII – the first two of whom actually reigned twice; seven reigns; and five changes of dynasty, in 1461, 1470, 1471, 1483 and 1485.

Yet this was not a 'frenetic and purposeless' collection of events, as Professor Carpenter dubbed it.[1] The next section groups these events in order and makes some sense of them. Further reference is available in the Chronological Table of Events and the family trees, or List of Pedigrees.

THE COURSE OF THE WARS OF THE ROSES

The Wars commenced in the reign of King Henry VI (1422–61), the third of three kings of the House of Lancaster since 1399. His father Henry V

(1413–22) was designated as successor to Charles VI of France (1380–1422), and so Henry VI was also the only king of England really to have reigned also as king of France. In 1445 Henry VI married Margaret of Anjou, a French princess, daughter of René I of Naples, Duke of Anjou. It was during Henry VI's reign, in 1449–53, that the English lost the Hundred Years War and all their French territories except Calais. These defeats contributed to the series of domestic disturbances, beginning with the *Crisis of 1450* and culminating in the *First War* in 1459. The *Crisis* began with the impeachment in January 1450 and murder of William, Duke of Suffolk, the king's principal adviser, the murder of Bishops Aiscough and Moleyns, and Jack Cade's Rebellion in Kent and Sussex in May. It ended with the emergence in the autumn of Richard, Duke of York, as principal critic of the regime, rival of the king's favourite Edmund Beaufort, Duke of Somerset, and leader of a programme of reform that he repeatedly sought to force on the king throughout the 1450s. Although rebuffed in 1450, York tried unsuccessfully to seize power in 1452 (the Dartford episode). After Henry VI lapsed into madness in August 1453, York became Lord Protector and figurehead of the regime (York's *First Protectorate*, 1454–5), but was superseded on Henry's recovery early in 1455. With his Neville allies the Earls of Salisbury and Warwick, York attacked the royal court at the First Battle of St Albans (22 May 1455), resumed control of the government, and was briefly Protector again until relieved of office early in 1456. A major attempt at reconciliation was made in March 1458, the *Loveday at St Paul's*, but failed. Instead York and the Nevilles tried to seize power again in 1459, thus instigating the *First War* (1459–61).

The *First War* began when Salisbury fought the royalist Lord Audley at Blore Heath in Staffordshire (23 September 1459). Forced on the defensive by Henry VI at Ludford in Shropshire (13 October), York fled to Ireland, Salisbury and Warwick to Calais. Although condemned as traitors by Parliament, Warwick and Salisbury invaded Kent in June 1460, defeated and captured the king at the Battle of Northampton (10 July) and York laid claim to the throne. Even his own supporters objected to him succeeding at once. The *Accord* kept Henry VI as king, but substituted York as his heir in place of Prince Edward of Lancaster and also gave him control of the government. This settlement was unacceptable to many, especially Henry VI's queen Margaret of Anjou. York was obliged to go northwards to enforce his rule, but was defeated and killed, along with Salisbury, at the Battle of Wakefield (30 December 1460). Queen Margaret and her troops marched southwards, defeated Warwick at the Second Battle of St Albans (17 February 1461), but failed to take London. Meanwhile, York's son

Edward had defeated the Welsh Lancastrians at Mortimer's Cross (2–3 February), met up with Warwick, proclaimed himself King Edward IV (4 March), and annihilated the Lancastrian army at the Battle of Towton near York (29 March). The Lancastrian King Henry VI had lost his throne and was replaced by the Yorkist King Edward IV (1461–83).

King Edward in turn reigned for the rest of the decade (his *First Reign*, 1461–70) before conflict resumed. The second phase or *Second War* (1469–71), resulted from a rift within the Yorkist regime that made his former ally Warwick the Kingmaker into his principal foe. Edward's ill-advised marriage to the widow Elizabeth Grey (née Wydeville) was a root cause. Along with his son-in-law George, Duke of Clarence (d. 1478), Warwick rebelled in 1469, defeated and eliminated Edward's new favourites at Edgecote (24 July 1469), imprisoned the king and took control of the government. When this broke down in the autumn of 1469, Edward came to terms with Warwick and Clarence, who early in 1470 raised a rebellion in Lincolnshire, this time to make Clarence king. Following the defeat of the Lincolnshiremen at Empingham (Losecote Field, 12 March 1470), Warwick and Clarence fled to France, where they agreed with Queen Margaret of Anjou to restore Henry VI as king. Warwick's other, younger daughter Anne was married to Henry VI's heir Prince Edward. Clarence now became the next heir. The combined invasion was entirely successful: Edward IV fled in September 1470 to the Low Countries and Henry VI reigned again for six months from 6 October (his *Readeption*). Edward was backed by his brother-in-law Charles, Duke of Burgundy, and invaded England on 14 March 1471. Landing first in Yorkshire and proceeding southwards, Edward took London and defeated first Warwick at the Battle of Barnet (14 April) and the Lancastrians at the Battle of Tewkesbury (4 May). Henry VI, his son Edward and Warwick all perished; only Henry's half-brother Jasper Tudor, Earl of Pembroke, and nephew Henry Tudor escaped abroad.

Edward IV's *Second Reign* (1471–83) was much more successful. Following the natural death twelve years later of Edward IV in 1483 and the automatic accession of his young son Edward V (1483), the third phase of the conflict (*The Third War*, from 1483) resulted from the self-conscious decision of the young king's uncle, Richard, Duke of Gloucester, to take the throne as King Richard III (1483–5). First, Gloucester ousted the queen's family (the Wydevilles) and then Edward IV's most trusted retainer William, Lord Hastings. Once king, however, Richard found he had numerous enemies determined to rid themselves of him. Although able to defeat a first rebellion in autumn 1483 (Buckingham's

Rebellion), Buckingham himself being executed, Richard was confronted by a large body of Yorkist exiles first in the duchy of Brittany and then in the kingdom of France who backed Henry Tudor. A largely French and Scottish army invaded England, defeated Richard at Bosworth (22 August), and made Henry Tudor into Henry VII (1485–1509), the first Tudor king. He married Edward IV's eldest daughter Elizabeth of York in 1486 and fathered the Tudor dynasty.

Yet this was not the end. A stream of Yorkist claimants continued to threaten the new dynasty in the 1480s, 1490s and even perhaps until 1525, the date of the death of the last serious contender, Richard de la Pole. As late as 1541, Henry VIII imagined Clarence's daughter Margaret, Countess of Salisbury, to be a threat to his throne: like his wives, she too was executed.

Clearly 1485 was not the terminus of the conflict, as Tudor propagandists claimed at once and repeatedly. It is arguable precisely when the Wars can be said to have finally petered out.

The Case for the Wars of the Roses

This book, therefore, discusses at least three Wars that were fought over different issues by an evolving cast list. Most of those who fought in the first two Wars had died by 1485. They were thus unaware that they were part of something called the Wars of the Roses. They had no idea how long into the future the dissension was to last until it had actually ceased. It was not even obvious when it had ceased. Not until 1485 was it realized that the Wars were a distinct period in history that had commenced, continued and now – it was hoped – had passed.[2] It was much later, in 1829, that Sir Walter Scott invented the collective title. In the process he lumped together all the civil strife that characterized the second half of the fifteenth century and attributed it to the dynastic rivalry of Lancaster and York.[3]

Looking back over half a millennium, it is convenient for us today to view the age as a whole and to explain it through that single acquisitive motive – the ambition to be king – of the principal participants. This perception dates back to Polydore Vergil, the official historian of Henry VII.[4]

However, the Wars had begun very differently in 1450, as a call for reform that only became dynastic in 1460 and that appeared to be over in 1461. William Caxton, England's first printer, typified a whole series of historians who ended their chronicles with Edward's accession in 1461 and looked ahead to the permanent return of peace. They believed that 1461 signalled not merely the end of the first phase or a pause in ongoing strife, but the end of civil war altogether. The *First War* would be the only War. At the end of his *Chronicles* Caxton was to pray to God 'to save & keep him [Edward IV]', to enable him to reign in accordance with God's will to the benefit of all his subjects, and to campaign against the Turks and heathen men.[5] Caxton was no prophet. No crusade happened and Edward was to be supplanted by Henry VI. Under the year 1470 the Second Anonymous Crowland Continuator (henceforth Crowland), a senior civil servant and the best historian of the time, wrote that:

> You might have come across innumerable folk to whom the restoration of the pious King Henry was a miracle and the transformation the work of the right hand of the All Highest; but [he goes on] how incomprehensible are the judgements of God, how unfathomable his ways: for it is well-known that less than six months later no-one dared admit to having been in his counsels.[6]

They, too, were mistaken. Crowland was amongst those who rejoiced when Edward IV returned victorious in 1471. Following the king's death in 1483, he looked forward hopefully to the reign of Edward V and had high expectations of Richard, Duke of Gloucester, as Lord Protector. Once Richard had apparently triumphed, in the spring of 1484, even his most bitter rival Elizabeth Wydeville, queen-dowager of Edward IV and queen mother to Edward V, felt obliged to make her peace with him. Again, in 1485, Crowland applauded Henry VII's decisive victory that had brought the Wars to an end.[7]

In 1461, therefore, and again in 1470, 1471, 1484 and 1485, most people surely believed that the conflict was over. Two chroniclers of the 1470s who looked back across thirty years saw the whole cycle in terms of reform, not of dynastic rivalry.[8] Nobody before 1483 could have predicted the eventual result nor could they have viewed it as a whole in the way that the Tudors were to do and their successors have done.

Yet it is not wholly anachronistic or unhistorical to talk of the Wars of the Roses or to identify Bosworth as a decisive moment. When Crowland sat down in November 1485 to continue an existing chronicle from 1470 to his own day, he chose to start in 1459 'so that it might be clear from the beginning how the kingdom of England was agitated by many warlike incursions before the calamitous incursion of the northerners' of Queen Margaret of Anjou in 1461. Already Crowland believed that the Battle of Bosworth had ended the civil wars of the fifteenth century and had ushered in an era of hope and peace. Bosworth was the decisive victory by Henry Tudor over Richard III. Bosworth was the end of the Wars that Crowland had lived through: 'and so ends the history', he wrote less than three months after the battle, in November 1485. 'Out of this warfare came peace for the whole kingdom.' The new king, he reports, 'had shown clemency to all' and thus 'began to receive praise from everyone [including himself] as though he was an angel sent from heaven through whom God deigned to visit his people and to free them from the evils which had hitherto afflicted them beyond measure'.[9] He did not notice the irony that he had written much the same of Henry VI in 1470!

Of course, it was not quite the end. There was to be another full-scale battle in 1487, further insurrections throughout the 1490s, and the last hope of the White Rose (Richard de la Pole) survived until 1525. Yet such was Crowland's perception and it was shared by Vergil and a host of other Tudor writers culminating with Shakespeare, who devoted eight plays to the history of the Wars of the Roses, which he too saw as a unity, an assessment which still shapes our views today.

Tudor historians, moreover, had an explanation for the whole sequence of Wars. They illustrate the workings of divine providence: Bosworth was God's solution to the deposition of Richard II (the Revolution of 1399). That explanation no longer works today, in an age where even most Christians no longer believe that God shapes events or intervenes in our world. Once stripped of God's underlying purpose, which gave them meaning, the plethora of events, of characters who change their names and their allegiances, of victories and overthrows, does appear both 'frenetic and purposeless'.[10] The Wars become quite inexplicable or, alternatively, explicable only in terms of the basest of human motives, the clash of blatant and ruthless ambitions. Hence our difficulties in grasping the whole conflict, setting it all in order, or explaining it. Yet once it is recognized that each War was actually different, that the causes of each were distinct, and that most of the participants changed from War to War, as outlined above, then every conflict becomes more manageable and its causes, course of events and consequences are easier to understand. By separating out the different causes and indeed the different principal characters, each War makes sense on its own terms. Great strides have been made here by modern historians in the last fifty years. Moreover, it becomes apparent that there are causes which explain not just each War, but the whole sequence of Wars. The Wars belong together. The 'Wars of the Roses' are therefore a meaningful and useful term to us today.

MILITARY ASPECTS OF THE WARS

There are other features that set these Wars apart.

The Wars of the Roses are renowned for their violence and ruthlessness. The slayings of Edward IV's teenage brother Rutland at the Battle of Wakefield in 1460, of that other teenager Prince Edward of Lancaster after the Battle of Tewkesbury in 1471, and of the Princes in the Tower in the 1480s are well known. Some of these scandals were exaggerated by Shakespeare, to wring out the horror and the pathos in his plays, yet they also register an essential truth. The Wars of the Roses were quite exceptional in the sheer frequency with which it was the army commanders who were killed and in the sheer numbers of aristocrats who were slain. This policy was quite deliberate. Warwick and Edward IV ordered that defeated rank-and-file should be spared, yet they presided over mass executions of captured leaders. Had Henry VI done like-wise and executed Richard, Duke of York, after the Dartford episode in 1452, there might have been no Wars. His ill-advised clemency to York and rigour towards Jack Cade's rebels in 1450 applied standards more normal at this time, both in foreign and civil wars conducted in accordance with the ethos of chivalry, namely, that aristocrats were spared for ransom and ordinary troops slaughtered, since their lives had no particular value. To them the laws of war did not apply. Participants in the Wars of the Roses appreciated that there was no surer way of curbing political foes than by beheading them. That was why so few of the leaderships carried over from one war to the next. Politics was brutalized.[11]

Bloodiness was only one of the ways in which the Wars of the Roses differed from continental wars. Each campaign was brief, merely a few weeks or a few months, and culminated in battles that were short and decisive. There were virtually no sieges – the staple of the fifteenth-century phases of the Hundred Years War in France that came immediately before. Brevity made the Wars much less destructive and economically disruptive than had been the English raids on and occupations of France, although we are quite unable to measure how the mobilization of the economically active and their deaths impacted on the economy. There was many a wife or mistress who waited endlessly for her husband or lover to return and never knew for certain why he did not. Probably the armies were smaller than those of the Hundred Years War and they certainly did not compare in size with those of the next spate of conti-nental wars. The armies raised so rapidly in the Wars of the Roses were much less well equipped than the expeditionary forces despatched to France after long and expensive preparations by Edward IV in 1475, Henry VII in 1492, or Henry VIII in 1513. Although there was some overlap of personnel in the first phase of the Wars with soldiers from the French wars, this was limited. The last English garrisons in France had consisted disproportionately of ageing veterans. The Wars of the Roses were fought primarily by aristocrats and the conscripted commoners who may perhaps have been adequately armed and even trained, but who lacked much first-hand experience of war. They were not career soldiers. Hence the exceptional importance of the Earl of Warwick's Calais garrison in 1459–71 – the only substantial professional force at the time – and of those northerners who were experienced in desultory warfare with the Scots. Kings and at least some noblemen, notably Warwick, did appreciate the potential of field artillery, hand-guns and perhaps even sixteen-foot pikes, especially when employed by foreign soldiers trained to use them, yet they proved ineffective at the battles of Northampton (1460), Second St Albans (1461) and Barnet (1471); although they *may* have played a significant role at Bosworth in 1485 and Stoke in 1487, but we cannot be sure. Militarily, the way the Wars were waged was primitive, outdated and insulated from the more advanced warfare practised on the continent.

Unlike the Hundred Years War that immediately preceded them, the Wars of the Roses were English conflicts that were fought for domestic reasons very largely by Englishmen to military standards that had no international currency. The Wars are of purely English significance. Yet, as we shall see in the ensuing chapters, not only was the loss of the Hundred Years War an important precondition, but the international rivalries of France and Burgundy encouraged domestic strife and contributed to the results. Burgundy, a state that no longer exists, included not only the province of Burgundy in France but also modern Belgium, the Netherlands and north-western France. The Wars can therefore also be viewed as conflicts between France and Burgundy that happened to be fought on English soil. In that sense, they succeeded and prolonged the Hundred Years War, and they ended when continental rivalries turned elsewhere, to Italy after 1494.

WHY THE WARS MATTER

Of course, the Wars of the Roses have generally been regarded as marking an important turning point in English history. In political terms they have been said to mark the end of the middle ages – that era when foreign wars were approved, when factious nobility warred amongst themselves and deposed kings, and when feudal or bastard feudal hosts engaged in wars or perverted the law. What followed the Wars of the Roses – and very largely resulted from them – was the modern era, symbolized by the Tudor dynasty, who curbed the nobility and bastard feudalism, ruled without fear or favour, and constructed a state that genuinely served the public good. As time has passed, of course, historians writing five hundred years on have conceived of themselves as living in 'Late Modern' or even 'Contemporary' Britain, that is far more modern than the Tudors. Instead, this book demonstrates the Wars to be a distinct historical era deserving study in their own right.

CHAPTER 2

❖ ❖ ❖

WHY DID THE WARS OF
THE ROSES HAPPEN?

That Henry VI supposedly recognized his nephew Henry Tudor as his ulti-
mate successor in 1470–1, as recorded by Bernard André and Polydore
Vergil, the official historians of the new regime, by Edward Hall and later
Shakespeare, is highly unlikely, given that the king's own son Prince Edward of
Lancaster, his designated successor, George, Duke of Clarence, and numerous
Holland and Beaufort cousins took priority. It is almost certainly a Tudor
invention.

That Crowland wrote as he did tells us just how effective was the propaganda of the new Tudor regime. His stories that Richard III had terrible
dreams, no chaplain to shrive him and no breakfast before Bosworth are just
as much part of the Tudors' propaganda as the tales of Richard's protracted
birth and crooked back reported years later by John Rows, Thomas More and
their successors. The Tudor Myth was to be perpetuated by André and Vergil,
by Hall, Raphael Holinshed and other Tudor historians. Above all, it was
continued by Shakespeare, who created the popular perceptions that we share
today.

The Wars of the Roses take their name from two badges of the warring
dynasties, the Red Rose of Lancaster and the White Rose of York. It is a
convenient label for a distinct era that is otherwise difficult to summarize. It
also makes clear that the cause was dynasticism – the incompatible ambitions
for the Crown of the two great families.

In reality, however, the two Roses were not the only, nor perhaps
even the principal badges of the rival dynasties. With the titles and estates
that Lancaster and York had inherited from various ancestors, there came a
host of other emblems. Particular family members chose distinct badges for

themselves. The primary badge of the House of Lancaster was not the Red Rose but the SS collar. King Henry VI seems not to have used the Red Rose at all. As for the Yorkists, the White Rose does indeed occur in much of the family's manuscripts and heraldry, yet it was the falcon and fetterlock that was the favourite badge of Richard, Duke of York (d. 1460). Although his son Edward IV was dubbed the 'Rose of Rouen' after his birthplace, he much preferred the sun in splendour, or sunburst, which commemorated the miracle of the three suns (or panhelion) that marked his victory at Mortimer's Cross in 1461. Richard III, the third Yorkist king, continued to use the white boar that had been his badge as Duke of Gloucester.[1] Neither Rose was the principal emblem at any of the key battles.

Only in 1485 did the two Roses come to the fore. This was apparently the invention of the victorious Tudors, who claimed simultaneously to have unified the Roses and to have brought the Wars to an end. The new-found importance of Roses was taken on board as early as November 1485 by Crowland, who already recognized the years 1459–85 as a distinct era: 'the tusks of the [White] Boar were blunted and the Red Rose, the avenger of the White, shines upon us'. Crowland explains that *he* chose his symbols from 'the banners and badges of today's victor [Henry VII] and vanquished [Richard III] and at the same time those of King Edward's sons [the White Rose] whose cause, above all, was avenged in this battle'.[2] Members of Parliament and the Pope appreciated how Henry VII's marriage to Elizabeth of York unified the warring houses. Both Roses and their Union in the Tudor Rose feature in Henry VII's joyous entry to York in April 1486.[3]

The fruit of the Union of the Roses was to be another Arthur, eldest son of Henry and Elizabeth, who was born at Winchester where the round table of the heroic king of British legend was still displayed. Unfortunately, Prince Arthur predeceased his parents so it was the coronation of his younger brother Henry VIII in 1509 that sealed the Union of the Roses.[4] This was the Tudor message publicized for five centuries by William Shakespeare, but he did not invent the term 'Wars of the Roses'. The term 'quarrel of the two roses' first occurred in 1646 and it was only in 1829 in his novel *Anne of Geierstein* that Sir Walter Scott coined the name Wars of the Roses.[5] The label has caught on and is familiar and indeed useful to historians and non-historians today. Cricket matches between Lancashire and Yorkshire have been called Roses Matches for over a century and the Amazon website catalogue records the Wars of the Roses as the title for 120 different books.

DYNASTIC CONFLICT

The rival Roses and the Tudor Union of the Roses made the Wars into a dynastic conflict between rival Lancastrian and Yorkist claimants to the Crown. The theme makes sense only after the Tudor victory at Bosworth and the marriage of Henry VII and Elizabeth of York on 18 January 1486. What came before also mattered. Whatever Richard, Duke of York, may privately have thought, it was not until 1460 that he overtly challenged the Lancastrian right to rule and claimed the throne for his own line. It had been quite different issues that had raised tensions and triggered the conflict that produced the dynastic trial of strength of 1460–1. It was Yorkist propaganda from 1460 that transformed disagreements about governance into dynastic rivalry. Thereafter, the Yorkists traced the Wars back to the deposition in 1399 of King Richard II, a legitimate king, and his wrongful replacement by Henry IV who 'unrightfully entered upon the same'. Hence the tribulations of the following 62 years. Edward IV asserted that back in 1399 the new king should have been Edmund Mortimer, the grandson of Edward III's second son Lionel, Duke of Clarence (d. 1368), to whom the Crown 'by law and conscience belonged', and from whom it should have passed to the house of York. Arbitrating on York's claim in 1460, the House of Lords had ruled that 'the title of the said duke could not be defeated'.[6] The usurpation of Henry IV was punished in 1461 when his grandson Henry VI was overthrown by the rightful Edward IV. 'These three harrys', so Edward IV's *Brief Treatise* observed, 'have occupied and kept the said Crown of England from the rightful heir this 62 years'. 'Ill-gotten gains cannot last', the chronicler Waurin remarked.[7] This was the Yorkist Myth. However, it was never universally accepted. Moreover, Yorkist chroniclers did not foresee the renewal of conflict of 1483–5, still less its astonishing conclusion. And certainly nobody before 1483 can seriously have anticipated Henry Tudor's succession, marriage, or the Union of the Roses.

As will be shown below in chapter 5, the Wars did not originate in dynastic rivalry. The *First War* and even the *Second War* were primarily about good government. From 1460, however, it made sense to Richard, Duke of York, to explain the *First War* in dynastic terms. After 1461, supporters of Henry VI found it easier to defend the Lancastrians' right to rule in terms of dynastic legitimacy. Yorkist propaganda and hence Yorkist historians read the dynastic contest back in time, re-categorized those who had rebelled against Henry IV and Henry V as supporters of Mortimer and York, and in 1461 allowed their heirs to recover what they had forfeited.[8] Even the Tudors came to accept without question the primacy of the Clarence and Mortimer title and the Yorkist Myth. None of them remembered that Edward III had entailed his Crown on his male (Lancastrian) heirs, nor did they accept the entail of it on the issue of Henry IV by Parliament in 1406.[9] Yorkist legitimacy was reconciled with the Lancastrian Henry VII because he was backed by the Yorkists and had married their heiress, Elizabeth of York. It suited the Tudors to present the Wars as a dynastic struggle and to downplay any more fundamental causes.

Yet it only makes sense to explain the whole of the Wars of the Roses in dynastic terms after 1485. Starting with the wrongful succession of the Lancastrians after Richard II's death in 1399, this interpretation (the Tudor Myth) traced the outbreak and continuation of the Wars to an idealized Tudor conclusion: Henry VII's succession satisfactorily remedied all the wrongs and solved all the problems. The sin of the original usurpation by Henry IV in 1399 was punished by the deposition of Henry VI in 1461. Although he had wrongfully been king, Henry VI had nevertheless been God's lieutenant and should not have been unseated, so his ouster Edward IV merited the punishment which fell instead on his son Edward V, whose usurper Richard III was duly supplanted by Henry VII, who reconciled the warring parties and brought the whole cycle to a close. Individual monarchs, however worthy, could not avert the inevitable retribution of God for the original wrong of 1399.

The Tudor Myth is the theme of Shakespeare's eight history plays set in the period from 1398 to 1485; his *Henry VIII* – an afterthought – took a very different, Protestant, theme culminating in the birth of a Protestant princess, the future Queen Elizabeth I. Each play stands by itself, but together they are the most convincing statement of the Tudor viewpoint. Into the story of the Wars, Shakespeare read the political assumptions of his own age, such as the concepts of order and non-resistance, which were not current in the fifteenth century. An anointed king was God's representative on earth. To depose him was offensive to God, punishable by God, and could never be justified. Tyranny was for God alone to punish and must be suffered patiently rather than that order should be upset, for disorder was much worse. However great had been Henry Bolingbroke's (later Henry IV) sufferings at the hands of the tyrant Richard II, they could not justify the overthrow of an anointed king.[10] 'Clearly Shakespeare, in common with most Elizabethans, regarded Henry IV as a usurper.'[11]

This theme of usurpation and punishment can be traced through all eight plays, which were designed to work both as separate dramas and as a single unit. Even when writing about the Wars of the Roses, Shakespeare took account of earlier events that he had not yet dramatized, and when he did write them up, he anticipated what was to follow. On the very eve of the national triumph at the Battle of Agincourt, therefore, Shakespeare makes his patriotic hero Henry V pray that retribution for 1399 be postponed.[12] Moving on two plays, Richard, Duke of York, in person presents his aspirations far more openly than he ever did in reality:

> Then will I raise aloft the milk-white rose,
> With whose sweet-smell the air shall be perfum'd,
> And in my standard bear the arms of York
> To grapple with the house of Lancaster
> And force perforce I'll make him yield the crown.[13]

York pursues his claims to the throne at the First Battle of St Albans (1455), up to his agreement with Henry VI to succeed him (1460), and to his own death later the same year at the Battle of Wakefield. Henry VI prophetically recognizes Henry Tudor as his heir.[14] In *Richard III* Shakespeare made the most of the potential for reconciliation after the Battle of Bosworth with the marriage of the new king, Henry VII, to Elizabeth of York:

> And then as we have ta[k]en the sacrament
> We will unite the White Rose and the Red
> Smile heaven upon this fair conjunction
> That long have frown'd upon their enmity.
> Now civil wounds are stopp'd, peace lives again,
> That she may long live here, God say amen![15]

It was Shakespeare who invented the celebrated scene in *Henry VI Part I* where the dynastic rivals pluck roses, immortalized in Henry Payne's Victorian painting.[16]

That the Wars were about rival claims to the crown was commonplace enough for Sellar and Yeatman to satirize in 1930 in their *1066 And All That*.[17] What Shakespeare presents in his history cycle became what every schoolboy knew of the Wars of the Roses. Despite all the efforts of the Richard III Society, it is Shakespeare's villainous Richard III, 'false fleeting perjur'd Clarence' and the pathetic Princes who remain most familiar today. Without him indeed, 'hardly anyone . . . would know of their existence'.[18] Richard III still needs to be continuously rehabilitated. Yet the explanatory framework of sin and punishment that made sense of it all has been out of date for two centuries and has yet to be satisfactorily replaced.

APPORTIONING BLAME AT THE TIME

Of course, all participants and all historians at the time deplored the civil strife, took up stances on the rightness or wrongness of the causes, and apportioned blame amongst the principal players. Until 1460 they saw each problem separately, looked to the immediate past for the causes, and proposed short-term and specific solutions. As early as 1449–50, there had been a public outcry against Henry VI's ministers and household. They were accused of treachery, for their collusion with the French and also for evil counsel, causing the king to break his coronation oath, and for incompetence that fell well short of the legal definitions of treason.[19] Richard, Duke of York, and the Yorkists heaped opprobrium on their enemies. York even persuaded Parliament to hold responsible those whom they had attacked at the First Battle of St Albans in 1455.[20] When the tables were turned in 1459, the Coventry Parliament blamed York for the whole series of clashes and condemned him as incorrigible.[21] The victory of the Yorkists enabled their arguments to prevail. In 1460 York placed the mistaken decisions of 1399 at the heart of the argument: the Lancastrians should never have ruled, and York, as heir to the Mortimers, was rightfully king. The Parliament of 1461 enshrined them both in its acknowledgement of Edward IV's title and its proscription of Henry VI and the Lancastrians.[22] Yorkist chroniclers writing in or after 1461 wrote up the 1450s in Yorkist terms.[23] York had stood consistently for reform and good governance.

Of course, contemporaries identified many sub-themes and often denounced their enemies' actions as sins that duly incurred divine punishment.[24] Shakespeare highlighted Richard III's crimes and made him into one of the greatest villains in history. All these Tudor histories simplified what they inherited by presuming at key points that what did happen was always intended. Thus York's dynastic aspirations were read back to 1450, Queen Margaret's machinations to the 1440s, Warwick the Kingmaker's collusion with the Lancastrians to the 1460s, and Richard III's crimes to 1471 and his preparations for usurpation to 1478.[25]

Although committed to Henry VI and his line, the Lancastrian propagandist (and ex-chief justice) Sir John Fortescue realized in the 1460s that there was more to the defeat of the Lancastrians than the hereditary title or the factiousness of York himself, and he accepted many Yorkist reforms as remedies. He

17

thought the king was too poor to exercise a proper ascendancy over his greater subjects. As remedies, he proposed the cancellation (resumption) of royal grants and more monies raised from the Crown estate, a more considered distribution of patronage managed by a council of functionaries like himself, and greater reliance on low-born bureaucrats over the nobility, whom he thought too self-interested. Here he directly contradicted popular preferences for the natural counsellors of royal blood over those 'brought up of nought'.[26] Although not influential at the time, Fortescue's diagnoses have been applauded by modern historians, who have stressed how the growth in Crown lands augmented royal finances and who share Fortescue's distaste for the hereditary nobility and the greatest magnates in particular.[27] Other circumstances propitious to their ascendancy were overlooked by Fortescue. His proposals, moreover, prioritized administrative efficiency over political management and hence were ignored by Lancastrians, Richard III and Henry VII alike. It was to be several centuries before any king regnant would consent to being sidelined in this way.

APPORTIONING BLAME IN LATER CENTURIES

Historical understanding of the Wars of the Roses has developed in three stages since the Tudors. First of all, in 1762, the Wars attracted in the Scotsman David Hume a historian who not only rejected the Tudor Myth, but could comprehend neither the religious and moral standards nor even the noblemen of the Wars of the Roses. He adopted the Yorkist interpretation that almost all later historians have followed. Profoundly hostile to an age so different to his own, Hume was contemptuous and dismissive of the motives and conduct of most of the participants. 'All we can distinguish with certainty through the deep cloud, which covers that period, is a scene of horror and bloodshed, savage manners, arbitrary executions, and treacherous, dishonourable conduct in all parties. There is no possibility, for instance, of accounting for the views and intentions of the earl of Warwick at this time.'[28] It was Hume's interpretation that researchers active in 1870–1940 clothed with detail. They revealed the fifteenth century as an era of uncontrolled baronial faction and of livery and maintenance, when the great nobility used gangs of uniformed retainers to oppress the localities, to pervert the law, engage in violence and even wage war in pursuit of their private interests, and also to oppose in battle and dethrone legitimate governments. The Wars of the Roses were the nadir: 'Civilisation . . . had gone back'. Yet the Wars offered scope for a better future – a 'New Monarchy', the

'New Learning' and a new Protestant Church of England. Bosworth was 'the last act of a long tragedy or series of tragedies . . . the unity of which lies in the struggle of the great houses for the crown', in which 'the strife of York and Lancaster is then allayed'.[29]

Hence there were still 'divided opinions about the real meaning of the Wars of the Roses'.[30] That was in 1936. The next seventy years witnessed more historical writing about the Wars of the Roses than during the previous five centuries. All is post-K.B. McFarlane, 'the one indisputably great historian to have worked primarily on the fifteenth century'. McFarlane came to realize that the practice of politics required multiple participants. It was not sufficient to write a king-centred history, in which the king could take the lead and any opponents, lumped together, were obstacles to progress. The nobility were partners of the Crown, each nobleman having his own interests to protect and advance, and bastard feudalism was just a 'convenient short-hand for certain types of social relations'.[31]

Most modern historians believe that the Wars did not start out as dynastic, but become dynastic over time.[32] The first alternative interpretation was that in 1966 of R.L. Storey, who attributed the outbreak of civil war to mounting lawlessness, exploited and fuelled by the feuds of the nobility, who allied with one another against their foes, and the inability of an inadequate king, Henry VI, to control them as he should.[33] A score of historians have expanded on these themes. Often there is sympathy for York, accepting that his 'close blood relationship to the king' entitled him to membership of the royal council, from which he was excluded, and to command in France, from which 'he was slyly superseded', and crediting him with 'some genuine and unselfish concern for the restoration of good government'. When constitutional means failed, York tried violence, but regrettably failed to distinguish between 'the champion[ing] of reform and retrenchment', which was acceptable, and 'taking up arms against his anointed king', which was not.[34] The best-documented popular uprisings – the two Kentish uprisings of Jack Cade in 1450, the Bastard of Fauconberg in 1471 and the Cornish Rising of 1497 – have been thoroughly investigated, but as isolated instances rather than as symptoms of popular politics more generally.[35]

What all these studies have in common is the prioritization of records over other sources, consequently the deduction of motives from actions, and thus an emphasis on the cynical pursuit of self-interest in preference to the many surviving declarations of principle and intent. 'With the assumption that rampant individualism was the norm' and the 'jumbling together of different hypotheses', the sum of understanding has not increased with the sum of knowledge.[36] Not surprisingly, there has been a reaction. Every man in whatever age imbibes the values of his time, appeals to them to justify his actions and expects to be judged by them. That the Lancastrians and Yorkists so frequently invoked their principles cannot always be rejected as mere lip-service. Participants in the Wars of the Roses were obviously moved by intangible motives such as self-interest and self-preservation, political and constitutional standards and expectations. Hence Professor Carpenter has placed 'the events of the century within a clearly delineated framework of constitutional structures, practices and expectations, in an attempt to show the meaning of the apparently frenetic and purposeless political events which occurred within the framework – and which sometimes breached it'. She rejected the notion that there was anything 'intrinsically "wrong" with the social system' and any search for 'long-term causes' rather than specific causes 'in a particular period'.[37] She shows what happened, not why.

Our understanding of the Wars of the Roses has thus moved from the obsolete certainties of the Tudor Myth and dynastic rivalries to the imponderable uncertainties of today. Many explanations have indeed been devised for the long lead up to the *First War*. Nobody, however, has revealed why it was that the late fifteenth century was so favourable to civil war, what it was that enabled and even encouraged so many noblemen to take up arms to overthrow successive governments. The particular problems of the 1450s, 1460s, 1480s and 1490s were, at least to some extent, expressions of underlying conditions. It is these circumstances which this book seeks to explore and to explain. It was not that mistakes were made or that the nobility were especially unruly, but that the circumstances of 1450–90 made it exceptionally difficult for any king, however capable, to hang on to his throne and to control events.

Nothing is inevitable until it actually happens. To explain the English Civil War after 1642, Professor Lawrence Stone divided the causes into *preconditions* (which he traced back to 1529), *precipitants* (from 1629) and *triggers*.[38] It was the triggers that turned the latent potential for conflict into reality. These distinctions are useful also for the Wars of the Roses, and they underpin this book.

The Wars ended conclusively in 1461 – and in 1471 – and in 1485. That these battles proved not to be decisive was due to the interaction of four factors. Two first appeared during the *Crisis of 1450*, the subject of chapter 5. These were the weakness of the crown – for the government was virtually bankrupt and remained so throughout the *First* and *Second Wars* – and the direct involvement in politics of the people. A third factor, already apparent in

1456–61, was the intervention of foreign powers in English politics. One result of the *First War* was the dynastic rivalry that removed the presumption in favour of the current king. This in turn, fourthly, persuaded the nobility that it was legitimate to overthrow the government. Combined, these four factors removed the military superiority of the monarchy and exposed all kings to effective challenge. Particular individuals under particular pressures took advantage. They thought they mattered – and within this framework, they did. Some episodes were quite unpredictable. Edward IV's leadership was crucial both on his accession to the throne in 1461 and upon his return in 1471, and he had more than his share of luck. Much did depend on the precise course that battles took, Edward IV's victories in 1471 being especially surprising,[39] yet much was beyond the capacity of contemporaries to control. When these four factors ceased to operate, the stability of government resumed. Prowess and charisma could no longer unsettle it. This book's final chapters will explain how it was that the Wars of the Roses ceased.

The next three chapters explore the preconditions to all the Wars. Chapter 3 examines the political system, chapter 4 particular problems with the system and chapter 5 with the *Crisis of 1450*.

CHAPTER 3

How the System Worked

THE NATIONAL CONTEXT

The kingdom of England during the Wars of the Roses included Wales, the lordship of Ireland, Calais and the Channel Isles. Scotland was separate. England was a realm ruled by hereditary kings, who progressed between a dozen palaces and castles in southern England. Hundreds of menials in the lower household handled catering and other support services. Manuscript illuminations frequently depict these kings sitting in state on their thrones in the inner apartments of their upper household attended by the well-born attendants, the courtiers, who constituted their courts. Everyday kingly life was much less formal. Courtiers kept kings company, shared such recreations as chess and hawking, gossiped, and thus kept them in touch with what was going on. Often they informally advised their monarchs as well. More formal advice was provided by infrequent sessions of Parliament, which was already crystallizing into the two houses of Lords and Commons familiar to us today. Meantime at Westminster the central administration implemented the king's wishes. In the three great departments – chancery, exchequer and privy seal – and the principal lawcourts – king's bench, common pleas, chancery and exchequer – hundreds of staff each year penned thousands of charters, writs, letters and warrants in the king's name, and recorded their actions on hundreds of membranes of parchment that were later sewn into rolls. They operated without need for the king himself or even ministers, undisturbed by the Wars of Roses. Some coordination was provided by a royal council of officials, which met several times a week. Decisions, however, were beyond mere bureaucrats. Even quite minor replacement appointments required the input and will of the monarch, who was also crucial for all issues of policy. Much support was provided by household offices, the signet (secretarial) and chamber (financial), which kept records, now lost, that we can only surmise.[1] In crises, the person as well as the name of the king was required, both to make the key decisions and to confer the necessary regal authority on what had been determined and what was to be done.

Rulers had to be impressive. Magnificence was expected. A king's houses had to be of the grandest style; furnishings and decorations too; clothes, jewels, diet, horses and everything else had to be of the richest quality; his cavalcade had to be the best born, best attired and best mounted; and everywhere and every day there ought to be ceremonial most elaborate and etiquette beyond compare. Yet behind all this splendour, at the hub, monarchy was hard work. The kings of the Wars of the Roses were never off duty. They were always liable to be waylaid by suitors, at prayer, at the chase, or at dinner. Much time was spent receiving and judging petitions and authorizing appointments and grants that often seem quite minor, but which were the lifeblood of politics. A king's patronage was a key exercise of his regal power. What kings had to give pandered to every taste and purse. A king always had rewards to covet, for every taste and rank, whether for the lowliest clerks and skivvies or the most blue-blooded in the land, whose aspirations, standing and very reputation depended on the king's response. Kings had to weigh up their decisions carefully – to eke out their bounty carefully, distributing it equitably, according to deserts, but also with their eyes open to consequences and implications. It was dangerous permanently to shut out any great man. Often, no doubt, they refused requests, although we know little of that, but necessarily without excluding the rejected from future rewards, hope of which could lure them into further service yet to be performed. A model king, an Edward I or a Henry V, held his ground, spoke firmly man to man, pressured, alarmed, coerced and even punished their proudest subjects. Man management was essential for effective rule. Edward IV, Richard III and Henry VII had the knack, not necessarily the consistency. Henry VI possessed it only sporadically and the child Edward V, obviously, not at all.

Late medieval governments did very little. They strove to keep things running and to pay their own costs, ideally from the king's ordinary resources – customs, estates and fees. They commandeered what they required through the system called purveyance and repaid it later. Their scope by our standards was narrow: not education, not health or social services, not the management of the economy. Defence of the realm, foreign policy, the maintenance of law and order, and justice were their focus. They had need of few policies, no aspirations for reform and no legislative programmes. Actually, most actions were started by the ruled and executed by them too. Individuals petitioned for royal patronage, individual victims invoked the criminal law and requested special commissions, and individual litigants launched an ever-increasing flood of cases to the central courts that occupied sheriffs, bailiffs and constables of the hundreds. This was a monarchical system highly responsive to the extremely varied demands of its subjects. When it did not respond, their ire was roused.

Kings had to decide and had to be able to decide, yet their freedom of action was limited and they were not expected to decide alone. A king was God's representative. He had to be virtuous rather than vicious, to practise the cardinal virtues and avoid the deadly sins, and act in line with God's commandments. What this really meant was that he should put the interests of his subjects first – in the public interest or for the good of all (the commonweal). Were his actions conducive to the commonweal was a question constantly asked by Parliament, critics, the people, and even in 1450 both by a group of the pirates and by Jack Cade's Kentish rebels.[2] Kings did not rule for their own pleasure. Kings had a social function – of which they were reminded every time they seemed to forget. The self-preserving *Prince* of Niccolò Machiavelli (d. 1527) had not yet been invented. Divine right meant having public responsibilities.

Kings were inundated with advice which they were expected to heed and, ideally, implement. When young, all read instructional books of advice, known as Mirrors for Princes, which had often been written specially for them. Ministers had rights of regular audience, council and councillors respectfully submitted guidance, great councils (the Lords meeting without the Commons) were consulted frequently, and Parliament was still primarily a forum for advice. These were the official, prescribed and regular channels. Additionally, courtiers and favoured aristocrats slipped in a word informally and often, indeed, much more than that. The principal advisers of Henry VI and Edward IV – William, Duke of Suffolk, and William, Lord Hastings – were not government ministers, although both had household offices respectively as steward and chamberlain. Not only had such men casual access to the king, they controlled access for others and could, if they desired, exclude them.[3] By the most elitist standards, both men were newcomers, not to be compared to those princes of royal blood who called themselves the king's natural councillors and who thought themselves entitled by birth to counsel the king. Such noblemen, so Jack Cade's rebels argued, were too exalted to be self-interested, unlike the courtiers, so often junior and conniving, who flattered their kings to please them and to secure their favours, and thus distanced them dangerously from reality.[4] The model *Book of the Courtier* of the Italian Baldassare Castiglione (d. 1529) was yet to be written. Too often real kings rejected honest advice as unpalatable – outvoted all their advisers – and went their own wilful ways. Such failings were not blamed on the king himself, but on his advisers: on evil councillors, who should be punished and could even make the king a traitor by inducing him to act against the common weal.[5] Once evil councillors were removed and punished, it was often hoped, good councillors would make all well.

Kings were sacred. Everybody owed them a duty of reverence and fidelity, called allegiance, that overrode the petty loyalties due to lesser men. Kings and their closest family were protected against murder or the waging of war by the statute of treason. Traitors were condemned to the most horrendous deaths and the forfeiture of all possessions not just by themselves, but by their wives and children. From this grew the doctrine of attainder: the blood of traitors was tainted – corrupted – so that their heirs could not inherit and were ruined too. Apparently first mentioned in 1450 and first applied in 1453,[6] the statute of attainder was developed in 1459 into the wholesale confiscation and the destruction of entire noble houses. This became the norm at every revolution and in the aftermath of every uprising. Attainder was a powerful deterrent to treason or, indeed, any political action, as traitors who had won forthwith attainted vanquished loyalists. Fortunately, circumstances permitting, attainders could be reversed. Assassination was not a feature of these Wars, although Henry VI and Edward V were quietly eliminated in custody, Richard III fell in battle, and most other claimants died violently.

Treason set practical limits to politics. Kings were also limited by their weakness. They could not rule alone or force their subjects to do their will. They had no standing army or police force. If they had more money and manpower than the most overmighty of their subjects, they did not outweigh all of them or even a section of them, nor should they wish to do so. That way lay tyranny. It united opposition and risked deposition. Wise kings saw that such rifts never arose. The realm was a limited or mixed monarchy in which power was shared by the king and his greater subjects (the nobility or magnates). Magnates accepted the sovereignty of the king, deferred to his leadership and generally worked with him. Consensus and collaboration were the norm. There were plenty of chances to remonstrate with and seek remedies from the king for bishops, noblemen, aristocrats, town corporations, and even, through intermediaries, for the humblest of subjects. Parliament, which represented everyone of rank, handled little else.[7] The constitution worked. It was not broken and did not need fixing. The theory and conventions of politics changed very little between 1300 and 1600, and remained perfectly familiar to Shakespeare. If the usual channels faltered during the Wars of the Roses, it was because the strains to which they were subjected were too great. Once relaxed, normal business resumed.

Always it was a big step to move beyond the established channels to oppose the king, to resist him or press him to change his mind. Loyal liegemen were entitled to disagree, to petition and to protest. Whether they could legitimately pressurize or coerce the king, even with majority backing, was a matter of dispute and was never really solved. Was reform compatible with allegiance? The Yorkists in the 1450s and Warwick in 1469 argued that it was. To overstep the mark was definitely treason, all kings always declared. It was audacious to constrain a king or dethrone him. It took a handful of magnates a whole decade – and then as the last resort – to dispose of Henry VI in 1461. So momentous was that decision that the Wars of the Roses were triggered and all the prime movers were slain. Anybody who took this step prematurely, before every option was exhausted, and rebelled, like York or Warwick, was destroyed by the majority. Before 1450 *coups d'état* actual or attempted were highly unusual and were rarely successful. Everyday politics was prosaic. Politics was the peaceful conversation and social interaction of men of similar upbringings, aristocratic lifestyles, world views and attitudes, who knew one another well and were generally cousins. Killing one's brothers-in-law, as at the First Battle of St Albans in 1455, was a break with normality. The Wars of the Roses defied political conventions: they were a social and political aberration.

Late medieval England was not always in upheaval. When Edward II was deposed in 1327, who came next was not in dispute: Edward II's son Edward III inherited the throne early. Henry IV in 1399 was the male heir designated in 1376 by Edward III.[8] It was because an alternative Mortimer line succeeded in 1461 that the 62 years of Lancastrian rule, covering the reigns of Henry IV, Henry V and Henry VI, are so often presented as particularly turbulent. Actually, the first two kings were followed automatically by their heir, the last being a tiny baby. There was violent opposition to Henry IV, which he defeated, and much criticism in his early Parliaments that dwindled with his success. Everyday life in Lancastrian England was mostly orderly and peaceful – until the Wars of the Roses.

THE RULE OF THE PROVINCES

The England of the Wars of the Roses was a unitary state. Government was everywhere alike. There was a universal and standardized pattern of local government – shires, hundreds or wapentakes, manors and boroughs – run by a standard set of royal officials – sheriffs, escheators, coroners and justices of the peace. It was the king's government and the king's justice that they administered and the king's writ that ran everywhere. Some units were private, such as the counties palatine of Chester, Durham and Lancaster, and the marcher lordships of Wales, yet all applied the same laws. Indeed, the devolved systems of central government in Cheshire and Lancashire were amongst the most effective and are certainly the best documented today. No arbitrary official could completely evade review and correction from the centre. There were also local financial networks – the sheriff and escheator again, collectors of the customs in the ports and of the indirect tax on wool (aulnage) in the counties, and estate administrators. 'Since his most faithful servants had been distributed all over the kingdom as keepers of castles, manors, forests and parks, no attempt could be made however stealthily by any man, whatsoever his distinction, without his being immediately faced with it'.[9] Although this is wishful thinking, royal judges did go down to the counties on assize every year, county courts did meet monthly, justices of the peace did sit every quarter and also handled much business at home. England was a much-regulated country.

Yet all this was 'self-government at the king's command'. Kings could pay few of their agents. Bar anything received from fees or other graft, all served for the prestige and the authority over others that royal office conferred. They were drawn from those of local rank, who brought their local standing to the post and had their authority legitimized by royal commissions. Boroughs were run by successful businessmen, but outside them offices were monopolized by those aristocracy – the nobility, gentry and lawyers – who were best able to ensure that royal commands were implemented. Carrying out the king's law and the king's will was therefore a partnership of mutual advantage. Kings had to rule with the local notables who were able both to enforce and also to thwart. Changing the personnel, as Richard III found, did not terminate the authority of those displaced or make the interlopers acceptable locally. Royal patronage could not transform local realities, at least not at once. In a real sense, the king presided over the provincial spheres of influence of his greatest subjects and had to work with them.

The precise complexion of such provincial elites depended on landholding and other circumstances. The lowliest gentleman could dominate his particular village or run his particular hundred. Esquires or knights, members of the county elite, governed their part of the county, just as Edward Guildford esquire did in the seven Wealden hundreds of Kent where he was too important for anyone to gainsay.[10] The Vernons of Netherhaddon 'ruled' the Peak district. Where there was no top family, the county community of gentry governed together. Noblemen – barons and upwards – oversaw whole counties or even whole regions. They – and even the leading gentry – often deputed the tiresome routine of offices to be exercised by lesser men with legal training. The powerful moulded the system to their own advantage, perverted or even flouted justice. These were the bastard feudal abuses open to those able to command committed manpower through the mechanism of bastard feudalism discussed below.[11] Peacekeepers also committed violent crimes, but generally escaped unscathed.

THE RULING CLASS

These officers were the rulers of the countryside. Aristocrats were landholders with inherited estates paying enough rent to keep them in comfort without the need to labour. They were a military caste, brought up to the practice of warfare and on chivalric values, whose whole intellectual justification, as passed down by generations of theorists, was to wage war on behalf of and to protect the rest of society. Many thousands strong, they ranged from the parliamentary nobility (the Lords), some with vast estates across many counties and huge revenues, to the country gentry, knights and esquires, who held a few manors. All were educated to and aspired to contemporary expectations. At the other extreme, much shadowier but more numerous, were the gentlemen, living amongst their fields and perhaps without any chivalric pretensions. The Cheshire gentleman Humphrey Newton was worth only £13 a year.[12] Honorary gentility was accorded to professional lawyers and estate officers. Full membership, the product of substantial landholding, was bought by those who invested resources amassed elsewhere – from the successful practice of the law (like the Pastons), arms (like Sir Andrew Ogard), or even trade (like the de la Poles). The typical aristocrat was a landowner or rentier, a countryman who resided on his rural estates in the English provinces and was supported by revenues from the estates that tenants cultivated. Aristocrats lived rural lives in well-staffed castles and manor houses, practised country sports in their own parks, and oversaw the management of their affairs. Like the Pastons, they watched the price of grain, looked out for reliable tenants, and guarded their boundaries and watercourses, which does not imply that they were uncultivated, uncultured, boorish or bucolic. The Pastons employed a bailiff in Richard Calle. Those of greater rank and wealth delegated much more to professional officials and councillors, and lived quite remotely from most of their possessions, most of which were leased out. They resided for longer periods in just a few houses and much more comfortably.

It was the aristocracy who commanded the armies that fought the Wars of the Roses. No civil war could have occurred without the manpower they deployed through the system that modern historians have called bastard feudalism. This manpower comprised distinct elements. The nucleus was a lord's household, scores strong for barons and hundreds for dukes, and all, but the indispensable laundress, male. Whether from the genteel upper household or the menial service departments, most were young, tall, of military age and militarily effective. Clad in their livery, it was they who made the great household of a magnate so impressive. A lord could call at any time on their protection and looked first to them when a show of magnificence or power was required. Most numerous were his tenants, who had unwritten obligations also to turn out for their lord. Perhaps they were loyal: more commonly perhaps they were compelled. All, theoretically at least, had their own weapons and were obliged to practise archery, although a Bridport muster roll of 1457 suggests unsurprisingly that few possessed complete armour and that weapons might be miscellaneous or home made. When Humphrey Duke of Buckingham scotched the depredations of Sir Thomas Malory, 60 yeomen from his estates sufficed. Eight hundred rustics and citizens of York were indicted as adherents of the Percies at their private battle at Stamford Bridge in 1454. Tenants were a latent force that had nevertheless to be mobilized.

Crucial, therefore, were the lord's estate officials, generally themselves gentry, the chief officers of his household, his councillors and extraordinary retainers who were the officer cadre that made latent force into a reality. Next, but strangely most emphasized by modern historians, were those extraordinary retainers separately contracted and in receipt of fees. Few in number, because too expensive to be otherwise, they were not resident in their lord's household nor primarily his tenants. Instead, they lived in their own households on their own rural estates and had independent standing in their own localities. Although seldom in their lord's company, they were summoned as required, to escort him clad in his livery and accompanied by their own men to family rites of passage, quarter sessions and county courts, parliaments and coronations, private and civil and international wars. They were luxurious extensions to a lord's own resources, but always few. The 33 knights, all heads of county families, that the Earl of Northumberland brought to meet the king in 1486, were quite exceptional. Finally, anybody could be recruited by receiving badges distributed in times of crisis and in defiance of the law: Humphrey Duke of Buckingham ordered 2,000 Stafford knots in 1454.[13]

Households were committed to their lords. The relationship of members of the household to its head – their master or lord – was comparable to that of a child to a father within a family. It created an absolute obligation of obedience and an absolute loyalty that was recognized, both by the law which made killing a master into petty treason – comparable to treason proper and punishable in the same way – and as political reality. Edward IV accepted as mitigation for treason a plea of the membership of the household of Henry VI.[14] Extraordinary retainers had choices: certainly at the point of taking service, sealing a contract or swearing an oath. They balanced this new obligation against others, to their families and friends, to other lords whose service they thought compatible, and sometimes indeed specifically excluded named individuals. Another choice may have occurred when service was demanded, for such men had political standing, political awareness and perhaps political preferences of their own. Although some did fail their lords, notoriously Henry Vernon in 1471 and Northumberland's men in 1489,[15] the fact that lords did generally bring their companies to battle suggests that such defaults were not normal. Bad service, of course, meant no reward. Such men could hold back a lord's tenants. The mass of tenants may not have been consulted or informed about why they were required and may have had little choice but to serve. John, Lord Howard, listed how many men he could levy from each manor in his account book, and somewhat later the Percies listed tens of thousands of the men whom they could raise. Under the early Tudors, lords itemized the tenants of monastic estates of which they were stewards alongside their own tenants amongst the men they could count on. Probably it was the listing that was new, not the compulsory conscription. Of 200 men of Canterbury involved in 1471 in the Bastard of Fauconberg's Rebellion, at least 92 successfully pleaded compulsion.[16]

All these categories owed fidelity to their lord against all men, except – as their contracts made clear – the king, to whom an overriding allegiance was due. Perhaps some were not too scrupulous about that – like Simon Milburn, whom York sought to retain in 1460 – but some were or at least exploited this escape clause. Hence the importance of royal commissions of array, which authorized noblemen to enlist their own men and those of others with the king's authority in what was intended to be the king's service. Towns added their own contingents, generally no more than a couple of dozen strong. Surely such levies made up the majority of the 4,000 men that George, Duke of Clarence, brought from the West Country in 1471. It was these rustics, hundreds and thousands strong, who made up the numbers of the armies of the Wars of the Roses. These were really the king's men, but kings needed aristocrats to raise and command them, even against themselves.

Remember the royal family, then as now, were aristocrats. Kings were the greatest of aristocrats. They were educated in the same way as dukes and knights and were often brought up with them, to pray, to ride and fight, to read the same escapist romances and to practise the same recreations, such as dicing, hunting and hawking. They shared the same religious, political and chivalric values. They were prepared for very similar futures: presiding over households, managing their financial and other affairs, disputing and resolving disputes, fighting wars and governing those around them. Although obviously kings had other functions, such as the conduct of foreign relations, what distinguished them was firstly the much larger scale of their canvas – the whole realm rather than a fraction of it – which made them first among equals, and secondly their supreme rank, which entitled them to the respect, service and obedience even of their noblest subjects. That kings had similar values and interests to their greater subjects, spoke the same language, approached issues from the same direction, and knew what made them tick, facilitated amicable relations and made it easier to manage them. Two of the Yorkist kings, Edward IV and Richard III, were noblemen before they became kings. Both were well-suited for monarchy, capable of military leadership and also of effective decision-makers. They worked and socialized with their magnates, yet also asserted themselves whenever required. Henry VI, in contrast, did not fit the model, shared neither the military nor administrative expectations of a king, and, whatever his private virtues, lacked the force of personality or inclination to pull rank with his lords. His natural councillors and suitors found themselves dealing not directly with the monarch, but with his chosen councillors or favourites, not noticeably their superiors in rank, who were not entitled to the authority to command them and who were suspected of moulding patronage, decisions and policy to suit themselves. Henry VII may have demanded respect, but he was remote. Strangely, the Wars of the Roses was a conflict between aristocrats who ignored normal chivalric standards, and that was most damaging to the aristocracy.

Pedigree 3 Rivals to the Crown 1447–61

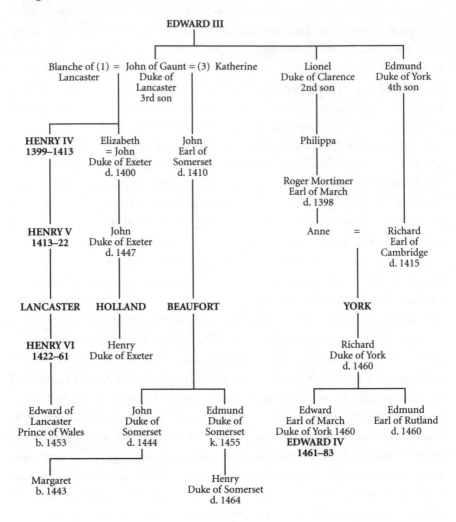

CHAPTER 4

PROBLEMS WITH THE SYSTEM

There was nothing fundamentally wrong with the system, but there were problems that were preconditions which applied to all three Wars. This chapter looks in turn at two such preconditions: the collapse of public order and the issue of dynasticism.

THE COLLAPSE OF PUBLIC ORDER

It is normal to locate a collapse of public order in the mid fifteenth century that was caused perhaps by the weak rule of Henry VI and was certainly not corrected by him. The records of the principal criminal court (king's bench) made Professor Storey conclude that 'the Wars of the Roses were the outcome of an escalation of private feuds'. Contemporary authors, he said, depicted 'a kingdom in a state of disintegration'. 'Internal peace . . . was poised on a razor's edge.'[1] Crimes of violence, minor riots and assemblies were so common that complaints were received at every Parliament. In London there were full-scale attacks on the men of law near Fleet Street (1459), the Lombards (1456) and the Flemings (1457). Because public order had collapsed, there was an upsurge in bastard feudalism and great landed magnates came to dominate every locality. 'Quiet and prosperity' depended on the keeping of the peace, proper administration of justice and due execution of the law, yet in 1450 'for lack hereof', so the Commons complained, there are '[m]any murders, man-slaughters, rapes, robberies, riots, affrays and other inconveniences greater than before'.[2] Obviously there was some substance to their lamentations. Had there not been, it would have been pointless for the Earl of Warwick in 1459 to deplore 'the great abominable murders, robberies, perjuries and extortions . . .

33

openly used and continued in the realm with great violence', and to complain how the 'good politic laws heretofore notably and virtuously used [were] piteously overturned'.[3] The first Yorkist Parliament and Yorkist chronicles of 1461 took such problems as read.[4]

Actually, however, such disorders had 'long preceded the final defeat in France' in 1453 at Castillon. Even though King Henry V did enforce good public order, any deterioration had began during the minority of Henry VI (1422–37), when there was no adult king, and was not corrected, as it should have been, by him when he came of age. Storey argued that the lack of order, politic governance and justice forced ligitants into direct and violent action, into perverting the law, and hence into bastard feudal associations and the patronage of the great. Thus they shared the political divisions of their masters and joined them ultimately in civil war.[5] The parties in these minor contests coalesced into the two 'sides' in the Wars of the Roses.

Crime, that is the breach of laws set by society, occurs at all times and in all places. Violent crime was commonplace in the later middle ages. All kinds of insults, disagreements and quarrels, often fuelled by drink, contributed to violence that was often lethal, since knives were universally carried, but which was also generally impulsive rather than organized. Knife-crime, however deplorable, was not organized, nor systematic, nor gang-related as it apparently is today. If identified and apprehended, offenders were liable to execution; however, many were pardoned and many others quietly relocated themselves. That there were many crimes of passion does not constitute a collapse of public order. It was possible for a relatively high incidence of violence to exist side by side both with the rule of law and indeed with respect for the law.[6] Hence both the savage criminal law, which summarily executed those who were caught red-handed, and the routine binding over (mainprise) of potential offenders by justices of the peace in order to keep the peace. Principals had to find sureties (mainpernors). Principals and sureties alike were obliged to recognize substantial debts that were forfeited (payable) only in the event of non-compliance: much like bail today.

Crimes of violence were committed by every class of people. Even Richard II's half-brother John Holland committed homicide in 1385. Many early fifteenth-century members of Parliament, especially in Cornwall, committed murders for which they escaped punishment.[7] If all aristocrats were violent on occasion, it is not surprising that judges and jurors of this rank, such as the peers in Parliament, were inclined to condone conduct they performed themselves amongst offenders of their rank. It is not likely that public order was any worse than in earlier times. There seem, for instance, to have been virtually none of the organized aristocratic gangs that preyed on the East Midlands a century earlier.[8]

What did make the Wars of the Roses notorious and did threaten public order were those quarrels of the great that escalated into organized violence, feuds and even battles: into what have been dubbed 'gentlemen's wars'.[9] Seldom have we explicit and objective statements of what was at issue. Disputes often loom into our vision only when they threatened public order, required special commissions to suppress them, and thus generated indictments. Unfortunately, indictments are merely the charges, often drafted by the other side, partisan rather than impartial statements of facts.

There were three root causes for such quarrels. First, but usually unrecorded, were those that originated in, or were underpinned, by clashes in personality, precedence, slurs on honour, or other insults.[10] Of course, the parties did not view them as frivolous, but deadly serious; often enough, as crucial to their public standing and reputations. Second, modern historians deduce, were conflicts over the 'rule' of particular localities, perhaps most often a byproduct of the third category. Third, what are best recorded, most easily understood and explained, are 'land wars'. All aristocrats were landholders. To hold land inevitably required litigation in the royal courts of three principal types: with adjacent properties over boundaries, watercourses, common rights and jurisdictions; over the running of the estate with tenants (rents, services, common rights, poaching) and with officers (arrears and malfeasance); and with rivals over the rights of possession to the land itself. Disputes over title were fundamental, because they made all the difference between high rank and wealth or ruin, and because they were so intractable. Land law had become very complicated and unpredictable, and the stakes were too high.

Originally there had been quite a simple system that produced clear heirs to all substantial properties, like those that interested the aristocracy. They were held in fee simple by primogeniture. Under primogeniture, the next heir to the current holder was in the direct line of descent: a landholder's son was preferred to the landholder's brother. Males in each generation were ranked in order of their births, and brothers took precedence over their sisters, who rated equally as coheiresses. The offspring of the deceased holder even if female took precedence over his next brother, so that a granddaughter in the direct line could shut out of inheritance her uncle or male cousin. Legitimacy was usually an issue: the great Armburgh and Plumpton lawsuits are exceptional here.[11] It was undoubtedly offensive to heirs apparent when the current landholders married again, because such second matches usually resulted in younger dowagers who encumbered what heirs apparent viewed as 'their' estates, in younger sons who supplanted their elder half-sisters, and children of the second marriage bed, even the youngest sister, taking priority over their elder half-siblings. Though women could inherit, this was seen as a problem because a daughter joined at marriage another family, and her inheritance was placed at the disposal of her husband. His interests inevitably took precedence over those of her original kin or completely excluded them, her uncles – the brothers of her father – and her cousins. Hence fourteenth-century lords had often resettled their estates to confine them to the direct male descendants of the first lord. Such resettlements were called *entails in tail male*. Sometimes they were designed quite explicitly to exclude particular females – to favour a younger son over the daughters of a deceased elder son, for instance. Should there be no male heirs, the property reverted to the right heirs under primogeniture, thus enabling women still to inherit. This happened to the Warwick inheritance in 1446 and in 1449, to the benefit of Warwick the Kingmaker.[12]

By the time of the Wars of the Roses, therefore, almost every major estate was entailed, inheritance being restricted to the heirs, usually the heirs male, of the conveyers. Entails inevitably favoured particular individuals over others less fortunate, often quite brutally and personally, but they did clarify who was the heir as long as the intended beneficiaries survived. Increasingly land-holders inherited agglomerations of property from different ancestors subject to different entails and with different heirs.[13] Entails could not be broken or revised. Yet lands already entailed were often resettled in tail jointly on husbands and wives at marriage and even transferred wholesale to the offspring of second marriages, as in the Neville–Neville and Mountford–Mountford disputes.[14] Which entail took precedence? By 1449, the most appalling jumble of settlements and resettlements of the Beauchamp estate had grown up which had to be resolved. Warwick the Kingmaker was the winner: at least four rivals felt wronged.[15]

On to this increasingly complicated situation there were superimposed trusts subject to a landholder's last will, sometimes conditionally, which were subject to a different system of law – equity, not the common law – and different courts – chancery, not common pleas. Often testators ordered the sale of family lands to the loss of the heirs. In such confusions it was not difficult to perceive arguable titles, such as that of the notorious Robert Lord Moleyns to Gresham (Norf.), bought by Justice Paston from the trustees of the last will of Lady Moleyns's grandfather.[16] Technicalities such as seisin (actual possession), whether tenure was unbroken, proper livery, and licences to alienate could make all the difference. Claimants entered properties illegally to establish actual possession. Resignation of rights (quitclaims) from all potential claimants born and unborn was essential for the establishment and conveyance of secure titles. Heirs might reject past transactions, to the eternal damage of the seller's soul, and those who had inherited land bought in good faith might find themselves dispossessed by the seller's distant heirs.[17] Landholders studied their pedigrees and noted their potential claims to properties in case unexpected deaths made them into reality.

Solving such disputes was difficult, since the formal government inquiries (inquisitions post-mortem) were subject to all kinds of external influence, from labouring and maintenance to intimidation and murder, and anyway did not cover trusts. Many such disputes were handled more informally, by mediation of outraged neighbours, by the arbitration awards imposed by lords, at a higher level by the royal council and king, and any violent ramifications were settled by royal commissions of oyer and terminer (to hear and determine). The public interest demanded that disputes were resolved peacefully, not necessarily justly. Usually they were, but a few, such as the Berkeley dispute, were repeatedly revived. George, Lord Abergavenny, coheir according to the 1450 inquisitions but actually excluded by his cousin the Earl of Warwick, resubmitted his claim whenever opportunity offered during both the *Second War* and the *Third War*.[18]

Since land was the basis of wealth, rank and standing within local society, it also conferred authority on landholders in the shape of jurisdiction over tenants and the right to a say as juror or officeholder in local society. It is uncertain whether a place on the commission of the peace was yet an essential badge of county status, but certainly such offices as justice of the peace or commissioner of array legitimized and extended a landholder's rights not only over their own tenants but over others in their localities. At higher levels, great landholding or such major roles as warden of the northern marches, conferred authority well beyond the boundary of the landholder's estates, even hegemony over a whole region. Thus 'land wars' could easily develop into struggles for local supremacy, in which retaining burgeoned, neighbours took sides, lords were drawn in to support their tenants, and violence broke out between individuals and private armies. Mortality happened, but never bloodbaths. Only one death each was involved in two of the outrages that most shocked contemporaries, the murders in 1457 of the Devonshire lawyer Nicholas Radford by the son of the Earl of Devon and in 1477 of the Dorsetshire widow

Ankarette Twynho by the royal Duke of Clarence. Forcible entries and riots could involve so very few people and were so ritualized that sometimes they seem to involve no physical violence at all. The ways in which such disputes were prosecuted were often underhand and unchivalric: for example, ambushes on Westminster steps. Jibes of cowardice or dishonourable conduct were defended in blood.[19] As disputes spread, often the original roots have been lost, and may not be apparent to us today.

There were disputes about title to land at all times and at all levels of landed society. It is quite unsurprising therefore to find them in the 1430s and 1440s. Perhaps the proliferation of settlements and resettlements, of overlapping trusts, and the growth of the land market meant that they had become more numerous than hitherto.

Escalation was not inevitable. Whenever they did escalate, the losers always sought royal intervention. It was a king's job to stop them. There had been major disputes in 1426–45 during both the minority and majority of Henry VI, such as the Gloucester–Beaufort, Neville–Neville, Fanhope v. Grey of Ruthin, and Percy–Archbishop of York disputes, all of which were resolved at the time. Some historians disagree. 'For them, the Crown's treatment of the Fanhope-Grey dispute (1437–9) and, more notoriously, the Courtenay-Bonville dispute, reveals that it was quite unable to impose any sort of workable settlement between "neutral" parties who were equally matched.'

Actually, however, order was restored in all these early cases and peace was imposed. Losers did not carry on the fight because the government made it impossible to persist. When the stewardship of the duchy of Cornwall was granted in error both to the Earl of Devon and Sir William Bonville, the royal council suspended its use. When John, Duke of Norfolk, attacked Wingfield (Suffolk), he was arrested, bound over to appear before the king's council, and was forced to abide arbitration. This was at least his third offence. When James, Lord Berkeley, laid claim to the Beauchamp and Lisle lands on the death of Earl Richard Beauchamp in 1439, he was instantly confined in the Tower and released only on sureties to abide arbitration. Repeated efforts to arbitrate the dispute maintained public order throughout the 1440s, even though the feud did revive in the less repressive conditions of the early 1450s. It is not clear whether it was deliberate royal policy to remove the ringleaders by sending them to fight in France, as the Earl of Salisbury did in 1436, Lord Bonville in 1442, and Lords Shrewsbury, Lisle and Moleyns in 1452. During their absences their rights were protected against attack by royal protections and thus the frictions were suspended temporarily, in some cases for decades. Shrewsbury,

Lisle and Moleyns all died before they could resume their quarrels. Moleyns's heirs abandoned the quest for the manor of Gresham (Norfolk). 'It is noticeable that several serious conflicts were successfully defused and contained'.

Admittedly this was rough justice. 'Those who were better connected to Suffolk and the cardinal [Beaufort] were every time triumphant'.[20] However, even such highly regarded kings as Edward I, Edward III and Edward IV bent justice in what they perceived as the wider interest. It was not just these temporarily suspended disputes that sometimes revived, but also those that had been first quelled by the strongest of kings. We must not expect too much of medieval monarchs.

Public order had not therefore broken down before 1450, nor had it degenerated decisively from the high standards of Henry V, which can indeed be exaggerated. Henry V's attack on such major crimes as West Country piracy was successfully resisted locally and had little long-term effect.[21] There were many other occasions, earlier and later, when Parliament complained about public disorder, the prevalence of violent crime and the perversion of justice.[22] Furthermore, the authority of lords, the retaining of their servants, and their deployment in all kinds of roles was not unique to the reign of Henry VI or the Wars of the Roses, but were structural features of late medieval and early modern society. Things were never so bad even during the Wars of the Roses that the courts stopped meeting, justice ceased to be purveyed, the rule of law or property rights were suspended.

Professor Storey's case is supported by the articles of impeachment of William, Duke of Suffolk, in 1449–50, the evidence of the *Paston Letters*, the manifestos of Jack Cade and indictments from 1450. All these assert that the Duke of Suffolk in East Anglia, James, Lord Say, and others in Kent used their privileged access at court to advance themselves in their home counties and to profiteer and oppress people, secure in their immunity as members of the ruling regime from effective prosecution or intervention by the king.[23] Whilst the sources emanate from their enemies, the general tenor is probably authentic. There is some contemporary confirmation for the offences of Suffolk and his fellows in the surviving letters of the equally partisan and perhaps disruptive Pastons, and in the indictments of local officers and royal household men.[24] For Pollard, 'the systematic abuse of power in the king's name ... had not been witnessed on such a scale since the reign of Richard II'.[25] Although the general impression of Suffolk's misrule may therefore be correct, the charges themselves need to be approached sceptically, as hostile and sometimes malicious. The definition of treason often departed from that recognized at law, and most offenders were never brought to trial. Even when there were trials, some ended with the indictments being quashed or in acquittals.[26] Such charges may still be true but cannot be assumed to be fact. Undoubtedly these cases came to light because Parliament attacked the regime and thus gave new opportunities for protests to be expressed. There is not much evidence beforehand for such offences, nor does it seem likely that these complaints would have been pursued had Suffolk not fallen, still less been recorded.

Again, there are parallels with all periods in history, since all royal favourites in the later middle ages abused their positions to advance themselves and to oppress. However this was not necessarily true everywhere. Although there were complaints on Suffolk's fall from other regions, there was not everywhere the flood of complaints, the explosion of resentment, the search for vengeance, or the universal revolt that happened in Kent and to a much lesser extent in Sussex, Surrey, Essex, Wiltshire and East Anglia. These excesses may have been a phenomenon of eastern and south-eastern England, the most economically advanced areas, where, as we shall see, such grievances were magnified by the *Great Slump* of *c*.1440–80.

That Suffolk and his allies behaved badly and abused their opportunities does not constitute a collapse of public order. Far from it. The evidence actually seems to indicate that they retained such a firm grip on affairs that opposition was effectively stifled and could have been suppressed indefinitely. It was not the *mismanagement* of East Anglia that brought Suffolk to book. It was the defeat of the English in France in 1453 and the consequent impeachment of Suffolk in Parliament that relaxed his hold on the localities, that enabled charges to be laid against him and then against others by Jack Cade, thus creating our evidence for their misconduct, and that permitted direct action in Kent, Sussex and Wiltshire. It proved extremely difficult to restrain the protesters in future. The breakdown of public order was a result of the *Crisis of 1450*. The *Crisis* did not result from deficiencies in local peacekeeping.

THE DYNASTIC ISSUE

Most people since the Tudors have regarded the Wars of the Roses as dynastic disputes about whether the Houses of Lancaster or York should hold the English Crown. They started in 1399, when the succession departed from its natural course. King Richard II (1377–99) had been an undisputed king. When he was deposed in 1399, he had no son, and a choice of successor was made from amongst his relatives of Henry of Bolingbroke, Duke of Lancaster, who became King Henry IV (1399–1413). Two other Lancastrian kings followed, Henry's son Henry V (1413–22) and grandson Henry VI (1422–61). In 1399 there were no recent or obvious precedents to guide the momentous decision.

The monarchy was hereditary within the royal family. Every king since the Norman Conquest of 1066 was descended from William the Conqueror (1066–87) and all since 1189 from Henry II (1154–89). All were Plantagenets and succeeded their fathers or grandfathers. Beyond the direct male line, there existed no rules to define precisely who was to inherit comparable to the system of primogeniture for knights' fees and peerages, albeit often modified by entails in tail male. From 1337 all new earldoms and senior peerages were entailed in the male line. But should the Crown also descend according to primogeniture or according to the now fashionable entails in tail male? Such issues were certainly in the minds of Edward III himself in 1337 and in 1376, and of the House of Lords in 1399 and 1460. There was no certain answer which land law to apply.[27]

A whole succession of kings felt free to resettle their inheritances, but in practice their decisions did not bind future generations.[28] Probably nobody thought it was acceptable to divide a kingdom between coheiresses or their descendants. When arbitrating the Great Cause (1290), Edward I had firmly decided against this with reference to Scotland, selecting the heir of an eldest daughter, even though the three daughters had actually inherited such English estates as Tottenham jointly. A male monarch, King John Balliol, had resulted. The same year Edward ruled that if he himself left no son, each of his daughters should inherit the crown of England in succession rather than his brother Edmund: tail general not tail male.[29] This was somewhat surprising, since for England precedent – admittedly decidedly ancient precedent – suggested that queens regnant were unacceptable, the Empress Matilda being the obvious example. Chief Justice Fortescue was to demonstrate just how many kingly functions no woman could perform. No English rule restricted succession to the Crown to the male line, like the Salic law which developed in early fourteenth-century France. Matilda had failed to rule, but she had transmitted her title to her son who did succeed as King Henry II in line with primogeniture. Edward III (1327–77) seems to have reached the opposite conclusion to his grandfather Edward I, preferring his heirs male in 1337, 1362 and more certainly in 1376 when he entailed his possessions on his heirs male to exclude his granddaughter Philippa, the daughter of his dead second son Lionel, Duke of Clarence (d. 1368). Instead, he preferred his third son John of Gaunt, Duke of Lancaster (d. 1399), who had a son living in the future Henry IV. That Richard II awarded the arms of St Edward and in 1397 highest precedence to both his senior first cousins in the male line suggests that he agreed.[30]

Yet this did not settle the issue. In 1388, when the Lords Appellant seem to have considered deposing Richard II, it was apparently the candidacy of Thomas of Woodstock, Duke of Gloucester, the youngest and third surviving son of Edward III, that was first promoted and contested by the future Henry IV, the next heir under the entail after his absent father Gaunt.[31] Perhaps it was already accepted that the Crown was different to a noble estate and that a dead king could not bind his successors. Hence perhaps Henry IV's decision to obtain parliamentary sanction for entails on his four sons and their male lines in order of birth, but this was not a true Salic law. Nor was the further entail that replaced it later the same year, which allowed the eventual inheritance of daughters of these sons.[32] Such an act, so Richard, Duke of York, was to argue in 1460, was not 'of any force or effect against him that is right inheritor of the said crowns as it accordeth with God's law and all natural laws'. God's law, York assumed, was primogeniture, to which the House of Lords, shorn of his enemies, acquiesced.[33] What may be missing here are different perceptions. To the high nobility, whose lands and titles were entailed in tail male, the statute of 1406 made sense, but to everyone else – Cade's commoners, the gentry and the baronage, who practised primogeniture – it was primogeniture that was normal, natural and hence right for the Crown.

Yet there was an alternative, less restrictive, notion of the royal family, even though scarcely regarded by the inner circle of royalty most closely related to the current king. About two hundred men and women could trace their descent from previous kings through the male and female lines. They cherished their royal blood. It was this much wider notion of dynasty that was symbolized by the surname *Plantagenet* that was adopted by Richard, Duke of York, in about 1460 and applied retrospectively and anachronistically to the royal house from Henry II onwards. By this definition the houses of Lancaster and York were both Plantagenet. The surname Plantagenet first used by Richard, Duke of York, in was coined from Henry II's badge of the yellow broom (*planta genesta*). It was a reminder to contemporaries that Henry II himself had derived his own claim from his mother Empress Matilda: even if unable to reign, a woman had transmitted her title to her son.[34] It was a title to the Crown of France derived from his mother Isabella of France, who was still living, that Edward III had claimed in 1340. York in 1460 asserted rights transmitted via both his great-grandmother

Philippa of Clarence, and his mother Anne Mortimer. Any personal claim of Henry VII to succeed to the throne in 1485 came from his mother Margaret Beaufort, who actually outlived him.

Yet in 1399, when Richard II was deposed, Henry, Duke of Lancaster, was the obvious successor. Son of John of Gaunt, the third son of Edward III, he clearly took precedence over the late king's fourth son, Edmund, Duke of York, and the heir of the fifth. Whether the 1376 entail was current or not, Henry IV was Edward III's male heir. Circumstances also mattered. He was an adult male. He was king both by consent – by acclamation – and by conquest. He was in actual control. Yet this evidently did not suffice. Other titles were sought, perhaps including the ridiculous suggestion that his rights through the female line of Edmund, Earl of Lancaster (d. 1296), the younger brother of Edward I, should take priority over those he derived from Edward III! In the absence of agreed rules, the toddler Edmund Mortimer (d. 1425) – grandson of Philippa (d. c.1378), great-grandson of Lionel, Duke of Clarence (d. 1368) – was the heir under primogeniture. Edmund was too young in 1399 to assert his claim and perhaps never did, thus retaining his head. Similarly, self-preservation, may explain why Richard, Duke of York, Edmund's nephew and heir, had sported the arms and livery only of York and not of Clarence until 1460. In the highly unlikely eventuality that York was unaware of this distinguished ancestry, the Clare Roll prepared c.1455 by Osbert Bokenham would have reminded him.[35] Yet such alternative titles were not passed over and were asserted for them by others – the Percies under Henry IV and the Southampton plotters under Henry V – and they were never forgotten. The Mortimer claim remained latent, capable of revival should another change of king be required, or if the house of Lancaster expired.

That situation appeared imminent between 1435 and 1453. Although Henry V had three brothers, each died without legitimate offspring to carry forward their claims: Thomas, Duke of Clarence in 1421; John, Duke of Bedford in 1435; and in 1447 Humphrey, Duke of Gloucester ('Good Duke Humphrey'). From 1435 to 1447 only Henry V's son Henry VI and his uncle Gloucester survived of the male line of Lancaster. Although heir apparent since 1435, Gloucester had been separated since 1441, when his duchess was gaoled for sorcery, and was therefore maritally in no situation to beget an heir. When Gloucester died in 1447, there remained only the king to continue the Lancastrian line. The situation was improved somewhat in 1453, when Henry fathered a son of his own, Edward of Lancaster (d. 1471), who was recognized at once as heir to the throne and thus stymied any immediate alternative candidates. Obviously, Prince Edward of Lancaster had yet to survive the perils of childhood, which he did, but another seventeen years were to pass until he married and he was never to beget an heir of his own. Who was to succeed Henry VI was therefore a pressing issue from at least 1435 onwards.

The problem was not a shortage of potential candidates, but a plethora representing conflicting hereditary principles. Nobody seems to have considered the foreign royalty descended from the daughters of Henry IV and John of Gaunt: it was a principle of English law that those born abroad could not inherit. At least another five alternatives can be identified. Firstly, there was John, Duke of Exeter (d. 1447), the son of Henry IV's whole-sister Elizabeth, daughter of John of Gaunt and his first duchess Blanche of Lancaster. In English law the whole blood was preferred to the half-blood or stepsiblings. Applying normal legal rules therefore, Exeter had a superior claim to the Beauforts' as the next heir to Henry IV and the Lancastrian kings. In 1454 Exeter's son Duke Henry (d. 1475) apparently asserted his rights to the protectorate of Lancaster as heir of his great-grandmother Blanche, first wife of John of Gaunt.[36] However, neither Duke of Exeter was the male heir of Edward III as the Lancastrian kings had been. That title belonged, secondly, to John Beaufort, Duke of Somerset until his death in 1444, and his brother Edmund Beaufort, Duke of Somerset (d. 1455), grandsons in the direct male line of John of Gaunt and hence male heirs of Edward III himself. However, their father was a legitimated bastard and step-sibling of Henry IV, whom the king himself had sought, with doubtful legality, to exclude from the throne.[37] Thirdly, Margaret Beaufort (1443–1509), the daughter of Duke John, was the heir under primogeniture (heir general) of the Beauforts. It was actually to be a charge against Suffolk in 1450 that he had betrothed his own son John de la Pole to Margaret 'presuming and pretending her to be next inheritable to the crown of this your realm for lack of issue of you sovereign lord in accomplishment of his said traitorous purpose and intent'.[38] Clearly the succession was a live issue of discussion and speculation. Fourthly, and quite independently of any Clarence/Mortimer claim, York represented the next direct male heir of Edward III – that is the legitimate male heir, in preference to the legitimated Beauforts – as the grandson of Edmund, the king's fourth son. Fifthly, albeit through a female, Humphrey, Duke of Buckingham (d. 1460), represented Thomas of Woodstock (d. 1397), the youngest son of Edward III.

Perhaps it was with a view to the legitimate succession to the Crown that Henry VI elevated his royal cousins Exeter, Somerset (twice) and Buckingham to dukedoms in the 1440s, and that these magnates were intermarrying their offspring to likely candidates.[39] We have no explicit statements to this effect: it is also striking that these magnates were competing for precedence rather than collaborating with one another.[40] Note that none of them took precedence over York. Perhaps the assertion of York's claim as next heir to the throne in Parliament by his satellite Thomas Young, MP in 1450[41] was in his capacities as premier duke and heir male to Henry VI through the York line rather than the Clarence line, but this is nowhere explicitly recorded. The same applies to the duke's selection as Lord Protector in 1454.

Most people did not practise entails in tail male and so presumed female inheritance to be normal and indeed right. In 1450 the rebel Jack Cade took the pseudonym of Jack Mortimer, certainly in order to lay claim fraudulently to kinship with the Duke of York to which he was not entitled, but conceivably also as an allusion to the Clarence/Mortimer claim. Indeed, one rebel manifesto denied promoting York's title to the Crown, an indication that the topic had been raised and was being used to smear the rebellion as treason. Amazingly, at least one individual preferred Cade to Henry VI as king![42] To look to the future and plan for the reversion should the ruling dynasty die out was perfectly permissible. It was quite different from promoting the explosive Clarence–Mortimer claim in preference to the ruling line. York certainly had it drawn to his attention, by Bokenham for instance, but neither he nor anyone else, so far as we know, dared promote this Clarence–Mortimer title before 1460. From 1453 Prince Edward of Lancaster was the accepted heir. We cannot tell what York may privately have thought, but he was surely behind the preparation of Mortimer tracts sometime before 1460.[43] When he did raise the issue in 1460, it appealed only to a minority. Dynastic rivalry was a result of the Wars of the Roses – like deposition, in 1326 and 1399, a last resort when all else had failed – but it was neither a cause nor a precondition. It was a means of cutting through the incompatible complexities.

PART II
WHY THE WARS BEGAN

CHAPTER 5

PRECONDITIONS: THE CRISIS OF 1450

The Wars of the Roses could have begun a decade earlier during the explosion of anger against the regime in 1450. Actually they did not. The *Crisis of 1450* was a precondition of the *First War* of 1459–61 and to historical understanding of what happened. It compares with other great late medieval upheavals – 1297, perhaps 1340, and 1376–81 – when everything seemed to go wrong at once. Explosive though each crisis was and effective also in forcing governments to reappraise the situation, none actually changed either the king or the dynasty. All the protesters vowed they were loyal subjects to their king.

Of all these crises, that of 1450 may have been the most significant. It needs to be explained. Whilst certainly a unique series of events with very particular precipitants, this crisis witnessed the first interaction of the crucial factors that were to condition all the subsequent Wars. Whatever the critics of the regime in Parliament and in revolt hoped for in 1450, their actions in the short-term failed to deliver their objectives or to alleviate the problems that they perceived. These problems became more acute over the next decade and shaped all three Wars of the Roses.

THE ECONOMIC FACTOR

For almost 150 years after the Black Death of 1348–9 the English economy shrank. There were ever fewer people, also fewer and less populous settlements, constant reductions in arable farming, lower agricultural and other forms of production, and falling prices and rents. Admittedly productivity per head rose, but it was because not much less was produced by far fewer people and because more was being consumed per head, so wages in money and

49

purchasing power increased. The economy did develop, as cloth-making for export expanded and farming was commercialized, yet overall there was contraction. Within this 150 years, the deepest trough occurred in the mid fifteenth century. It was a 'pan-European' rather than purely English recession due principally to a desperate shortage of silver bullion, which meant that the actual coins and the credit necessary for trade were lacking. The recession led indirectly to protectionist measures that further damaged commercial relations. In England the recession is called the *Great Slump* of *c.*1440–80. 'An extraordinary range of powerful depressive forces combined to impose an enduring and wide-ranging slump of precipitous proportions upon the long-term recessionary trend.' Although most conspicuous 'in those branches of England's overseas trade which are able to be quantified', it was also apparent everywhere, North and South, town and country, and affected everything from wine exports to rabbit prices. The recession began in the late 1430s in the North and in the 1440s spread elsewhere. Although the economy was to plunge further in the 1450s, 1460s and 1470s, and was an essential context for each phase of the Wars of the Roses, yet very significant falls in commerce in wool, woollen cloth and wine had already taken place by 1450.[1]

The *Great Slump* hurt all types of people. It affected the high nobility, whose rents fell, especially in the Welsh marches, and whose costs rose. It hit cultivators, whose products sold for less if at all, manufacturers who encountered falling demand, artisans who were underemployed or unemployed, and landholders who could not lease their lands or collect their rents. Even an innovative landlord like Winchester College that invested its annual surplus in urban inns derived only derisory revenues from them.[2] Those able to prosper were principally those with additional income, such as noblemen who accrued other inheritances – they were all richer than their fathers[3] – and successful lawyers who bucked the trend. There were also those who diverted royal revenues to themselves by amassing royal grants, took a percentage of royal dues, or who charged for access to the king or justice. Accordingly, hard-pressed and jealous Kentishmen derided Henry VI's courtiers, sheriffs and commissioners as 'traitors' to justice and reform. They wanted the king's grants to be cancelled, or resumed, and the income used to defray the king's expenses without need for taxation: this was called resumption. Even 'though standards of living were high by the standards of earlier centuries',[4] and the most extreme deprivation of earlier centuries was avoided, yet there was a sharp economic downturn even for farmers and artisans who had been prospering, and hence economic discontent everywhere. There was acute deflation: rent reductions, unoccupied land, reductions in entry and common fines, a shortage of coin, barter and truck, unsaleable grain, stock and wool, falling prices and purchasing power.[5] Two related groups that suffered particularly in the late 1440s were sheep-farmers and cloth-workers, whose livelihoods depended on the export of wool and woollen-cloths. Following hard on prosperity and expansion, between 1446 and 1450 cloth exports fell by 35 per cent, causing 'acute problems of over-production and unemployment' in the cloth-producing areas of Wiltshire and the Cotswolds. Exports of broadcloths from Sandwich (Kent) in 1449–50 fell from 2,078 to 237 and woolsacks from 182 to 25. Imports of wine fell from 1,042 tuns to 271. Doubtless it was a glut of unsold wool and cloths that caused the severe drop in wool prices.[6]

London was a special case. It was the seat of government and justice. The City was the wealthiest and most populous town, with perhaps 50,000 inhabitants. It was the largest port, the largest market and retail outlet for luxuries and manufactures, and the largest employer in fifteenth-century England. It contained substantial alien colonies, notably Hanseatic merchants from North Germany and the Baltic based at the Steelyard, Flemings in Southwark, and merchants and bankers and 42 servants from Italy in 1456–7. Aliens were valued by the Crown, paying alien poll taxes, higher customs, and often purchasing licences of exemption from customs, but they were suspected by native Englishmen as trading more preferentially than themselves. Although London was the only cosmopolitan city in England comparable to Bruges and Antwerp in the Low Countries, and the great towns of northern and central Italy, the relations of Londoners with their enclaves of privileged aliens and lawyers were delicate, fraught and sometimes exploded into violence. London's merchants had long recognized that there was a relationship between commercial prosperity and the money supply, in medieval terms the actual number of coins. Hence they deplored any export of cash that reduced the stock of coin, and sought to prevent it. It was generally believed that these foreigners imported frivolities at inflated prices, bought cheaply, engaged in all kinds of sharp practices, and drained the country of its bullion in an era when coin was in desperately short supply. This was the diagnosis of London's merchants, whose recipe was therefore to regulate alien traders, to deprive them of their unfair advantages, to stop them from carrying their earnings abroad, and to make them invest their profits in English products. London's merchants of the staple were behind ordinances of 1429 that forced purchasers of English wool at Calais to pay one third in bullion and foreign coin. For seven years from 1440, a hosting statute had made aliens lodge with native

English people and under their supervision. Such measures curtailed the buying power and commercial freedom of foreigners. Inevitably they provoked reprisals, such as the Burgundian blockade of 1435–9, and reduced the amount of commercial activity, but these unfortunate repercussions did not cause Londoners to modify their policies.[7]

The life-blood of London was foreign trade. The principal importers and exporters of wool, cloth and foreign luxuries were London merchants: the staplers, who had a monopoly of English wool exports through Calais, and the merchant adventurers, who monopolized the English cloth trade to Bruges and Antwerp. When national commerce slumped in the late 1440s, it was London that was hit hardest. London merchants were victims. So too inevitably were London's mercers, grocers, haberdashers, anybody else retailing such imports, and the mass of lesser Londoners whom they employed and who depended on their custom. They blamed the aliens in their midst and hence the government that (in their opinion) had failed to regulate them adequately.

Economic distress did not propel the people automatically into blind revolt and violence, nor were popular rebels the lowest of the low. Where they can be identified, popular insurgents usually prove to have stakes in society as small landholders and heads of families. Often they were the leaders of their communities and office-holders who had something to lose and preserve, some sense of causation, and who hoped by direct action not merely to protest or destroy, but to relieve their distress. Such men were the retailers, artisans, servants, labourers and even merchants of London, who exploded into violence in 1450 and the following decade.

Similar figures were prominent in the rebellions that took place during this acute recession in Wiltshire, Kent and Sussex. 'The available evidence suggests that there was a general correlation between those areas that were heavily disturbed in 1450 and the major cloth producing areas.' 'Thus in both Kent and Sussex, as well as in Wiltshire, economic distress may have combined with political dissatisfaction to produce a volatile mixture of ideas that ultimately exploded in revolt.' There were two potential targets, national and local. As the recession deepened, 'even . . . small amounts become burdensome', as Sussex protesters sought to rid themselves of common fines, chevage, and other customary emblems of the authority of their lords, with some success as certain landholders made concessions. In Kent, other seignorial and local governmental abuses were additional burdens, from the court of Dover, forest courts, the greenwax, or purveyance, some of which amounted to 'great payments of the people' and stemmed directly from government policy, as the rebels realized.[8] Although an elitist body, the Parliament of 1449–50 declared in strangely modern socialist terms that 'God and all wisdom suggest that they who are most able and right able to bear such charges should be charged and the poor people eased.' Parliament put a stop to the commandeering of transport for purveyance and the extortion by exchequer officials that had harmed ordinary subjects.[9]

Unlike their counterparts of today, medieval governments did not purport to manage the economy, which was indeed generally beyond their control. There was nothing governments could do about the onset of plague and other disruptive epidemic diseases. It was the weather, not man, that determined the success of the harvest, which in turn affected supplies of food, prices, wages, employment, transport, demand for manufactures, and was also, quite literally, a matter of life and death. It was the independent operations of the weather and of little-understood animal diseases that caused murrains and other misfortunes of livestock. England's crippling shortage of coin was a symptom of an international bullion crisis that was Europe-wide and beyond the control of any single state. The government of Henry VI did not cause the *Great Slump* and could do nothing about it. It was not until 1516 that Thomas More indicated how society and the economy could be moulded, and not for a further thirty years till the Tudor commonwealthsmen started making their interventions effective.[10] Yet medieval people, just like ourselves today, blamed economic problems on the government. 'The king's subjects were similarly disposed to believe that some aspects, at least, of economic recession were the result of misgovernment.'[11]

Actually they were right. The *Great Slump* itself was an external force, but many of the particular aggravating problems of 1450 were the fault of the government. The collapse of the wine trade was the direct consequence of the war with France and the loss, with Gascony, of the Bordeaux wine region. On 23 May 1449 Robert Winnington attacked the Hanseatic Bay fleet, capturing 110 ships, including 'all the chief ships of Dutchland, Holland, Zeeland, and Flanders'. He had been commissioned to cleanse the sea of pirates by the government, some of whose principal members profited from Winnington's exploit, and Henry VI's government refused Hanseatic demands for redress. Understandably, the Hanse reacted by excluding English goods from their key markets of north Germany and the Baltic. Restoration of this trade was an important objective of the Kentish rebels under Jack Cade in June 1450. Similarly, it was the English bullionist legislation advocated by protectionist merchants that had provoked Burgundy in 1447 to exclude English cloth from its principal markets. In 1449 this was reported in Parliament as a source of unemployment and economic distress, 'unto the right intolerable hurt of all the commons of this realm, cloth makers: that is to say men weavers, fullers, dyers; and women combers, carders and spinners; and other buyers and sellers thereof'. Strangely, those who had pushed for such legislation did not see the Burgundian ban as a consequence of their own actions. Instead, in and after 1449 they urged further restrictions on alien trade.[12] It was again the government that restarted the war with France. Without necessarily being wrong, all these actions partly explain why clothworkers found themselves thrown out of work, why Kentishmen complained to King Henry that 'his merchandise is lost', and why Wiltshiremen saw the killing of that 'traitor to the king' Bishop Aiscough as a remedial step.[13]

Violence did not work, for government policy at most aggravated the pre-existing depression, which persisted and indeed deepened in the years that followed. Hence blame continued to be heaped on the government. The people became disposed to direct action in appropriate circumstances. Some of those hit by the Burgundian embargo 'became as idle people', unemployed, 'which provoketh them to sin and mischievous living'.[14] The recession was a contributory factor to disturbances in York in 1453–5.[15] Londoners wrongly blamed it on the misconduct of foreigners and especially those aliens who drained England of its bullion. The solution, as they petitioned repeatedly, was further to regulate the movements and trade of aliens. Such beliefs underpinned the attacks in London on the Lombards and Flemings in the 1450s.[16]

Acute economic distress thus predisposed not just individuals but whole categories of people and whole communities to complain, protest, take to the streets, engage in self-help and violence. The government was blamed indirectly through its officials and directly, as the root cause through its policies. Yet those most affected were responsible members of society, with much to lose: often, indeed, protests were coordinated by local elites and local officers.[17] A predisposition for insurrection need not be triggered into action, and in most of the country it was not. A dozen seditious mutterings in the 1440s resulted only in the arrest, trial and punishment of the offenders. There were several small uprisings early in 1450. On 24 January, in the extreme south-eastern tip of Kent, a rising was led by the labourer Thomas Cheyne, who called himself 'the hermit Bluebeard'. On 9 January Adam Moleyns, Bishop of Chichester and keeper of the privy seal, was murdered at Portsmouth in Hampshire by troops he was trying to pay. His assassins raised the people at nearby Bishops Waltham on 1 February. On 3 March there was another rising at Ipswich, apparently in favour of Richard, Duke of York, who was actually in Ireland. If its 10,000 adherents seem highly improbable, the other two risings were substantial enough for captains to be appointed and for each to be directed against the government: Bluebeard's men explicitly sought the deaths of William, Duke of Suffolk, James, Lord Say, Bishop Aiscough and Abbot Boulers. Other bishops and abbots were attacked. Although unusual in their national focus, such small-scale insubordination was well within the capacity to cope of the local authorities and the commissioners of central government, who quickly restored order and administered justice: Bluebeard himself was hanged, drawn and quartered.[18] The rebellion of Jack Cade in June was much more serious.

Execution and forfeiture were strong deterrents for everyone with property and dependants. The particular and locally focused complaints of Cade's first manifesto were not sufficient to induce such responsible citizens to hazard everything, nor for their discontent to escalate into a regional revolt. Prerequisites included more widely shared grievances and objectives, the relaxation of the forces of repression, some further irritants to drive the disgruntled into direct action, and a confident conviction of the rightness of their cause.

All these came together in the spring of 1450 with the trial in Parliament of William Duke of Suffolk, his murder in the Channel by pirates, and the expectation of government reprisals on Kent. Beyond a certain threshold, everybody was prepared to rise up, including the London mob, and discipline degenerated into general violence, pillage and piecemeal vengeance. Although popular protesters subscribed generally to the political conventions of the elite, they were more extreme in their judgements. In their eyes, maladministration and corruption were transmuted into treason, and the penalty that they demanded was always death. Several ministers were lynched. Some protesters even thought to change the king.

MILITARY DEFEAT

Henry V had been a king of great strength and charisma who made himself into the national hero, not merely to contemporary Englishmen and supporters of the Lancastrians during the Wars of the Roses, but also to their Yorkist rivals, who dared not criticize him, to Shakespeare nearly two centuries later, and even into our own time. Henry V had renewed the Hundred Years War with extraordinary success. Besides his amazing victory at Agincourt in 1415, achieved apparently against great odds, Henry systematically conquered

Normandy and, by the Treaty of Troyes (1420), secured his own recognition as successor to the French throne by the current French king Charles VI in lieu of his own son the dauphin. Henry V took on the government of France itself. However, he died too soon to taste the fruits of his victory. It was therefore his infant son Henry VI who succeeded in 1422 as king both of England and of France, and his brother Bedford as Regent who carried the task of conquest forward, winning further victories (notably Verneuil in 1424), extending his rule further through northern France, and in 1431 orchestrating the young king's coronation at Paris. Such victories and Henry VI's *Dual Monarchy* of England and France were sources of English national pride and came to be expected. After a generation, the occupation of so much of northern France was normal and routine. The threat to Calais in 1436 was presented as a national crisis, and its relief featured in many a chronicle and poem as yet another national victory.[19] Withdrawal from France, the renunciation of Henry V's legacy, and defeat were inconceivable, not just to English warriors and English settlers with vested interests and raucous voices, but to the English public at large, to whom the French wars and English victories were genuinely popular. This remained true as late as 1475, 1492 and 1513, when Edward IV, Henry VII and Henry VIII invaded France in pursuit of their French Crown.

Yet this very enthusiasm was a problem for the Lancastrian regime, since it denied the government any flexibility of policy and strategy. It was a problem to which no satisfactory solution was ever found. Public opinion took English military prowess for granted. Defeat or French superiority were inconceivable. If defeat happened, therefore, it was attributed not to the superiority of the French but to English treason. Had Henry V survived another twenty years, perhaps he could have convinced enough Frenchmen in person of the validity of his title and he might have made a reality of his agreement with Charles VI. Minus Henry V, with only a baby to inspire and obviously incapable of persuading, this proved impossible. In retrospect, English success had peaked before 1429, when their siege of Orléans failed. The Treaty of Troyes of 1420 had never enjoyed general approval from the French. Most of eastern, central and southern France remained unconverted, and the Dauphin Charles – the 'king of Bourges' – was widely recognized as King Charles VII. Although his cause faltered initially, the phenomenon of Joan of Arc, who brought him success, his coronation at Rheims Cathedral and a revival in patriotic self-belief, ensured that the English never made a reality of Lancastrian France. It had been a serious setback in 1435 when Burgundy had withdrawn from its alliance with England. Paris fell in 1436, leaving the English with mere enclaves – substantial admittedly – in the north (Normandy, Maine) and south-west (Gascony) of France when Henry VI came of age. Even had he been another Henry V, Henry VI probably could not have reversed the deterioration in English fortunes, but of course he was not. Forced on the defensive, it became ever more difficult for the English to retain what they already held, to finance the war from their French resources, to rely on the loyalty of King Henry's French subjects,[20] or to mobilize sufficient money and men from within England. The superior resources of Charles VII gradually told. The financial strain on the government in England became increasingly insupportable. What Henry V had bequeathed, it gradually emerged, was an unwinnable war.

Henry V's triumphs, moreover, ruled out retreat and a diplomatic solution. It had been impossible, both at the Congress of Arras (1435), when Henry VI was still under age, and later, to surrender his title to sovereignty over France. Yet this concession was essential for any agreement that might have preserved English territory intact on a permanent basis. After Bedford's death in 1435, four great magnates in turn took command in Lancastrian France as lieutenants to the king: Richard, Duke of York (1436–7), Richard, Earl of Warwick (1437–9), John Beaufort, Duke of Somerset (1443), York again (1440–6), and Edmund Beaufort, Duke of Somerset (1446 on). On balance they did well and stabilized the situation, so that very little was lost to the resurgent French, although the inhabitants of the occupied territories became less and less committed to the *Dual Monarchy*. There was even a popular uprising in Normandy in 1435.[21] The war effort cried out for the leadership of the king: ideally, another Henry V, but such charismatic monarchs occurred infrequently. An adult male king of reasonable competence and bellicosity could have provided leadership, inspiration, more recruits and more resources from England, especially taxation from Parliament, than any noble lieutenant. Whether success could even then have been possible, one cannot say. But Henry VI was not like that. After his coronation as king of France in 1431, he never revisited France. He shrugged off his military responsibilities onto a succession of noble lieutenants, who could not completely fill his shoes. Serious errors were made in the direction of the Hundred Years War, notably the division of command and hence diffusion of the exceptional financial and military investment in 1443,[22] but they were not in fact decisive.

Henry VI also seems early in his reign to have decided on a peace policy, perhaps because he was naturally peaceful – hence his ill-advised clemency to domestic foes during the Wars of the Roses – and initially at least on the persuasions of his great-uncle Cardinal Beaufort and others about him. A key moment came in 1439–40, when it was decided to release Charles, Duke of Orleans – a captive whom Henry V himself had ordered never to be freed – to work with the French for an enduring peace. This was opposed by the late king's last brother, Humphrey, Duke of Gloucester, now heir to the throne, self-appointed custodian of Henry V's memory and legacy, and leader of a significant group committed to waging the war. Gloucester was overruled, clearly with Henry VI's approval. Such opposition may have stopped Henry from negotiating away his title to France, which he was prepared to suspend in 1444 in return for Gascony and Normandy in full sovereignty, although it does not appear that Charles VII was ever willing to partition his kingdom or to compromise his overriding sovereignty. The principal achievement of the peace policy was the Treaty of Tours (1444), a two-year truce. It solved none of the substantial issues, but it gave the English government a breathing space and the chance to curb war expenditure. The treaty was regarded and indeed widely welcomed in England as a triumph, accompanied as it was by the king's marriage in 1445 to Margaret of Anjou, a princess of the French royal house, albeit one who brought no dowry and whose wedding was at English expense. The condemnation of the match by *Caxton's Chronicle*, highly influential in future generations, dates after 1464 and was informed by hindsight.[23] Under the circumstances it is difficult to see what else Henry could have done. It was very much his policy.[24] Perhaps naively, he saw it as the first step to a lasting peace.

Whatever the benefits of this pause in hostilities, they were surely counteracted first by the surrender of the county of Maine in 1447 and by English aggression towards Brittany (and, as described above, towards the Hanse). Although it may well have appeared illogical to King Henry to withhold this county from the rightful holder, who was now his father-in-law King René, the surrender of Maine was an unnecessary concession, not an integral part of the treaty, and was surely a personal decision, as Henry was later to confirm. Implementation was strongly resisted, but ineffectually, by his commanders on the ground, led by Edmund, Duke of Somerset, who lost those lands he held in Maine by the handover. These commanders recognized Maine as an important buffer against French attack, the loss of which exposed the heart of Normandy to any future French assault. They sought to exculpate themselves from future blame for carrying out orders with which they profoundly disagreed.[25] Four times the French renewed the truce of Tours.

By the late 1440s, therefore, any hope of making Henry VI's French kingship into a reality had passed. Humphrey, Duke of Gloucester's fruitless exhortations and continual carping at the betrayal of his brother's legacy became intolerable.

In 1447 Gloucester was arrested, but died before whatever was intended could be done. The ideal of a *Dual Monarchy* had failed. Whatever nostalgic loyalty the Gascons still felt towards England, for the Normans the English had become an oppressive occupying power. The French used the truces to re-organize themselves militarily: to establish a permanent standing army of well-trained and well-equipped professionals funded by France's much greater resources. The English could not rearm: Parliament refused the opportunity to reinforce and revictual.[26] The peace dividend had to be taken and defence expenditure had to be cut. There is no reason to doubt Richard, Duke of York's later charges that experienced officers were dismissed, troops were disbanded, unpaid, unvictualled and unmunitioned, for without money from England – as York well knew – Norman resources alone were insufficient, and indeed by 1449 the Norman Estates were refusing to finance even the peacetime establishment.[27] Henceforth Englishmen and Frenchmen would meet on very unequal terms. A lasting peace might have confirmed possession of Lancastrian provinces in France, but it was achievable only if Henry renounced his French crown, which was politically unacceptable at home. In the longer term the situation was untenable, although apparently neither side realized this.

Early in 1449 Parliament was briefed on how strong were the French and how weak their own defences, so that 'if the war should befall, as God forbid, the country of Normandy is in no wise of itself sufficient to make resistance against the great puissance of the adversaries'.[28] Nevertheless, veterans and public opinion alike in England seem to have been unaware of French military reforms and still took victory in any future conflict for granted. The French also overrated the English defences and were surprised by their collapse. In retrospect, it is clear that English retention of Normandy, perhaps Gascony, and even Calais depended on the prolongation of the truce, which was indeed repeatedly extended. The expiry of each truce did offer the French regular opportunities, if required, to apply their greater resources and military machine to the extinction of Lancastrian France. Charles VII seems to have seen no urgency in completing the job. It was the English who foolishly broke the status quo.

It was imperative for the English to maintain the truce and to avoid offending the French. Strangely, they miscalculated and in 1449 provoked a resumption of the war by seizing the Breton town of Fougères. From a position of weakness, they had categorized Brittany as an English ally in the truce agreements, without the knowledge or consent of either the French or the Bretons, who did not see themselves as such. The English mistakenly supposed that their seizure of the Breton castle of Fougères concerned only them and the

Bretons, not the French. Since the relevant clause was not acceptable either to the French or the Bretons, neither was the Fougères episode, so hostilities resumed. Even so, war could have been prevented by a prompt recognition of Breton subjection to France and by English withdrawal from Fougères, yet the regime intransigently refused.[29] The instructions to Edmund, Duke of Somerset did not permit him to conciliate, as York later said he should have done.[30] The government's policy was discussed and approved by the House of Lords as late as the Winchester Parliament of June 1449.[31]

Yet the war turned immediately against the English who, to French surprise, proved quite unable to resist. Suddenly, unexpectedly, King Henry needed massive sums of money for new armies to defend Normandy, all that remained of Lancastrian France. They were not forthcoming. He was able to send only 2,500 men under Sir Thomas Kyriel. When Somerset finally capitulated at Caen, his 4,000 men may have been outnumbered fivefold.[32] Somerset dared not commit his tiny forces to the field, left his garrisons to their own devices, surrendered Rouen almost at once and other places without a siege at all. Such conduct offended the chivalric code of honour, dishonoured the duke and exposed him to the penalties of treason.[33] If Somerset was indeed a coward and a poltroon, who failed to fight to the last, it was surely because he knew how frail English defences were and how improbable were adequate reinforcements or supplies. Indeed, he had foreseen such an eventuality when negotiating compensation for the loss of his Maine domains in 1447.[34] York was later to imply that Somerset had ample funds from Norman sources, but this was incorrect.[35]

Disappointed in their wages, it was soldiers awaiting embarkation at Portsmouth who murdered Bishop Moleyns on 9 January 1450. A few repatriated and again unpaid soldiers joined Cade's Rebellion in June and many more shared in the riots in London that accompanied the autumn Parliament. After capturing Normandy, Charles VII swiftly swallowed Gascony, whilst the Burgundians threatened Calais, whose mutinous garrison appeared willing to hand it over to whoever would pay them.[36] In May commissions were issued to array all men between the ages of 16 and 60 to repel an anticipated French invasion.[37] The *Crisis of 1450* took place at a time of national emergency. Contributing to it with first-hand information and the most bitter and malicious resentment were those thousands of unexpectedly unemployed ex-servicemen, who had suffered utter defeat of the most humiliating ease and rapidity, and who now wanted their back-pay, compensation, and justice on the commander and ministers responsible.

The Bankruptcy of Lancaster

The recession impacted also on royal revenues, on the ability of the government to defend Lancastrian France, and on the capacity and willingness of English taxpayers to make up the shortfall.

Cade's rebels expected the king to live in kingly style. They deplored in 1450 that Henry was 'himself so poor that he may not [pay] for his meat nor drink', that 'he oweth more than ever did king in England', and could do none of these things.[38]

Waging the Hundred Years War was an enormous drain on English resources. Even when successful, the war in France cost more than could be comfortably afforded. Foreseeing that the French war would become an open-ended charge on the English taxpayer, Henry V's Parliament had insisted on the separation of the finances of his two kingdoms of England and France. The Regent Bedford did indeed fund his rule and continuing war in France from Henry VI's French subjects. The burden on the latter, however, became too great, especially as Lancastrian France contracted and was economically exhausted, and as Charles VII made his greater resources tell. The relief of Calais in 1436 required a supreme English military and financial effort. So too did Somerset's expedition to France in 1443.[39] Diplomacy was scarcely cheaper. The war effort and peace negotiations alike had increasingly to be funded from English resources that were insufficient.[40] Suspension of hostilities in 1444 was financially necessary. Collection of the peace dividend came close to total disarmament.[41]

Reluctantly, Parliament acknowledged the king's necessity and voted taxes regularly, but at the rate of only a half fifteenth and tenth a year, with exemptions after 1433 reducing them to a mere £15,500 a year. This was adequate only slightly to ameliorate the annual deficit and quite insufficient to remove the need for purveyance or to contribute to the repayment of accumulated debt. Whatever contemporaries may have felt, the 1440s was *not* a period of high taxation. By earmarking whatever taxes there were to particular purposes, to ensure that these at least were properly funded, parliament diverted funds from other necessary purposes and could not significantly alter the global situation.[42] At a time of economic recession, when everyone was hard up, the half tenth and fifteenth due in November 1449 was perceived as heavy – and purveyance equated to paying twice – and the weight of taxes and exactions was identified as another area where financial burdens could be relieved. There was a 'widespread (erroneous) belief that excessive taxation was a principal cause of lower incomes'.[43] Rather than voting the immediate and substantial taxes that alone might have averted defeat by the French, the Parliament of 1449–50 insisted first on resumption (cancellation) of royal grants and the appropriation of existing revenues to particular purposes. Rather than levying another fifteenth and tenth with a guaranteed return, Parliament experimented with a new income tax that was designed to transfer the burdens elsewhere. Predictably it failed to raise enough money.[44] An easier way out that would cost taxpayers nothing seemed to be to resume grants made since 1422 and thus enable the king to manage on his own without any need for parliamentary taxation. At first, in mid 1449, this demand for resumption implied no criticism of the government's French policy, which was explicitly endorsed, but was predominantly financial in motivation. MPs were so unwilling to vote taxes because they realized the general impoverishment arising from the acute economic depression.

'Even had the country been at peace, however, it is unlikely that Henry's government would have been able to pay its way.'[45] By 1450 the royal finances were in a most parlous state. Henry V had died in debt in 1422. As early as 1433, accumulated debt totalled £164,815; by 1450 it had accrued to £372,000; and almost certainly it continued to grow afterwards. In 1433 only £8,000 remained uncommitted after meeting such fixed and inescapable charges as the Calais garrison and the royal household, and in 1450 only £5,000 was available.[46] Successive treasurers of England faced daily problems in matching their commitments to revenues: those of Bishop Lumley, treasurer from 1447 to 1449, have been explored in depth.[47] Faced by such grave and deteriorating deficits, Lord Treasurer Ralph, Lord Cromwell in 1433 and his successors took to declaring the true state of the king's finances to Parliament, hoping thereby to secure a more sympathetic understanding from the Commons and practical financial help.[48] The king's poverty was commonplace. However, by at least 1450, contemporaries were blaming his financial difficulties not on the intolerable burdens of the French war and the collapse of normal revenues, but on the extravagance, corruption and incompetence of his ministers and household, who were viewed as enriching themselves at the king's and the public expense.[49] The king's patronage and its misuse became the top political issue. Hence the call for acts of resumption that would cancel royal grants, return alienated revenues to the Crown, enable the king to fund his government and war from his own resources, and thus remove any need to relieve him through taxation. This was quite unrealistic.

Actually Henry VI never had very much land to distribute in patronage. His three uncles of Clarence, Bedford and Gloucester had been modestly endowed, principally from exchequer annuities, and he had no access until 1443 to those duchy of Lancaster lands held in trust for the fulfilment of the will of his father and later himself.[50] Moreover, in 1445 he had to find £4,500-worth of endowments for Queen Margaret. Yet most historians have accepted Henry's outrageous extravagance as a fact. Henry had 'wantonly squandered' the royal demesne: between 1437 and 1449 he 'was moved to alienate his lands outside the circle of princes of the royal blood to an extent probably unprecedented in English history'. In response to the first act of resumption in 1450, there was a review of patronage to members of the king's household, which distinguished between what income each must surrender (£1,000) and what each could keep (£3,570). Yet if all had been resumed and not regranted, for resumed offices had to be filled, and even if as much again had been resumed from beneficiaries outside the household, resumption 'could have had little immediate or ultimate effect on the state of the king's finances'.[51] At most 5 per cent of the revenues that had been available to Richard II and to Henry VI could have again become available. What was resumed had at once to be appropriated to the royal household and was not available to repay the king's debts or for extraordinary expenditure. 'We may seriously doubt whether a very substantial, permanent contribution to the national finances could be secured by any resumption that they proposed, however drastic it might be.' Even the most far-reaching act of resumption was therefore not the panacea for all the king's financial problems that contemporaries repeatedly and obdurately supposed. When in 1451 'the extraordinarily lavish grants and alienations of 1437–49 were almost entirely undone', the king's resources remained 'gravely inadequate for the legitimate expenses of government'.[52] For critics of the regime, unfortunately, the failure to achieve this result did not indicate how inadequate were the resources in question (correctly), but rather (incorrectly) that royal favourites had obstructed full resumption and that the priority was to overcome their opposition to it.

Such accumulated debt might have been manageable had royal revenues remained at the £110,000 of Richard II's last years, but they did not. By 1450 royal revenues had dropped by at least 40 per cent. The fall was to continue thereafter, quite how low is uncertain, since the records of the exchequer deteriorate and much revenue was spent before it arrived there. Obviously the king shared in the decline in rents that affected all other landholders. By far the most important development was the plunge in customs revenues, which plummeted from £40,677 in 1421 to £28,100 in 1446–8, and (probably after some recovery) to a mere £25,000 in the early 1460s. Even 'while recognizing that some extravagances of expenditure were Henry VI's own fault, it is difficult to avoid the

conclusion that shortfalls of royal revenue, accompanied by incessant allegations that the kingdom was over-taxed, fed directly into the discrediting of his
government'.[53]

Throughout the 1430s and 1440s, therefore, Henry VI's government found
itself faced with the inescapably escalating costs of war, with diminishing
revenues, and with grudging and inadequate votes of taxation that were spiced
with strictures for not living within its means and with appropriations designed
to remove its flexibility in deploying what few revenues there were. Reducing
costs, by terminating the French war, was strongly criticized. Diplomacy also
cost money. Queen Margaret brought no dowry and had to be dowered.
Curtailing military expenditure from 1444 alleviated rather than solved the
problems and had disastrous military side effects. In 1450 the government was
to make serious efforts to cut household expenses from an uncontrolled total of
£24,000 to £11,000, a difference of £13,000.[54] Retrenchment and resumption
combined saved £18,000, probably more than a third of royal revenues, but
quite insufficient to cover ordinary expenses, fund the war effort, or make
much impact on the mountain of debt. It also had political repercussions.
People lamented that Henry no longer maintained what was seen as the
appropriate state for a king.

Henry's household and troops had been supplied by taking what was
required, through extension of the scope of the legitimate device of purveyance,
and by non-payment of suppliers, military commanders, soldiers and creditors,
some of whom had to wait many years for repayment. Those owed money did
receive assignments for repayment against particular sources of revenue, but
found themselves in competition with more pressing current commitments
that usually took precedence. Too many of these assignments proved bad and
went unpaid. That army captains could at least defer payments to the troops
under their commands had the most serious of repercussions: soldiers
mutinied, deserted, looted those they were meant to protect, and irrupted into
English politics. That soldiers went unpaid was a most damaging political
critique throughout the 1450s.[55] The gap between income and expenditure
could not be bridged by borrowing, for who would lend when there was so little
chance of prompt repayment? Coin and credit were alike in short supply. 'By
1449 the Lancastrian regime was truly bankrupt.'[56]

It was on top of this desperate and deteriorating situation that there were
suddenly imposed extreme necessities. The three interruptions mentioned
above to trade with the Hanse, Burgundy, Gascony and France in 1449–50,
which almost terminated English exports, also drastically cut customs

revenues. Simultaneously, the renewal of the French war demanded massive sums in cash that Henry could raise neither from his own resources, nor from borrowing, nor from Norman revenues, for 'the general povert[y]' there was too great,[57] nor (it emerged) from English taxpayers either. The king should live of his own, cried parliament and populace alike, as they focused on achieving that result rather than in funding the defence against the French that all agreed was the top priority.

Englishmen disliked taxation anyway. Now, in economic recession, they found it extremely burdensome and were not prepared to increase their contribution. That it was apparently insufficient, that monies meant for defence had been spent on other purposes, that monies that were supposed to be in hand actually were not, and that the king was resorting overmuch to purveyance – taking what he required – and not repaying what had been borrowed, could only (in their view) be due to mismanagement by the king's ministers and even to embezzlement. Critics of the regime believed that Suffolk, the king's ministers, favourites, and members of the royal household had been advancing themselves financially by persuading the king to grant them his lands, by soliciting bribes for royal favours, and by perverting the law to their financial advantage.[58]

The solution in this national emergency was not to throw good money after bad or to vote extra taxes, but to try and transfer the load from traditional taxpayers through an experimental taxation poll tax, to ensure that what had been voted was actually spent on the intended purposes, and to resume into the king's hands what had been given away, so that he could meet his ordinary expenses. The staplers did shoulder some costs of Calais, but only on condition of reduced customs for themselves and an end to the sale of licences to trade wool staple-free,[59] which the government did not – indeed could not afford to – honour. Instead of alleviating a desperate situation, Parliament exarcebated it. And after one Parliament insistent on resumption was dissolved, its successors (1449–50, 1450–1) took up the cause – which admittedly King Henry could and perhaps should have conceded – rather than focusing on the national necessity.

THE CRISIS OF 1449–50 AND THE FALL OF WILLIAM, DUKE OF SUFFOLK

If it was errors in foreign policy that brought about the renewal of fighting in 1449, it was the virtual bankruptcy of the Crown that made effective defence impossible and the economic recession that deterred Parliament from prioritizing the taxes essential for survival. Without speedy reinforcements, defeat was inevitable, and relief was not really conceivable. So, we may suppose, thought Henry's lieutenant and commander-in-chief Edmund, Duke of Somerset, who did not prolong resistance in the hope of relief that he recognized to be in vain. Having witnessed his brother John's long imprisonment in France and ruinous ransom, Edmund did not intend suffering likewise without serious hope of reinforcements, and capitulated quickly on good personal terms. The English garrisons proved powerless to resist the reformed military machine of a resurgent France. Normandy was lost, then in 1451 Gascony. Despite all its difficulties, the English government somehow raised another army and despatched it to Gascony in 1452 under the command of the Earl of Shrewsbury, initially with startling success. Total defeat followed at Castillon in 1453, marking the end of the Hundred Years War.

These disasters caused the domestic crisis that brought down the regime. It seems that Englishmen of whatever rank found it impossible to conceive that the French were militarily superior – more numerous, better resourced, equipped, trained, and more professional. Defeat had to be for other reasons. The king's principal counsellor William, Duke of Suffolk, was accused of treasonable collusion with the French. Henry himself, as always, was above criticism, even when he defended those whom he said had just acted on his orders, but it stood to reason that the advice that he had received was evil counsel: the traditional explanation for all such disasters. Almost everyone blamed the government, alleging cowardice, financial mismanagement, evil counsel, corruption and – at home – misgovernment and perversion of justice. The king's ministers, councillors, royal favourites and household were attacked and ridiculed in seditious rhymes that circulated widely and set the political scene:

For you have made the king so poor,
That now he beggeth from door to door;
Alas, [that] it should so be.[60]

The parliamentary House of Commons agreed. Such a crescendo could not be ignored. Lord Chancellor Stafford and Lord Treasurer Lumley resigned late in 1449, but Suffolk was no quitter. Confident in his good intentions and in the confidence of the king, he chose on 22 January 1450 to face his critics and to defend himself against all charges. The Commons immediately charged him with plotting the betrayal to Charles VII of Wallingford Castle, well inland in Berkshire and certainly not on Charles's list of priorities. 'Fantastic though it may seem to us today, this specific, concrete charge merited investigation in

January 1450.' Suffolk was imprisoned in the Tower on 29 January. Bishops Moleyns and Aiscough were already or soon to be murdered. The three chief ministers of the late 1440s had now gone.[61]

The Commons impeached in Suffolk the moving spirit in the regime. Impeachment was a form of trial in which the Commons acted as prosecutors and the Lords as judges. The Commons were concerned primarily with the military defeat and the accountability of Suffolk. Hence they started with nine charges of treason of a traditional kind: disclosing details of English defences, revealing the instructions of English ambassadors, encouraging the French to invade, impeding English relief efforts and betraying England's allies. Their story began in 1440 with the release of Charles, Duke of Orleans, which was reinterpreted as deliberate favouring of the enemy. Suffolk himself was charged with surrendering Maine. The charges were 'based on well-authenticated incidents, whose real significance was purposely misrepresented by the Commons' managers in a way that ignored the sincere hopes of the peace negotiators'.[62] To these, Suffolk had a complete defence, since he had never acted alone or without the king's authority, which Henry now explicitly affirmed.

Anticipating the duke's acquittal, the Commons then submitted 18 further charges. Most were military, but others alleged domestic misgovernance, mistaken appointments, oppressions, misapplication of taxes and unauthorized actions. 'The articles prove that nothing tangible could be adduced against Suffolk.' They were 'a truly formidable hotchpotch of half truths and untruths'.[63] Misconduct did not yet include the local oppressions and collapse of order condemned by Jack Cade's rebels and only two counts, 16 and 17, were about misgovernment. One was instigated by the elder statesman Ralph Lord Cromwell, whose enemy the Lincolnshire esquire William Tailbois had been protected by Suffolk from the penalties for his crimes. Count 17, much more vaguely, accused Suffolk of appointing sheriffs for money and hence pliable, for favouring his own supporters and his own lawsuits, and for spreading perjuries.[64] It reads like an afterthought and indicates that such matters were not really preoccupations for the Commons. 'These were flimsy grounds indeed for charges of treason, distorting, exaggerating, even inventing where it could be done plausibly to destroy the power of this royal minister.'[65]

That indeed was the point. The Lower House was set not on justice or dismissal for incompetence, but on Suffolk's destruction. Undoubtedly they were pressurized by the baying for Suffolk's blood of a London mob, which probably did not recognize any such distinction and which was spurred on by disappointed and understandably malicious veterans who had been ousted from jobs and homes in France. Those anonymous 'commons' managers', who crafted the charges and deliberately misrepresented the facts, knew what they were about. Although Suffolk's defence implicated many of the other peers, who surely feared attacks would follow against themselves, yet evidently Suffolk could not count on acquittal by the Lords. Doubtless the Lords shared much of the public dismay and desire for accountability, certainly some had personal differences with Suffolk, and perhaps crucially Lord Cromwell may have joined Suffolk's enemies. Cromwell was certainly behind charges relating to Suffolk's maintenance of the Lincolnshire squire William Tailbois, who had attempted Cromwell's own assassination, most probably on Suffolk's prompting.[66]

In response, the king first deferred the trial, then shielded Suffolk as acting on his command, and finally stopped the proceedings. Henry rejected the charges of treason, but for the misprisions (knowledge of offences) he exiled Suffolk for five years. He hoped thus to end the matter. Revealingly, Henry was concerned also to protect the accusers from any vengeance to be wreaked in future by Suffolk. The king acted on his own initiative, without counsel of the Lords. The Lords appeared not to have approved the decision;[67] nor did the Commons; nor indeed the London mob, who sought to lynch Suffolk; nor the crew of the *Nicholas of the Tower*, who intercepted and murdered him on 2 May 1450; nor Cade's rebels, who took his guilt for granted; nor future Houses of Commons in later parliaments that sought his attainder.

JACK CADE'S REBELLION

At this point, late in May 1450, the *Crisis* moved beyond normal political parameters and institutions, as the people engaged for the first time in politics: a defining characteristic of the Wars of the Roses. Led by Jack Cade, the people of Kent and Sussex rose, demanding remedy of their grievances and reform. Their grievances consisted both of highly local irritants and more general dissatisfaction with the economy and misgovernment, which they identified with the strictures of the Commons against the government and the parliamentary reform programme. They thought the remedy for their grievances was the purging of the whole Suffolk regime and its replacement by disinterested councillors whom they could trust.

There is no comprehensive list of the rebels, but every social class seems to have been involved, even including some of the gentry and urban elite. The specific grievances came from men of substance, who had property to lose, to be taxed or forfeited, held office and sat on juries, elected MPs, sued and were sued, had businesses to be distracted from and trade to be damaged. They were the leaders of local communities, the sort of prosperous tradesmen and farmers of demesnes who inhabited many surviving black-and-white houses, now adversely affected by the economic downturn. Such local leaders were also the constables and bailiffs of 60 of the 65 Kentish hundreds, whom it appeared mustered their communities – presumably all the able-bodied men aged between 16 and 60 – and subsequently secured pardons for all of them. All Kentishmen were therefore involved,[68] not just those most acutely affected.

The people brought to politics a clarity of vision – that the issues were black and white, that politicians were friends or foes with no neutrals in between, foes being 'traitors'. They contributed a summary brutality, in which legal definitions, due process and justice itself gave way to lynchings and the summary killing of such traitors. Such misperceptions, shorthand judgements and indeed brutalization of politics were to prevail for thirty years, and to infect not only popular but elite and even court politics. They made routine of the extermination of the vanquished and even potential opponents. The arrest of Suffolk was the crucial decision that removed the government's lid on protest, first of all in London. It unleashed more widespread attacks on the regime as a whole in and out of Parliament, propelled the people into national politics, stimulated further assassinations and popular insurgency, and upset public order. 'The weakness of the government encouraged men to express their economic discontents in direct action.'[69] The fall of Suffolk had let a genie out of the lamp that was not entirely returned for another thirty years.

At first this was not apparent. However strident and vengeful the articles against Suffolk were, they were part of an established political process that required the cooperation of both Houses of Parliament. What the Commons sought was relatively narrow, elitist, and was focused on one individual. It was not yet the attack on all the king's councillors and household that it was to become later in the year, nor did it yet encompass the economic grievances and petty oppressions that concerned the people. Normal parliamentary discussions continued on defence and on the revenues needed to finance it. The Commons were not opposed to 'relieving' the king, but 'your said commons been so impoverished' that a resumption was essential, which Henry at last conceded in late spring 1450. Economic reprisals to the Burgundian trade embargo were agreed.[70] The regime still commanded the allegiance, obedience and attendance of the political elite that Parliament represented. It dealt effectively with the murderers of Moleyns and Suffolk, with the rebel labourer Bluebeard. Magnates still believed in the need for order, for disciplining and deterring plebeian dissent, seditious words, assemblies and rebellions. They presided over judicial sessions that convicted and executed plebeian dissidents.

Similarly, the populace saw themselves as acting within their constitutional limits. Far from being aggressive, they had 'inkennelled' themselves by 11 June 1450 at Blackheath (Kent, now south-east London), where they fortified their camp, petitioned en masse as past and Tudor commons were to do, and waited for the government to negotiate. Their captain, Jack Cade, 'called himself and his people petitioners' who had come, not 'to do any harm, but to have the desires of the Commons in the parliament fulfilled'. They proved too numerous to be suppressed: a delegation of lords was sent to them, who on 16 June promised that 'all things should be redressed', but nothing concrete that the rebels were prepared to accept. Next, therefore, the king approached 'with a mighty power'.[71] Cade's rebels were loyal. They were not prepared to confront their king when his banner was displayed, which was tantamount to treason, so they withdrew instead on 18 June to Kent. The rebels would have dispersed peaceably if they had not been attacked by royal supporters (the Staffords) near Sevenoaks. After the defeat and deaths of the Staffords, the king withdrew from London to the Midlands. The rebels re-grouped, returned to Blackheath on 29 June, and on 3 July crossed London Bridge into the City, where they enjoyed widespread sympathy and were admitted by the mob. They started implementing their programme directly. James, Lord Say, then treasurer of England, and others were executed, and yet other royal favourites were indicted of treason, pillaged and destroyed. Only when the rebels' depredations became too damaging did the City authorities expel them, on 5 July.

Suffolk's plebeian murderers had seen themselves as representing 'the community of the realm' and acting on its behalf. So likewise, at Potterne in Wiltshire on 29 June, did the murderers of Aiscough, the king's confessor, who denounced the bishop as a 'traitor to the king'.[72] Even when pledging their commitment to the interests of king and realm, Cade's manifestos declared that the rebels knew better than Henry himself what these were. They, too, sought resumption and wanted the resistance of the king's favourites, most of whom were exempted from the act of resumption, to be overridden. They added a whole string of their own grievances, for instance about non-repayment of purveyance, the sale of office and consequent profiteering, fraudulent trusts, denial of bail, and abuse of greenwax, the hunting laws, and castleward. Specific cases emerge in their later indictment against local and household officers.[73] The rebels were petitioning en masse for redress of grievances: not for revolutionary change, but for reform and a reversion to what they saw as proper constitutional processes. They felt themselves to be part of the same reforming cause as the Commons. So did the retainers of some lords who declined to crush the rebels.

After Suffolk's death, alarming rumours spread 'that Kent should be destroyed with a royal power and made [into] a wild forest [in retaliation] for the death of the duke of Suffolk'.[74] Whatever their other grievances, it was these fears of government reprisals that were the necessary trigger that precipitated the Kentish commons into armed protest later in May 1450. Ironically, it was the commissions of array that Henry had issued for coastal defence against French invaders that brought the loyal commons to arms that were then turned against the regime itself. Mustered and led by the constables of the hundreds, they were overwhelming in number, but actually engaged in loyal protestation as petitioners, not rebels or traitors.[75] Here was an opportunity for negotiation, as many specific demands were easy to satisfy, but unfortunately this was not realized. The king did not reply to the rebels' manifestos and did not even – or ever – offer remedies to even the most easily sorted of their complaints. Understandably rattled, Henry advanced in force, and the opportunity for peaceful reconciliation passed. Cade himself was captured on 12 July at Heathfield in Sussex and died of his wounds.

YORK'S FIRST BID FOR POWER, AUTUMN 1450

At this point two new players appeared on the political scene. Neither had been implicated in Suffolk's fall and both were absent during the domestic crisis. The first was Edmund Beaufort, Duke of Somerset, the defeated commander in France, whose excuses for defeat the king accepted and who resumed his place on the royal council. Second in time was another royal cousin, Richard, Duke of York, who had been resident in Ireland throughout the *Crisis of 1450* as the king's lieutenant and who returned to England in October 1450, most probably because he did not receive the revenues that he had been promised and required. Somerset quickly took the lead in defending the regime. York gravitated at once to leadership of its critics.

Cade's Rebellion was a direct threat to the regime and was defeated. Cade's cause, however, was not discredited, and was reiterated in Parliament in the autumn. Uncoerced, Kentish jurors indicted the local agents of the regime.[76] Back from Ireland, York requested justice be meted out to the king's favourites, and demanded authorization to undertake the reforms himself, which the king skilfully sidestepped, offering him only a place on the royal council.[77] How

York responded is unknown, but certainly he and the Commons in a new Parliament in autumn 1450 now pursued a reforming agenda. It was taken for granted henceforth that Suffolk and these others were guilty as charged. In October, York demanded that those accused by the rebels be put to trial.[78] York now campaigned against 28 other named individuals accused of domestic misconduct and also against Somerset, now the king's favourite, against whom such charges were impossible, but who had presided over England's humiliating defeat. The people, riotously assembled in support, raised a great shout in Westminster Hall, and sought to lynch Somerset. He was imprisoned in the Tower. The pressure for reform and for a purge that was exerted on the king in Parliament and by the London mob was intense and almost irresistible. King Henry, however, was no politician. He simply declined to give way and rode out the storm. Christmas arrived, Parliament dispersed, Somerset and the other 28 remained, and the intensity relaxed.[79] The *Crisis of 1450* was over.

THE POLITICAL LEGACY OF 1450

That the *Crisis* receded did not mean that the grievances and demands of the Commons, Jack Cade's rebels, the London mob, or York were satisfied. They were repeatedly revived. Sporadic gatherings persisted for several years, requiring intervention from the centre to repress, both reform and revenge retaining their popular appeal for another two decades. These were leavened by disappointed ex-servicemen, unpaid, unemployed and displaced, 'which non-payment and poverty', in York's later words, 'causeth also daily great inconveniences within this your land'.[80] The duke had constituted himself the champion of reform for the next decade. He saw the new popular politics as an opportunity and accepted the people's priorities, rage and brutality as the necessary price for their support. Although thwarted in 1450, the campaign for reform of counsel and policies was continued repeatedly over the next twenty years.

Whilst the social and political issues identified by contemporaries in 1449–50 were not redressed, it is questionable whether these were the real issues or that correcting them could have prevented the military, political and financial collapse that had occurred and that was to persist. In retrospect, the *Crisis of 1450* was a mistake. The peace policy of the Crown had enjoyed the support of members of the royal council and in Parliament, yet in the light of the military defeat it was rejected and blamed on the Duke of Suffolk, who was not personally or alone to blame. Once the disaster had befallen, Parliament, the commons and even the king's soldiers had been very quick to diagnose what was wrong and to blame the government. Yet surely they reached the wrong conclusions. The Maine and Fougères episodes did constitute misman-agement and perhaps Edmund, Duke of Somerset had surrendered too easily. However, it is not self-evident that the root causes were bad governance or were to be explained by evil councillors, or that the cure was better councillors of the blood royal. Obviously Suffolk, Say, Moleyns and Aiscough were removed and many others earmarked for dismissal.

It is not obvious that substituting 'lords of his royal blood' for 'persons of lower nature exalted and made chief of [the] privy council' would really make for more disinterested and good governance.[81] Reformers focused principally on domestic politics, especially royal patronage, not the real causes, the revival of French military strength and the financial bankruptcy of the regime. Although repeatedly told and acutely aware of the unfortunate side effects, the House of Commons did not recognize how hopeless the financial situation was. 'You are greatly impoverished', the Commons told King Henry. 'The expenses of your said honourable household and the wages and fees of your menial servants [are] not paid ... and your other ordinary charges not paid, satisfied, or done'. So, too, lamented Cade's rebels.[82] However, the underlying causes were not understood and the remedies that were proposed – retrenchment and resumption – were not only incapable of delivering financial solvency, but actually impeded the counter-offensive that was required. That the king's poverty was due to excessive generosity and the cure was resumption had become a commonplace throughout the 1450s that could not be dispelled just because it happened to be untrue. There were lessons from the *Crisis*, but unfortunately they were not understood.

The politics of the ensuing decade took for granted the humiliation of foreign defeat and the complicity of the government in it, the financial helplessness of the government and the frailties of Henry VI himself, and the inadequacy of the central administration of justice. Throughout the 1450s the regime was on the political defensive and unable to take significant political initiatives. To this the *Crisis of 1450* added three other key ingredients: the demand for reform, in particular the resumption of royal patronage and the dismissal of the king's evil councillors; the involvement in politics of the people; and the existence in York of a leader who encapsulated reform and was prepared to invoke popular support. Obviously York focused on Somerset, the principal obstacle to reform and most formidable of the king's agents. Somerset alone could not be tarred with Suffolk's brush, but he was vulnerable because of his military defeats. It was because this was the only way to strike at him that York repeatedly raised these issues. Against such criticisms, the king and his advisers could not defend themselves effectively, in part because they were so weak – the king himself took no initiatives and his resources were so limited – but also because their critics, both greater and lesser, resolutely and repeatedly drew the wrong conclusions from the disasters that had befallen. Hence the next decade was fought over these misapprehensions and, in a real sense, the escalation to civil war was founded on misunderstandings.

CHAPTER 6

PRECONDITIONS:
PERSONALITIES AND ISSUES

What happened in 1450 was a mass movement: an explosion of wrath that had national dimensions, but was actually concentrated in the south-east. It swept away the ministry, but it was not revolutionary. A change of king was never an option. Anger diminished, yet there remained underlying popular discontent for a skilled politician to revive. The politics of the 1450s, in contrast, is about individuals and personalities, albeit only dimly perceived: the king himself; York; the Nevilles; and a succession of evil councillors – Somerset, Buckingham, Shrewsbury, Wiltshire, Beaumont and even Queen Margaret of Anjou. Continuity was provided by the king and York, who are difficult to integrate into the course of events. This chapter examines them, seeks to establish what their debate is about, and to establish what each thought permissible and what not.

THE INANITY OF HENRY VI

King Henry was a factor in what went wrong in the 1440s and in 1450. It had been in his name that the unsuccessful foreign, military and financial policies were pursued. He it was who had appointed and relied upon Suffolk, Aiscough, Moleyns, Say, other evil councillors, and the so-called oppressors of the people of the 1440s. He also directed the patronage from which they bene-fited. This chapter therefore looks backward as well as forward in its analysis of Henry VI's kingship.

Obviously Henry VI was a profoundly unsuccessful king. He lost both his thrones, that of England twice. Low on the list of causes was the fragility of his hereditary title, the latent Mortimer claim, and the potential alternative always offered by his cousin York. Personal inadequacy, even dynastic alternatives, could not and did not threaten Henry's right to reign. For Henry undoubtedly was king: the son and grandson of past kings. He was also a good man, whose virtues – piety and innocence – were the qualities that political theorists advocated in a king. Back in 1422 the House of Lancaster had established itself strongly enough for a baby of nine months to succeed without question. It was fifteen years before Henry VI could rule for himself. Minority governments both in England and France ruled effectively in the absence of an adult king, and they handed over their responsibilities unimpaired when Henry came of age. The Lancastrian regime had not merely survived or endured, it had triumphant successes in foreign policy that had enhanced national prestige. Henry was acknowledged by the whole political establishment in Parliament, and enjoyed the fealty and allegiance of every significant aristocrat. Breaking their oaths was a step too far. Even in 1460 most refused to do that. Lack of success did not imperil Henry's crown.

Henry VI, it was said at the time, did not look like a king. As late as 1446, when he was 25, so critics said, he looked like a child, behaved like a fool or simpleton. It has been difficult even to establish at what point he was regarded as of age.[1] Even if Henry lacked the imposing height of Edward I or Edward IV or the charisma, magnetism and sheer force of personality of Henry V, he knew what kingship entailed and, unlike his immediate predecessors, he had been brought up for the role. Henry never knew a time when he was not the king. He never knew a superior or an equal. Only kings could talk in equal terms to kings. Henry was ingrained with the formal ceremonial and etiquette of court life, embracing not only formal audiences from his throne, but also his daily worship, meals and recreation. At a public level he operated appropriately, receiving embassies, presiding over parliaments, judicial sessions and lovedays, even on occasion addressing ambassadors and the parliamentary peerage.[2] He was profoundly conscious of his regal dignity and the respect due to him as king. Henry believed in showing his face, vigorously traversing his realm, to Durham and York, Chester and Hereford, Norwich and Walsingham. He spent many summers away from London and the Thames Valley and presided over judicial sessions in his troubled provinces every summer from 1450 to 1459,[3] except those of 1453–4 when he was mad. Henry believed in the majesty of his justice, in the deterrent value of terror, and in using his prerogative of mercy to mitigate its effects. He recognized and deeply resented affronts to himself and his queen, whether criticisms popular or parliamentary, presumptuous usurpations of his authority, or personal insults and seditious words, which he punished with death.[4] Often he attended the actual executions himself.[5] He insisted on his prerogatives, especially that of mercy.[6] The royal blood that set him, his queen and Prince Edward aside, also distinguished the princes of the blood royal, from whom he condoned conduct that he was prepared to tolerate in nobody else and on whom he imposed lesser penalties than those on other noblemen. He was more lenient to them than to mere gentry or mere commoners. This was fortunate indeed for York, for Henry, Duke of Exeter, and for Thomas, Earl of Devon, but not for their unfortunate agents, retainers and tenants. His chaplain John Blacman reported how Henry forgave four noblemen convicted of treason and even the rebel Yorkists in 1459, subject to their submission to his authority.[7]

Yet Henry has often been identified as the root cause of his own disasters. McFarlane identified 'the inanity of Henry VI' as a cause of the Wars of the Roses.[8] Certainly no English king has ever been weaker than the infant Henry VI in 1422, none was for so long under age, none before George III went mad, and no adult English king, many historians have agreed, was so unsuited for and inadequate in the role. That Henry was 'an exemplar of late-medieval spirituality' did not make him into a more effective king, although it makes his actions and inactions more understandable to us.[9] Was Henry there at all or was there merely a king-shaped vacuum at the heart of the body politic?

Although there are many thousands of surviving documents that record actions taken in the king's name, by themselves they cannot prove that the king personally initiated them.[10] The same applies to every one of England's medieval kings. All actions in the king's name resulted from decisions at the beginning of an administrative process when warrants were issued that moved the various seals. The original decisions need not have been made by the king. The consensus is that Henry's decisions were influenced most during the 1440s by Suffolk and his allies, in 1451–3 by Somerset, in 1454 and 1455–6 by Lord Protector York, and in 1456–60 by Queen Margaret.[11] Their initiative is assumed and read into the story, sometimes without being qualified at all. It is a short step to suppose (with John Watts) that it was these advisers who actually did the deciding rather than the king.[12]

But this is not credible. The agency of the king's evil councillors rests largely on outside testimony, almost all of it hostile, from the charges of their enemies, often distributed widely and perhaps couched for wider appeal, and from Yorkist chroniclers writing later who had been influenced by such propaganda. Against such evidence can be set those chronicles and observers who record the king's anger, sorrow, or disapproval. Although conceding that Henry did not engage consistently or willingly in public affairs, John Blacman left no doubt that the king himself was behind his grants and pardons, as his warrants confirm. Within the surviving records of government there is virtually no direct evidence that Suffolk, Somerset, or Margaret did decide anything. On the contrary, there are hundreds of documents authorized with the king's sign manual, including many that are endorsed with the king's wishes – 'the king will' – or with humble recommendations to the king, all of which indicate that the king did do the deciding.[13] Henry may indeed have been managed, but his compliance could not be taken for granted. Blacman also testifies that Henry took many of his decisions himself. 'In those things which interested him, such as the outward forms of conventional moral behaviour, the strict observance of the letter of the law in religious observance and catechising candidates for bishoprics, Henry could be ominously extrovert and censorious.'[14] That suitors invoked Christian festivals in their petitions or concocted elaborate sob stories was because they believed that these influenced the king and that they improved their chances of success.[15]

It is not credible to attribute to others the peace policy and religious foundations to which Henry devoted so much personal attention and energy, and that he resolutely drove through regardless of disagreement and opposition. Nor need we dispute Henry's personal willingness to suspend his title to the Crown of France, his personal decisions to surrender Maine, to intervene in Suffolk's trial, to acquit him and yet exile him, to forgive Somerset for his utter defeat, and to reconcile the warring magnates in 1457–8. King Henry stood consistently for conciliation, mediation, compromise, reconciliation and arbitration, repeatedly seeking to settle the differences between York and Somerset and then between York and Somerset's heirs. He had a remarkable capacity to forgive and to start again. He insisted on retaining his prerogative of mercy in 1459 even for those attainted of treason against him, and again in 1460, in the teeth of his Yorkist minders, for those who withstood the new *Accord*.[16] Henry was strong enough (stubborn enough?) to stand out against the will of the Commons, Parliament as a whole, and even apparently everyone else, to approve, veto or defer parliamentary bills, and to resist demands backed by military force. He was cordial in 1456 to York when his queen was not, and he rejected advice to hold the Earl of Warwick to account in 1458.[17] He possessed both the moral courage and a willingness to shoulder responsibility for himself rather than shrug it off onto his ministers and councillors. It was undoubtedly Henry's own excessive clemency and superfluous generosity that his councillors sought to restrain in the 1440s, Cardinal Kemp *c.* 1450 and Sir John Fortescue during his *Readeption* in 1470–1.[18] Too much is inexplicable without his obstinacy. His loyalty to his ministers, councillors and courtiers, too often dangerously identifying them with himself, blinded him to the justice of any personal charges of personal misconduct against them. Declaring responsibility was not the same, of course, as accepting liability or willing the consequences. To attribute all his acts to his agents is to swallow the necessary political conventions of an age when the king himself could not be criticized with impunity. Henry could be managed, probably he usually was, but there were directions in which he could not be driven and he was never a mere cipher.

Perhaps Henry did not attend sufficiently to business, master the details and complexities, or provide sufficient direction, yet he presented himself as a good king. He committed himself verbally and repeatedly to good governance and to the public interest, he protected the Church and practised openly his personal piety, he appointed those of appropriate rank to high office and military command, and he tempered his justice scrupulously with mercy. Rarely did he act on his will alone. He was certainly no arbitrary tyrant. Kings were meant to seek counsel, listen to counsel, and to act on it. It was Henry's prerogative to choose his ministers, officers and councillors, to be counselled by whom he chose, to choose which counsel to follow or to disregard. Here Henry could not be faulted. He was constantly counselled informally, listened to the advice of his formal council and usually acted on it, frequently convened great councils and met regularly with Parliament, especially for every important decision. On occasion, as with the peace negotiations of 1439–40, he allowed himself to be overruled.

What was deplored, usually in retrospect and after failure, was not Henry's rejection of counsel, but that the winning counsel was evil and purveyed by evil councillors. Henry may have left much more than was usual of the ordinary business of government to his ministers and councillors, perhaps even allowing them to make key decisions. He was easily influenced and perhaps even managed and manipulated by them. It was Suffolk and Aiscough, so it was alleged in 1446, who really ruled.[19] Yet Henry's uncle Cardinal Beaufort, Suffolk, Somerset or the queen were appropriately qualified to advise him, and each moreover acted within wider consultation and with the sanction of the Lords. Of course, they sought to control access and information to their king, for example through censoring the sermons that he heard.[20] What favourite did not? Yet Suffolk was steward of the household, not chamberlain, and never controlled access to the king, Somerset held no household office at all, and the queen was often separated from him. As each favourite was cut down, Henry found others on whom to rely, because he was the king and the greatest of magnates – Buckingham, Shrewsbury, Wiltshire, or Worcester – were proud to serve him. 'That Henry was always controlled by a never failing succession of bad men beggars belief, but such an assumption was the only possible alternative to direct attacks on the king himself.'[21] Moreover, Henry never had a favourite with that monopoly of advice or patronage that all favourites sought, because Henry's easy pliancy allowed him to be advised and persuaded by mere courtiers – by those who, in Fortescue's words, could not (or should not be allowed to) advise him.[22] Each petition was judged on its merits – or what the king perceived as merits – rather than on the basis of policy or wider considerations, such as solvency, and the restraints on his pardons or grants were repeatedly broken by his unfettered will.

To admit that Henry made many of his own decisions does not make them wise or sensible. The quality of his decision-making has to be judged by results. Much has been written on the failings of government during his majority, though generally with insufficient allowance for the impossibility of the situation. What choices did he have? Often, no doubt, Henry was naïve or even wilful,[23] arising from a failure to understand the real issues. Certainly he was frequently inflexible and seems to have misunderstood the pragmatism implicit in politics. He vacillated and sometimes issued contradictory instructions: here underdeveloped record-keeping in the signet office may be a factor.

One understudied area where unfortunate consequences of the king's own actions can be detected is in the peerage, within which he not only made many promotions, but repeatedly adjusted precedence to reward particular individuals. Rewards for some in this instance were definitely at the expense of others. Three royal dukes were created in the 1440s with precedence over John, Duke of Norfolk, who prided himself on being royal himself. Although Humphrey Stafford was created Duke of Buckingham in 1444 and followed it up with a grant of precedence over any future duke, he found himself supplanted only the next year, when the dispute required a judgement of Solomon from the Lords collectively. Both Arundel and Devon, contenders to be premier earls, were disappointed when Richard Neville, Earl of Warwick, was formally granted this position. Warwick in turn found himself supplanted by the king's two stepbrothers, who were granted precedence over all other earls including the premier earl. The topic of precedence reveals Henry responding in turn to each petitioner individually, seeking to gratify them, and incidentally creating unnecessary resentment amongst Buckingham, Norfolk, Arundel, Devon and Warwick, to name only a few.[24]

The son of a military hero could not fail to appreciate his role as commander-in-chief. Several times Henry VI declared his intention to take command himself. He never did. Circumstances intervened, but they would not have prevailed had his heart been in it. Hence Henry never took the military lead. Perhaps he lacked military aptitude: he never took hands-on command of his army. Although he must have had the military training of all young aristocrats, he was a passive passenger in battle and perhaps a poltroon. He showed little interest in winning the war in France, being personally more inclined to peace, and he was no more effective in government or justice. Yet this does not appear to be due to a lack of ability – he certainly mastered the intricacies of his new colleges at Eton and Cambridge and drove their establishment forward – but due to a lack of inclination. His court was oddly domestic and peaceful in tone even in the 1440s when a major war had still to be waged and won.[25] Religion and learning were certainly worth kingly attention, but as well as, not instead of, foreign policy and defence, finance, justice, or order, in which Henry lacked the constant application already expected of a king. Hence perhaps his ill-considered spending, his lack of foresight, prudence and calculation. Historians write appositely of his 'disengagement from the world of politics' and find him 'incapable of a sustained political role'. Henry regarded an audience with a 'mighty duke of the blood' (perhaps York?) as an interruption.[26] He was certainly dilatory. Henry did not engage constructively in detailed discussions or negotiations and was only too happy to leave such matters to others. Besides foreign policy, administration and military commands, even arbitration between lords was shuffled onto others,[27] who could not deliver verdicts with the authority of the king.

Yet these deficiencies did not render Henry unable to rule or to carry on the business of government. In fact, he lasted for thirty-nine years under circumstances that would have strained any ruler. He rode out the multi-sided crisis of 1450 and his own insanity in 1453–5. If he undoubtedly contributed to his own failures, it was the impossibility of the situations in which he found himself that brought him to catastrophe, and in particular the refusal of York to allow him to rule. From inadequacy, Henry was to deteriorate. After his two-year insanity he may never have altogether recovered his former mental health, although there is evidence of him making decisions right down to 1460. Insanity forced interim expedients on the political nation, which stressed that they were temporary and looked forward to Henry himself resuming his kingly authority. A great deal more evidence of Henry's failings – and especially repeated challenges to his authority – was needed to persuade in 1460 even a significant minority to support a transfer of his rule. Few came even then to doubt his right to reign. That Henry VI's capacity to rule became a factor was because of the conflict with which he could not deal. And in 1470 an overwhelming majority of the politically active wanted him back.

RICHARD, DUKE OF YORK

York was an improbable revolutionary. He was, after all, first cousin to the king, a prince of the blood royal of three kingdoms with a good claim to be heir presumptive to England, the premier duke and the best-endowed of contemporary magnates, twice the king's lieutenant in France and his lieutenant in Ireland almost continuously from 1446. He was moreover imbued with contemporary values about allegiance, rank, royal blood, hereditary rights and honour.[28] He had vested interests in the status quo and was pre-programmed by class outlook to resist threats to it, to depress insubordination and the presumption of social inferiors, to rebut threats to rights of property and to the existing political system that so advantaged him. Such factors, together with his own personal limitations, arguably contributed to his failure as a radical reformer.

By the 1450s York no longer saw himself as a subject, as a mere nobleman, but as the greatest of them all. His inheritances had made him the leading magnate not only in England but in Wales and Ireland also. Besides the duchy of York, he was the heir of Clarence, de Burgh, de Clare and Mortimer, as the monks and friars of his patronage at Wigmore Abbey and Clare friary remembered and reminded him in their abbey chronicle, Osbern Bokenham's *Legends* and the *Clare Roll*,[29] all of which he probably read. In York's veins there coursed the blood royal of England, France and Castile, to all of which he cherished hereditary claims. Certainly he aspired to a crown: if not for himself, for his heir. In 1444–5 Duke Richard had investigated his title to the Crown of Castile. It was a dynasty that he was breeding. By the mid 1440s, when none of his children had reached double figures, he was already seeking a French princess for his heir Edward, he had contracted his daughter Anne to the future Duke of Exeter, and he was constructing a landed patrimony in France for his second son Edmund, titled Earl of Rutland[30] – only the second younger son ever to have such a courtesy title, the first being York's own father Richard, Earl of Cambridge. In 1458 another duke was secured for York's second daughter Elizabeth.

Always a royal prince, York moved inexorably closer to the English throne on the childless deaths of the king's paternal uncles in 1435 (John, Duke of

Bedford) and in 1447 (Humphrey, Duke of Gloucester), when probably – and certainly in 1451[31] – some saw him and perhaps he saw himself as heir presumptive. York took precedence over Norfolk and all the other royal dukes that Henry was to elevate. Eminence was thrust upon him. Prematurely and unwillingly king's lieutenant (commander-in-chief) in France in his mid twenties, he had been glad to relinquish that office in 1437, but it was very much on his own terms that he resumed command in 1440, and he definitely wanted to continue when superseded under suspicion of corruption. Had he retained his command, he would not have embroiled himself in English politics in the 1450s.[32] Again, York wanted to be lieutenant of Ireland in 1447 – as Earl of Ulster and the greatest of Irish magnates such service was a family tradition – and in 1454 he appointed himself to the principal remaining military command, the captaincy of Calais.[33] Such offices carried vice-regal prestige and renown, vice-regal revenues and lifestyle. They brought into York's service captains of experience and renown, such as Sir John Fastolf, Sir William Oldhall and Sir Andrew Ogard, who saw in the duke first the protagonist of their aggressive military policies and then thereafter their hope for revenge against those responsible for defeat and for compensation for their losses. Apparently they flattered him. They also preyed on him financially, purchasing properties he was forced to sell and extracting lucrative terms for their loans.[34]

Already by far the richest English magnate with about £5,000 a year and thus able to live in a genuinely princely style, York was lured into the most conspicuous consumption at royal expense, commissioning for instance a £608 state dress for his duchess, a collar priced £2,666 13s. 4d., retaining the Earl of Shrewsbury at an excessive annual fee of £200, and committing himself to the largest known dowry (£3,000) for his eldest daughter. Yet such display outstripped his means. His £20,000 annuity of France was in arrears from the second year, £26,000 (or five years of his own income) being due by 1446, and that of Ireland (£2,666 6s. 8d.) quickly fell behind. Income from the two lieutenancies, his captaincy of Calais (2,000 marks, £1,333 13s. 4d., a year), his two protectorates (2,000 marks, £1,333 13s. 4d., a year plus expenses), and as heir (10,000 marks, £6,666 13s. 4d.) in 1460, was important to him. His pay from his *First Protectorate* (1454–5) was still outstanding late in 1455, when he demanded it: the Lords agreed, subject to the availability of funds. Meantime his Welsh revenues plummeted – it seems that York did not recognize the decline to be permanent – and his French estates were first wasted and then lost when reconquered. To make ends meet, York wasted his capital assets, selling off timber, seigniorial rights and outlying properties, mortgaged manors, pawned jewels, and borrowed on unfavourable terms. Yet he may not have cut his cloth, since in 1450–1 his household was still costing him at the rate of £5,000 a year[35] – probably equivalent to the whole of his normal income and double the household spending of his only equal in wealth, Humphrey, Duke of Buckingham. It is unknown whether York economized thereafter. York's management of his finances, it appears, was no better than Henry VI's.

Unlike the king, York had both a scapegoat and a remedy. No doubt he was wrong to suppose himself particularly unfavourably treated,[36] yet the totals owed to him of £26,000 were larger than those due to anyone else, had been run up very quickly in 1441–6 at the rate of £5,000 a year, and had first to be laid out by him in royal office from personal resources that were scarcely greater. From 1446 he complained repeatedly about his losses. It was for 4,700 marks (£3,166 13s. 4d.) in assignments not honoured that he threatened withdrawal from Ireland in 1450.[37] Securing control of the government, he probably hoped, would bring him the preference at the exchequer that would restore his finances. Perhaps there is an element of truth in Professor Storey's statement that 'the bankruptcy of Lancaster drove York to rebellion'.[38] From 1450 onwards York wanted to be the king's chief councillor, to be captain of Calais and Lord Protector despite all the risks of further unrequited expenses. By 1449, when pay due to the Calais garrison reached £19,395, Buckingham wisely resigned the captaincy.[39] In fact, York had received neither pay nor expenses 'for the great and outragous costs and expenses' of his *First Protectorate* as late as November 1455, when he agreed to take pay pro rata and 1,000 marks (£666 6s. 8d.) down.[40]

York was no foe to the Suffolk regime. He was a royal councillor in 1434 aged 23 and again in 1447, and he shared in the key decisions of the 1440s that were condemned in 1450. Hard though historians have searched, they have found no signs of hostility to the Suffolk regime, nothing to identify York politically with the isolated Gloucester, nor with disapproval at his fall, no evidence that York was exiled to Ireland, to which it appears he went very willingly, reserving the right to return whenever he chose.[41] York had benefited considerably from Henry's patronage.[42] If inadvertent, it was his good fortune not to be in command when Normandy was lost in 1450, not to be blamed for the surrender of those towns where he was absentee captain, and not to be remembered as the lieutenant of France at the time of the Treaty of Tours in 1444, and therefore implicated in that treaty. It was Cade's rebels who attributed bad governance to 'mean persons' and who demanded instead the king's 'natural councillors' of the king's blood, of whom (following a series of deaths) there was a current shortage. Amongst these they listed 'Good Duke Humphrey' and John, Duke of Exeter, both dead, as well as York, who seems to have secured the devotion of the March rebels as well as themselves without any opportunity actually to earn it. They first circulated the myths of 'Good Duke Humphrey', York's exile and his enthusiasm for reform, and his potential as heir apparent,[43] all of which the duke chose to exploit. York's honour may have suffered when Somerset surrendered uncontested those fortresses where York was officially captain.[44] He certainly did suffer materially: from the loss of France, which dispossessed both him and his son Edmund, and from the first act of resumption, for which he had no proviso of exemption. Apart from wanting payment of his dues, perhaps from resumed property, York had no personal quarrel with the indicted courtiers and expressed no intention of holding Somerset to account for his defeat in any of his five bills of 1450 to the king.[45] As a prince of the blood royal and the beneficiary of all these myths, York was able to seize the leadership of a programme that had already been formulated. He directed it specifically against Somerset only when he found it brought him a clientele and when Somerset proved to be a stumbling block to reform. This may already have been in November/December 1450, when Somerset was first held militarily culpable for the loss of Normandy. Holding Somerset to account (and hence destroying him politically) was the avowed aim of York's coups both in 1452 (Dartford) and 1455 (First Battle of St Albans).

What is clear, however, is that York returned from Ireland not merely to share in government, but to run it. This was his position for ten years from 1450. Regardless of who was advising the king, they were all evil councillors, whom he sought to remove, if necessarily by force and at least six times, in 1450, 1452, 1453–4, 1455, 1459 and 1460. Still only thirty-nine in 1450 and in the prime of life, York was already exceptionally experienced in governing English overseas dependencies and had good grounds for supposing himself best equipped to conduct English government. The king's officers and courtiers fled from him, tried to impede his progress, and sought his protection, whilst the king sent emissaries to learn his intentions, reassure him and negotiate with him. Once his assurances of allegiance were accepted, York demanded reform – especially the punishment of those whom Cade's rebels had indicted – and urged to be allowed to undertake this task himself. York had no intention of counselling the king, in the sense of joining the ranks of his councillors, but demanded the role of chief councillor, much like Gloucester or Suffolk, and to govern on behalf of or even instead of the king.[46] He regarded himself as different in kind even from the other great lords of royal blood, almost certainly as heir apparent, and certainly to be treated by the government as an individual rather than amongst the Lords. When offered by Henry VI membership of 'a sad and a substantial council',[47] York declined the option and chose instead to achieve his objectives by pressure and violence. In 1450 he progressed to Parliament with his sword uppermost. His invitation to the 'true lords of the king's council . . . and especially the lords of the mighty royal blood' to join him in purging and punishing traitors 'brought up of nought' contained veiled threats towards any who were not 'true'.[48] The dukes of Norfolk and Exeter, the two Neville earls of Salisbury and Warwick, and the earls of Arundel, Devon and Northumberland allegedly supported him at this point; the dukes of Buckingham and Somerset opposed.[49] York encouraged aggression towards the government and royal household by the House of Commons, of which his chamberlain Sir William Oldhall was speaker and others of his retainers were MPs. If not actually the fomentor, which is unprovable, York encouraged riotous demonstrations to pressurize the king, government and Parliament by the retainers both of himself and his allies, by demobilized soldiers, and by the London mob. It was York's adoption of all the different programmes of the diverse critics of the regime, his appeal simultaneously to the Commons, the people, to chivalric noblemen and to ex-servicemen, and his willingness to invoke popular support in politics and to direct mob violence that made him so apparently irresistible in 1450.[50]

However well endowed, no nobleman normally had resources to rival those of the Crown. Just like Thomas of Lancaster, Edward II's greatest magnate, York found that his resources at a time of exceptional weakness of the Crown sufficed to make of him an overmighty subject. He, too, was an independent power, to be treated apart from the rest of the lords. Starting in 1451, he decided which councils, great councils or parliaments to attend and he ignored royal summonses to meetings at which his will was not guaranteed to prevail. He ignored summonses from the council to account for his conduct and its attempts to discipline him both before and after his protectorate, when he himself had legislated to make others more compliant. York expected to negotiate his own terms in person with the king and through no intermediaries in 1450, 1452, 1455 and 1459. Such a man as he (in his own eyes) was incapable alike of treason and of rebellion. Normal constitutional conventions did not apply. York's forceful protests or armed self-help, what contemporaries called 'the way of fait' and we today call *coups d'état*, were actually forceful expressions of counsel befitting the king's natural councillor and hence entirely legitimate. They should not therefore have been confused with the otherwise identical insurrections of lesser men, which were treasonable and should be punished as such. Hence the highly explicit oath against resort to 'the way of fait' that York was three times obliged to swear did not prevent him (so he thought) from further forceful counselling, nor mean that by such actions he had perjured himself.[51] He was clear that he had not. Neither had his backers. In 1454 he complained that the punishment of his fellow rebels at Dartford (1452) had slurred his honour. He insisted that the penalties be revoked, that the Lords acknowledge that he had always been loyal, and that his allies Thomas, Earl of Devon and Lord Edward Cobham be exonerated also.[52]

York was no conciliator. He had no time for compromise. He preferred to go for the jugular. Repeatedly he sought the destruction of Somerset with complete disregard for the verdict of the king. In 1454 he hazarded his new-found hegemony by trampling over the privilege of the House of Commons, imprisoning their speaker Thomas Thorpe, and insisting they elect another. He pursued Thorpe vindictively, ousting him from office, resuming his fees and officers, and sought his financial ruin.[53] He raised the political tempera-ture and political tensions. York it was who called the people into politics, York who resorted first to violence and to bloodshed, York who attacked the court and had his rivals slain. And if he himself could not be pre-eminent, Henry VI and his current advisers, whoever they might be, were not to be allowed to rule either. That he never had majority support among the Lords – not in 1452, 1454, 1456, 1459, nor 1460 – did not impede him. Opponents were eliminated.

What did York stand for? He stood for the cause of reform. But what was that?

The *Crisis of 1450* had identified the issues and set the tone of political debate for the 1450s. Justice and order were important themes to which York had been committed as lieutenant of France.[54] Defence of the realm was also crucial. Recriminations about defeat and the punishment of the guilty were less so. So far as is known, there were no further attempts to impeach Somerset or the others that the 1450–1 Parliament had wanted excluded from the king's presence. From 1450 there were attempts to attaint Suffolk for treason, unavailingly, and to rehabilitate Duke Humphrey, successfully at last in 1455.[55] The parliamentary Commons (and apparently also the populace) attributed much of the economic distress to foreign merchants, whom they wanted controlled – they must be made to pay better prices for English products and placed under the supervision of English hosts – and on the licences to export wool customs-free that detracted from the staple monopoly.[56] Although repeatedly informed how parlous were the Crown's finances, the Commons consistently opposed taxation, preferring that the king should live of his own and hence favoured comprehensive resumption of grants even though this had already happened in 1451. They targeted members of the royal household, who were still believed to be restricting access to the king, improperly dominating his counsels, and exploiting royal favour out of their own 'covetousness'. Both in 1450-1 and in 1456 the Commons sought resumption even of the endowments for the king's religious foundations and the duchy of Lancaster trusts of Henry V and VI, which they found burdensome, the cancellation of licences to export, and the punishment of offenders without the possibility of pardons. Since each infringed the royal prerogative, Henry found them offensive and adamantly refused.[57]

York subscribed to this programme and tried to implement it when he had the chance, in 1454 and in 1455-6. Combining household cuts with resumption could significantly improve royal solvency and was a realistic, if modest, programme. Whether he was altogether sincere has been debated – after all, he knew the realities of royal budgeting and resumption – but his stance brought him valuable support. He struck at his enemies in the royal household by cutting the staff in 1454 and its funding in 1455.[58] Somerset held no official household office and was abroad during the final years of Suffolk's ascendancy, so he was not vulnerable to such cutbacks or associations, but he was exposed by his abject military performance in France. Issues of honour could therefore have motivated York's pursuit of Somerset and certainly were important to the Duke of Norfolk,[59] who had also served abroad and as earl marshal had particular responsibility for chivalry. Somerset's military record was the best way to oust him from government and to let York himself in. Whilst clearly committed to justice, law and order, and defence during his two protectorates in 1453-5 and 1455-6 – for what English government was not? – York did not display any originality in his policies.

Different Visions

Two very different notions of what constituted acceptable political conduct conflicted in the 1450s.

What held the line between what was acceptable and what was not was the statute of Treasons of 1352. This protected the king, queen and immediate royal family against violence – assassination or mere attack. Levying war against the king or the king's army when his banner was displayed was forbidden. All such acts were treason, the most heinous of offences, and carried the death penalty and the forfeiture of possessions for the perpetrator.

Seven earls were condemned by Henry IV and V under this definition. Moreover the concept of treason was extended in the fifteenth century: judicially, to enmesh plebeian offenders guilty of treasonable words, and in the popular imagination against those acting against the popular interest who were eliminated in 1450.[60]

For peers, the situation was rather different. Like all subjects, they owed allegiance to the king, for each individual took extra oaths of allegiance in 1454, 1455 and 1459.[61] All peers were entitled to trial by their fellow peers who, in the words of Sellar and Yeatman,[62] would understand. In 1403 the Lords had found that Northumberland's self-evident complicity in the Percy revolt was felony, not treason, and he was pardoned. In 1450 they acquitted the Duchess of Suffolk and in 1454 the Earl of Devon, and in 1454 declined to convict Somerset. In 1535 the peers found Lord Dacre not guilty of treason. Admittedly, the circumstances of each case differ, but collectively they indicate a reluctance amongst the Lords to treat fellow peers as harshly as their social inferiors.

When York tried to seize power at Dartford in 1452, the king and the courts treated his offence as treason.[63] York himself was obliged to swear a long and detailed oath that was made as explicit and wide-ranging as possible. He would obey all royal summonses. He would act as befitted a subject to his sovereign. He would not attempt anything or do anything against the king, consent to anyone else so doing, or conceal their intentions. He would withstand any such offenders. He would not array or gather men without the king's licence or commands, any interpretation being not for him but the king or his fellow peers. He would not take direct action ('way of fait') against the king or anyone else, nor 'take upon me [royal authority] against your royal estate or the obeisance that is due thereto'. If he felt wronged, he would seek his remedy in the courts according to the law. The oath was as absolute and inclusive as possible – 'anything', 'in no wise', 'at any time hereafter', 'to the uttermost of my life'. The penalties for non-compliance were defined as loss of worship (honour), his rank and title, and as being 'unabled [dispossessed of his property] and foresworn' as a perjurer. York declared that he swore of his own free will and explicitly denied duress: a common escape clause. The oath was sworn in the most solemn way possible – on the Bible, touching the Holy Cross, and receiving the sacrament from the Cardinal Archbishop in St Paul's Cathedral – and York signed the written record with his own hand and sealed it with his seal of arms.[64] A more comprehensive and watertight oath cannot be conceived. Henceforth York's political activity should have been confined to constitutional and peaceful channels. He should have needed to work with and win over his peers. What should have restrained him was not military force, nor any penalties for breaking his bonds, but moral issues – the potential damage to his honour and reputation of perjury.

Yet the oath did not work. York broke his promises, attacking King Henry at the Battle of St Albans in 1455. He swore the oath twice more[65] – it could not be tightened any more – and yet in 1459 he broke it again on the Blore Heath and Ludford campaign. The battles both of First St Albans and Ludford, at which he waged war against the king with his banner displayed, were breaches of the statute of Treasons.

Yet York convinced himself that he had never rebelled, committed treason, or perjured himself. Persuading his followers was more difficult. Sir William Skipwith, his steward of Conisburgh in Yorkshire, refused to serve his lord against his allegiance in 1455. In 1459 many were not prepared to fight the king. Persuading them required more than angry protestations of his own innocence. Hence York always denied that King Henry was the real source of the rejections of his demands and requirements to submit. It was a Yorkist tale, retrospective and probably invented, that at Dartford York had been deceived into swearing the first oath – that it was his enemies who had perjured them-selves[66] – and that York was not bound to honour an oath exacted under duress. Hence also his argument in 1460 that oaths of allegiance to Henry VI had been sworn on a misapprehension.[67] In 1459–60 any obligations of alle-giance were relieved by claims that the king was dead and that Prince Edward was illegitimate (and not therefore entitled to allegiance). In 1454 York angrily repudiated the aspersions on his honour. He had rewritten in 1454, 1455, 1459 and 1460 the histories that presented him as traitorous or perjured.[68]

The distinctiveness of the royal family was enhanced from Richard II onwards in many honorific and material ways. York and his allies Norfolk, the Nevilles and Devon were all of royal blood. The Mowbray dukes of Norfolk were heirs of Edward I's second son Thomas of Brotherton and prided them-selves also on descent from the earls of Lancaster. Norfolk himself was son of Katherine Neville, daughter of Joan Beaufort, half-sister of Henry IV. Salisbury was Joan's eldest son and Warwick her grandson. Thomas Courtenay, Earl of Devon, was husband/widower of Margaret Beaufort, daughter of Henry IV's half-brother John, Earl of Somerset. Joan Beaufort's eight married children spread the blood royal of Lancaster very widely.[69] All were members of the Lancastrian royal family. Norfolk and Devon were repeatedly imprisoned. All their claims to be royal were sidelined in the 1440s and 1450s by Henry's creation of his own nuclear family and by the preference (and precedence) he showed for the male line of the Beauforts and the Holland dukes of Exeter. Here was a clash between different concepts of royalty that involved, one might say inevitably, the downgrading of older collateral loyalty in each generation.

There was a psychology of royalty. In 1388 Edward III's son Thomas denied that he had committed treason. 'Lord Duke', replied Richard II's spokesman, 'you have sprung from such a worthy stock, and you are so near us in a collateral line, that you *cannot* be suspected of devising such things'.[70] (The italics are mine: a royal prince *cannot* commit treason.) As we shall see, this was the attitude also of the Yorkist peers. The psychology of the Yorkists themselves has to be deduced from their actions, from a debate at Calais in 1460, and from the *Somnium Vigilantis*, a hostile tract dating from 1459 that nevertheless sets out the Yorkist case most cogently if only to refute it.[71] These two late sources make sense of some of their conduct and utterances, although the Yorkists may well have taken time to rationalize what they felt.

York, Norfolk and the Nevilles were extremely touchy about their royal blood, rank and honour. York clearly felt that his treatment after the Dartford coup had dishonoured him and asked the Lords to exonerate him. Even when in exile and convicted of treason, his son March and then the Nevilles reacted furiously at allegations of treason. York and the Nevilles felt themselves justified in their direct action in 1452, 1455, 1459 and in 1460. All critics of the regime in 1450 experienced a tension between the common good – which was what government was for – and allegiance to the king, whose function was to pursue the common good. The tension was partly resolved by purging the king's agents whilst keeping the king. York claimed that the tension persisted for the whole of the next decade. His main justification at each juncture was that he was acting in the public interest and in the interest of the king. The common good did not override allegiance to the king. The two went hand in hand. The Yorkists knew Henry's interests better than he did himself. They were not acting against the king, but against such as 'were odious to the God and to the people for their misrule'.[72] These are common themes in every uprising from 1450 to 1460. York and the Nevilles themselves were the king's natural councillors, with a right to summonses to Parliament and great council, and access to the king to put their case.

How this excused them from the normal obligations of obedience and the statute of Treasons was not made explicit until 1460, when the attainted Yorkist earls upbraided their Wydeville captives. Salisbury berated Lord Rivers 'that he should be so rude to call him and these other lords traitors, for they shall be found the king's true liege men', rather than 'a traitor &c'. Warwick berated Rivers for his presumption 'to have such language of lords, being of the king's blood'. Royal princes could not commit treason.[73] Princes were not the same as other peers. Hence they could subscribe to ordinances of the great council against arrays and direct action, and even promote an act in the 1454 Parliament, and yet engage in the proscribed activities themselves. Hence also their readiness in 1454 and 1460 to condemn their opponents for treasonable acts that they denied when applied to themselves. That York was not wholly discredited by his repeated insurrections, nor dishonoured, is shown by the willingness of the Lords to exonerate him in 1454, again in 1455, and in 1456 and 1460, two occasions when they declined to go along with his more radical proposals. That Henry himself felt York to be special and was uneasy emerges from his unwillingness to treat York as harshly as lesser offenders among the peers. It was this immunity that enabled York to attempt further coups.

CHAPTER 7

PRECONDITIONS:
RECOVERY ABORTED 1451–6

The *Crisis of 1450* was a precondition for the Wars of the Roses that fell short of civil war because there were not two sides to fight – almost everybody was enraged and only the king could rebuff the critics – and because there was no demand to change either King Henry or his dynasty. Civil war was not inevitable. There was no continuous build-up of tension over the next eleven years. Tensions first relaxed, resumed and fluctuated, two sides emerged, and in 1460 the issues metamorphosed into something distinctly different.

Of all the sequences of events during the Wars of the Roses, none appears more random and hence incomprehensible today than those of 1450–61. Actually they make good sense when divided into distinct phases, which started but were never completed because prevented by chance circumstances, the first and most important being the chance of the king's insanity. The sequence is complicated, but meaningful and comprehensible to us today. The years from 1451–9 need to be viewed as six distinct phases of politics.

The regime recovered until the king's lapse into insanity in August 1453. An attempted *coup d'état* by York in 1452 (the Dartford episode) failed and left the regime stronger. From this unprecedented dilemma, York emerged as Lord Protector in 1454–5. His *First Protectorate* ended with the king's recovery. This third phase, from February to May 1455, was terminated by York's successful coup at the First Battle of St Albans (22 May 1455). York's *Second Protectorate* (1455–6) collapsed in February 1456. The first four phases from 1451–6, including two periods of rule by York, had left the king as much in control if not more, and York more excluded from power than before. Here surely was the opportunity for recovery to continue. Two attempts were made. Unfortunately, recovery was not achieved. Civil war began in 1459.

RECOVERY OF THE REGIME 1451-3

The *Crisis of 1450* passed, the complaints unredressed and perhaps beyond the government's capacity to resolve. Those who wonder why so long passed and so many experiments intervened before Henry VI was deposed presume that it was Henry who was the root problem. He was not. His forces were defeated in France in 1450 because of insufficient resources. The government could not manage within its means without economic recovery, still two decades away. It needed more income to finance the recovery of Gascony, to pay off its debts, and to rebuild its credit. MPs proved just as unwilling to vote taxes to the reforming Lord Protector York in 1454 and 1455 as to Henry VI. Yet the regime did revive, it did strive to restore order, it did prosecute the Hundred Years War, and it did continue. Neither in 1450, nor in the next decade, could York exert pressure enough to cause the Lords to abandon their king.

Obviously there were factors militating towards further political crises. To the loss of Normandy was quickly added that of Gascony: Bordeaux fell on 5 June 1451. The humiliation was the essential backcloth for chroniclers as late as the 1470s.[1] At home, as we have seen, the people had been invited into politics and their potential had been revealed. They had learnt that they mattered. They expected their wishes and their interests to be taken into account. There were to be sporadic disturbances and uprisings that demanded intervention from the centre to repress. Even though Suffolk was never convicted, it was generally accepted that he had been guilty of treason, that there had been misconduct in the defence of France and bad governance at home. The guilty men, the so-called traitors of 1450, had escaped unpunished. There was an awareness of unfinished business, reflected in the re-issue and continued relevance of Jack Cade's manifesto as late as 1460,[2] but actually no pressing reason why it should be completed. To convert all this into conflict required a catalyst, a man who knew how to exploit such opportunities. York thought himself, mistakenly, to be that man. He was to press his case by force both in 1452 (the Dartford episode) and in 1455 (First St Albans), both discussed below. Henry VI's government could cope with all the challenges it faced, albeit feebly, but not, unfortunately, with York.

The years 1451-3 were ones of recovery that indicate what governance the king could offer, and did in 1456-60 after York's two protectorates. 'By the summer of 1453, it was beginning to look as though Henry VI's reign was set on a new and more steady course.'[3] The immediate stresses were relaxed. If the economic recession was still profound, the commercial collapse of 1450, which had impacted so much on those engaged in foreign trade and on clothiers, was alleviated. Terms were reached with the Hanse and the Burgundians that enabled trade with them to resume. Fearful aliens, who in 1450 dared not travel and exported no more than four woolsacks, re-emerged and started trading once more.[4] There was therefore some recovery in customs revenues. The act of resumption of 1451 had been comprehensive and had retrieved substantial grants of property and offices.[5] Royal revenues were increased so that, on a day-to-day basis, the government was able to survive on its own resources ('live of its own') and even face some of the challenges posed by the continuing warfare. The pursuit of Edmund, Duke of Somerset moved down the political agenda. Ex-servicemen joined the enlarged garrison of Calais, the fleet to keep the seas, and the expedition to recover Gascony. Initially, perhaps amazingly, this counterattack succeeded, as the Earl of Shrewsbury did indeed recapture Bordeaux on 23 October 1452. This prompted a display of generosity from the much more tractable Parliament at Reading in the spring of 1453, including taxes to fund 13,000 archers,[6] although what the Commons regarded as affordable remained as always insufficient for the government's needs. The inner royal family was strengthened by the creation of the king's two Tudor half-brothers as earls of Richmond and Pembroke and by the pregnancy of the queen, which on 13 October 1453 produced an heir, Prince Edward of Lancaster. Edward's birth ended speculation about the succession and carried on the Lancastrian line. The trajectory of the regime was upwards from the nadir of 1450.

Problems remained. The economy was depressed, the government impoverished and entrapped in an unaffordable war. It took several years to pay off arrears due to the Calais garrison and before permanent funding was agreed by the merchants of the staple. Virtually none of the mountain of debt could be repaid, without which the government's credit could not be restored. The Channel was now the front line: invasions threatened and piracy burgeoned. That Shrewsbury was annihilated at Castillon on 17 July 1453 and Gascony was lost forever was almost overlooked in the domestic conundrum of the king's madness (August 1453 – February 1455).

Usually any vigour in the government or any achievements in these two years are credited to Somerset rather than the king. Somerset, it is assumed rather than proven, had replaced Suffolk as the mastermind of the regime.[7] Nevertheless, Henry remained the figurehead – and often seemingly much more than that. On 25 January 1451 he reasserted his right to decide and to direct by repudiating control by the council in certain areas that he had previously conceded.[8] King and government retained the respect and obedience of all subjects.

The key domestic issue was public order, which was disrupted as offenders both popular and aristocratic took advantage of the collapse of the regime in 1450 and of the usual forces of repression and deterrent. There were further uprisings in Kent late in 1450, 1451 and afterwards. None of the popular outbreaks were dangerous in themselves, although they did reveal the persistence of grievances encouraged by Cade's successes and threatened another such large-scale insurrection that the king, government and elite so greatly feared. Some of the 'gentleman's wars' escalated into murders and ambushes, tit-for-tat feuding and even private warfare, both sieges and battles. Not all happened at the same time, however, nor did they continue unchecked. Those of 1451–3 that have been studied most fully by historians are the revival of the Berkeley–Lisle and Courtenay–Bonville disputes in the West Country; the depredations of Gruffydd ap Nicholas in West Wales; the Harcourt–Stafford of Grafton feud; the misconduct of Sir Thomas Malory in the West Midlands; the Warwick and Despenser contests in South Wales and the West Midlands; the Ampthill dispute in the East Midlands; the strife amongst the gentry of the North Midlands; and the celebrated Percy–Neville war between the earls of Northumberland and Salisbury in Yorkshire and Cumbria.[9] There were others: for example, John, Duke of Norfolk's dispossession of the Wingfields and his defiance of an arbitration that the council was trying to enforce on 20 June 1452.[10] It is an impressive and perhaps unparalleled tally.

The Earl of Warwick may have stilled the feud between the Harcourts and Staffords, both his retainers.[11] The Berkeley–Lisle, Warwick, Despenser and Ampthill disputes originated in contested inheritances; the Courtenay–Bonville and Percy–Neville ones are more obscure, but certainly became struggles for county or regional hegemony.[12] What was new was that disputes outgrew the usual mechanisms of peaceful mediation and arbitration – offenders hoped to win rather than as usual be forced to compromise – and their sheer number. That such a list can be recited for so many areas does not mean that disorder was general, though some petitioners to Parliament and some commentators reported as though it was.[13] Actual mortality even in the so-called battles of Heworth, Stamford Bridge (Yorks.) and Clyst seems to have been in single figures. However violent was everyday life, such feuds were exceptional in the later Middle Ages and were as shocking to contemporaries as they are today.

Henry's government took these threats to public order very seriously and deserves some credit for controlling lawlessness. Against popular uprisings it despatched magnates to suppress them and authoritative commissions of royal judges and magnates to impose justice on offenders. Sometimes the king accompanied them, often presiding in person over the gruesome executions, following which heads and quarters were posted on town gates as deterrents. Aristocratic feuds were always drawn to government attention by the aggrieved party, to which the council responded with injunctions, summonses, and, on appearance and pending settlement, by binding both parties to keep the peace on pain of ruinous financial penalties. Twenty-two peers were bound in this way between 1437 and 1458. 'It seems that the king and council were at this time using such instruments to quell the recalcitrance of nobles and the personal feuds between magnates.'[14] Contempt of the king's messengers, one of whom was urged to eat his mandate, seal and all, by Derbyshire rioters,[15] or disobedience to summonses, brought stronger privy seals from the council threatening more extreme punishment – which, however, offenders knew would never be enforced. That may be why Henry promised the Commons in Reading a nominated council, perhaps with the enhanced powers to which the Lords subscribed in November and that was enacted at the next session of Parliament.[16] Those who disobeyed the council next faced the king in person.

It seems that Henry preferred to impose order in disputes himself and to leave the real issues wherever possible to be settled at the common law, in the courts, by arbitration and/or in Parliament. It is a fair criticism that Henry did not engage with the detail: some awards, notably York vs. Somerset, really demanded his personal involvement. Following William Tailbois' murderous attack, Ralph, Lord Cromwell, had petitioned in January 1450 for his imprisonment and procedure by bill on heavy security. The king agreed to the first, consigning Tailbois to the Tower, which enabled Cromwell to sue at common law, win ruinous damages and keep his foe out of circulation until 1455.[17] When Henry, Duke of Exeter, seized Cromwell's castle of Ampthill (Bedford) on 5 June 1452, the king and council promptly forced arbitration on him, which it is presumed that he lost; on 1 February 1453 they also rejected his allegations of treason against Cromwell himself. Cromwell pursued his case in the courts, which Exeter strove to impede by riots both in Bedfordshire and Westminster Hall, to which the king again responded extremely promptly by arresting all the principals.[18] Whilst undoubtedly both cases were marred by the sharp practice so commonplace in fifteenth-century disputes, Henry did not turn a 'blind eye' to the seizure of Ampthill, nor 'proved incapable of that personal assertion of royal power so necessary to the restraint of local conflict', nor 'allowed the processes of law to be manipulated by and in favour of the ruling clique at Court',[19] of which Exeter was certainly not one. The process has not been fully understood: even when the ringleaders were pardoned – too lightly, declare Henry's critics – that was not the end of the story, as those forgiven were habitually bound over on heavy sureties afterwards.

In company with his judges and an impressive number of magnates, Henry toured southern and western England in the summers of 1451 and 1452 imposing order and justice. He also presided in August 1452 over sessions at Ludlow in Shropshire at which supporters of York's Dartford uprising were indicted. Another tour was scheduled for the summer of 1453.[20] However unimpressive physically, Henry VI was the king, to whom the utmost reverence was due. At his approach even the most recalcitrant nobleman submitted. So many lords accompanied him on these tours that nobody could withstand him. Judicial commissioners presided over the indictment and summary trials of offenders, some of whom were executed and others, on submission and on sureties, pardoned. To be pardoned was not tantamount to escaping scot-free. Sureties for good behaviour were normally required. The prerogative of mercy, it is important to remember, was not just about letting off the guilty, but was a mitigation of rigour that was necessary if justice was to be respected and culprits were to be induced to submit rather than to resist.

Noble ringleaders were sometimes indicted, but never tried. Peers were entitled to trial by their peers, in great council or Parliament. Yet they were not unscathed. Trials by peers were staged for Devon and Somerset and probably also for Exeter and Bonville.[21] Usually disruptive lords were imprisoned, whether to cool off or in punishment, and were thus removed from circulation: an effective measure, which seems to have stilled the disturbances that they had orchestrated. Already in 1440, Henry had signalled his displeasure to Norfolk by a brief imprisonment; in 1443 it was the Earl of Northumberland and in 1448 Norfolk again for six days who were confined in the Tower.[22] When the Courtenay–Bonville dispute revived spectacularly in 1451 with Devon's raids on Bath and Taunton in Somerset, King Henry, so *Benet's Chronicle* reports, was enraged. Devon's victims, the Earl of Wiltshire and Bonville, though both royal favourites, were gaoled at Berkhamsted Castle (Herts.) and Devon's allies Lords Cobham and Moleyns at Wallingford Castle (Berks.),[23] albeit briefly. Moleyns indeed joined Shrewsbury's ill-fated expedition to Gascony. So of course did Shrewsbury and Lisle, parties in the Berkeley and Warwick inheritance disputes. Devon, saved by York's intervention, did not submit and was humiliated instead by removal from the commission of the peace. Again at liberty, Devon and Cobham joined York's Dartford escapade in February–March 1452, a much more serious treasonable offence. This time Devon was imprisoned in Wallingford Castle, possibly for a whole year – he attended a great council in

November 1453 and was formally tried only in 1454 – and lost his ancestral precedence among the earls that he had valued so highly. Cobham was consigned to Berkhamsted Castle, where he stayed for two years.[24] In summer 1452 the king progressed through the West Country, visiting Crewkerne in Somerset, the Earl of Devon's abbey of Forde in Dorset and Bonville's seat at Shute in Somerset, and oversaw there the indictment and trial of their dependants.[25] In 1453 Henry imprisoned Exeter at Windsor Castle, Cromwell at Wallingford Castle and Lord Grey of Ruthin at Pevensey Castle.[26] Although Lord Admiral, Exeter was not among those commissioned to keep the seas. York was to incarcerate him for another six months in 1454–5. The king was again to imprison both Devon and Bonville late in 1456, keeping Exeter incarcerated until the summer, and then he imprisoned him for a fourth time in 1459.[27] Although the evidence is much patchier than for Henry V or for Henry VII, normally such noble offenders were bound over for good behaviour on pain of heavy financial penalties for themselves and their sureties, which appear to have operated as real deterrents. Order was imposed. Far from being partisan, Henry and the council were equally severe on the ringleaders on all sides. Except for York, who alone escaped imprisonment for his uprisings.

Modern historians have tended to judge the government's efforts at peacekeeping both as partisan and ineffective, principally it seems because the Courtenay–Bonville dispute revived later, surely because of York's intervention on Devon's behalf in 1454, and because the Ampthill, Glamorgan, Percy–Neville and North Midlands disputes raged on. Arguably they persisted because Henry's madness intervened. Yet the Ampthill, Warwick and Despenser disputes were all terminated in these years – not necessarily justly, but were medieval disputes ever resolved fairly? – and both the Courtenay–Bonville and Berkeley–Lisle disputes were temporarily aborted. As always, the absence of contending parties on war service, such as Shrewsbury, his son Lisle, Moleyns and a Berkeley, imposed some deliberate intermissions, in these cases nearly two decades in duration. Henry's West Country progress in 1452 was 'exemplary as well as punitive' and marks 'Henry's re-establishment of order and confidence in the regime. . . . The King was now ruling his kingdom.'[28]

Following the adjournment of the Reading Parliament on 2 July 1453, the council in London was contending both with the Percy–Neville feud in Yorkshire and Richard, Earl of Warwick's occupation of George Neville's Despenser lordship of Glamorgan. Nothing, it is well known, came of their efforts. Lord Chancellor Kemp forecast Henry's visits to various regions 'to the intention and end that maintenance, extortion, oppression, riots and other misdeeds . . . might be destroyed and the doers . . . punished according to their demerits' before the next parliamentary session in November.[29] Henry was at Clarendon near Salisbury in August 1453. Probably he intended first to quell the Despenser dispute in Glamorgan, where Warwick had just ousted Somerset as guardian of the rightful heir George Neville in defiance of a whole series of conciliar injunctions; possibly also the depredations of Gruffydd ap Nicholas in West Wales; and then conceivably the Percy–Neville feud in the North.[30] Strong letters were still despatched in Henry's name to the rival earls of Northumberland and Salisbury and their sons as late as 8 October 1453. 'But these matters seemed well in hand.'[31] Had King Henry actually appeared at Cardiff, Warwick could not have resisted without making himself a traitor and prematurely ending his career. Submission, surely inescapable, entailed the partition of his estate with George Neville, much reduced resources, and a decidedly less overmighty career. We can never know what might have been. At this stage the government was acting resolutely and had some success in the restoration of order. ' "No escalation of private feuds" was allowed.'[32]

Madness, wholly unpredictable, intervened and prevented Henry from proceeding. This was early in August 1453. Warwick was not therefore held to account. He followed up his victory in Glamorgan by intervening in the Neville–Percy feud, specifically the stand-off on 20 October between the two armies at Sandhutton near Northallerton in North Yorkshire.[33] The king's breakdown ensured that Warwick was never punished for his forceful misappropriation of Glamorgan, nor his Neville kinsfolk for their disturbances in Yorkshire. The two Neville earls – Richard Neville, Earl of Salisbury, and his son Richard Neville, Earl of Warwick – wisely backed York during Henry's insanity. Their support contributed to York's appointment as Lord Protector and helped him rule. York in turn found for the Nevilles against the Percies.

The Dartford Incident 1452

On many issues with legal implications Henry VI consulted the judges – *his* judges – who attended great councils and the House of Lords. They were chary of committing themselves on politically sensitive cases. The Lords reserved to themselves cases involving other lords, such as precedence and title, but appeared reluctant to decide for or against anyone or to upset the status quo.[34] They insisted on trial by peers, but acquitted those impeached in 1450 and Devon in 1454, refused to convict Somerset in 1454, and only retrospectively and posthumously convicted him and the other victims of the First Battle of

St Albans.[35] Although obliged as royal commissioners to preside over the trials of local rioters who might include peers and prepared to destroy those who were not peers, guilty like Sir William Oldhall or innocent like Thomas Thorpe,[36] the Lords were unwilling to convict noblemen like themselves and perhaps sympathised with York's assertions that his rebellions were legitimate protests. Hence perhaps their readiness in 1454-6 to overturn the acts that proscribed the Dartford rebels and in 1460 the attainders of 1459,[37] in both cases at the demands of the politically dominant Yorkists. The Lords were not servile on such essential issues as the 1455-6 resumption, nor on the change of dynasty. The king could also direct their actions: at the Reading parliament of 1453 against the Dartford offenders, in great council at Coventry, when the Duke of York was apparently convicted; and later in 1459, when the Yorkists were attainted.[38] From 1459, however, there was wholesale proscription of the defeated, including peers, by all parties.

York had been unable to cow the king into purging the court and thorough-going reform in the winter of 1450-1. Following the dissolution of Parliament late in May 1451, he did not pursue his case in court or council. His attempted *coup d'état* of spring 1452 – the Dartford episode – should be grouped with that of 1450. Apparently he declined to attend a great council at Coventry in September 1451, probably when his differences with Somerset were scheduled for arbitration. The great council coincided with Devon's attack on Bonville and Wiltshire in Somerset that so enraged the king. Although the feud took place well away from his home territories, York stepped in to restrain Devon, to still the disturbances, and to protect the recalcitrant earl, who had ignored summonses from the royal council, against the consequences of his acts. Whilst effective in restoring order, this was both a partisan act and a usurpation of royal power that annoyed King Henry. Allegedly York's chamberlain Sir William Oldhall was already organizing the assemblies that later indictments identified as the treasonable preparations for York's rebellion early in 1452. Oldhall took sanctuary in November 1451.[39] Almost certainly York wanted, as he said, to punish Somerset for the mismanagement of his command in Normandy. Clearly, however, he also wanted to supplant him as prime-mover in the government. There is no conclusive evidence whether he intended thoroughgoing reform if successful.

York had determined to revive his ascendancy of autumn 1450 by recreating the circumstances. Again he planned to array his own retainers and those of his allies, this time Devon, Cobham and a host of towns. Oldhall and others organized musters on his estates. Open letters were circulated in York's name to various towns. Again York was to march to London from the periphery, this time from Ludlow rather than from Ireland, and was to invoke the support of ex-soldiers, Londoners and the Kentishmen. Again, therefore, he labelled his enemies as traitors, naming specifically only Somerset, whom he wanted tried and punished for the loss of Normandy. Again, as a preliminary and to ensure that his protest was not confused with the treasonable rebellion that it so closely resembled, he formally swore allegiance to the king on the sacraments before witnesses (9 January 1452), had his oath publicly certified, and despatched the record to the king. Once again, he justified his resort to force by reference to the machinations of his enemies, who, he claimed, intended the corruption of his blood – his conviction for treason, forfeiture of his estates and hence the destruction of his dynasty. Again, York purported to be pre-empting a strike against himself, for which there is actually no other evidence.[40] Once again he disregarded the king's inquiries and prohibitions. He also ignored Henry's summons to discuss his grievances at a great council at Coventry and he avoided meeting the king en route.

In one key respect York's insurrection was a success. Even in the absence of reliable figures, he seems to have raised a very considerable force, too large surely to be made up solely of the retainers of the three noblemen, and hence suggesting considerable popular support. Some towns rejected his overtures. He was refused access to London, hence deflected over the Thames at Kingston and proceeded to Dartford in Kent, where he capitulated. The disturbances of the previous autumn, his failure to appear at council, and above all his declaration of allegiance and circular letters to town councils, several of which were forwarded to the king, forewarned Henry of York's intentions and gave him time to raise an army to withstand him. If York hoped to repeat the level of backing from the nobility that he had enjoyed in autumn 1450, he was disappointed, only Devon and Cobham joining him. Arundel and the Neville earls, like most other magnates, were with the king, who raised a substantial force, probably larger than York's, that grew as more loyal subjects arrived. Apparently also York had counted on mass support from the Londoners and Kentishmen – hence his otherwise eccentric march to Dartford – who did not rise up or rose too few and too late, like John Wilkins in Kent in May. Possibly they were deterred by 'the harvest of heads' of the previous spring. Most probably their discontent had eased as the economy recovered.

York's appeal to the people was misdirected. His surviving manifesto was extremely vague about bad governance, the principal concern of Cade's rebels, and was patriotic and precise only about Somerset, never part of Suffolk's regime and the target principally of French veterans. The manifesto did not start from the concerns of the populace. York knew that he needed popular backing for his coup, but he had not yet diagnosed what his message required for popular appeal, nor had he found the knack to bring out the masses.

York also made several tactical errors. His declarations of allegiance and his widespread recruitment forewarned the king, enabling him both to offer constitutional means of redress, which it was damaging for York to reject, and to recruit an army himself. Regardless of York's professions of loyalty, his activity looked like treason, in which neither town corporations nor magnates wanted any part. In the last resort, so York found, the nobility always rallied to the king when summoned, whether against rebels (especially popular rebels) or in Parliament. Finally, of course, when confronted by the king with banners displayed, York's only alternative to submission was treasonable war against the king – too stark a choice for him to take and one for which he lacked support.

Anxious to avoid unnecessary bloodshed, the king sent envoys to negotiate an armistice (1–2 March). To them, York passed his articles against the Duke of Somerset. Later it was claimed on his behalf that he surrendered only on condition of the arrest and trial of Somerset and was double-crossed, finding Somerset at liberty in the king's tent, but all the (related) sources for this are post-1461 and can be classified as later Yorkist propaganda, devised to justify the duke's subsequent actions.[41] That York was released only because of the approach of an army led by his son Edward, Earl of March, then twelve years old, was surely apocryphal, a contemporary rumour that became established fact in the later *Brut* and London chronicles.[42]

Acts passed by the Reading Parliament in the spring of 1453 made it clear that those 'assembled in your field of Dartford' were like Oldhall and even Cade, 'your traitors [acting] unnaturally and against the duty and faith of his allegiance'.[43] Yet their leader York was treated as a very special case and got off lightly, if not wholly unscathed. King Henry condescended to accept his protestations of loyalty. Whilst rejecting York's demands for Somerset to be tried and indeed repeating Somerset's exoneration, Henry confided any private differences between the two dukes to a panel of arbitration, who were to investigate and impose a settlement. Both dukes were obliged to obey the award on pain of £20,000, potentially a ruinous penalty.

York was not summarily executed, as he could have been, nor charged with treason, nor did he even suffer the spell in prison that was de rigueur for other offending dukes, Exeter, Norfolk (and also Gloucester, Somerset and Suffolk), earls and barons. He did have to submit with the utmost ceremonial publicity at St Paul's Cathedral, where he swore on the sacrament in the most explicit terms never to pursue his political objectives by 'way of fait' (violent self-help), but only by constitutional means. The original certificate of his oath that he had signed and sealed was lodged at the royal exchequer, and copies were widely circulated.[44] York was pardoned. 'Humiliating though it was, York's oath was an extremely light penalty for what could have been regarded as a treasonable conspiracy and could thus have destroyed the duke utterly.'[45] Surely he would have been destroyed by a stronger king, Henry V or VII, for instance? York's supporters – Devon, Cobham, and Oldhall, Sharpe, Halton and others – were treated as traitors. Many lesser men were indicted of treason with Devon and Cobham, who were imprisoned and lost their precedence in Parliament. Several were executed. Those who were pardoned had to beg for the king's mercy, clad only in their shirts, on their knees in frost and snow, and had to provide sufficient sureties for their good behaviour in future.[46] Parliament attainted Oldhall of treason in 1453 and coupled him with Jack Cade: King Henry signed both original acts.[47] The 1453 Parliament also resumed all the grants and offices of those on the wrong side at Dartford.[48] The gravity of their offences was certainly brought home to the rebels by a combination of majesty, justice and regal mercy designed to deter them from further uprisings.

York's later conduct and protestations show that he thought himself harshly treated and not at fault. He considered that he was not bound by the oath, which he had sworn under duress:[49] rightly, but it was the legitimate compulsion of the king acting with the proper advice and consent of the Lords. Later York was to rewrite history to that effect. Nothing came of the arbitration: neither the first panel nor a second one were able to reach a decision. How could they decide, given that Henry had settled the public issues and there were no real private ones? York's reputation had suffered a serious blow and amongst his peers he was politically discredited. More materially, several of the grants and appointments that he had received in the 1440s were resumed: the Isle of Wight, which was leased to another; the lordships of Builth in Wales, Hadleigh (Essex), and his London house to the king's under-endowed half-brothers; the chief justiceship of the forests south of Trent to Somerset; and, most painful of all, the lieutenantcy of Ireland that he certainly cherished, to his erstwhile deputy, the Irishman James, Earl of Wiltshire.[50] Apparently, however, York retained his precedence among the dukes. Supposedly, Henry directed him to stay on his estates, which seems to be confirmed by his itinerary.[51] There is no concrete evidence for the next eighteen months that York attended the sessions of the royal council, great council, or (in 1453) Parliament, although he was sent the customary summons. On his duchess's admission, he was 'estranged from the grace and benevolent favour' of the king, which presumably means that he had no access either to him or to his bounty for himself or his clients. She asked Queen Margaret to intercede for him with the king, perhaps first about April 1453 at Hitchin (Herts.) – evidently without result, whether forwarded to the king or not – and petitioned her again, most probably that summer, assuring the queen (and hence the king) of York's loyalty and his willingness to do Henry's will. What appears the most exemplary and humble of supplications for forgiveness and for restoration to normal political life is reminiscent of similar protestations in 1450, 1452 and 1455. That the letter survives as an undated copy indicates that it was circulated and therefore that it too was an open letter designed to put York's case more widely and to pressure Henry to relent.[52] York was not ready to give up political dominance. Henry, however, did not re-admit him to his favour.

The Dartford episode, therefore, not only failed to remove Somerset or to place York in command, but it also deprived the latter of the political consideration to which he felt entitled. He was still in the cold when the king went mad in August 1453 and was not therefore invited to the opening discussions of what to do about it.

MADNESS AND THE FIRST PROTECTORATE

The insanity of the king, however, eventually enabled York to achieve the political eminence to which he aspired. The king and his infant heir Prince Edward of Lancaster were incapable of ruling. Ministers, councillors and courtiers carried on as normal at first, but needed a consensus on what to do next. York had to be included in any decisions. On the precedents of 1377 and 1422, the king's authority devolved on the Lords, who reluctantly did whatever was essential. The Lords feared the anger of the king when he recovered and the blame of the Commons for the dire financial situation.

In this uncertainty, York knew what he wanted and did not hesitate. In November 1453 he thrust forward the programme thwarted at Dartford. He found powerful allies in the two Neville earls, the father Salisbury and son Warwick, who had private quarrels with Somerset and the Percies and needed power to avert the equitable verdicts that were bound to disadvantage them. Now York's ally, the Duke of Norfolk charged Somerset with treason: he was lodged in the Tower. What to do next was certainly not agreed. York, Exeter and the queen claimed the right to rule when Parliament reconvened in February

1454. Probably the Lords ruled Exeter out, but both York and the queen took their cases to Parliament. The death of Cardinal Kemp broke the impasse, since government could not operate without a chancellor. Parliament appointed York as Lord Protector on 27 March 1454 and his ally Richard Neville, Earl of Salisbury, as chancellor. York used his authority to advantage his allies: Warwick was assured of his countess's inheritance; Devon was acquitted of treason at Dartford; and commissioners convicted adherents of the Percies. The Ampthill dispute was settled in Cromwell's favour and the Percy-Neville feud in the Nevilles' favour. York made himself captain of Calais and lieutenant of Ireland.

Yet York's triumph was far from complete. He was the best candidate in a field of three. The others were Queen Margaret of Anjou – a foreign queen in a country with no tradition of female rule – and Henry, Duke of Exeter, the most irresponsible of magnates and also York's recalcitrant son-in-law. York's powers were restricted to actual defence, merely until the infant prince came of age, and alongside a nominated council. Not only did the Lords appoint him, but they even allowed him to bridle the compliant Commons of the previous year by forcing out the speaker Thomas Thorpe and by retracting their condemnation of the Dartford rebels. Yet Parliament was dissolved as soon as possible (16–18 April) without implementing the reform programme. Perhaps it was still unsympathetic: perhaps also York miscalculated that he had plenty of time. The council did agree to substantial cuts in household expenditure, which was reduced to £5,193, and even diverted £1,000 a year from the duchy of Lancaster trust-lands designated for Eton and King's Colleges. The cuts were not merely theoretical, but were applied in detail to all ranks of individuals, dozens of whom were purged.[53] Although still insufficient to achieve the desired reductions, these savings could have assisted materially in balancing the government budget, if not addressing the issues of government debt and credit.

Otherwise, however, the nominated councillors were wary of difficult decisions and controversial meetings, absenting themselves in preference, notably for Somerset's trial: York had to veto Somerset's release.[54] Although protector, York could not count on the Lords for his reform programme.

York's authority was contested, first by Derbyshire rioters who denounced the regime as traitors, and more seriously by the Duke of Exeter in alliance with the Nevilles' foes the Percies. Exeter regarded himself as next heir to the duchy of Lancaster and heir general to the king. He was the grandson of Henry IV's whole sister Elizabeth and great-grandson of John of Gaunt and his first duchess Blanche, the Lancaster heiress. Exeter had contested York's Protectorate and now joined the Percies at arms against the Nevilles. In his 'private' letter of

8 May 1454 to him – actually another open letter for circulation – York took his stand on the obedience due even from 'princes of high and noble blood' to our 'sovereign lord and the laws of this his land' and his own duty as 'defender of England' to enforce it.[55] In practice, most rioters and rebels acknowledged York's authority, submitting, fleeing, or taking sanctuary as Exeter did. York had Exeter removed and imprisoned at Pontefract Castle on 24 July, where apparently he was to remain without trial indefinitely.[56] York went on tour in the summer of 1454, presiding over judicial sessions just as Henry had done and brought the warring provinces to order. There was no pretence of impartiality. The Yorkshire sessions placed almost all the blame in the Percy–Neville feud on the Percies and Exeter.[57] Council proceedings against Salisbury in the North and Warwick over Glamorgan were dropped. Again at liberty, Devon and his rival Bonville were bound to good behaviour on penalty of 4,000 marks (£2,666 13s. 4d.).[58] Nor was this justice necessarily any more effective.

York's protectorate might have continued indefinitely, but he had been appointed only for the duration of Henry's incapacity and at the king's pleasure. Once Henry had recovered, it was bound to end and did, on 9 February 1455. Henry found to his delight that he had fathered a son and heir, also that both Lancastrian royal dukes were imprisoned without trial. Obviously he could not accept decisions that overrode his own, such as the proceedings for treason against Somerset or York's self-appointment as captain of Calais. Henry was not precipitate. He met several times with his councillors, with the great council at Greenwich (4–7 March), and then, he hoped, at Leicester in May: 'an impressive display of public consultation'.[59] He relieved York of his protectorate and Calais captaincy, not reappointing Somerset (or, at least, not yet), but assuming the captaincy himself, day-to-day management obviously remaining with the commanders on the spot. York stayed lieutenant of Ireland. Henry first released Somerset and bound him on heavy sureties to answer the charges against him (great council, 5 February), and then on 4 March at yet another great council at Greenwich exculpated him of treason and cancelled his sureties. Complaining about his fourteen-month confinement, 'without any results proved or lawful process', Somerset challenged any detractors to combat, an offer that was not taken up. Henry channelled Somerset's differences with York once again to arbitration, both dukes again being bound on 20,000 marks (£13,333 6s. 8d.) to abide the award, for which the new deadline was 20 June.[60] He removed Exeter to Wallingford, ostensibly to try his 'riots and offences', for the duke was never in favour with the king, but in the face of opposition from Exeter's custodian Salisbury, whose resignation as chancellor on 7 March 1455 may have been for this reason.[61] If so, the king's replacement – Archbishop Thomas Bourchier – was decidedly traditional and uncontentious. So, too, was the Earl of Shrewsbury, the new treasurer.

York was to argue that the great council at Leicester was scheduled to destroy him – hence his pre-emptive strike. Many modern historians have agreed, often condemning Henry's actions as precipitate and provocative and directly responsible for the violence that followed.[62] Yet this presumes that York was entitled to override the legitimate and formal decisions of the king and the Lords and to appeal to arms, and that he was right to take this extreme and treasonable step. Moreover, it is hard to see what less Henry could have done. York could not continue as protector. Decisions overriding those of the king himself could not be ignored. It was scandalous that Somerset had not been brought to trial and the king was bound, surely, to confirm his earlier verdict. Once again that issue, as far as Henry was concerned, was closed. The king's actions were measured, taken in consultation with his two great councils – as representative and authoritative a body as was possible short of Parliament – and there is no evidence that he overrode the consensus in any detail. These councils did include some figures, such as the Earl of Northumberland and Lord Clifford,[63] who had not attended Parliament, great council or council during the protectorate, but whose presence was certainly necessary for consultation to be fully representative. Certainly it was not, as York claimed, a secret council.

If York and the Nevilles did not attend or absented themselves, it cannot be confirmed (as they asserted) that they were uninvited. The king's escort to Leicester was certainly not sufficient in scale or equipped militarily to overawe them by force. No such royal cavalcade ever was in time of peace. And account should always be taken of the king's track record: neither in 1452 nor in 1459 did he wish to proceed with extremes. Apart from a Milanese comment that 'my lord of Somerset ruled as usual',[64] there is nothing to confirm that Somerset was in charge. Henry had never given Somerset the power to strike at his tormentors, and at the First Battle of St Albans he placed Buckingham in command both militarily and in negotiations. Moreover, account must be taken of the parallels between York's stance and conduct in 1455 to 1450 and 1452, and the similarities with his pre-emptive strikes of 1452 and 1459. Possibly, the award of the arbiters in York vs. Somerset was expected at Leicester: York could not expect much from it, particularly since Somerset had good grounds for complaint in his confinement over the previous year, but he had nothing much to lose either. Arbitration awards were compromises that mitigated any losses. Probably Exeter was also to be tried.

It does not appear, therefore, that York actually had anything to fear from the return to rule of the king and potentially of Somerset. He wanted Somerset held to account for his military misdemeanours in Normandy, he said, and would not take no for an answer. When Somerset died, however, York also took over the government and launched the programme of reform for which he had insufficient time during his *First Protectorate*. What he actually did casts light on what were surely his intentions. Also, of course, power brought him rewards – the repayment of royal debts, offices for himself and patronage for his followers. The Nevilles, in contrast, had more urgent grounds for concern. Warwick could not expect the Glamorgan issue to be forever forgotten, and whatever solution was found for the Neville–Percy dispute could be expected to be more equitable than the judicial sessions of the previous year. However, no such worries could justify an attack on king and court, even under the pretext of purging evil councillors. What was planned and happened was treason, however fervently the Yorkist lords denied it at the time and even though retrospectively they defined it as legitimate.

In 1455, unlike 1452 and 1450, York decided to forego popular support, which was overwhelming when successfully mobilized but which had failed to materialize in 1452, and which anyway took too long to assemble and thus enabled the king to exploit the allegiance owed him by everybody. Instead, York trusted in bastard feudal retainers and in surprise – the unexpected application of limited numbers. What happened was that York and the Nevilles (henceforth for convenience the Yorkists) mustered a private army in several locations, certainly in the North – the Nevilles brought borderers and York called out his constable of Conisburgh in Yorkshire[65] – and probably in the West Midlands and Welsh marches, where the king was later to try offenders. Next the rebels met up and proceeded towards London, evidently extremely rapidly, arriving on 20 May at Royston in Hertfordshire on the Great North Road. These manoeuvres may have lasted several days. News had reached the king at Westminster by 18 May, when Henry summoned military support to Coventry. More explicit information arrived by 19 May, when letters under the great seal commanded York and the Nevilles to disband on pain of forfeiture, in line with the oath that all had sworn in 1453.

York, Salisbury and Warwick replied from Royston on 20 May. They protested that their intentions were misrepresented by their enemies about the king, who were trying to alienate Henry against them and against whom they themselves needed the armed protection that they had assembled. They declared themselves to be loyal, assured the king of their protection, and directed Lord Chancellor

Archbishop Bourchier to threaten excommunication against all those wishing ill of him. Finally, they urged Bourchier to do his duty, so that he would bear no responsibility 'if any inconvenience . . . must befall, which God forbid':[66] this was apparently a threat of violence and a denial of any personal liability. Most probably they intended an armed demonstration in London, where they were strong, and wanted to ensure they were admitted to the City on arrival, but actually the king was already en route for Leicester when their missive reached him at 10 a.m. on 21 May. Not more than twelve hours later, having received no reply, the Yorkists repeated their message, this time addressed to the king and apparently accompanied by articles (petitions) denouncing Somerset of treason. Interestingly, the letters – but not the articles – were circulated, as evidence of York's exemplary innocence to those who might otherwise oppose them. They were delivered to the Earl of Devon at Watford at 2 a.m. on 22 May. Not surprisingly, no answer had been received by the Yorkists at 7 a.m. at St Albans, when they demanded Somerset's surrender to them. Only an affirmative response was acceptable to them. Brief negotiations were conducted through the neutral heralds of the marshal and admiral of England (Norfolk and L'Esparre), neither of whom was present, Buckingham instead representing the king. He assured the Yorkists that he was not protecting Somerset. He relayed to them the king's reply that he had not yet been able to consult on how to respond. Henry declined also to repute the Yorkists as loyal liegemen. He refused to concede their demands even when threatened by force.

Although fewer in numbers, civilian and unmilitary in character, King Henry's escort was protected by his banner displayed – which no loyal subject dared defy! – and by the streets of the substantial unwalled town of St Albans. Nevertheless, the Yorkists attacked: they were the first to shed blood in these civil wars. York's forces were at least twice as large as the king's and far superior in firepower. Frustrated nevertheless by barriers at the gateways, Warwick broke through the backs of houses into the streets. Somerset was slain deliberately, together with about 60 others, including the Earl of Northumberland – brother-in-law to both York and Salisbury – and Lord Clifford. Perhaps both peers were also targeted, but later, conveniently, their deaths were explained away by the Yorkists as collateral damage. Buckingham, Devon and Somerset's son Dorset were wounded. The king, though slightly wounded, survived and fell into York's hands. The Yorkists were first to import the brutality of the populace into the aristocratic faction and made politics into an altogether more lethal affair.

The First Battle of St Albans on 22 May 1455 was a more successful re-run of York's abortive coups at Westminster in November–December 1450 and at

Dartford in February 1452. It, too, was a pre-emptive strike, against what York's enemies supposedly intended against him. Once again, the duke declared his loyalty both to the king and for public consumption. Once again, he ignored royal commands to disperse and declared his protest to be loyal: evidently this was not to be regarded as a *coup d'état* ('way of fait'), which he had sworn never to repeat in 1452. Once again, his attack was directed on Somerset in person, apparently on the same old charges as those that Henry had twice dismissed. York wanted Somerset handed over for what was surely at best a kangaroo trial. It is not credible that he wanted (as he claimed) no more than 'the removal of Somerset and others from the king's presence'.[67] It is striking that, the unfortunate Thorpe apart, nobody else was persecuted during York's *Second Protectorate*. Any other demands in the petitions are unknown, so what else was intended if the king gave way is also not known.

What made St Albans a more successful coup than Dartford was York's brutal application of military superiority. Although he had fewer men this time, for a general appeal to popular support was eschewed, York brought several thousand armed and armoured retainers. Against him stood a lesser company, perhaps 2,000 strong, made up mainly of domestics and civil servants who had not brought their weapons or armour with them – because they had not expected to fight. York's superiority was assured by surprise. This time he had issued no circular letters to forewarn his opponents or to allow the king to call on the allegiance of his loyal subjects, undoubtedly more numerous than Norfolk or any other Yorkists who failed to arrive before the battle. Envoys sent by the king were detained to prevent them reporting back. However sympathetic to York's demands, as Lords Devon (who was wounded) and Fauconberg probably were, those noblemen with the king were obliged on their allegiance to stand by him when he was attacked. Thirteen peers fought for the king, only four for his assailants. Probably the king failed to take more effective action, by arraying troops, retiring to the Tower of London, or taking an alternative route, because neither he nor Buckingham could believe that York really intended such a blatant act of treason. York was more successful at St Albans also because he refused to accept any delays, the king's rebuttal of his demands, or any commands to disperse; because he was more ruthless, for nothing but Somerset's death was sufficient; because he was prepared to commit actual treason by attacking when the king's banner was displayed; and because of the no-holds-barred nature of the fighting. Showering the king's men with arrows and firing ordnance at them, however effective, was hardly a surgical strike. The king was injured: he might have been killed. Although not necessarily wishing such a result, with all the potential alarming repercussions for the future, that was a risk which the Yorkists were willing to take.[68] If they had thought that far ahead, they may have hoped to dominate Prince Edward's long minority, since this was a *coup d'état* rather than a usurpation or dynastic revolution. In the resolute pursuit of military objectives, past historians have perceived the single-mindedness of the Nevilles rather than the fumbling of York, very likely correctly. Quite possibly it was now Warwick, rather than his father Salisbury, who was 'the dominant, and more headstrong, of the two. . . . If one can detect a new ruthlessness and single-mindedness in the Yorkist camp from 1455–6 . . . it probably came from Warwick.'[69]

YORK'S REFORMING GOVERNMENT 1455–6

The reaction to First St Albans could have been violent, perhaps should have been violent, as the rest of the loyal peerage and subjects united against those who had attacked their king. That this did not happen was not because the rebels' actions were approved. Only a fraction of the peerage was prepared to work with the victors. One factor was certainly that the most prominent noble leaders, Somerset, Exeter, Buckingham and Northumberland, were dead or in custody. Several peers were confined, Lord Dudley (in the Tower) and the new Duke of Somerset. Buckingham and 'his brethren', presumably his half-brothers Archbishop Bourchier, Henry Viscount Bourchier and John Lord Berners, had to find sureties for their good behaviour.[70] By placing king and administration in their own hands, the battle, if handled right, could give the victors control of the country. Somehow a means was found of enabling Henry to appear, to be accessible, even to make certain decisions, and to use his name for their government. The revolution was minimized by retaining Viscount Bourchier as Lord Treasurer and Archbishop Bourchier as Lord Chancellor,[71] besides Lord Cromwell as household chamberlain.

York determined this time to secure his power and to implement his reform programme. A new Parliament was summoned at once. Ostensibly it was to maintain 'restful and peaceable rule', but actually, to consolidate his military ascendancy, Lords were ordered to bring to Parliament only modest escorts[72] – not, as in 1450 or 1454, private armies. To disarm resistance or even a counter-coup, the Yorkists needed first of all to demonstrate their loyalty. Hence the profound reverence that they rendered their prisoner the king in public, both at St Albans and Westminster. Next they needed to show that they had not committed treason and to justify the unjustifiable. They asserted their loyalty and blamed the court as the aggressors. With Somerset's death, his treasons were no longer relevant, and in the interests of reconciliation blame was focused on him, Thorpe and Joseph. This was in the *Parliamentary Pardon*, an act of Parliament that rewrote the history of the episode and excused the rebels. It was now Somerset, Thorpe and Joseph who had deceived the king, who had concealed the truth of York's loyalty, who had withheld the two letters to the king, and who had caused the battle.[73] Not obviously a prisoner or unfit, but not allowed to rule, Henry presided in person from the throne over the opening of Parliament on 9 July 1455, over the charges laid on the Lords (on the 10th), and at the nomination of the speaker (the 11th), and also personally declared York, Warwick and Salisbury to be loyal as set out in the *Parliamentary Pardon* that he had initialled. On 24 July the king personally received the oaths of allegiance and fealty renewed by each individual lord. It is probably at this session also that Henry set his sign manual on the act that declared 'Good Duke Humphrey' loyal and blameless. Since Humphrey Duke of Gloucester (d. 1447) was credited, just like York, with resisting Suffolk's corrupt regime, York wanted him rehabilitated. Henry presided at the prorogation on 31 July, when a general pardon was announced. Two London chronicles report that Duke Humphrey's exoneration was proclaimed in London. 'Item the Saturday the 16th day of August Humphrey Duke of Gloucester was proclaimed in the City abovesaid and soon after in other places [to be a] true and faithful liegeman to the king and a true prince up to the hour of his death.'[74] The Yorkists did everything possible, in short, to make their *coup d'état* legitimate and to foster unity among the Lords: one of the six objectives listed by Lord Chancellor Bourchier.

Although the tiny Yorkist faction at St Albans was somewhat expanded by the addition of other sympathetic peers – Norfolk, Devon, Salisbury's brother Fauconberg, and Viscount Bourchier – and although efforts were made to rebuild bridges with Buckingham and Wiltshire, it remained a small minority. The Lords were riven by acute frictions, signalled by the blazing row of Warwick with Cromwell, the king's chamberlain, and Shrewsbury.[75] 'It would seem, therefore, that there was no large party even in the comparatively thin House of Lords which assembled at the end of June likely to endorse any extreme demands which York might feel disposed to make.' Some MPs found the whole situation odd and even opposed the passage of the *Parliamentary Pardon*. This may indeed be almost all that happened at the opening session, which lasted only until 31 July.

The second session of Parliament in November–December 1455 and the third session in January–February 1456 were quite different. The focus was on York's reform programme. Most probably the first session had revealed the Commons to be sympathetic – there was a big overlap of membership with the radical Houses of 1449–51 – but the king and Lords less so. Henry did not attend these later sessions. York was commissioned as lieutenant to preside on 12 November and then, at the insistence of the Commons, he was again made Lord Protector (the 19th). It seems certain that this was not because Henry was again insane, although he may have been unwell. The council appointed to assist York was to report to the king and keep off his prerogative. Maybe it was because Henry was not a cipher and not easily manipulated that he was shouldered aside. Since the Lords were also unresponsive, York had to rely on the backing of the Commons. Presumably it was because the speaker at least was cautious, perhaps also the knights of the shire, that the necessary pressure was exerted instead by York's retainer, William Burley, and that support was curried by the duke's assertion of a radical programme of reform that appealed to Londoners and merchants over the opposition of the Lords. It was apparently a section of the Commons, rather than the Commons as a whole, who were induced to back York's promotion. The Lords agreed, somewhat reluctantly,[76] even though the only lay magnates present were York's supporters: notably the three Neville lords, Salisbury, Warwick and Fauconberg.

Probably three-quarters of the peers were elsewhere. A letter of complaint dated 15 December to all those absent, and a demand for attendance at the third session, was addressed to no fewer than ten bishops (out of 19), Norfolk, eight earls including the king's half-brothers (out of 12), twenty abbots and priors (out of 26), and to 27 barons, at least two-thirds of the total membership.[77] This demand was ignored: York's protectorate and programme did not receive the consent of most of the Lords.

Instead of serving merely at the king's pleasure, York specified this time that he could only be removed by king and Lords in conjunction. Members of his newly nominated council were instructed to treat everybody alike, regardless of rank, kinship or political stance. They were to be selected from those who would not shirk difficult decisions, a problem with York's previous protec-torate, and their payment (and York's too) was given as high a priority as royal finances permitted.[78] York hoped thereby for lasting control of government. How York may have perceived himself is suggested by the translation of the Roman poet Claudian's *Stilicho* by York's partisan Osbert Bokenham, which may have dated to this juncture. It presents a noble but under-appreciated statesman who was recalled to lift his country out of corruption and decline.[79]

It was at the later sessions that most of the other legislation proposed at this Parliament belongs. This business was of three types. First of all, York's previous behaviour was more completely rehabilitated and the penalties against his adherents were reversed: the resumption of the grants of the Dartford rebels was cancelled; the attainder of Sir William Oldhall for offences since 1450, which the king had initialled himself, was revoked; and the penalties against York's adherents, to Walter Devereux from 1452, and even Thomas Young from 1451, were cancelled.[80] It was to these sessions, secondly, that belong the more vindictive attacks on Thorpe and Joseph. Their grants were resumed and the penalty of £210 on a bond from Thorpe to York was exacted. The royal household defeated militarily at St Albans was the core of opposition to York, and hence it too was curbed.[81] Other bills failed. Thirdly, there was the reform programme, which is discussed below.

The immediate justification for York's *Second Protectorate*, 19 November 1455, was to restore domestic peace by repressing rebellion. Actually, the First Battle of St Albans and consequent change of regime seem to have provoked a resurgence of violence that was only curtailed, if at all, by decisive victories for the Nevilles in the North and by the Courtenays in the West. If nothing else, the Yorkist coup signified dissension, weak government, and hence an opportunity to pursue private quarrels by force. The slaughter of Northumberland and Clifford at St Albans, even though it was decided not to blame them for the battle, aggrieved the Percies. With 200 others, Northumberland's son Egremont was at Salisbury's manor of Stamford Bridge (Yorks.) on 31 October 1455, perhaps on another raid, when he was met (ambushed?) by Salisbury's sons Thomas and John Neville, and was captured. In preference to trial by his peers, a process unlikely to result in conviction, or judicial commissions that might have found his captors at fault, the Nevilles sued Egremont for damages. The amount of £11,200 was awarded, an unpayable sum, and Egremont was consigned to the London debtors' prison at Newgate.[82] If the Nevilles had won, the root causes remained. And the Percies' ally Exeter, although pardoned in August 1455, was not actually released until 16 January 1456, when he was bound on his own recognizance of £20,000 and on sureties to appear in chancery on the morrow of All Saints (1 November 1456).[83]

In the meantime Thomas Courtenay, Earl of Devon, proceeded to restore the untrammelled Courtenay hegemony in the West Country that had been so seriously upset in recent years. Although demonstrating his military ascendancy, his raid of 1452 had led to his humiliation, imprisonment, the alienation from him of even minor gentry, and to the ascendancy for Bonville, who was now constable of Exeter and Lydford, keeper of Dartmoor, member of a whole string of commissions, and the 'supreme figure in south-west England'. So, too, Lord Bonville himself seems to have thought, forgetting both Devon's many more numerous tenants and the traditional appeal of the Courtenays, else he would not have goaded the earl into a fair fight. The Courtenays started flexing their muscles in October 1455, overawing the quarter sessions at Exeter. On the 24th, shockingly, Devon's heir murdered the lawyer Nicholas Radford, before occupying Exeter from 3 November to 23 December and pillaging its Close, and besieging Powderham Castle, the seat of Bonville's allies, the Courtenays of Powderham. It was Bonville who challenged Devon to battle, Bonville who on 15 December was defeated at Clyst, and Bonville's seat at Shute that was sacked on the 19th. Appalling though the conduct of Devon and of his sons was, the actual battle, conducted in the spirit of chivalry, was Bonville's fault. Having vowed to settle the quarrel in person 'on thy body' and having escaped in flight, Bonville was dishonoured and discredited. In terms of brute force, Devon still had the decisive edge.[84] In two decades Bonville had not been able to construct a connection to rival a hegemony four centuries old, and whatever remained of his connection at his death was to die with him.

In the meantime the Radford cause célèbre and soon after other exaggerated reports caused great alarm in Parliament, presumably to York's acute embarrassment. Apart from one bill from Radford's heir and others against adherents of the earl, yet another recommended the arrest of both Devon and Bonville and warned that the sheriff of Devonshire was a Bonville man. On 5 December, Devon was ordered to appear before the council, obviously unavailingly, and ten 'worshipful lords and other persons' were summoned to accompany York, 'by whose help, strength and advice he may settle ... such misgovernances and rebuke them that would bear up the contrary'. Proceeding westwards and now fortified with the king's authority, Lord Protector York received the submission of the earl and brought him to London. It was 'by counsel of the king' that Devon was again imprisoned, this time in the Tower; Bonville, who had fled to the king at Greenwich, was confined in the Fleet prison. Devon's trial by his peers in Parliament was scheduled for 9 February 1456. This coincided with a Yorkist attempt to overawe the Lords by force and was deferred ('countermanded').[85] Most likely there was then a hearing and Devon was released on bail, ahead of the pardon of the Courtenays and the indictment of their men in the summer, and the binding over to keep the peace of the earl and his sons in the autumn: the pattern of 1452. Bonville stood surety for at least two of his men on 22 November 1456.[86] By then, however, the *Second Protectorate* was long over.

The new regime had committed itself to the business of reform. Back on 26 May 1455 a new parliament had been summoned. When it met, on 10 July, the chancellor's opening sermon declared that action was needed on national unity, the funding of the household, Calais and Berwick, the keeping of the seas, Wales and the export of bullion, for each of which there were Lords committees. No committee minutes exist at so early a date. Not much can be shown to have resulted on unity, Berwick, Wales, or indeed the keeping of the seas, but there was much legislative activity on Calais, the household and bullion. At the core of York's reform programme was the curbing of the royal households, those of the king and prince to £6,522, and a thoroughgoing resumption, which (as in 1450) had the potential to improve rather than radically transform royal finances, but which of course had political objectives and implications too.[87]

Almost all the legislation, proposed and actual, took the form of Commons bills. At least some of the Commons were radical in outlook, much like their counterparts of 1450-1. Their programme mirrored that of the London mercantile community. In the depths of a recession that affected their very livelihood, how could they be other than 'deeply concerned about trading relations with Burgundy, the staple monopoly of the wool trade and royal attitudes to alien merchants, and be involved in the wider debate about bullion flows and the balance of trade'?[88]

Perhaps, therefore, London's MPs as well as the Calais committee had some input in the deal with the merchants of the staple of Calais, mainly Londoners, that York had commenced during his *First Protectorate*. The customs of Calais were transferred from the exchequer to the staplers to repay them for clearing the arrears of pay to the Calais garrison: a short-term fix that did not resolve how to fund the garrison in future. It mattered more to the staplers that Calais should be defended and that the garrison did not mutiny than that the Yorkists should control Calais. If they were to pay the outstanding arrears, they did not want their own repayment from the customs to be postponed by licences granted to aliens to trade custom free, nor of course did they want their own trade to be undercut as a result.[89] Away from the northern marches, of which the Earl of Salisbury was warden, and the keeping of the seas, for which the earl since 1453 had been a commissioner, the Calais garrison was the only professional force funded by the Crown. Now both the captaincy of Calais and the keeping of the seas were confided to the Earl of Warwick, although he had not actual possession of Calais (which remained under the command of Somerset's captains). Probably, York and government alike valued the command of Calais only for defence and not for its potential in domestic politics. Warwick engaged first in large-scale piracy, perhaps necessary when funding was uncertain, but also appealing to English patriots and to Englishmen hostile towards those foreigners who were blamed wrongly for the recession. He also deployed the garrison and fleet as never intended in domestic politics. This was to prove crucial. With popular backing and the continuing weakness of the Crown, it enabled the Yorkists to triumph in 1460.

York's regime committed itself to the highly popular bullionist and anti-alien policies of the London merchant community. As we have seen, they blamed the recession, obviously mistakenly, on the shortage of coin. 'A country's well-being depended', so it was generally believed, 'on the possession of an ample store of gold and silver. . . . Any commercial activities which led to a drain of specie from the country must be stopped.' The culprits were believed to be malicious and self-interested foreigners, who were importing expensive foreign fripperies, exporting coin, and exporting also English wool and cloth that they had acquired too cheaply.[90] The staplers, merchant adventurers, mercers, clothiers and wool producers were all interested in restricting alien traders, ensuring that they paid the just price, and stopping them from carrying any coin abroad. Hence, surely, the group of Commons bills against licences to export wool free of customs, against licences to exempt exports from the Calais staple, to prohibit Italian merchants from travelling beyond designated ports, and to ensure that foreign wool-packers paid the right rate. All such bills were forcefully expressed. The clerk to the treasurer, John Wood, was singled out for particular punishment. Even more vindictive punishments were proposed for Thomas Thorpe. Equally forceful were restrictions planned for the benefit of clergy.[91] Licences to export wool had been limited by an act of Parliament in 1449, but only for five years that had now expired. Repeated representations for its renewal by Londoners had failed. Now, it appears, was their opportunity. Presumably it is not a mere coincidence that London's share of national wool exports rose sharply to 93 per cent in 1456–7.[92]

Most of these bills passed both Houses of Parliament and presumably were approved by York, but were then rejected by the king,[93] presumably after he resumed control in February 1456. We cannot tell whether York as Lord Protector was entitled to give the royal assent to parliamentary bills or indeed ever did so, but clearly in these instances he did not. Henry's veto thus identified the king himself with opposition to London's commercial interests. From Henry's angle, however, such measures invited boycotts by England's trading partners and other commercial repercussions, the loss of the higher customs duties and/or sale of licences that aliens paid, and hence they imperilled almost the only significant revenues available to him in his dire financial circumstances.

However sympathetic to some policies of the new regime, the Commons refused any fresh taxation to repay either the accumulated debt or to fund current spending. Some of the gap was bridged by cutting the expenses of the royal household and by resuming royal grants, although there were political reasons for these too. Staff in the upper household had been significantly reduced during York's *First Protectorate* and household funding was now sharply curtailed.[94] Its members, still evidently regarded as over-rewarded and undeserving, were the target of a new act of resumption yet more draconian than its comprehensive counterpart of 1451. The Commons intended even to cancel Henry's duchy of Lancaster trusts, to disendow his two colleges of Eton and King's, to dispossess his Tudor half-brothers of their estates, and to cut back even the dower of the queen. All these trespassed beyond the conventional bounds of political debate. The Commons also urged the resumption of all grants of wardship of feudal tenants since 1448. If implemented, this act would have augmented royal resources somewhat, but at a high price in the display and authority that were expected of the Crown. Once back in control, King Henry accepted the principle of resumption, but referred exemptions to a Lords' committee that York did not control. It is not obvious why it 'would, even if implemented, have significantly reduced the crown's freedom of action and made it more answerable to conciliar control',[95] or indeed that this was the objective.

All these measures were parts of a radically different Yorkist economic policy. The customs were used to repay past debts rather than to cover current costs. Implementing the bullionist policies of London's merchants would deprive the government of revenues from selling licences to trade that Henry VI had valued so highly and risked protectionist countermeasures by foreign countries. Solvency might be improved by economizing on the royal household and by a comprehensive resumption, even though savings and gains alike were relatively small. How could York's salary and backpay as Lord Protector and the future costs of Calais be financed? These measures do not betoken a financial policy that was likely to succeed.

It is not quite clear what was happening. The *Parliamentary Pardon* was driven through despite opposition from 'those that grudged sore'.[96] On his past and future record, Henry would oppose anything that infringed his prerogative to grant licences or pardon offenders. He signed the bill rehabilitating Duke Humphrey and assented to at least one bill each in the first and second sessions.[97] Any problem with his royal assent was overcome by those proceedings that were expressed in the first person and hence as his wishes, such as the *Parliamentary Pardon* and endowment of the prince of Wales. The Lords were not to be moved by the flurry of radical bills passed by the Commons (and thus captioned 'soit baille aux seigneurs') that failed to become law. Two were endorsed 'To this bill the lords have not agreed'. Another three others were put off (respited), one for extra information. Regarding a sixth, on wards, it was noted (presumably late in February 1456) that it 'is thought to the king and all the Lords that this bill is unreasonable'. York had overstretched himself. That so many proposals of York and the Commons were rejected by the Lords suggests more substantial divisions in principle,[98] which York was never able to heal.

A little more is known about the resumption, which became the confidence issue on which the future of the protectorate hung, and which the Yorkists tried to drive through by overawing the Lords. On 9 February, 'My Lords York and Warwick came to the parliament in a good array, to the number of 300 men', all in padded jackets and armour. However, the ploy failed – the House of Lords, indeed all the Lords according to *Benet's Chronicle*, refused to be cowed or to yield – and the regime collapsed. Unable to command a working majority in the Lords, York's regime was defeated in Parliament in a strangely modern way. It was not that York feared physical attack, for those were right who 'think verily there is no man able to undertake any such enterprise'.[99] His *Second Protectorate* fell after only three months because it no longer enjoyed the consent of the Lords and probably never had. In the last resort, York did not reassert his local military dominance, but accepted their verdict.

There was no physical restraint on the king. King Henry was induced to resume power, appearing in the House of Lords on 21 February 1456 to assent to a bill about Sandwich vicarage, and again on 25th, with the assent of the Lords, to relieve York of office. This was the king's decision and was formally taken precisely in line with the terms that York had insisted upon at his appointment. Henry was in the Lords once more on 9 March, when he assented to three bills, one being for York to be paid all the arrears of pay and expenses from both his protectorates.[100] The bill of resumption was shorn of its extreme features and received the royal assent as an act. Far from being 'severely emasculated', this resumption was as comprehensive as the 1451 act and was modified by relatively few provisos of exemption, only three for members of the queen's household.[101] Most of the radical Commons bills were refused:[102] generally deservedly, as impractical, however popular. But the Crown may well have tarred itself as pro-alien, anti-London and anti-commercial to subjects who still did not appreciate how intractable were its problems.

CHAPTER 8

PRECONDITIONS:
NO PROGRESS 1456–9

Between the end of York's *Second Protectorate* in February 1456 and the *Accord* of November 1460, York did not govern and Henry VI, at least nominally, did. Although ousted from power, York refused to bow to defeat. This fifth phase of the political kaleidoscope of the 1450s comprised two years of stormy rule by the king. Henry may have forgiven the victors of the First Battle of St Albans, but other victims and their heirs had not and sought revenge; so too, it appears, did some reformers whose aspirations were disappointed by the failure of York's *Second Protectorate*. It was King Henry himself who in March 1458 engineered a new reconciliation in the *Loveday of St Paul's* that was meant once again to clear the political air and put past frictions firmly in the past. It did not work. The eighteen months following, regrettably very obscure, culminated in a further Yorkist coup that failed and the exile of the Yorkists, who returned in 1460 to wage the *First War*.[1] In retrospect – and especially from a Yorkist angle – this was a disastrous regime, which usually receives a damning verdict from those modern historians who have read Yorkist accounts such as the *English Chronicle*:

> In this same time, the realm of England was out of all good governance, as it had been many days before, for the king was simple and led by covetous counsel and owed more than he was worth. His debts increased daily, but payment was there none. All the possessions and lordships that pertained to the crown the king had given away, some to lords and some to other simple persons, so that he had almost nought to live upon. And such impositions as were put to the people as taxes, tallages, and fifteenths, all that

came from them, was spent in vain, for he held no household nor maintained no wars . . .[2]

The chronicler's verdict is generally accepted.

Yet most of it is either demonstrably false or misrepresents the facts. The 1456 act of resumption had not been rejected, but was passed and was as comprehensive as that of 1451 that critics applauded. King Henry had not alienated all or indeed much of his wealth. Yet such was the popular perception. If Henry were to resume what he had given away, so the reasoning ran, then surely he would not need the taxes, nor the purveyance that enabled him to keep afloat. The Parliament of 1455–6 had voted him no supply. The king was poor, unable to pay his debts or to keep a splendid court not because of improvident largesse, but because he was burdened with debts of war accumulated before 1450 and because his ordinary revenues had collapsed due to the recession. The absence of parliamentary taxes made it impossible for him to do other than he did. Even his revenues from customs were largely appropriated to the staplers to repay the arrears of past wages that they had advanced to the Calais garrison.[3] Not even Lord Protector York had found a solution. 'In any event, the needs of the government and the household were already well beyond the financial resources available.'[4] Yet unquestionably Henry needed some resources. Loans were scarcely feasible. On nine occasions Lord Treasurer Shrewsbury had tendered sums totalling £2,411 from his own pocket; his successor, the much criticized Wiltshire, paid out over £1,000.[5] Staying at monasteries was a saving for the king, but not for the monastery: a third of the years 1456–60 was subsidized in this way.[6] Hence also Henry's attempts to maximize income from the sheriffs, to exploit feudal incidents, to collect cash at the local source, competitive leasing, to maximize income from the prince's estates, to appropriate any chance windfall to the king's chamber, and even – somewhat desperately – to locate new seams of precious metals and to transmute base metals into gold.[7] Probably none of these made much difference – they merely shifted monies to petty cash from the exchequer and from the repayment of debtors – but maximizing ordinary revenues or living of one's own, as Charles I was to find, was unpopular too. It certainly is not credible that 'the queen was gathering riches innumerable'.

A government so impoverished could do no more than tick over, but tick over it did. The realm was not 'out of good governance' as the chronicler claimed. Writing after 1461, the pro-Yorkist *English Chronicle* was projecting back in time the propaganda that the Yorkists had promulgated after their victory, and in certain instances in partisan manifestos beforehand.

THE RULE OF QUEEN MARGARET?

To explain his unfavourable and mistaken assessment of the government, the *English Chronicle* (echoing the Earl of Warwick's 1459 manifesto) blamed 'covetous counsel' who led the king, in particular and especially 'the queen with such as were of her affinity [who] ruled the realm as she liked'.[8] The chronicler's verdict has been widely accepted. The queen has been blamed for the failure of York's *Second Protectorate*. 'From 1455 Margaret of Anjou exercised an extraordinary degree of control over the affairs of her husband and son.' 'The queen ... took over the leadership of the Beaufort faction after 1455. ... By April 1457 it was clear that the Queen and the court party coalescing around her were in the driving seat.' Supposedly she pursued a stridently anti-Yorkist line: 'That the fundamental intention of [Queen] Margaret and her supporters was the outright destruction of those who had engaged in treasonable activity by accroaching the royal power there is, of course, no doubt.' 'Rash and despotic', it was Margaret who raised the tensions and provoked the conflict with York, who should have been allowed to rule. The breakdown in autumn 1459 has even been seen as the result of three years of planning by Queen Margaret to humble and destroy York and his allies.[9] Most historians treat the royal actions in these years as the work of the queen and regard every commission or purchase of weapons as sinister evidence of her malign machinations to destroy the Yorkists, even though, in every case, no destruction followed. This interpretation derives from chroniclers that were indeed contemporaries,[10] but who were also committed Yorkists who told essentially the same stories after the Yorkist revolution of 1461 and relayed to us Yorkist propaganda, some of it admittedly from contemporary documents. If these retrospective accounts are set aside, there is very little to substantiate Margaret's agency in the records, and much to discount it.

Once married to Henry in 1445, Margaret indeed scarcely occurs in the chronicles before 1456 and rarely in a political role. Margaret's surviving letters reveal her small-scale exercise of her patronage as landholder, her influence, and perhaps also petty oppressions and rebuffs.[11] Undoubtedly on occasion both queen and king wanted the same things and wrote independently to the same effect, usually no doubt at the insistence of the same supplicants. Margaret exacted all the obeisance to which she was entitled. Queens did have a legitimate political role, principally as conduits for petitioners and intercession with their husbands. Before 1456 her national political activity amounts to two incidents: receipt of a petition from Cecily, Duchess of York, for her intercession in 1453, which if pursued was ineffective; and Margaret's own claim to the regency next year,[12] which failed.

On 9 February 1456, however, in a letter replete with rumour and specula-tion, John Bocking reported that 'the queen is a great and strong laboured woman, for she spareth no pain to sue her things to an intent and conclusion to her utmost [power]'.[13] This slight evidence has usually been taken to indicate that Margaret had a role in terminating the *Second Protectorate*, which actually was not yet over and which, on current evidence, did not need her contribution. Bocking's literal meaning is that she pressed her requests to the king as vigor-ously as she could. The immediate context was really the act of resumption, from which she had good reason to want exemption and which she did indeed secure. It was probably the clauses seeking to reduce significantly the incomes of the queen and the prince of Wales 'that galvanised her into direct political action'.[14] The act did not of course affect Margaret's own patronage and she did not actually secure exemption for many of her household.[15]

At that stage, so Bocking also indicated, the rumour was that Henry wanted to keep York on in some capacity.[16] Certainly there was no sudden change in personnel or policy. Judicial sessions in London and Kent were conducted by an impressive showing of peers. The sparse councils from March to July 1456 were most regularly attended by Salisbury, Warwick and the Bourchier brothers, and the most important business related to Warwick's captaincy of Calais, which was settled to his entire satisfaction.[17] From 1456 to 1460 Warwick, his countess and daughters were in continuous residence at Calais. He devoted himself to the highly aggressive sweeping of the seas.[18]

Queen Margaret was protected by the same treason laws as the king and prince and was also entitled to the same allegiance. If she did become the king's principal counsellor and the prime mover behind the regime, she could not be criticized at the time as an evil councillor in the same way as Somerset and Suffolk had been. In 1460 it was actually Shrewsbury, Wiltshire and John Viscount Beaumont that the Yorkists denounced.[19] Undoubtedly Margaret was the victim at the time of hostile smears, such as the scurrilous bills of the Middle Temple lawyer John Halton, but regrettably none of these actually survive and much of the contents can only be speculated about. In prison for another offence, Halton was released on bail, which he failed to keep in April 1456. Obviously it was afterwards that he was tried and executed for alleging that the prince was not the queen's son, an improbable allegation that he then withdrew on the scaffold, and which was later superseded by the slightly more feasible story that Prince Edward was the product of the queen's adultery – a story that was repeated by the *English Chronicle*.[20] Whatever the facts, they made no difference in English law, which attributed any offspring of adultery to the adulteress's husband. The *English Chronicle* also asserts, obviously falsely, that Margaret wanted Henry to abdicate in favour of his son. She distributed the prince's livery of the swan to the men of Chester: their denigration as 'galants' – young, fashionable, effete and sinful – hints at satirical verses, perhaps the undated ones that survive.[21]

Three charges against Queen Margaret are more substantial. Firstly that her whole marriage had been the result of a diplomatic error and the cause of all disasters, from the surrender of Maine onwards, a charge that appears in the *Brut* of 1464–9.[22] Secondly, that she was the government: 'Margaret of Anjou's dominance of her husband was far more complete in the late 1450s than ever Suffolk's or Somerset's had been earlier.'[23] And thirdly, that she 'placed the king more completely in her thrall by removing him to the enclave of her midland estates',[24] which features also in the Yorkist chronicles, all written in London in 1461 or later.

Yet these three charges were also current at the time, since they first appear in the theological dictionary of the Oxford academic Thomas Gascoigne, who died in March 1458. Dating his comments so early is his principal value as a source, since he was notoriously obsessive – about bishops who did not preach and Bishop Reynold Pecock – and credited such wild stories as Henry VI's plan to surrender all his possessions outside England to Charles VII! Gascoigne's interpretation is highly Yorkist, in the case of the First Battle of St Albans *because* he had been reading Yorkist propaganda, the *Parliamentary Pardon*. Gascoigne's critique of Margaret's marriage, which he repeated three times, was unfounded and demonstrates his susceptibility to slanderous rumour. After two such lengthy diatribes, Gascoigne wrote that in 1456 the queen had drawn to her house in Chester both king and prince, that she might make (or rather mismanage) all the business of the realm. 'God knows where it will end!' 'And what kinds of things happen from the actions of the queen, in the year, 1457, God knows!' Prophetic rather than factual, his testimony is corroborated not by fact or evidence, but by rumour, 'as it is said' (*ut dicitur*) and 'as it is believed' (*ut creditur*),[25] which demonstrates extremely valuably what was thought or said at the time, not that such interpretations were actually reliable.

Certainly Gascoigne's geography is misleading. That Henry VI withdrew to his secure Lancastrian laager in the Midlands appears in most of the chronicles and commentaries of these years.[26] It needs to be remembered, however, that almost all the chronicles – Bale's, Benet's, Gregory's, the *Brut*, the *English*

Chronicle and the London chronicles – were products of London or the Home Counties, notably St Albans (Whetehamstede) and Oxford (Gascoigne). Foreign despatches and the Pastons' news were also garnered in London.[27] It is not surprising, therefore, that all such sources take a London stance, regard government from London as normal and the king's continuous absence elsewhere as odd and indeed aberrant.

In fact, absence from London was not unusual. Henry had held previous parliaments outside London and Westminster, at Bury St Edmunds, Coventry, Leicester, Reading and Winchester, for instance, travelled widely, and had a particular partiality for the Midlands.[28] That Henry chose Coventry cathedral priory as the site for a great council in October 1456 was not therefore sinister, as claimed by the London-based chroniclers, nor was it probably prompted by disorders in London that had actually been silenced. The venue appears indeed to have been a last-minute decision, prompted as the *Brut* suggests, since as late as 3 September Henry was planning to meet in the capital.[29] He himself stayed at Coventry from 20 September to 14 October 1456. What was unusual was that he went next to Chester, not back to London, returned to Coventry for Christmas, and was not to return to the environs of the capital until September 1457.[30] This may have been due to a chain of circumstances rather than a deliberate plan, although as time passed some administrative rationalization did take place. That the principal disorders were nearby, in the marches and principality of Wales, may be explanation enough. What the sources minimize is that Henry returned to the Home Counties in September 1457, perhaps particularly because of the French raid on Sandwich, and remained there for twenty-one months, until May 1459. Yet his Midland sojourn has traditionally been blamed on the malign influence of the queen – *Benet's Chronicle* writes of Margaret's hatred of London[31] – and seen as her opportunity. Henry's acts henceforth have been interpreted as her's.

There is no doubt that Margaret became the arch-defender and decision-maker of the Lancastrian cause late in 1460, as she had to, but it is far from obvious that she played such a key role before that date. If the judgements of the Yorkist chroniclers informed by hindsight that appear to read her role back in time are set aside, there is precious little evidence for it. Knowing that she was in command and planning the long-term destruction of York has caused a succession of modern historians to interpret the rather opaque and uninformative records in this way. What is certain about Margaret is that from mid 1456 she did reside much of the time in the Midlands, particularly at her castle of Tutbury in Staffordshire, perhaps as *Benet's Chronicle* says, because she justifiably disliked the riotous and dangerous city of London. Her itinerary in earlier years has not been worked out. In 1457 also the four-year-old prince was granted possession and the issues of his appanage in Chester, West Wales and the duchy of Cornwall, which was managed for him by a council supervised by the queen.[32] (Edward IV was later to mirror these arrangements for his son Edward V). Inevitably, Prince Edward's tenure impinged on the sphere of the Duke of York, who had to surrender some of the prince's possessions in Wales. Coventry, the principal Midland city and within the Earl of Warwick's Midland hegemony, was 'the prince's chamber'. Margaret may have been able to exercise the prince's patronage, naturally to her own servants, and hence the north-west Midlands may have become her power base just as it had been for Richard II. If so, her activities were neither exceptional nor improper. The use Margaret made of the Midlands may have been. But that remains to be demonstrated.

Moreover, initiative in government always rested with the king. The great officers, like their departments, the central courts and the council, most probably remained at Westminster, where his commands were implemented. It was there that Lord Chancellor Waynflete received most of the warrants for the great seal.[33] Indeed, the principal evidence about who was in charge for the whole period 1456–60 consists of the warrants for the great seal (C 81) and privy seal (PSO 1), and the patchier council warrants (E 28). Only a single file of warrants to the privy seal for 1454–9 survives, but there are sixteen files of direct warrants from the king to the Lord Chancellor for 1456–60: thirteen files of signed bills, every single warrant bearing the king's signature, three files of signet warrants, a third of them additionally initialled by the king, and two files of warrants of the council which was still meeting at Westminster (E28/87), many of them countersigned by the king. Why should these not be accepted as the king's decisions? On four signed bills, the king specified that a licence should be for three years only; that half the goods of Adam Polesworth should be applied to the relief of the poor; that a general pardon should run from Good Friday and not later; and that the suppliants should be pardoned in honour of the Passion.[34] These sound authentically the voice of Henry VI. When additional comments say 'the king granted this bill' or 'the king wills [woll]',[35] should they not be accepted as his decisions? A number contain additional statements specifying the king's wishes, two authorized by his chamberlain Sir Thomas Stanley: the authorization of a chamberlain had also been a common authentication for Richard II and for certificates of homage whenever taken. Another was signed by the king on the advice of the council. One he referred to the discretion of his chancellor and the lords of his council.

In another Henry insisted that the chancellor do as he commanded.[36] Six memoranda state: 'If it please the king, it shall be done/be passed/signed', once by the advice of the council.[37] Obviously, these indicate that the king was advised, perhaps managed, and even perhaps that warrants were pre-vetted: there are none surviving where the king overrode recorded advice, nor where he rejected the recommendation of his advisers. The deferential tone of such comments leaves no doubt that it was King Henry who was deciding. This is also one conclusion from a ruling of Lord Privy Seal Bothe that a signed bill initiating an exchequer standing order should be filed in his office and used then to warrant periodic payments under the privy seal.[38]

Not one of these thousands of warrants refers to the advice or authority of the queen. Apart from licences for chantry foundations that included masses for the royal family, Margaret and her staff feature infrequently and insubstantially in the patents of these years. There are no recorded decisions taken by the queen and her council.[39] It was Henry personally who was making appointments and distributing what little patronage there was. Moreover, he was taking advice as he should. How long he was taking to make such decisions cannot be established from these warrants, which merely reveal that decisions were being made and that the king was making them.

The bulk of these memoranda relate to two periods, when the king was at Coventry in 1456–7 and in 1459, but not to his period in the Home Counties in between. Perhaps this arises because the advice he was seeking and was securing was from the councillors at Westminster and required less formal mechanisms when he was at hand. Indeed, many of these council minutes are themselves initialled by the king himself:[40] did he attend? Those advising him were few in number and predominantly administrators. Reliance on a distant council when he was in the Midlands may well have caused the delays in, or lack of, decision-making of which contemporaries complained.[41] However, the king did consult regularly and much more widely than with his entourage and council. Admittedly there was no Parliament until November 1459: what was the point of convening one when it was unlikely to vote supply? Henry did, however, convene a whole series of great councils, at least nine in the period 1456–9. These seem to have been fairly well attended by the bishops and lay magnates, who also turned out regularly when required for judicial commissions to enforce order. Although the king's government was limited in its ambitions and achievements, impotent domestically, internationally and financially, it seems to have enjoyed the consent of the Lords. Even Margaret's critics admit that she could not always get her way in great councils.[42] And if

Margaret really wanted to destroy Warwick or the Yorkists in 1459, she failed: she was rebuffed by the king.[43]

The great council at Coventry in October 1456 has a key place in the hypothesis of the queen's seizure of control over the government. Like all great councils it is poorly documented, although three London sources, perhaps independent, namely, *Benet's Chronicle*, John Bocking and James Gresham, agree on essentials. Bocking relied on what tidings and forecasts he could pick up at his pub (the *Chequers*), not all correct. It is Gresham who stresses the role of Humphrey, Duke of Buckingham. On 26 September 1456 Lawrence Bothe was appointed Keeper of the Privy Seal in place of the deceased Thomas Lisieux, and on 5 October the Earl of Shrewsbury replaced Viscount Bourchier as Lord Treasurer. The great council opened on 7 October. York, still at Sandal in Yorkshire on 30 September, and Warwick did attend and were received most graciously by the king:[44] perhaps surprisingly, given the misconduct of York's retainers Herbert and Devereux that came before the assembly, and should have resulted in their imprisonment. York was commissioned to sort out the Scots, which he did.

Admittedly, York's relations with the queen were reported as poor by Gresham and *Benet's Chronicle*. Yet Margaret clearly could not determine her husband's attitude to York. Since, moreover, she was at odds with Buckingham, who disapproved of the replacement as ministers of his two Bourchier half-brothers, she did not have everything her own way. Buckingham it was who intervened on 11 October to stop local men from lynching Henry Beaufort, the new teenaged Duke of Somerset.[45] All three dukes of Buckingham, Somerset and York witnessed the transfer of the great seal from Archbishop Bourchier that same day at Coventry Priory.[46] It is therefore on very thin and dubious evidence that Margaret has been charged (in rather strong language) with a *coup d'état* at this great council, when apparently *she* changed all three great officers of state to her own creatures and then in October 1457 'reshaped [the government] ... on more partisan lines to the liking of the queen'.[47] Actually, there is no direct evidence that Margaret changed or could change any of them. That the three ministerial appointments were staggered over three weeks in September–October 1456 makes this a very gradual coup. Bothe may have been Margaret's protégé, but Waynflete if anything was Henry's own man and Shrewsbury was a great magnate. The political component to these appointments is not obvious.

On occasion Margaret did come publicly to the fore, when both were received ceremonially at Coventry in 1456–7,[48] but actually she was not well placed for micro-management. King and queen normally lived in different residences, the king at Kenilworth Castle in Warwickshire and in monasteries, she especially at Tutbury Castle in Staffordshire. They may only have united for the string of great councils at Coventry Cathedral priory in October 1456, February–March 1457, and at Leicester (June 1457), and for major festivals, such as Christmas 1456 at Coventry, Easter 1457 at Hereford, which coincided with the sessions against William Herbert and Walter Devereux, and Easter 1459 at St Albans. It is a modern assumption that, on *all* such occasions, Margaret was in control and that when they were apart she was also in charge. The records reveal Henry presiding over his own regime, undertaking routine tasks, perhaps unenthusiastically, and taking advice widely. Nobody, not even his queen, could override or disregard him.

GOVERNANCE 1456–9

Post-protectorate, the new regime did face grave challenges. There was still no settlement with France. If the English were in no position to take the offensive against France, which Charles VII fortunately did not realize, yet a French raid on Sandwich in 1457 had a massive impact on contemporaries. The incursion was not repeated. A grant of taxes by the Reading Parliament in 1453, originally for 13,000 archers, was resurrected, after the event and inevitably temporarily. At once Warwick was commissioned to keep the seas. Not much else could have been done. Warwick used his command to molest foreign shipping of many nationalities, thus funding himself and making himself a popular reputation at the price of considerable future international repercussions. It may well be that by 1458 his removal was being mooted, but it proved beyond the government's power.[49] The Scots were also aggressive, but not very effective, on the northern borders. Violent crime was particularly prevalent, if John Hardyng and other critics are to be believed.[50] However, the Percy–Neville feud in Yorkshire had ended in 1454 in a Neville victory and private war there was not to resume; the Glamorgan dispute of 1453 remained shelved. There remained disturbances in London, which were not resolved, and in Kent, the West Country and Wales, which the government – and the king in person – effectively quelled. The most serious feuds, between the victims and victors of First St Albans, are treated in the next chapter. It is not true that feuds were escalating. If the underlying frictions remained unresolved, major disorders wherever they occurred were quashed. On the face of it, the regime was managing defence and order effectively. Under the circumstances, stagnation was good. Things were never so bad that the Lords abandoned their king.

A Kentish uprising at Erith in November 1456 was easily suppressed.[51] The Percy–Neville feud was muted, although Lord Egremont broke out of Newgate prison in 1456 – the explanation, no doubt, why the keepers of the Marshalsea required his brother Richard Percy and other noble prisoners to take out ruinous sureties not to escape.[52]

Much more serious was the Courtenay–Bonville feud in Devon, which was far from over. There were further depredations by the Courtenays in spring 1456. Admittedly, 38 Courtenay adherents had been attainted, whatever that means, by Parliament, but it was the visit of the king in June 1456 and judicial sessions at Exeter that brought the disturbances to an end. It was almost entirely Courtenay adherents who were indicted, at least one of the murderers of the lawyer Nicholas Radford in October 1455 – Nicholas Philip – being tried and executed in London on 28 June 1457. Most were pardoned.[53] The Earl of Devon's heir Thomas Courtenay married the queen's niece Margaret of Maine in about September,[54] thus joining the royal family, which may partly explain why Devon and his two elder sons were pardoned in November. It is not true, however, that 'nothing was done' about their crimes. All were bound over on sureties to keep the peace.[55] Devon was still not completely rehabilitated before his death on 3 February 1458. Peace, however, had been restored and was not to be again broken. Just as the Nevilles had won in the North, so effectively had the Courtenays confirmed their dominance of the far west.

Admittedly, the regime found no satisfactory answer to the disorders in London, where feeling against the aliens and lawyers ran very high. Alien sharp practice was blamed for the ongoing recession. Not only did Italians control a quarter of foreign trade and all the related financial services, but they also dabbled in the depressed retail sector. Complaints to Crown and Parliament were unavailing. An assault on Alessandro Palastrelli on 28 April 1456 escalated into serious riots that enjoyed widespread and perhaps overwhelming support from both the populace and parts of the patriciate, notably Alderman William Cantelow, the master of the Mercer's Company. Although the king intervened in person and a commission of magnates at the Guildhall secured indictments against the ringleaders, three being executed, such measures did not resolve the problems, nor cow the actual rioters nor their sympathizers amongst the merchants (especially staplers) and patriciate. The City authorities conducted their own investigations and probably compensated the victims. In September, Cantelow was required to explain himself before the great council and was then confined at Dudley Castle. He was bailed for £1,000 marks (£666 13s. 4d.) in December. In January both he and the mercer John Seyncle were bound to appear before the council again in May and February 1457 respectively. The mercer Ralph March, the master of two rioters, was bound over to ensure their good behaviour in future.

On 16 June 1457 March's servants attacked Galiut Centurioni, one of those Lombards licensed to ship wool. Vigorous measures were needed by the City corporation to prevent a full-scale assault on the Lombards. The king progressed in force through the City and gaoled 28 Londoners at Windsor Castle,[56] yet the Italians nevertheless abandoned London. The Genoese capture of the Englishman Robert Sturmy's ship in the Mediterranean in 1458 exacebated the situation.

There were also riots against the Fleet Street lawyers. According to *Benet's Chronicle*, it was the lawyers (not the courtiers) who displayed dead dogs in Fleet Street accompanied by offensive, but opaque, verses: it is not obvious that these were attacking the Duke of York.[57] On 13 April 1459 the lawyers erupted from the inns of court to attack their neighbours, who fought back for a day and won. Nine lawyers and five citizens were killed. Order was restored by a combination of the government, bishops and the City corporation. A formidable group of magnates processed through the area. King and council imprisoned 27 ringleaders, 24 citizens at Windsor Castle and the three principal lawyers at Hertford Castle.[58]

Also intractable was the legacy of First St Albans. The heirs of those slain in the battle wanted revenge and the royal household, even the lower or menial household, rightly saw the Yorkists as their foes. There were several alarming incidents. In November 1456 there was an attempted assassination at Coventry of the new Duke of Somerset: still a teenager and certainly not the power behind the throne, he may have been associated with opposition to York's reform programme. There was a clash between a royal domestic and a Warwick man at Westminster in November 1458 that exploded into the near-lynching of Warwick by royal cooks and scullions within the verge of the household. Although some blamed the Earl of Warwick and he should perhaps have been lodged in the Tower, Henry firmly declined to hold him to account. No wonder that Warwick was to complain, like Lord Cromwell before him, of the disrespect shown to the king's councillors, lords and judges.[59] He may also have been thinking of the Duke of Exeter's arrest of a pleader in Westminster Hall on 30 January and his imprisonment in the Tower, where Exeter was constable. This was disrespectful of royal justice, disrupted the courts, and was committed within the verge of the court, the king being resident at the time. Hence Exeter found himself incarcerated at Berkhamsted Castle: he was bound on sureties for good behaviour and to appear before the council.[60] Whether nearby or afar, Henry's itinerary certainly did not signify his 'abdication of his responsibility towards his capital.'[61] He seems indeed to have intervened regularly to calm London's alarming turbulence, even if he discovered no solutions.

The governments of Henry VI in 1453 and Lord Protector York in 1455 had despatched a stream of injunctions and summonses to Gruffydd ap Nicholas in south-west Wales without apparent effect.[62] Gruffydd may have been next on York's list for direct action. Other disturbances in Wales were attributable to York's own principal retainers Herbert and Devereux, who had been forcefully asserting themselves since 1452–3. Devereux had been implicated in the Dartford episode and was only rehabilitated by Parliament in 1455.[63] Although Lord Protector York had appointed himself constable of Carmarthen and Aberystwyth in 1455, effective control remained with Gruffydd, until the intervention around midsummer 1456 of the king's half-brother Edmund, Earl of Richmond, probably acting on behalf of his brother Jasper, Earl of Pembroke. Richmond took over the Welsh castles. Rather than applauding, Herbert and Devereux marched 2,000 men across Wales to recover them. They captured and imprisoned Richmond and illegally commissioned themselves to hold illicit great sessions. (Richmond died on 3 November.) Such outrages eclipsed even those of Gruffydd.

All the ringleaders quickly submitted. Devereux, Herbert, Gruffydd and his sons all appeared at a great council at Coventry in September 1456. Gruffydd and his sons were pardoned, probably bound on sureties, and featured hereafter in the service of the king's other half-brother Pembroke, henceforth the prime authority in south-west Wales. On 28 September the great council ordered Devereux to be imprisoned first at Windsor and on 13 May 1457 at the Marshalsea prison in London, where he surrendered on 28 May: in June he was pardoned and released on sureties. As early as 8 February 1458 he was again bound on sureties for good behaviour and to keep the peace until Michaelmas, when he appeared in chancery and the sureties were discharged. Herbert was also consigned to the Tower, but returning instead to Wales and committing further offences, he had to be declared a rebel with a price on his head before submitting at Leicester in June 1457 and being pardoned at Coventry on 7 June. Evidently his confinement at the Tower and in Windsor Castle reported in *Benet's Chronicle* followed rather than preceded his arrest.[64]

Henry progressed next year to the marches. Sessions were held in Hereford at Easter 1457 during which the offenders, York's retainers, were indicted.[65] The reality of royal authority was brought home in his heartland to York, who surely lay behind the outrage, but once again he escaped unpunished. That April, 'humble and obedient', York 'fully agreed at your special desire and commandment for to grant his estate of the said offices' of constable of Carmarthen and Aberystwyth to the king's other half-brother Pembroke, receiving in return £40 a year until appointed to another office of equivalent value.[66] Obviously, the constableships had been worth more than £40 to York!

Perhaps York was indeed held to account in the spring of 1457. Perhaps it was this episode at a Coventry great council that is reported in the act of attainder of 1459.[67] Some sort of trial had even been conducted in Henry's presence. Lord Chancellor Waynflete recited the charges ('divers rehearsals') against York, the Lords apparently consulted together and convicted him, and the Duke of Buckingham, acting as their spokesman, 'rehearsed full notably to make the said duke of York to understand how badly he had behaved [of what demeaning he had been]' and how he had no defence. Henry had then pardoned him, again. At Buckingham's petition, all resolved that this was his last chance and that next time he would 'be punished after their desert', to which both York and Warwick swore. Their oath was that which York had first taken at St Paul's not to resort to forceful action ('the way of fait'), perhaps beefed up to make it even more explicit.

One copy states that this oath was actually sworn three times, at St Paul's in 1452 and at Coventry and Westminster: it is not stated when.[68] Unfortunately, this council act once appended to the original attainder has disappeared and there is nothing to establish to which Coventry great council it belongs: October 1456, which seems unlikely since York left on good terms with the king; December 1456 or this session in March–April 1457, about which nothing whatsoever is known; or June 1459, at which the Yorkists were supposedly indicted and for which there is a strong case, but from which *Benet's Chronicle* states they were absent.[69] No sureties from York or pardons to York are recorded on the earlier occasions. The Nevilles (and Warwick) were negotiating a marriage for John Neville with the queen in spring 1457, surely evidence of good relations.[70] Whichever the correct date, the show trial did not interrupt their tenure of their key offices, nor indeed the stream of commissions on which they were named. If it happened in 1456 or 1457, it had no permanent repercussions.

RELATIONS WITH YORK

On 9 March 1456 York had had his chance to rule and had failed. That was why he was not ruling in 1456–8. His regime had collapsed. However popular with the House of Commons and hence perhaps with the populace, his faction lacked the confidence of the Lords, who did not sanction attacks on the royal family. His *First* and *Second Protectorates* had proved to be no substitute for Henry VI. York had pursued partisan policies that were unacceptable to those who mattered. In the last resort – and clearly York and the Commons had reached that limit – an adult male king could not be overridden nor restrained. It was at the request of the Lords that Henry resumed direct rule on 25 February 1456.[71] Whatever his intentions following York's *First Protectorate*, the king seems to have forgiven York for the Battle of St Albans, for the deaths of Somerset, Northumberland, Clifford and others, and for his successful *coup d'état*. Never until another attempted coup in 1459 did Henry attempt to correct or reverse the Yorkist version of events set out in the *Parliamentary Pardon*. He does not seem to have resented York's *Second Protectorate*, to which indeed he apparently agreed.

Initially Henry kept on all three of the great officers – Archbishop Bourchier as chancellor, Viscount Bourchier as treasurer and Thomas Lisieux as keeper of the privy seal – all of whom he had appointed in the spring of 1455. A bill that he approved on 9 March 1456 provided for payment of the arrears in York's salary and expenses.[72] By then York had left Parliament, but Warwick and his father Salisbury had not. Indeed, they and Viscount Bourchier were present at many of the poorly attended meetings of council at Westminster up to June 1456,[73] during which period Warwick's takeover as captain of Calais was finalized. The king could still have rescinded it. Warwick's brother George became bishop of Exeter, although he was too young to perform the functions. York remained lieutenant of Ireland and Salisbury chief forester of the North. If one adds to the control of Calais and Ireland, Warwick's keeping of the seas and Salisbury's wardenship of the West March towards Scotland, then the victors of St Albans still controlled every significant command except the East March and spent most of the government's defence budget. There are no grounds here to suppose their services went unrequited.

There is really no convincing evidence that York broke with the court in 1456. Admittedly, neither he nor Warwick nor Salisbury attended court and council regularly over the next three years. York's movements have been tracked mainly on his estates.[74] Warwick, unusually, chose to reside continuously at

135

Calais with his countess and daughters. Advancing years may have caused his father Salisbury to absent himself, but most probably he was also preoccupied by deteriorating relations with Scotland. Hence, perhaps, why Warwick and Salisbury were not summoned to every great council, yet all three peers attended several. There is some evidence that Henry still valued York's services. The king may not have been even the same inadequate man that he was before his lapse into insanity. He slept a great deal. He realized his defects. He appreciated that York had his uses, both in council and in protection of the realm, internal and external. Thus it was York who responded forcefully to James II of Scotland, both in 1456 and in 1458. Although Bocking speculated before the end of the *Second Protectorate* that Henry wanted to find a way of retaining York with less extensive powers,[75] nothing formal resulted. Complete dominance or rule by the duke were not acceptable options, either to the Lords or the king, and perhaps this remained the least that York wanted, ruling out his participation in government as a mere courtier or continual councillor.

The government attempted a new beginning. York and Warwick were paid. New diplomatic efforts to make an alliance with either France or Burgundy included proposals for the marriage of York's heir Edward in March 1458. York and the Nevilles had little cause for complaint. The Earl of Salisbury was sent £1,578 for defence against the Scots as late as June 1459.[76] The Yorkists received a string of government commissions right up to their rebellion in 1459. Admittedly, Warwick's 'rogue command at Calais' and especially of the seas created commercial and international problems. If the regime wished to remove him, as rumoured, it could not. Some purchases of munitions and commissions at various junctures that have been perceived as sinister preambles to projected strikes against the Yorkists also came to nothing:[77] probably, therefore, they were nothing of the kind.

CHAPTER 9

THE FIRST WAR 1459–61

For three years from 1456 to 1459 King Henry ruled without Parliament, but with the constant consent of the Lords, whom he consulted every few months in a string of great councils held at Coventry and Westminster. These were years of routine, when government operated adequately rather than well, and in which foreign policy was almost entirely defensive. However, they were not years of domestic harmony. There were troubles in the West Country, Wales and London, clashes between magnates, and attempted lynchings and assassinations in Coventry and London, which the government repressed fairly effectively. They remained ongoing problems. Two alternative remedies were proposed: reconciliation with the Yorkists in March 1458, what was called in shorthand the *Loveday at St Paul's*, and a further *coup d'état* by York in October 1459. It was the latter that escalated into the *First War* of the Roses.

THE LOVEDAY AT ST PAUL'S, MARCH 1458

Time was certainly no healer, and the need for reconciliation and a fresh start was obvious to all. No role was found for York in government. Moreover, feelings ran high: amongst those who had supported reform and amongst the victims of the First Battle of St Albans. It became dangerous for York, the new Duke Henry of Somerset and for Richard, Earl of Warwick, to attend the great councils that were also frequented by their enemies, whether peers or of inferior rank. Witness the huge escorts that were brought by the contending lords to the capital in November 1457 – February 1458 and the drastic peace-keeping measures that were adopted by the City corporation.[1] Tensions had to be defused. Hence a whole series of great councils convened from the autumn of

1457 to bring peace and unity to the Lords, especially the victors and the heirs of the victims of St Albans, which culminated in three months of sustained mediation by the bishops and the arbitration of all outstanding differences. A great deal of time, effort and trust were invested in the proceedings by the king, all parties, the bishops and many lay lords too. An initial council in November 1457 was attended by York,[2] who evidently trusted in the king's good faith. It was reported that Warwick ignored threats to his life to participate.[3] The Percies were persuaded to commit their feud with the Nevilles to arbitration. All parties were bound to abide the award on huge bonds totalling £78,000.[4] This great council laid the ground for another on 28 February 1458, which all the principal parties attended. The mediators referred back at intervals to the king himself at Hertford. 'Rejoice, England, our lords accorded be', a poet sang.[5] The agreement, the famous *Loveday*, was universally applauded as the start of a new era of domestic peace. Disillusion and cynicism came later.

It is important to realize that the arbitration was not about who ruled, the king's right being unquestionable, nor about who advised him, since that again was Henry's choice, nor even about differences between York and Queen Margaret – whose quarrel still lay in the future – but about the resolution of the private differences between the victors and victims of First St Albans. Even with such a narrow focus, settlement was difficult to attain. The Yorkists regarded their actions as justified by the treason of Edmund, Duke of Somerset, and considered themselves cleared by the *Parliamentary Pardon*. That Somerset was a traitor was never conceded by his family. Moreover, the widows and heirs of Somerset, Northumberland and Clifford – the new duke, earl and baron – rejected the Yorkist case and thirsted for revenge, ideally blood. Since the Yorkists had no corresponding grievances, any solution was bound to involve concessions by them.

The whole arbitration process has been explained by the king's removal from the Midlands to the capital and his liberation therefore from the malign influences of the queen or alternatively the lords of the council,[6] but there is no need for such explanations with a ruler so committed to peaceful solutions, to mediation and arbitration as King Henry VI – witness the three attempted arbitrations of York vs. Somerset – and especially to reconciliation with York. That the parties were brought to negotiate and to compromise was surely because the king himself was so determined, persistent, insistent, and in the end could not be refused. Henry had long since abandoned any demand for justice on the aggressors at St Albans or for the offences committed there against him. The *Parliamentary Pardon* that exculpated and protected the Yorkists was allowed to stand. The Yorkists were not to be punished for rebellion. However, they could not deny that they had slain the three peers, even if accidentally (as they claimed regarding Northumberland and Clifford). The award therefore required them to endow a chantry at St Albans Abbey for the benefit of the souls of those they had dispatched. They were also to compensate monetarily Somerset's widow and heir with £5,000 and Clifford's heir with 1,000 marks (£666 13s. 4d.), albeit from arrears due to them from the government that might be hard to collect.[7] Such blood money, or wergild, occurs in other awards of the time. The ruinous damages due from the Percies to the Nevilles were cancelled: sureties for £15,000 from Richard Percy were relaxed on the date of the award, but his brother Thomas, Lord Egremont, was bound over for ten years to keep the peace towards the Nevilles. He was also to go abroad on pilgrimage.[8] In return all the heirs withdrew their demands for vengeance. Both the national feud and the specific Percy–Neville dispute were appeased. Provision was made for future mediation on some details. The Yorkists appear to have been pleased with the result. The first instalment towards the chantry was paid early in 1459, and Salisbury commissioned a certified copy of the award.[9] The whole arrangement was sealed by a public ceremony, the *Loveday at St Paul's* on 25 March, at which all the principals were reconciled and committed themselves on oath.

By reconciling past differences and by re-admitting the Yorkists to the public life from which they had absented themselves, the *Loveday* restored a political system in which the king ruled and the Lords participated. Although the Mountford and some other disputes were yet to emerge, existing feuds were not escalating and indeed almost all had been terminated or suspended. Tensions were calmed. The government tried its hardest to raise sums due to York and Warwick. York's son Edward was honoured by inclusion in plans for a triple marriage alliance with princesses of either France or Burgundy.[10] That this broke down, supposedly because the Yorkists pursued their own foreign policy, had no obvious domestic repercussions. There was no inevitability to the progression to further conflict over the next eighteen months, still less for the dynastic revolution that followed. Yet when the *Loveday* failed, there was a track record to fall back on of incompatibility, violence, treason, broken promises and mere missed opportunities.

PRECIPITANTS: THE YORKIST COUP, SEPTEMBER – NOVEMBER 1459

Most modern historians say that the *Loveday* was bound to fail because it only papered over the cracks dividing the parties and did not handle the real issues.

In one sense, this is not fair, since the award tells us only the solution found to the differences between the victors and the heirs of the victims of First St Albans. Each side had put their case, answered the others' arguments, and had resubmitted their case, supporting each point with evidence. Over a period of weeks the full range of grievances was surely aired and measured, leaving, as the balance of ills to be healed, only the cancellation of the damages due from the Percies to the Nevilles, compensation to the dependants of the deceased, and the chantry. The award presumed that these were the parties who really mattered. The very real grievances of lesser victims were ignored and were revived as opportunities arose. The king's household, such as the cooks who rioted late in 1458, had been threatened by the battle, expropriated by the resumptions, and regarded the Yorkists as their foes, surely correctly. Such resentments might not have resurfaced had the principals remained at peace. Nor did the *Loveday* address Yorkist demands for reform. Henry VI was left in charge, advised by whomever he chose, including – but not principally or solely – York. Not only was the Yorkist coup of 1455 not condemned, but the Yorkists were free to contend that their actions on that occasion were legitimate. Again, there was nothing here to make a further breakdown inevitable.

And yet, eighteen months after the *Loveday*, in September 1459, another *coup d'état* was staged by York, Salisbury and Warwick, this time with the assistance of two barons, Grey of Powys and Clinton. The Yorkists mobilized all their forces to seize power. This was the forceful coup ('way of fait') that had been forbidden at the Coventry great council and that York had personally sworn three times not to undertake. The provocation alleged of the queen, for which there is no convincing evidence, did not make their actions permissible. What happened was an illegal uprising. The firing of cannon at the king constituted waging of war by the standards of the time and hence treason under the 1352 statute. It deserved the most serious punishment. Some historians have nevertheless taken the side of the Yorkists, have excused their actions and condemned those of their opponents, and have considered the Yorkists to be harshly and unreasonably treated. 'War actually broke out in 1459 because Queen Margaret was finally, by then, in a position to destroy York and his friends once and for all. Queen Margaret wasted no time in pressing home her advantage' at the Coventry Parliament.[11] Yet there is evidence as early as November 1458 of Salisbury committing himself and his men to 'take full part with the full noble prince the duke of York', presumably in the Wars, and actively enlarging his retinue with recruits from outside his core estates.[12] Contemporaries recognized treasonable insurrection when they

1 *The Two Roses*, engraving of a painting by J.D. Watson. Depicts Shakespeare's invented scene in *Henry VI part 1* in the Temple Garden, where the dukes of York (left) and Somerset (right) pluck the rival roses, white and red.

2 John Talbot, Earl of Shrewsbury, the hero of the French war slain in the final battle at Castillon in 1453, kneeling, presents a book to Henry VI and Queen Margaret of Anjou on their thrones. A typical court scene.

EURIDUS DUX

3 Richard, Duke of York (d. 1460). A serene and rather sad image of the great nobleman whose dynamic populism and ambitious scheming made it so difficult for Henry VI to rule.

4 Genealogy showing the rights of the house of York to the crowns of Castile and England. In the centre Henry IV with his sword cuts off Richard II: Henry VI (top left) faces the victorious sword-bearing Edward IV (top right).

5 Reconstruction of Ludlow Castle as it appeared *c*.1450. The round building is the chapel and the chamber block (top right) was probably where the young Edward IV as Earl of March and Edward V as Prince of Wales resided.

6 Richmond Castle, Yorkshire. Re-drawn from the Register of the Honour of Richmond, early fifteenth century. The banners mark the defence responsibilities of the tenants of Richmond Honour, the saltire (bottom right) denoting the Nevilles of Middleham.

7 The Relief of Calais (1436), from the Beauchamp Pageant. England's sole colony was Warwick's base for launching three invasions. The formidable defences witnessed the repulse of Somerset's attack in a very similar scene in 1460.

8 The victorious Edward, Earl of March (afterwards Edward IV) kneels before the captured Henry VI outside his tent following the Battle of Northampton, 1460. Next York claimed the throne.

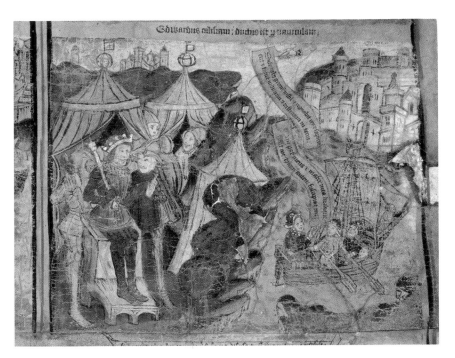

9 King Henry VI, on his throne with sceptre (left), watches the flight of the Yorkist earls for Calais after the Battle of Ludford, 1459.

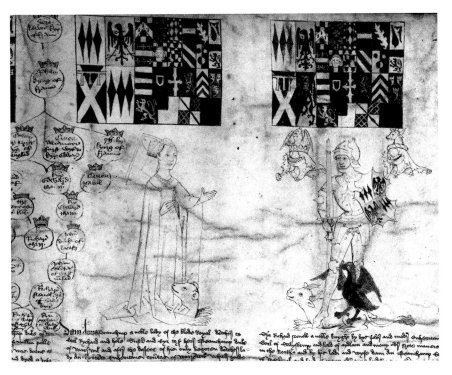

10 Richard Neville, Earl of Warwick (the Kingmaker) and his wife Anne Beauchamp. Their great estates and retinue derived from their inheritances from many noble houses shown by the coats of arms in their banners. Note the rather domestic Warwick bear at Anne's feet.

11 Warwick Castle Barbican and Guy's Tower (right). The seat of the Beauchamps, the Kingmaker and Clarence, Warwick was rebuilt with stupendous modern towers that provided the most modern facilities for the earl's court.

12 Frieze of bears and ragged staffs (the Kingmaker's emblem) over the entrance to the Beauchamp Chapel at Warwick College.

13 Arrest of Edward IV in bed by Archbishop Neville (left) following the Battle of Edgecote, 1469 (right). Note the king's armour in an open case above the bed and the cannon firing outside.

14 The Battle of Barnet. The work of a Burgundian artist, this depicts the battle as a combat between mounted and armoured knights, whereas infantry in leather jerkins were much more numerous.

15 Sally against the Bastard of Fauconberg's attempted storming of London, 1471. Following the Battles of Barnet and Tewkesbury, Warwick's shipmen and Kentishmen assaulted the eastern gates.

EDWARDE IIII

16 Portrait of Edward IV (1461–83), the best general and most successful king of the Wars of the Roses. We no longer admire the broad white face that was considered so handsome in his day, and that was inherited by his grandson Henry VIII.

Edwardus princeps Wallie
primus filius Edwardi quarti

17 Edward Prince of Wales, later Edward V, from the Royal Window, Canterbury Cathedral. Although aged 12 at his accession in 1483, Edward V was dethroned by his uncle Richard III, and probably murdered in the Tower.

18 Drawing of the two dukes of Burgundy, Philip the Good (d. 1467, left), and his son Charles the Bold (k. 1477, right). Duke Charles's rivalry with Louis XI secured foreign backing for invasions in 1470 and in 1471.

19 Margaret of York, Duchess of Burgundy (d. 1503) and her stepdaughter Mary of Burgundy (d. 1482) kneeling before St Anne. Mary wed Archduke Maximilian of Habsburg: their grandson was Emperor Charles V. Margaret backed both Lambert Simnel and Perkin Warbeck against Henry VII.

20 Thomas Rotherham, bishop of Lincoln, kneels before the Trinity, with King Edward IV (left) and Queen Elizabeth Wydeville, the king's mother Cecily Duchess of York (right), and members of the confraternity of Luton in Bedfordshire.

21 Portrait of King Louis XI of France. The 'Universal Spider', who orchestrated the *Readeption* and the fall of Charles the Bold, was nondescript and dressed extremely plainly, with badges of saints pinned to his hat.

22 Portrait of Prince Arthur, the 'Union of the Roses', eldest son of King Henry VII and Queen Elizabeth of York. Instead of a new Arthurian golden age, Arthur died in 1502 and his role was taken by his brother Henry VIII.

23 Perkin Warbeck. An authentic contemporary portrait of the young Frenchman who caused Henry VII so much trouble. The resemblance to Edward IV, his supposed father, is apparent, but not the courtliness that captivated the Duchess Margaret, Archduke Maximilan, and James IV.

24 Henry VII (left) and Elizabeth of York (right) with notably Henry VIII and his third queen Jane Seymour (front). A mid-1530s image of the victorious Tudor dynasty that had come to stay.

25 The House of Lords in the Parliament of 1523. The king on his throne presides over the Lords Spiritual (bishops and abbots, left) the Lords Temporal (right) and the secretariat (centre). A delegation of the Commons are top right.

saw it. The Coventry Parliament that followed, which was properly constituted and exceptionally well attended by the Lords both spiritual and temporal, pressed for more rigorous penalties than Henry VI was willing to concede.[13] If Margaret was indeed directing the Parliament, she failed to get her way and was moreover too half-hearted in enforcing its decisions.[14]

The only possible practical justifications for what was strictly treason and unjustifiable was that the situation had become intolerable: either because the Yorkists themselves were acting in self-defence, which this time they did not claim and which was not so, or because the state of the realm had worsened disastrously and could not be remedied, which was what they asserted. Historians have pointed to disagreements over foreign policy and Warwick's piracy,[15] but neither was a grievance *for* the Yorkists *against* the Crown and neither occurs in their surviving manifestos. It is argued that from spring 1457 the Yorkists realized 'that they were going to have to bide their time before they could make a further bid for power', that they had agreed on another coup by November 1458, that 'there can be little doubt there was an air of crisis in the first half of 1459', and that 'they decided to get their retaliation in first'.[16] If credible, this was a long-term treasonable conspiracy, but the Yorkists' situation was not untenable. Normal political life continued. There was a great council in June 1459 which the Yorkists did not attend and where they were indicted: perhaps for grave offences but perhaps merely for non-attendance. Even if that was where York and Warwick were held to account and were required to re-swear their oaths, as discussed above, that closed the issue and had no repercussions.[17]

Two Yorkist publications sought to justify their conduct. The first, undated, manifesto was issued by Warwick. The second was a letter from them all dated at Ludlow (Salop.) on 10 October 1459 that refers to the first and presumes acquaintance with its contents. The manifesto claims that law and order had broken down and that justice was being perverted, trade was interrupted, the king was impoverished and hence purveyance was impoverishing the people. All these ills were attributed once again to unspecified evil councillors: 'certain persons [who] for their own covetousness' were hostile to 'the true [very] lovers of the said common weal' and of the king's profit and who 'subtly and craftily hide' the truth from him. This was another fiction. Asserting their loyalty to the king, which at this stage there is no reason to doubt, Henry's 'true lovers [very lovers]' – York, Salisbury, and Warwick – intended to inform the king of the situation and 'by the advice of the great lords of his blood . . . [to] redeem his land and subjects from the jeopardy of the said mischiefs', and to punish those responsible.[18]

Public order is always difficult to measure, but it does not appear to have been worse in 1459 than before. In particular, noble feuds had ceased. Specific charges of widespread perversion of justice like those alleged for East Anglia and Kent in 1450 are lacking. Certainly the economy remained depressed and from 1459 plunged again into acute crisis,[19] perhaps forcing greater reliance on purveyance and exacerbating popular discontent. English overseas trade was again suffering in line with the international recession. It was made worse by Warwick's piracy, yet was popularly attributed to the licensing of alien merchants.[20] The fundamental cause of the recession was certainly not, as Warwick alleged, because of the king's alienation of his wealth, nor from his failure to live of his own. There had been a comprehensive resumption in 1456. It was impossible for the king to break even under such circumstances. It was a matter of fact that no parliamentary taxes had been granted since 1453 – although the archers voted then were actually raised and financed in 1457[21] – and therefore any royal impositions could add only marginally to popular discontent. These problems were not therefore attributable to evil counsel and could not be remedied by another coup to oust the king's current councillors and to replace them with the Yorkists. 'While they protested their loyalty to the king and the "good and worthy lords", they could hardly escape from the fact that they had risen against them all.' 'It was the verdict of the Lords that they now rejected.' The Yorkists represented few people besides themselves.[22] Since the other three royal dukes of Buckingham, Exeter and Somerset were already closely associated with the regime, it cannot have been they who were scheduled by the Yorkists for more prominent roles: indeed they may have been among those targeted. Certainly the household men were. In 1460 it was to be the earls of Shrewsbury and Wiltshire and Viscount Beaumont that the Yorkists specifically denounced.[23] Obviously Queen Margaret, who was protected by the statute of Treasons, could not have been named, but she could have been sidelined. Whilst Warwick denied unconvincingly that any old grudges were to be settled and advocated highly desirable ends to which all could agree – the rule of law, greater respect by foreigners for England, and prosperity at home[24] – the main objective of the Yorkists was once again control of the government. 'The real purpose of their action' was

> a determination to seize power, by force if necessary, in the king's name. . . . The nation as a whole was not prepared to take up arms against a king to whom it was still loyal and perceived them, however much they attempted to present themselves otherwise, as pursuing private interests and personal resentments.[25]

In his attempted coups of 1450 and 1452 York had appealed for popular support, which he had stiffened with his own retainers. In 1455 popular backing had been jettisoned in the interests of secrecy and surprise. The parliamentary Commons had pushed him into the protectorate, but it had proved insufficient to keep him in power. At no point did York enjoy enough support from the Lords to carry through his radical proposals. Normally indeed he was in a small minority: only five peers rebelled in 1459. In that year the Yorkists appealed once again to the people – the issues that they highlighted had been aggrieving the populace since 1450 – but probably failed to mobilize them. This may not be because the Yorkists lacked support – Warwick was able to enter London unopposed – but because too little time was allowed for recruitment in the Home Counties. Henry tried to appease those commoners 'blinded' by the Yorkist blandishments. As in 1455, the forces used in the 1459 coup were the household, tenants and retainers of the three magnates, plus the Calais garrison, and were apparently much more numerous than those they faced. In their enemies' words, they 'proposed to come to Kenilworth', where the king was, 'thinking you should not have knowledge beforehand, but suddenly to have fulfilled their traitorous entent'.[26] Salisbury's 5,000 northerners (probably the men of Richmondshire in north Yorkshire) might have done the task on their own had they arrived unexpectedly and seized the king, to be joined by York later. They appeared 'genuinely threatening. Their assembly of three forces to approach the king from different directions has to be interpreted as a military offensive'.[27] Moreover their total force, much larger than at First St Albans, was too numerous merely to be for the safeguard of their persons or for a peaceful protest, as York and the Nevilles alleged.

Unfortunately, Salisbury's march from Yorkshire towards Coventry was foreseen. He was intercepted by a substantial royal force at Blore Heath (Staffs.), where on 23 September he chose to fight – a decision that placed the Yorkists conclusively in the wrong. 'He could have withdrawn his forces or disbanded them without penalty.'[28] The royalist commander Lord Audley was killed. Warwick meantime had brought a substantial segment of the Calais garrison ashore – itself a gross misapplication of the national armed forces, a breach of trust and probably treasonable – and conducted them via London (on 20–21 September) to join his father Salisbury at Ludlow (Salop.), from which York and his marcher retainers had not yet stirred. It had not been part of the original plan as now proved necessary to confront the king and his forces directly or to engage him in pitched battle – definitely treason. Even at this stage, in spite of the act of the Coventry council declaring that any future insurrection would be punished,

King Henry via a herald offered York, Warwick and their followers pardon of their lives and the preservation of their lands and chattels from forfeiture if they submitted within six days: 'for he forgave all, both the leaders and the men under them, for what they had maliciously designed against him, provided they submitted themselves to him'. Salisbury and others at Blore Heath were not included. They had crossed the line beyond what could be condoned. 'For York and Warwick a return to the *status quo ante* was surely better than any defeated rebel could reasonably expect'.[29]

The king's offer was not accepted. At the very least the Yorkists wanted Salisbury included in the royal pardon. What the Yorkist lords did next, therefore, was to commit themselves to stand together, in something like a brotherhood of arms, the obviously short-term beneficiary being Salisbury. Such a contract was itself a seditious conspiracy. Next they sought better terms, at the very least forgiveness for Salisbury, perhaps even acceptance of their programme, by winning over peers in the royal army. Warwick's original manifesto had appealed for popular support. Now the Yorkists formally swore allegiance before witnesses at Worcester. Certified copies of their oath were sent not just to the king but to the lords in his company, assuring them that they had never intended treason.[30]

The tactic failed: Blore Heath was evidence enough. Still at arms, the Yorkists manoeuvred, before returning to Ludlow on 10 October, whence they despatched yet another open letter to the king protesting their loyalty and innocence, complaining that their (rebellious) tenants had been molested and their letters had not been answered, and asking for an audience to put their original case. Whilst phrased in reasonable language, this was not an offer to negotiate, but rather further defiance. Actually, it contained no admission of blame, no explanation why they had not obeyed the king's commands nor accepted his offers, no willingness to submit, no retreat from their original demands.

Anyway it was too late. The king had already issued writs for a Parliament, obviously to condemn the Yorkists, and on 12 October his army confronted them near Ludlow. A full-scale battle was scheduled for the following day. However, many Yorkists, especially those from Calais, declined to commit treason. Henry still offered a pardon, but his terms were too humiliating for the Yorkist lords to accept. Rather than submit, they abandoned their army and fled abroad: York and his second son Rutland to Ireland; Warwick, Salisbury and York's eldest son March to Calais. This astonishing decision categorized them as cowardly and dishonourable. Their flight reveals them as utterly uncompromising. They refused to bow to the opinion of the majority of their peers. They certainly intended continuing the struggle, both in Parliament and from abroad. Apparently they expected to be able to counterattack.

In their absence, the Yorkists were convicted of treason by Parliament at Coventry and their possessions confiscated. Although expressed intemperately and probably wrongly in associating York with the rebel Jack Cade, the act was surely correct to portray York as an incorrigible and ultimately intolerable conspirator and rebel.[31] There was nobody else in the 1450s whom York was willing to let rule. Treason did not need to be multiplied to incur the penalties of treason, which could as legitimately have been imposed on him in 1452 or 1455.

The Blore Heath and Ludford campaign was not a fair trial of strength between the rival armies. With contingents from the North and Calais as well as the marches, entrenched and equipped with ordnance, the rebels might well have matched the forces about the king had he been taken unawares. The loss of surprise enabled resistance to be organized and forced the Yorkists instead to unite all their disparate forces, a fall-back position that proved too ambitious, took time and enabled the king to rally his lords against the insurrection. The longer the campaign went on, the stronger Henry became, as he was joined from everywhere by further lordly retinues and shire levies. Five lords, however overmighty, could not withstand the rest of the king's subjects combined. Once these Yorkists were exposed as traitors actual or potential, any sympathizers amongst the politically respectable were deterred from joining them. The Bourchiers for instance were unwilling to tar themselves with treason and could not refuse to suppress rebels. The shame and penalties of treason also made the Yorkist army into unreliable combatants. The ploy that Henry VI himself was dead – and thus no treason was risked – was exposed when Henry himself appeared in the royalist lines. The king's moral authority could not be resisted.

The Yorkists had not been driven into the impasse where they found themselves. They arrived there through a series of choices. First of all, they had decided to resort to force. They may even have prepared for it a year or years in advance. Although they pleaded once again to be pre-empting the malice of their enemies, there is no evidence that they faced any such threat. Getting retaliation in first was not a permissible course of action. Since they still regarded forceful protests like those of 1452 and 1455 as legitimate, this latest coup seemed not so momentous to them as a treasonable insurrection, nor (to their minds) as risky to their lives, honour, family, or inheritances. The Yorkist lords did not regard themselves, in the words of York's oath, as perjured or dishonoured. From their angle, their last coup had not raised the stakes.

Salisbury could have declined battle at Blore Heath and could have withdrawn, probably unscathed. Fighting yet another battle and shedding more blood made retreat and compromise more difficult. They could have accepted the king's terms, with a reasonable expectation for Salisbury of a cooling-off period in prison, followed by rehabilitation. This was what York, Devon and Cobham had accepted after the Dartford coup in 1452. Every culprit in every feud so far had submitted to royal authority. Salisbury in 1459 did not. York and Warwick chose to back Salisbury and to defy the king. The Yorkists could still have submitted at Ludford and thrown themselves on Henry's mercy. How could the king have foreseen their flight and therefore forestalled such dishonourable conduct?[32] Warwick needed much luck to reach safety.

At this point the king's decision to abandon euphemism, to treat the Yorkists as the traitors that they were, and to condemn them to forfeiture certainly did raise the stakes. Yet although Parliament had been summoned to Coventry with a view to trying them for treason, King Henry actually fined and forgave most of the rebels before Parliament met, accepted the submission, fines and sureties for good behaviour of others during the Parliament, and reserved to himself the right to pardon and restore even those who had been attainted.[33]

The Yorkist label of the *Devils Parliament* (20 November–20 December 1459) is not really appropriate. The Coventry Parliament was exceptionally well attended: 66 peers, including three dukes, five earls, both viscounts and 23 barons. The Commons were not packed.[34] If Parliament was strongly anti-Yorkist, this surely represents the general and genuine shock at the treasonable conspiracy and waging of war against the king by the Yorkists. Yet the act of attainder – the first blanket condemnation of adherents of either party – was not nodded through. Two fragmentary tracts reveal protracted, agonized and tortured debates, for and against the legitimacy of the Yorkist protests, between rigour and justice. Although the Coventry great council act had declared that future offences would receive their deserts, clearly there were lengthy and anxious debates about implementing it. Some of the Yorkists' enemies wanted more rigour. They wanted more to be condemned and tougher penalties. They even tried to attaint Thomas, Lord Stanley separately when he was deleted from the main act. The contemporary tract known as *Somnium Vigilantis* tells us what arguments were put on behalf of the Yorkists, evidently formally and at the length. They were not at all conciliatory or submissive. The Yorkists were not engaged in treason, it was evidently argued, but sought the common good. To convict them carried dire consequences and risked reprisals in the future.[35] The Yorkists still had relatives in Parliament to plead for them. Even Henry was unconvinced by the more draconian demands. He still preferred reconciliation and forgiveness, subject to genuine submission sealed by what Yorkists thought an unnecessarily humiliating public ceremony. There were negotiations, complete and partial pardons, compromises and compounding of penalties.

The act of attainder did represent rigour. It marked a new stage by condemning six peers, a peeress, 19 gentry and their heirs to forfeiture.[36] That was a marked escalation and aggravation of differences. Condemnation of peers was something new, although executions still befell only those who were not noblemen or gentry. The government saw here a chance to re-endow the Crown – to enable the king to live of his own – by exploiting the forfeitures as sources of revenue rather than dispersing them as patronage.

But the scale of condemnation was modest. Only 37 out of many thousand individuals were attainted and nobody was executed for waging war against the king. Serial offenders like Devereux who submitted, in his case for the third time, were spared their lives and possessions. Even the penalties of attainder were negotiable. Henry continued to offer terms in return for submission, even though the Yorkist lords rejected them all. If they had been prepared to give up their hopes to govern, they could have returned to their allegiance and recovered their estates, perhaps after an initial period of confinement and certainly under sureties for their future good behaviour. To become once again loyal and obedient subjects was not on their list of options. The only terms acceptable to them were that they take over the government: not a basis for negotiation. It was Yorkist unwillingness to step back from the brink or to compromise even in defeat, not the oppression of the king and his advisers, that made this particular coup so much more serious than what had gone before. It might have become yet more serious. Making York king was the objective, one Yorkist Robert Radcliffe allegedly confessed before his death.[37] Whether York himself intended to usurp as in 1460 cannot be known. Publicly, the Yorkists never ceased professing allegiance to Henry VI.

RIPOSTE

The Coventry proceedings were 'a dangerous combination of weakness and forcefulness'.[38] In the sense that its decisions were unenforceable, this is true. Ironically, it was victory that exposed the military weaknesses of the government and that enabled the Yorkists to maximize their strengths. Their flight to Ireland and Calais meant that Henry could not carry out the sentences passed against them. Still defiant, highly effective in their resistance, and indeed able to take the counter-offensive, their unfounded claim to have been harshly treated was believed by the pope's agent Francesco Coppini, Bishop of Fermo, by the Burgundians, who saw advantage in English divisions, and at home amongst the bishops and the London elite, who came to blame the government for the suspension of trade to Calais that the rebels held against it.[39] Although the Yorkists had lost the military campaign, they won the propaganda war. Some saw the attainder as 'a perilous writing' or 'mischievous indicting', liable to be counterproductive, and even as confirmation that the king's advisers had been seeking York's ruin since 1450![40] Parliament's decisions were not regarded as permanent or conclusive. Coppini, the bishops, Londoners and doubtless others thought it was for King Henry to make concessions in the interests of domestic peace, even though the Yorkists had first resorted to political murders and who still pitilessly and routinely eliminated anybody who stood against him. When they returned from exile in June 1460, ostensibly to recover their inheritances and in the interests of reform, their stance resembled that of the returning Henry Bolingbroke, who had claimed only his duchy in 1399, and indeed that of the Duke of Exeter in 1454. Edward IV was to take the same line in 1471. To a fifteenth-century audience, claiming one's inheritance was entirely reasonable. Inheritance was a sacred right that could not be denied. And the Yorkists besides invoked God's will, the good of Church, king and common-wealth, and addressed very specific concerns of the populace and merchants.

Also perhaps there was a recognition (as in 1453) that the Yorkists had to be encompassed in any settlement since the regime was too weak utterly to scotch them. The Yorkists made the most of their naval strength, the only professional garrison, and the popular discontent that they had so assiduously nurtured to expose the financial prostration of the government. Again they were ruthless towards royal officers who fell into their hands. They did not flinch from despatching those whose only offence was loyal service to the king.

The fleeing Yorkists were never displaced and penniless refugees like their Lancastrian counterparts in the next decade. They retreated instead to safe havens: to the commands in Ireland and Calais to which Henry had appointed them, across the seas that Henry had confided to Warwick's keeping, and to the only professional garrison maintained by the crown and now loyal to Warwick. Winkling them out required the recruitment of new soldiers and the comman-deering of further ships, probably inferior in quality and certainly in leader-ship to Warwick, who boxed in the Duke of Somerset's expedition to Calais, captured a consignment of pay for his troops, pre-empted Lord Rivers at Sandwich in a destructive raid, and faced down Exeter's fleet at sea. The government's attempts to ban trade to Calais and to sever the town from its neighbours, moves that were dangerously characterized as colluding with the (foreign) enemy, did not work, and may have been counter-productive. Apparently they prompted the Calais staplers to bankroll Warwick. Already on good terms with Burgundy, the Yorkists may also have colluded with the Scots.[41] The regime had to call out the shire levies, to their discontent. Preparation of such ineffectual countermeasures stretched Henry's resources beyond the limit, leaving him unable to forestall any Yorkist landing which, from bases abroad, could fall anywhere. It was now that the king's financial weakness was directly transmuted into political weakness. Now was also when the Yorkists combined their message and the various elements of support to enable them to win the war.

Warwick's fleet and Calais garrison were securely funded locally by the staplers and by his piratical forays in the Channel. He could land anywhere on the south or east coasts of England and could disgorge at any time a force superior to whatever might confront his landing. And of course it might instead have been York who landed somewhere on the west coast, perhaps in his Welsh strongholds, or alternatively Salisbury in the North, or perhaps all might land simultaneously on all sides. That was why Henry was forced into an essentially negative strategy. How could his forces halt the enemy near their point of disembarkation when that was unknown? A central base in the Midlands was how Edward IV in 1470 and Richard III in 1485 were to confront similar challenges, equally unsuccessfully. These overseas resources were an important reason for the Yorkist triumph in 1460.

York, Salisbury and his son Warwick were great magnates, with large numbers of committed retainers concentrated in the North, West Midlands and in Wales, the wrong places for the 1460 campaign, insufficiently close to the jugular that was London. Little use was made of those retainers. This was a matter of choice. As in 1399, 1471 and 1487, the landing could have been in the North. Instead the Yorkists called out the people of the South-East. York had experienced the power of the masses in 1450 and had tried to mobilize them again in 1452, without success. In 1459 Warwick had appealed for popular support in Kent and London, and most probably learnt at first hand its potential, which he now determined to exploit.

The root cause of popular discontent was economic. The recession was long-term. The particularly acute crisis of 1450 had receded, as trade with the Hanseatic League and Burgundy resumed, yet trade with France and Gascony remained suspended and the worst then returned. Cloth exports fell by a further fifth, wool prices to below 2s. a stone in 1459–60, and everywhere there was what Professor Britnell calls 'a crisis in sheep farming'. In 1442–61 imports fell 31 per cent in value and exports by 34 per cent.[42] Landlords, tenants, farmers, artisans and merchants were suffering adverse economic effects throughout the decade, their standards of living suffered, and hence economic discontent persisted. As has been shown, the root causes were deep-seated and international, notably the international bullion crisis which reached its nadir in the early 1460s. Responsibility rested not with any government, nor was it within the capacity of Henry VI's or York's regimes to cure, but this was not understood. One cause of the recession, it was believed, was the misconduct of foreign merchants. Although bound to be both unavailing and counterproductive, these remedial parliamentary bills were vetoed by the king, who was thus failing to deal with the situation. Worse than that, the regime was seen as favouring the aliens. Its firm measures towards the anti-alien rioters in 1456–7 and against the Fleet Street rioters in 1459 were unpopular, not just amongst the lower orders, but amongst the merchants and City elite. Further licences granted to export wool independently of the staple were seen as unfair competition and a source of financial loss to the staplers. A major inquiry into Italian malpractices in 1458–9 was undermined by the royal pardons that the Italians invoked. For many merchants and Londoners, the fruits of this mistaken policy appeared obvious, as wool exports tumbled to their lowest level in 1459–60 – to 2,119 sacks, a mere third of most of the 1450s, and London's share of 1,249 also reached its nadir – only a fifth of the level of 1455–6.[43] The diagnosis was wrong, but the government's commercial policy was seen as inimical to the public interest and in particular the interests of all those engaged in the cloth industry, foreign trade, or cash transactions.

Warwick, in contrast, was sorting out the foreigners. His piratical attacks on shipping of all nationalities, whether hostile and French or friendly Hanseatic, Burgundian, Spanish, or Genoese,[44] must surely have disrupted normal commerce, yet his depredations were applauded at home. Appropriating much of the customs to repay to the staplers the £40,000 that they had provided for pay for the Calais garrison actually deprived the government of revenues to meet current wages and normal expenses. Therefore, it sold licences to trade free of customs: what choice did it have? Such licences inevitably postponed the repayments to the staplers and were widely interpreted as preferring those foreign merchants, who were the cause of commercial depression.[45] Warwick himself surely believed this cacophony of expert complaint which, moreover, justified what he was doing anyway. Already in 1459 he had lamented the 'great hurt of merchandise' and 'great hurt of merchants', which he blamed on the government.[46] There was a further sharp downturn in trade in 1459–61: wool exports followed cloth. 'There was a virtual stop of trade in the late 1450s. . . . This caused real poverty. . . . There were multiple and deep-seated grievances against the government in mid-century into which Warwick tapped.'[47] If hardly the government's fault, the political situation was certainly contributory. With Calais occupied by rebels, the regime certainly did try to prevent trade with the town, both from England – whence it was supplied with wool by the London staplers, food and other supplies from Kent – and from its Burgundian neighbours.[48] Since this failed to dislodge the rebels, the only hope for staplers became a Yorkist victory. Unemployment waxed in the cloth industry, shipping, distribution and transport, and in commercial agriculture.

Financial hardship was aggravated by taxation. However necessary for royal solvency, any extra payments to the government were therefore to be deplored. Actually, however,

> there was no new parliamentary taxation levied at all after 1453 . . . [so] resentment can only have been caused by household purveyance, by the exploitation of the hereditary revenues of the household at Coventry and, possibly, by an attempt to levy the grant of archers made by the Reading parliament in 1453 to the circumstances of 1457.[49]

Scarcely solvent, Henry could not afford to surrender those revenues to which he was entitled. Only these could enable him 'to live of his own', as Warwick well knew. The staplers did not recognize how their trade and finances were being worsened by the treasonable occupation of Calais and piracy of the Yorkists, but rather (and strangely) identified their interests with the Yorkists, to whom they and the City elite lent substantial sums that they denied the government. Through Warwick's connections with the merchants of the staple, the West Country pirates that he employed, black market suppliers on the mainland and even sympathizers in London, the earl was kept informed about popular and mercantile discontent in England and its sources. Having understood and internalized the situation, he exploited it. In comparison to York in 1452, he was able to represent their sentiments in his propaganda, and was thus able to mobilize popular discontent and direct it militarily.[50]

Warwick recognized broad similarities between 1460 and the *Crisis of 1450* and therefore reissued one of Cade's original manifestos, thus ensuring that he touched those themes that he knew had popular appeal and built on popular perceptions that nothing had changed. He developed the dominant 'Yorkist' version of the *Crisis of 1450*. Warwick tarred thereby the unfortunate councillors of 1460 with the same brush as Suffolk. The root cause of all ills was still evil councillors – 'traitors' prompted by covetousness, who controlled the king and kept the truth and truthful petitioners from him.[51] The new manifesto that Warwick issued was addressed once again to the king in York's name as a true liegeman who was drawing the king's attention to the misgovernment of his evil councillors. It deplored, as everyone must, the sufferings (unrecorded) of the Church and the perversions of justice, also unrecorded, by the king's entourage, and anticipated that there would be 'hanging and drawing of men by their tyranny'. Like Cade, Warwick blamed the economic problems on the depredations of the king's councillors. The king should live of his own without burdening the people. He should also, illogically, live in more magnificent state. Warwick fed popular patriotism and hostility to foreigners by harking back a decade to the shameful loss of France. He perverted the government's isolation of rebellious Calais into consorting with the enemy. The failed blockade of Calais, as we have seen, had struck at the livelihood of its trading partners, the suppliers and cloth producers of London, Kent and Sussex. The earl's manifesto threatened, untruthfully, that the government was inviting in Irish rebels. Duke Humphrey of Gloucester had been murdered and so too now were to be York, Salisbury and Warwick, all faithful subjects and petitioners, 'for no other cause but for the true hearts that God knoweth we ever have borne and bear to the profit of the king's estate, to the common weal of the same realm, and the defence thereof'. The events of 1459 and the Coventry Parliament constituted a malicious plot to destroy the Yorkists, as hatched by the evil councillors, the Earl of Shrewsbury, the Earl of Wiltshire and Viscount Beaumont:[52] not the Duke of Somerset, presumably because he was neutralized at Guines, and not the queen. However disingenuous and untruthful this was, the manifesto touched directly on popular grievances and presented the Yorkists as the solution. It worked. When the Yorkists disembarked on 26 June 1460, large and apparently overwhelming numbers turned out for them in Kent, at Canterbury, and then at London, where the cannons fired from the Tower into the City confirmed to Londoners that it was the regime that was their enemy. The Yorkists seized the capital, the machinery of government, and strove also to win over to their cause the moral authority of the Church.

Meantime the king was in the Midlands, wondering what to do. The evidence of the signed bills and council warrants from March to June 1460, as in 1456–7, is of decisions being made by a king with decided opinions on the advice of the council at Westminster, without any reference to the queen.[53] If Cade's raising of Kent and Sussex back in 1450 was formidable, how much more so it would have been if stiffened by hundreds of the Calais garrison, led by politically and militarily experienced magnates, and enjoying the sympathetic support of reputable, if naïve, bishops and even the papal nuncio?

A lack of military leadership for the Crown may have mattered at this juncture. York, Salisbury, Warwick and the captains in Calais, all key commanders, were on the other side. Somerset, Rivers and his son, and some barons in the Tower, were neutralized. It was therefore the Yorkists, once again, who took the military initiative. The army that Warwick led northwards from London had a core of Calais veterans, at most a handful of retainers, and a huge host of commons that one chronicler estimated at 60,000 or even 160,000 strong. Although obviously an overstatement, the inflated numbers make the point that the 'host' was exceedingly large and supposedly three times more numerous than King Henry's.[54] However, this time all the insurgents were prepared to fight against the king and to brave the penalties of treason. That they took with them bishops, whose mediation was declined, gave them the moral authority that was lacking in 1459. The forces that confronted at Northampton, nevertheless, were substantial. Buckingham, Shrewsbury, Beaumont and Egremont were all there.[55] Queen Margaret herself was elsewhere. Although unlucky in the weather that made their ordnance unusable, an army of aristocratic retainers and tenants in an entrenched defensive position was a formidable obstacle over which the Yorkists certainly could not guarantee victory. As in 1455, they sought to negotiate access to, and to coerce, the king, thus claiming any consequent bloodshed was not their fault. Actually, of course, they sought nothing less than a complete capitulation – the reversal of their condemnation in 1459 and control of the government – which Buckingham, again the king's front man, declined. Already attainted traitors, the Yorkists were not deterred from attacking when the king's banner was displayed.

The Lancastrians had entrenched themselves in a strong defensive position backing on the River Nene near Northampton that should have been secure against direct attack. That they nevertheless lost the Battle of Northampton on 10 July 1460 was not due to a fair trial of strength, but to treachery, as Edmund, Lord Grey of Ruthin, on the royalist left wing welcomed the Yorkists over the barricades. Their flank turned and, their retreat barred by the river, the royal army was enveloped. Again, it was the Yorkists who shed the blood and murdered the principal royalist commanders. Shrewsbury and Beaumont were eliminated, together with the Nevilles' enemy Egremont, and Buckingham, 'a great lord of the royal blood', who could never be named as an evil counsellor, but who was nevertheless the substance and perhaps the steel within the ruling regime. Henry was captured once again.[56]

Here surely was the opportunity for a change of king and dynasty, if that was the plan, but instead there are remarkable resemblances to what had happened after First St Albans in 1455. The Yorkist earls denied any treason, intended or committed, and asserted that the blood that they had shed was necessary in the public interest. The formal assurances of loyalty of 1455 were repeated, including expressions of the humblest obeisance, renewed oaths of allegiance, public processions and singing of the *Te Deum*. There was public rejoicing at the victory of Northampton and the destruction of the king's 'evil councillors'. As in 1450, the murder, judicial or otherwise, of Lord Scales and other 'traitors' who had garrisoned the Tower for the king was highly popular.[57]

Although the king had to appear at liberty, housed at first in the bishop of London's palace in the City, and actually did initial a few warrants over the next months, his patronage was at the disposal of the Yorkists. They installed a new treasurer in Viscount Bourchier (again) and a new chancellor and a new chamberlain of the household in Warwick's brothers George, Bishop of Exeter, and John, shortly to be Baron Montagu. Vengeance was wreaked on those lawyers who had devised their attainder. Apparently the king did as the Yorkists wished.[58] As in 1455, a new Parliament was convened on 7 October 1460, not to replicate the specious *Parliamentary Pardon* – for the Yorkists felt they needed no justification – nor to repeal the act of attainder of 1459, but brusquely to revoke the whole *Devils Parliament* – a better attended assembly – and all its acts. This was a far more complete, absolute and indeed contemptuous repudiation of the past judgements of the majority than had been the more piecemeal and measured reversal of the penalties for the participants at Dartford in 1454–6.

Yet the Yorkists' appeal to arms, their assault on the king, their shedding of blood and elimination of five further peers to add to the three of 1455, was profoundly shocking, especially perhaps to the Lords. Hence, perhaps, far fewer noblemen attended the Parliament of 1460 than in 1455–6, albeit rather more peers were committed Yorkists in 1460 than hitherto. That a comprehensive programme of reform was envisaged is suggested by a proviso of exemption that was sought from the expected act of resumption.[59] All that was needed to complete the formal transfer of power was a *Third Protectorate*. Here was an opportunity to implement the programme of 1455–6 on a sounder basis of noble and popular support. Thus far what had happened in 1460, however bloody, was not strikingly different from the St Albans coup of 1455. But it remained strictly limited and impermanent.

TRIGGERS

What made 1460 different from 1455 were two interconnected factors. Those who were defeated at Northampton or were merely absent now refused to accept the verdict of battle. Contributory to their decision was the first factor: Richard, Duke of York's claim to the Crown, which moved the whole debate from the arguably legitimate presentation of grievances by force to an avowedly treasonable dynastic revolution. It was a crucial raising of the stakes and an elevation of domestic disagreements to a much higher and more dangerous plane. By ascending the throne, York could make the Yorkist coup complete and permanent and could forever exclude his rivals from power. Obviously, York had been aware since childhood of his descent via the Mortimers to Lionel, Duke of Clarence, the second son of Edward III who was senior to the third son and Lancastrian patriarch John of Gaunt, Duke of Lancaster. Arguably, this offered him an alternative title to the Crown potentially superior to his own descent in the male line from Edward III's fourth son Edmund, Duke of York. His claim was stridently advanced both in the Latin chronicle of Wigmore Abbey and the Clare Roll of c.1456.[60] The alternative line of descent was commonly included in the de luxe royal pedigrees that were being published commercially in London.[61] Significant historical research on his behalf had been undertaken on the pedigrees both of York and Lancaster, for example to establish the precise dates of birth of Edward I (17 June 1239) and his brother Edmund, Earl of Lancaster (16 January 1245), thus discounting any Lancastrian argument that Edmund had been the older of the two, and to rule out descendants of other lines. Given the amount of work involved, it is scarcely conceivable that John Hardyng had not already written much of the *Second Version* of his *Chronicle*. So, too, surely had the composers of other Yorkist tracts – the *Prophetic History of Britain*, the *Brief Treatise* and York's annotated pedigree.[62] Whilst in exile, but more probably earlier, clearly York was aspiring to the Crown of England. Whether his principal allies realized or consented is much less certain.

Increasingly, historians have argued that, when Warwick visited York in Ireland in 1460, the two must already have planned for a change of dynasties and of kings. After York's landing in North Wales, it has been argued, Warwick cannot have been unaware that York was claiming the throne.[63] Yet the Yorkist manifestos of 1460 still professed their loyalty to Henry VI.[64] This proved not to be just a ploy when victory placed the king again in their power. It appears that none of these sectors of Yorkist support – neither the London elite and mob, the populace of the South-East, the pope's agent Coppini and the bishops, nor even the Lords – were prepared to take the logical next step and make the revolution complete, by substituting a Yorkist king for the Lancastrian Henry VI. Warwick was popular. York, if the Burgundian historian Jehan de Waurin is to be believed, was not, perhaps because he wanted to usurp the throne.[65] The formal protestations of loyalty after Northampton actually made a change of allegiance more difficult. Henry's fault was not tyranny, but weakness. If usurpation had been their original object, the Nevilles had quickly found that it was unacceptable to most of their supporters and had changed their minds.

It remains possible that York's usurpation was not the agreed plan, but York's own opportunist extemporization. As in 1450 and 1452, Duke Richard had waited until victory had been achieved before proceeding to London. Again landing in North Wales (8–9 September 1460), he once again processed in triumph, this time and differently donning the arms of England unquartered and the livery of his maternal ancestor Lionel, Duke of Clarence. He drafted indentures of retainer that did not reserve allegiance to the king.[66] To all intents and purposes and perhaps overtly, York had renounced his allegiance, but he had not proclaimed himself as king. He did, however, plan to be crowned on 13 October. Again he arrived late at Parliament. Entering the parliament chamber, he seated himself on the royal throne and moved into the king's apartments, displacing King Henry. These were serious misjudgements. Instead of hailing him as the king, Archbishop Bourchier asked tentatively whether he wished to see the king. Although probably few in numbers, the Lords vetoed York's coronation. Mere military ascendancy, York discovered, could not cause the Lords, even the Yorkist earls, to abandon their allegiance to the king, nor the respect that was due to him.[67] Perhaps the churchmen, probably a majority of the Lords, were crucial here. Even the Nevilles did not back York. There was a blazing row. The immediate accession of York was unattainable.

How different were the circumstances of 1460 from 1399! Then it was the pretender Henry of Bolingbroke who was in control of the government and was king. Then the consent of King Richard to his abdication was achieved in private and probably indeed fabricated. In 1460, in contrast, Henry was not shut away, was asked his views, and was able, very publicly, to withhold his agreement. Moreover, in 1399 the victor was militarily ascendant over the whole political elite assembled in the Lords, whereas in 1460 not just Queen Margaret and Prince Edward, but the Lancastrian royal dukes of Exeter and Somerset, the king's half-brother Pembroke, and also the earls of Devon, Northumberland, Westmorland and Wiltshire were all absent from Parliament, did not consent to its acts, and could not be regarded as bound by them. The process could not be unanimous, nor as carefully orchestrated and controlled as in 1399.

Yet York had the military might on the spot. Once again he insisted on forcing the issue. On 16 October 1460 he presented his claim to the House of Lords in the form of an annotated pedigree, much like those presented in other peerage cases, which he had prepared in advance to justify his accession, but which had now to be submitted to adjudication. The Lords sought direction from King Henry, hoping for a clear rebuttal, which it seems likely would have been decisive. At this stage Henry must have been acting as a free agent, since he did not concede the case as York surely desired, but rather weakly referred the matter back, albeit asking the Lords to find arguments against. They passed this hot potato to the judges, who passed it back, then to the serjeants-at-law, who also returned it, whilst York firmly pushed down the arguments that the Lords devised and insisted on a verdict. If the Crown was governed by primogeniture, as York assumed but never demonstrated, Parliament's entails on the Lancastrians in tail male and the obligations of obedience to the king that resulted were alike invalid. It may have been important here that almost all the senior nobility who held their titles in tail male, like the Lancastrian kings, were absent or already dead. Those present were predominantly barons for whom female inheritance was normal. Anyway, the peers who were there concluded that York's claim could not be defeated. But they still refused to depose Henry VI. Indeed, the Yorkists did not trust Parliament to approve their settlement – perhaps doubting the Commons rather than the Lords – for the *Accord* (like the *Parliamentary Pardon* of 1455) was not actually made into an act of Parliament and some aspects may never have enjoyed majority support.

The outcome, therefore, was that York and his sons Edward and Edmund were to supplant Prince Edward as heir, and York was to rule as heir presumptive. Henceforth he was sacred and protected by the treason laws, but he was not yet a formal protector. Formally, Henry was to continue to reign. York now had the permanent and legitimate hold on government that he had sought since 1450. King Henry agreed to this *Accord*, which he swore to observe.[68] Fearful perhaps that York might seek to advance his succession, most probably by forcing the king to abdicate, the Lords required him to swear that he would not try to injure the king or deprive him of his 'freedom [of action] or liberty'.[69]

That this had real meaning is suggested by some of the provisos of exemption, such as that excluding the king's enfeoffments from the appropriation of the duchy of Lancaster and reserving 'the king's prerogative and power royal'.[70] In the meantime, York and his sons were allocated the revenues of the Prince of Wales, Prince Edward being excluded not just from the line of succession but from all his hereditary expectations. His exclusion may have been eased by allegations of bastardy,[71] though these were never made official and were anyway inadmissible in English law.

If the *Loveday* of 1458 was one kind of compromise that was designed to heal wounds and put the past behind everyone, to enable King Henry to rule and to restore the Yorkists as faithful subjects, the *Accord* of November 1460 was another kind of compromise that gave York the power and prestige that he craved, that promised an end to his disruption of government, that allayed the consciences of faithful subjects, and that permitted King Henry to eke out his days as a powerless regal figurehead. Obviously, it granted York less than he had first sought, but more than the Lords had initially conceded. However, it was a compromise cobbled together *amongst* York's supporters, a minority of the peerage, not between him and his opponents, whose interests were not considered and who lost out completely. If not yet a dynastic revolution nor a usurpation, that was what it betokened. The *Accord* therefore went far beyond what York's absent opponents were prepared to accept.

York had overcome opposition before. Not everyone had supported the *First Protectorate* in 1454, yet neither Exeter nor the Percies had been able to defy the Lord Protector's legitimate royal authority. Brute force had prevailed at First St Albans, yet afterwards the Lords had been prepared to accept York's leadership up to a point – there had been no counter-strike – and the rival westcountry peers had then again bowed to him as Lord Protector. In 1460 the opposition was much more determined. Blood had once again been shed. Neither the queen nor the prince and heir apparent were in Yorkist power. Obviously the disinheritance of her son was unacceptable to Queen Margaret. Nothing at all had been reserved to him, not even the duchy of Lancaster. The deaths of Buckingham and Shrewsbury and the marooning of Somerset at Guines may now have forced her for the first time to take the political lead. 'With Henry's captivity she emerged as the acknowledged and avowed leader of a genuine Lancastrian party'.[72] Certainly it is now for the first time that her political actions can be distinguished in the records from those of others. Moreover, the *Accord* overrode the rights of the Lancastrian royal dukes of Exeter and Somerset to the Crown as heirs in reversion to the House of

Lancaster and drove them into alliance with Margaret. Exeter, son-in-law to York and repeatedly disciplined, certainly did not belong to some court party.

Regardless of what Parliament had decreed, most peers still rallied to the ruling house. Quite what they were going to do about it was unclear: perhaps passive resistance. Margaret was a political leader rather than a general. She seems to have doubted that she could raise sufficient military support in England and hence sought it abroad. This was the first of many times that contending actors invited the intervention of foreign allies. Margaret's own concessions of English possessions to the French and Scots gave priority to her faction over national interests. Apart from confirming Yorkist charges of collusion with aliens and feeding Yorkist propaganda, it brought her no significant reinforcements at this stage and did not affect the outcome of the *First War*.

From immediately after the Battle of Northampton, there were disturbances in the North, by 24 August associated with the Earl of Northumberland and his Percy retainers, who ignored the repeated orders and summonses of the new government.[73] Recalcitrance, however, is not war and for five months no military strike was launched to avenge or reverse the battle. It was conceivable that some sort of compromise with the Yorkists was possible that kept the Lancastrian dynasty on the throne and allowed York to become chief councillor. But the *Accord* was itself a dynastic revolution: it presumed the replacement of the ruling dynasty by York and his heirs. There could be no negotiation about that. The *Accord* decisively had raised the stakes and made some sort of conflict inevitable. The majority of lay peers, who had never accepted it, now actively rejected it. They now had a comprehensible and defensible cause to fight for. Not support for maligned evil councillors and an unsuccessful regime, but rather allegiance to the universally recognized king, to his queen, to his legitimate heir – to whom all had pledged their faith several times, most recently less than a year ago – and to the Lancastrian dynasty, and *against* those who had revealed themselves as traitors. Hence the *Accord* was not a settlement, but a cause for war. Gradually the Lancastrians regrouped. After many vicissitudes, the queen and Prince Edward assembled an army in the North. The Duke of Somerset and Earl of Devon marched their forces from the West Country to join her.[74] The earls of Pembroke and Wiltshire recruited in Wales. The new regime may have controlled London, the Home Counties, East Anglia and the East Midlands. Its hold on the West Country, Wales, the West and North Midlands, and the North was imperfect. For the first time, there was a geographical zoning between adherents of one side and another. Some who later professed themselves to be Yorkists, such as the northerners

Lord FitzHugh and Lord Greystoke, found themselves on the wrong side of the line. As in 1459, Queen Margaret looked abroad for support, this time to Scotland, but it was to be English resources that determined the result.

To impose Yorkist rule on the provinces, York's eldest son Edward, Earl of March, was sent to York's marcher estates, whilst York himself, his second son Edmund, Earl of Rutland, and Salisbury went northwards. They still spoke in the king's name. Doubtless York and Salisbury expected resistance to melt away and to encounter the same respect and subservience to their established authority as in 1454 and 1455. This time, after all, York had been declared heir to the throne, to be sacred and protected by the law of treason by Parliament, and hence resisters to him now became rebels and traitors.[75] These acts were rejected by many as illegitimate. Instead, York and Salisbury found themselves faced not by a faction, nor by rioters who were fundamentally loyal and respectful to royal authority, but by a coalition of magnates, who were ranged behind the queen and rightful heir and ideologically opposed to them, and who were prepared not only to take the offensive but also to apply to York himself the ruthless elimination of opponents pioneered by the Yorkists. Hence York and Salisbury found themselves isolated at York's little castle at Sandal in South Yorkshire. When they emerged, they were defeated on 30 December 1460 at the Battle of Wakefield. York, Salisbury and their sons the Earl of Rutland and Sir Thomas Neville were all killed. This was revenge for the deaths at St Albans, Northampton and in the Percy–Neville feud. Salisbury was captured and executed next day not by the Lancastrians but by William Plumpton[76] and other northerners who hated him: obviously not his own Richmondshire retainers. Apparently the acute slump in the North had not set the commons against the Crown.

Margaret meantime was in Scotland. Taken with her willingness to treat with the Scots and even to concede Berwick for Scottish support against the Yorkists, a polarization had occurred that had regional, popular and even international dimensions. Shadowy though it was, Margaret of Anjou was presiding over a rival shadowy government at York with its own council and council minutes.[77]

The Battle of Wakefield had been another decisive moment. It raised the stakes yet further. Hitherto only the Yorkists had deliberately eliminated their opponents. From Wakefield on, every victorious side systematically despatched any opposing leaders who fell into their hands, thus making the results more decisive – *they* would never fight again – and adding yet more bitterness and lust for revenge to the causes for conflict. It revealed that the Lancastrians had a constituency of committed supporters sufficient to contest the *Accord* and the Crown. On very limited evidence, they appear to have enjoyed popular support in parts of the North. Wakefield clarified what the queen and her allies should do. They were emboldened to complete the task by recovering control by force of King Henry, London and the government. Back from Scotland, Queen Margaret and her Lancastrian supporters assembled a large army in Yorkshire and marched slowly southwards, reaching St Albans in Hertfordshire on 17 February 1461.

Obviously the defeat at Wakefield and the deaths of both York and Salisbury were unexpected disasters for the Yorkist cause. Secure in their possession both of London and the king, however, the Yorkist regime in London headed by Warwick was determined to resist. Probably it expected reprisals and certainly seems not to have been interested in negotiation. Nonetheless, the City corporation continued to back the Yorkists. Two battles then changed the position. The queen's forces defeated Warwick at the Second Battle of St Albans on 17 February 1461, recaptured the king – thus assuring their cause of legitimacy – and threatened London. Warwick did not withdraw into the City, which probably he thought could not be effectively defended, but instead retired westwards, most probably to meet up with the deceased York's eldest son Edward, Earl of March, now Duke of York. However, the opportunity to make Second St Albans decisive was missed. Margaret hoped to negotiate her way into London rather than attack it and was prepared to spend time doing so. The City corporation recognized what appeared to be reality and were prepared to do business with her. However, the mob were not and she was refused access to the capital. The identification of the Yorkists with reform was popular with them and they refused to temporize.[78] Fear of the wild northerners had been skilfully fostered by Yorkist propaganda.[79] Meantime, Edward, Duke of York, had fought the Welsh Lancastrians at Mortimer's Cross near Ludlow on 2–3 February. Had he failed, history would have been very different. However, he won, thus giving himself both the military reputation and apparent divine approval that he needed, and unlike the queen he was able to enter London. The Lancastrians under Queen Margaret retreated to the North. The parallel with Bonnie Prince Charlie's retreat from Derby in the '45 is obvious.

At this point, again, there was scope for decision. With king, queen and prince in their hands, the only possible stance for the Lancastrians was on their established hereditary right to rule. There was scope for some concessions to their foes where possible, especially to the young Duke of York. But the Yorkists had a real choice. Now they had lost possession of King Henry, they could not take a stand on the *Accord*, which had completely failed. They could negotiate away the *Accord* in return for immunity for themselves as reconciled subjects of Henry VI. Edward Duke of York, could thereby have saved his duchy. Another strategy, which offered them much more but at much higher risks, was to convert Edward Duke of York into their king – to complete the dynastic revolution. Doubtless the Yorkists still wanted revenge for the deaths at Wakefield and feared for themselves in the longer term whatever settlement they had agreed. Doubtless they thought their own retainers, the Calais garrison and popular support offered a sporting chance of victory. The City also had committed itself too far to be confident about pulling back and now contributed the money that it had consistently denied King Henry. It was this option that the Yorkists selected. It was the final escalation. There could only be one king – Henry VI or Edward IV – and henceforth the politically committed had to choose whether to be Lancastrians or Yorkists.

The inevitable sequel was a fight to the death. King Edward IV dated his reign from 4 March 1461. The justification for proceeding at once to a new king that was presented was that Henry VI had broken the *Accord* by being captured:[80] an argument capable of convincing only those already convinced, but relieving them in their own minds of the stain of treason. Although Edward IV was elected by a faction, the mere handful of peers committed to the Yorkist cause, formal processes of inauguration were devised that aped those of normal accessions and of Henry IV in 1399, and gave the appearance of legitimacy. There was a carefully staged acclamation and ceremonies at Westminster Abbey and Westminster Hall. These were of value primarily to persuade their own supporters of the legitimacy of their actions and anybody uncommitted. The new king's proclamation renewed the denunciations of Lancastrianism for the loss of France, decay of trade, lack of governance and partial justice. The most savage slanders against Margaret and her son Prince Edward were invoked to make Yorkist propaganda effective, to deter people from supporting Henry VI and to persuade them to back the Yorkists.

The Yorkshire Battle of Towton on 29 March 1461 was the decisive trial of strength between the supporters of the two kings and their two dynasties. There is general agreement that it was the biggest battle of the Wars of the Roses, between two evenly matched armies, although little is known or can be known about the detailed composition. Although the Yorkists mustered fewer peers, at most seven, they did include the retinues of the three greatest magnates left following the deaths of Buckingham and Shrewsbury – York, Norfolk and Warwick – and presumably large numbers of 'the people' from the

South. There was a small contingent of Burgundian handgunners. Both sides included members of the Calais garrison. Henry VI enjoyed more general support among the political elite, at least 19 peers – perhaps half those able to bear arms – amongst them Somerset, Exeter, Devon, Wiltshire, and Hungerford who came from the distant West Country. They had brought some of their retainers with them, the Westcountrymen surely diminished by desertions, but the Lancastrian army comprised primarily northerners: not, however, the Nevilles' men of Richmondshire. Northumberland, the Nevilles of Raby, Cliffords, Dacres, Scropes, indeed almost all the northern peers were on their side.[81] On the defensive and isolated in the North, the Lancastrians had mobilized a mere fraction of the residual allegiance due to a king who had reigned for almost forty years. The Yorkists forced the passage of the Aire at Ferrybridge on 28 March and the full-scale engagement followed on the 29th. The Battle of Towton was a hard slog that lasted several hours, ebbed, flowed and could have gone either way. At first the Lancastrians had the upper hand, but the late arrival of Yorkist reinforcements reversed the trend and resulted in a major Yorkist victory and mass slaughter of the Lancastrian leadership. The Battle of Towton proved in due course to be decisive: although the Lancastrian royal family escaped, the *First War* had been won by the Yorkists.

PART III
WHY THE WARS RECURRED

Pedigree 4 The House of York 1461–83

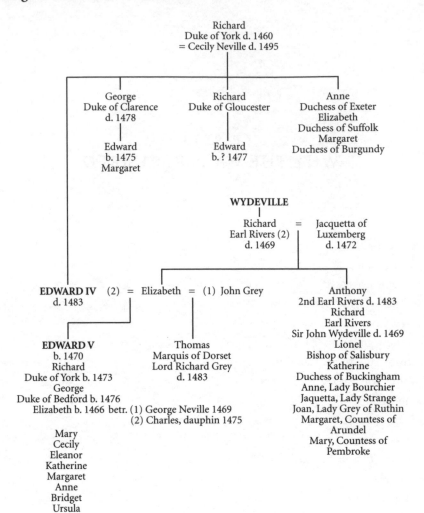

Richard
Duke of York d. 1460
= Cecily Neville d. 1495

George
Duke of Clarence
d. 1478

Richard
Duke of Gloucester

Anne
Duchess of Exeter
Elizabeth
Duchess of Suffolk
Margaret
Duchess of Burgundy

Edward
b. 1475
Margaret

Edward
b. ? 1477

WYDEVILLE

Richard   =   Jacquetta of
Earl Rivers (2)   Luxemberg
d. 1469   d. 1472

EDWARD IV   (2) = Elizabeth = (1) John Grey
d. 1483

Anthony
2nd Earl Rivers d. 1483
Richard
Earl Rivers
Sir John Wydeville d. 1469

EDWARD V
b. 1470
Richard
Duke of York b. 1473
George
Duke of Bedford b. 1476
Elizabeth b. 1466 betr. (1) George Neville 1469
                          (2) Charles, dauphin 1475

Thomas
Marquis of Dorset
Lord Richard Grey
d. 1483

Lionel
Bishop of Salisbury
Katherine
Duchess of Buckingham
Anne, Lady Bourchier
Jaquetta, Lady Strange
Joan, Lady Grey of Ruthin
Margaret, Countess of
Arundel
Mary, Countess of
Pembroke

Mary
Cecily
Eleanor
Katherine
Margaret
Anne
Bridget
Ursula

CHAPTER 10

WOUNDS UNHEALED 1461–9[1]

The Battle of Towton was a decisive victory. The Lancastrian army was destroyed. It proved impossible to put another of equivalent strength into the field. Towton gave the Yorkists untrammelled control of the whole kingdom bar the extreme peripheries – the Scottish borders, north-western Wales and Jersey. Civil war ceased everywhere else. There was peace throughout the realm. The new government sought through every means available to promulgate its right to rule to all its subjects and to secure their compliance, obedience and loyalty. For most people almost everywhere in 1461–70, the Yorkist dynasty established itself as a permanent fixture. The War of the Roses was over. There was no reason to expect either the *Second* or *Third Wars*.

Several fundamental causes of conflict remained. The *Great Slump* had yet to reach its nadir and any government therefore remained impoverished and weak. Having once been invited into politics, the people insisted on participating in future. Their interests (which they styled the common good) were symbolized especially by no taxation, resumption and reform. These remained the touchstones for good governance and convincing reasons for public intervention in national politics. Unreasonable expectations had been aroused, for every government of this era was impoverished and weak. The people expected especially that kings would live of their own, which was impossible, and that they would rule with the counsel of great lords of royal blood rather than those most devoted and most useful to them, which was unrealistic. Royal patronage was an essential cement for every regime and a vital instrument of political management, yet it was popularly characterized as illicit rewards for the covetous and corrupt. (The 2009 furore over MPs expenses, over-generous but also essential, is a modern parallel.) Warwick, a demagogue much more skilful than York, had learnt how to address the commons, how to touch the right buttons, how to mobilize them and how to direct them effectively, perhaps genuinely in their own interests. France and Burgundy increasingly intervened in English affairs, not to conquer England as in 1066, but rather to destabilize English regimes, to emasculate English foreign policy, prevent English expansion in France, and to strike at one another.

The new Yorkist regime faced significant threats therefore, which however it successfully defeated. Why, then, was it overthrown during the *Second War* in 1470 and twice more during the *Third War* in 1483 and 1485? Because in each case the ruling faction divided, as first Warwick from 1469 and then Edward IV's youngest brother Richard, strove to take the control. These contests are examined below: first Edward IV's disastrous Wydeville marriage that propelled Warwick into opposition (in chapter 11), and then Richard III's usurpation and overthrow (in chapter 12). Before them, however, this chapter treats Edward's struggle with irreconcilable Lancastrians in 1461–9 and his victory over them.

By 1461 force had become a normal and acceptable practice of English politics. Protagonists of the still living and until 1465 still free Henry VI refused to accept the Yorkist victory and continued the struggle. Even after Henry's death in 1471, until at least 1525 there were always rival claims to the throne to justify rebellion against the current monarch and his overthrow. Other great and ostensibly loyal noblemen, other overmighty subjects after York, were prepared to coerce the king, even to attack the king, and to turn to force at once. The Crown of England was to become a legitimate aspiration and usurpation a legitimate career option. Warwick and Clarence took only six months in 1469–70 – and perhaps much less, in 1469 itself – to move from constraining a reigning king to supplanting him. Changing the king and dynasty ceased to be the last resort: for Richard III, it was the first resort.[2] The whole political process, from protest and dissent to usurpation and revolution, was accelerated. Richard III took a few weeks to reach the usurpation that took his father York so haltingly and reluctantly a decade to achieve. Governments could rely less on the automatic support of all subjects and thus became ever easier to overthrow. After 1485 first the people and then the great powers withdrew from English politics and left it to the politicians.

For politics had become ever more perilous. For those identified as enemies of the people and the common good, the risks were to be denounced as traitors and condemned to violent death. Eliminating political rivals was an efficient way to achieve and to secure political power. Attainder and execution, which in 1459 were introduced so reluctantly, applied so sparingly, and were so deplored, were to become commonplace. They came to be employed whole-sale, and often indeed were reversed almost casually. Political choices became more momentous, potentially both more rewarding and more disastrous, the penalties became ever more lethal and indeed ruinous for whole families. No wonder that for John Lord Mountjoy, in 1485 politics had become simply too dangerous.[3]

Yet further conflict was not inevitable. If the chances of successful insurrection were much improved and the recipe of 1460-1 was several times replicated, yet there still needed to be preconditions and particular justifications for each government or dynasty to be overthrown. Repeated disappointments had been needed in 1450-61 to fuel the popular outrage that swept away Henry VI's government. Only one further popular explosion was to succeed. The easier option, the noble *coup d'état*, remained feasible. And battles were still won in the field, where surprise, professionalism, quality and generalship all counted for so much. It is not obvious that the victors of 1471, 1483 or even 1485 represented the public will, which of course is not easy to measure now.

EDWARD IV's FIRST REIGN 1461-70

Sadly, Edward IV's *First Reign* failed to meet the expectations of the commons and was not unchallenged, yet a renewal of full-scale civil war was far from inevitable. For that a catalyst was necessary, eventually provided by Warwick in 1469.

In 1461 Edward's new regime had offered fresh hope for the future and remedies to the poor governance of the recent past. The rulers were neither associated with past failures nor tarnished by them. A clean sweep had been made of Henry VI's household and evil councillors. Instead, there was now a new king of a new dynasty. Much was made of the 'Rose of Rouen' – a young, handsome and vigorous king who was both a military hero and possessed all the people skills that Henry VI had so conspicuously lacked. Edward IV was genuinely popular and was celebrated in verse.[4] He was backed besides by capable men – four Nevilles and the two Bourchier brothers – who knew what they wanted and how to govern. The new regime had a direction to it: it was a new beginning and offered new hope. The evil counsel, lack of governance, the local disorders and feuds, economic difficulties and foreign humiliations were all relegated to the past as 62 years of Lancastrian misrule were erased from the record and the Yorkist reform programme was implemented.[5]

The revolution of 1461 had overturned an established dynasty and a long-reigning king who had enjoyed the residual support of most subjects. It was settled militarily on a field of battle that might have gone either way. What made it possible were the bastard feudal retinues of the greatest magnates, foreign resources in the shape of the professional Calais garrison, mass support in London and the South, and a dynastic case that were combined against an enfeebled Crown and those who supported the incumbent monarch, only a minority of whom were at the battle. Most of the committed Lancastrian nobility were slain at or after the Battle of Towton, were dispossessed, duly mopped up in the next few years, or fled into exile. Many like the Wydevilles accepted that their cause was irretrievably lost, submitted, accommodated themselves to the new regime, and even prospered under it. So indeed did the gentry of the shires, town councils, and rulers everywhere. But not all. The Lancastrian royal family survived and remained at liberty, albeit displaced from country to country. Within the realm also significant individuals declined to accept the usurpation as permanent and hankered after the return of Henry VI. New plots and handfuls of identifiable plotters emerged throughout the next decade, alarming the regime, dividing it, and destabilizing what ought to have been a united realm. The change of dynasty was never clearcut or absolute. The House of York always faced a rival with claims to legitimacy that were cogently argued, particularly by Sir John Fortescue, and publicized.

Many hopes engendered by the new regime were disappointed. The slaughter at Towton resolved the rivalry of York and Lancaster and terminated many private quarrels, but it did not address either the economic slump or government finances, deliver the reform that the populace expected, nor did it restore national pride. High expectations were raised that the Yorkists had promised to fulfil, but did not and indeed could not. To achieve these objectives, insofar as they were achievable, required much more than military victory. The opportunities were missed as Edward IV ruled much like other medieval kings. The new regime was to prove a disappointment and its accession came even to be regarded as a mistake. Both the *Warkworth Chronicle* and the *Vale Chronicle* in the 1470s testify in retrospect to the numerous pinpricks that fed popular dissatisfaction in Edward's *First Reign*.[6] Preconditions of conflict and grumbling discontent persisted and indeed revived, but these alone were insufficient basis for further civil strife. New tensions and new leaders arose that enabled conflict to resume, not just once in 1469–71, but a second time, in 1483.

DISCONTENT AND DISILLUSION

'These three harrys have occupied and kept the said crown of England from the rightful heirs these 63 (*recte* 62) years.'[7] So argued the Yorkists, who ascribed all that was so conspicuously wrong with the 1450s to the Lancastrian usurpers. All those who resisted the new regime were traitors, as the Yorkists borrowed the king's argument of the Lancastrian *Devils Parliament*. Many more were attainted and had their possessions confiscated than in 1459. Sixty-two years of history since 1399 could not so easily be obliterated. Lancastrian creations of peers, charters to boroughs, and acts of Parliament had to be accepted and confirmed. Much time at the first Yorkist session of Parliament in 1461 was spent squaring the circle, determining how the overthrow of the previous illegitimate regime could be accommodated with the preservation of so much of its legacy. The royal family and many officials were changed, but not everyone. The clerks in the great offices of state and the judges had to be retained. The Yorkists could not remain a regime comprised purely of a few thousand of their own committed partisans. Their faction had to be extended, ideally to embrace the whole nation. And whatever the lip service, the political system did not change and its new masters had no notion or desire to govern it differently. The professional meritocracy advocated by the Lancastrian Sir John Fortescue was not seriously considered and was anyway politically impractical. The power brokers behind the revolution and the successful War took their ascendancy in peacetime as their reward.

Edward IV had many qualities desirable in a medieval king. Very tall, imposing, militarily effective, brought up as a conventional aristocrat and with aristocratic tastes, he was at one with his nobility, demanded their respect, could indeed browbeat them and impose his will on them. Edward could speak in public and could refuse requests. Charming, articulate and affable, he was able both to win over and to persuade. He could make up his mind, initiate actions, and at times engage in sustained administration and arduous interviewing campaigns. Edward knew whom he trusted, rewarded them, and was not afraid to withdraw his patronage from those who failed to perform. Initially the new king rewarded his own family and those who had made him king: those who were already Yorkists. They amassed a swathe of offices in the royal household and provinces from which Lancastrians were comprehensively purged. Edward's brothers became royal dukes, his uncle Henry Bourchier both Earl of Essex and Lord Treasurer, his friend William Hastings chamberlain of his household and a baron. Edward was exceptionally generous to his brothers and in-laws: in 1467 he set his brother Clarence's expectations at £3,733 6s 8d, well above the 2,000 marks (£1,333 6s. 8d.) that was the qualifying level for previous dukes, and he found (or created) earls for all the sisters of his queen (Elizabeth Wydeville), whom he married in 1464 – two wholly new earls and three partly endowed with forfeited properties.[8] Above all, his Neville cousins were allowed to add ever more titles, lands and offices to those they already held. He extended the regime from a mere faction, in part through the marriages that he had arranged through his consort's Wydeville sisters and son that bound the great houses of Arundel, Bourchier, Grey of Ruthin, Herbert, Holland and Stafford more closely to the Crown. By the late 1460s Edward presided over a much more broadly based regime, albeit one in which the most ambitious parvenus eagerly sought advancement at the expense especially – and dangerously – of the Nevilles.

There was mass production of the Yorkist propaganda that presented Edward IV's title as superior and unquestioned. His *Brief Treatise* and the varied types of popular rolls are striking examples.[9] His Yorkist myth eclipsed any Lancastrian counterpart. However, the *First War* had not been primarily waged over dynastic issues, but between protagonists (as they were perceived) of 'good' and 'bad' governance. In place of the corruption and ineptitude of Henry VI, the Yorkists offered wholesome and wholehearted reform – to implement the programme sought by Parliament and populace alike and that had been thwarted by the old regime. However, the Yorkist programme had not proposed a reformed system of government. It entailed rather the better management of the existing system by good rather than evil councillors, in short, themselves. Good governance certainly meant the maintenance of justice and law and order, which Edward IV personally took seriously, sitting symbolically in judgement himself and taking effective remedial action, in the form of judicial commissions wherever required and especially legislation. Edward was not strong enough and not willing to coerce the nobility, notably his brother-in-law John, Duke of Suffolk, for destroying the Pastons' manor house at Hellesdon (Suf.). If it is not really possible to demonstrate improved standards of order in the 1460s, there were noticeably fewer land wars than immediately before and after. Knyvet vs. Ogard, over Buckenham Castle in Norfolk, was an isolated instance that was successfully contained.[10] A revival of the Derbyshire feuds in 1468 that sucked in rival magnates was firmly quashed. Judicial sessions were held and the rival peers were bound over to keep the peace.[11] But resistance to the regime did persist.

On the international stage, tensions were relaxed. King Edward needed foreign recognition. Early in his reign he asserted his claims not just to England but to Normandy, Castile and France. If these were ever serious aspirations, his claim to Castile was shelved initially in the interests of better relations,[12] whereas in May 1468 King Edward committed himself by word of mouth in Parliament to renewing the English claim to France in his own person.[13] Alliances were forged with Brittany and Burgundy, the latter sealed in 1468 by the marriage of his sister Margaret of York to Charles the Bold, Duke of Burgundy. Parliament supported what was a genuinely popular venture, to invade France. It was an opportunity to reverse the national humiliations of 1449–53. However, no invasion followed, due both to internal and external impediments. The Treaty of Péronne in 1468 secured for Charles the Bold the Somme towns without recourse to war. By taking sides between the rival great powers of France and Burgundy, Edward unwisely made an active enemy of France. He gave King Louis XI grounds to strike at him to get at Burgundy and materially to aid his own Lancastrian enemies. That Margaret of York's marriage gave Burgundy stronger reasons to support him proved less immediately valuable.

The new king had no solution to the economic crisis, which was still largely shaped by external factors and especially the international bullion crisis. Although somewhat recovered after 1461, the economy remained depressed, and was to plunge into a further acute crisis at the end of the 1460s. Subjects in and out of Parliament opposed every financial burden from the government, however minor. The bullion famine was at its worst early in the 1460s. Burgundy, England's principal trading partner, banned English trade from 1464 to 1468. After recovering somewhat, wool exports receded to 30,000 sacks, whilst the lowest totals during the *Great Slump* were recorded for imports of wine and miscellaneous items in 1469–71.[14] Acute economic misery in the commercialized South-East could again be exploited by demagogues in 1469–71, when the people once again exploded in large numbers into politics, this time against a Yorkist government.

Similarly, Edward IV found no quick or effective cure for the bankruptcy of the Crown. Even the debts of the outgoing regime had to be honoured, and they hung over Edward IV for twenty years or so. The sum of £37,000 was due in wages to the Calais garrison, and mutiny loomed again. To these were added the accumulated debts of Edward's father York and the borrowings of the victors of 1461. King Edward did enjoy the enormous spoils of victory, regrettably incalculable. These included a vast number of moveables: the jewels, plate, furnishings, etcetera, of King Henry, Queen Margaret and Prince Edward, and the moveable wealth of the slain, defeated and eventually attainted, wherever they were. To these should be added the largely unrecorded fines or ransoms promised by those vanquished who were allowed to buy forgiveness, such as Sir William Plumpton who was bound over on £2,000 for good behaviour.[15] Whilst some of this money must have been pillaged or spirited away, most must have come into his hands. The royal lands were also greatly extended. Until 1464 Edward had no queen and until 1471 no prince to draw on the ancient Queen's lands, the principality of Wales, duchy of Cornwall, or earldom of Chester. Edward's own duchy of York and earldom of March were merged with the Crown. So, too, was the duchy of Lancaster shorn of all its Lancastrian en-feoffments. An act of resumption in 1461 placed in his hands all the patronage dispersed by his Lancastrian predecessors, including special items exempted in 1456 such as the honour of Richmond. Edward secured a host of wardships (for example, of the Duke of Buckingham and Earl of Shrewsbury) arising from the hostilities, and, above all, no fewer than 114 forfeitures of the Lancastrian nobility and gentry, including two dukes and four earls. Here, surely, was the means to pay off much of the accumulated debt, to re-endow the Crown and to enable it to live of its own, which was what subjects in and out of Parliament so stridently demanded.

Eventually Edward did re-endow the Crown,[16] but not in his *First Reign*. Little of York's own inheritance was available to him. Much more than the customary dower was needed for the Dowager-Duchess Cecily, now the king's mother, who survived until 1495, and much was assigned to the repayment of his father Duke Richard's debts.[17] Most of the offices and annuities that were resumed had to be reallocated to new officers and to members of his own household. The remaining estates were spoils of the victors. Edward did mean to exploit them for income, but in practice they were dispersed by 1464 in an orgy of giving, revis-ited and somewhat revised by acts of resumption in 1461, 1465 and 1467.[18] Rewarding those who had made him king and sharing out the spoils took prece-dence for Edward over the re-endowment of the Crown. Politically, it was imper-ative to win over all the Lancastrians he could, even Henry Beaufort, Duke of Somerset in 1462, despite the price of returning to them the estates that they had so recently forfeited, to the loss of loyal Yorkists who had received them as rewards. Inheritance was a right, to be honoured for heirs even if their fathers had offended. Many attainders were reversed: most were after 1471 or 1485.[19] King Edward could not endow his queen or brothers in 1464 without raiding the duchy of Lancaster and the appanage of his eldest son.[20] Any opportunity to re-endow the Crown and even to live of his own was missed. To break even without direct taxes, moreover, Edward had to exploit to the full any revenue-raising devices that did not require consent, all highly unpopular.

In a golden speech to Parliament in 1467, King Edward declared in person that 'I propose to live of my own and not to charge my subjects but in great and urgent causes'[21] – except when national emergencies demanded financial support. However, this was not how it appeared. Edward counted the customs that he had been voted for life among his ordinary revenues, yet he did not apply them to the keeping of the seas. He did appropriate much of them to the staplers, who took on the financing of Calais in 1466: a permanent solution to an intractable problem. He did resume grants as desired, but he reissued all of them and more. Like all kings, he had recourse to purveyance. He made extensive use of forced loans or benevolences to raise monies towards emergencies – and was slow, of course, to repay them. There were complaints in 1469 about impositions, charges, taxes, prests and inordinate charges 'upon their subjects and commons, to the great undoing and impoverishing of them, which caused all the people of this land to grudge'. When King Edward responded to the shortage of bullion by reforming (and devaluing) the coinage, he made a profit for himself supposedly of 3d a groat 'to the great harm of the common people'.[22] No doubt he had to act in this way, to eke out his limited resources. In 1464, moreover, he devoted taxes voted specifically for the Scottish wars, terminated by a long truce, to Calais. Again in 1468 Parliament voted two fifteenths and tenths for a foreign war that did not happen. Collection of these last taxes coincided with a sharp downturn in the economy.[23]

The obvious reason for such malfeasance was alleged once again to be the peculation of evil councillors who enriched themselves at public expense. And so in 1469 Edward was urged, as Henry VI had repeatedly been, to reserve enough lands to cover his ordinary charges without recourse to his 'true commons and subjects' except 'for great and grievous causes ... according to the promises that he made in his parliament openly by his own mouth unto us'.[24] Edward's unfulfilled promise was quoted back at him. Levying extraordinary taxes for two abortive wars was the clearest indicator to contemporaries of bad governance, of a failure to live of his own and up to his own promises. These were devastating and justifiable criticisms. It was in time of peace and in the economic abyss of 1470 that he collected the fifteenth intended for war and thereby further '[an]noyed the people' and confirmed their adverse assessment of him.[25]

If Edward was less hard up than Henry VI, it was because there was some recovery in customs revenues and he could borrow modestly in the City. Even so, each campaign in the North against Northumbrian rebels required a great financial effort. Recapturing Berwick was quite beyond his means. Hence in

1464 the 54-year truce with Scotland that left Berwick, shamefully, in Scottish hands.[26] Jersey was left unsubdued until 1468. Edward IV could not afford constantly to finance the keeping of the seas against potential Lancastrians. If not prostrate, his government remained financially weak and ill-prepared for any military threat.

LANCASTRIAN RESISTANCE

It was not at once apparent to those Lancastrians who had survived the Battle of Towton or who had missed it that Edward's victory was decisive. Only time revealed that. It was the experience of trying and failing, still more their inability seriously to challenge the new regime, that confirmed the result. However, that did not make the 1460s into an easy or stable decade for Edward IV.

Three of the elements that had undermined Henry VI and that had enabled the Yorkists to triumph in 1461 had Lancastrian counterparts that also destabilized Edward IV's *First Reign* (1461–70). The chronic financial weakness of the Crown has been mentioned. Secondly, there was always a dynastic rival. The Lancastrian cause continued to appeal to those who had personally served King Henry, sworn or owed allegiance to him, but it was also fostered by Lancastrian propaganda. Sir John Fortescue took up the debate that had not happened in 1460, to put the case for the Lancastrian male heirs and to refute that for the Yorkist heirs general. His works were distributed in England,[27] how widely we cannot tell. Henceforth Edward's foes could justify their resistance to themselves, even if they were just as liable to execution and forfeiture for treason if caught. Thirdly, the Lancastrian court was based abroad, out of reach, enjoyed limited subventions and other support from foreign powers, and was able to launch attacks on coastal areas as far afield as Northumbria, the Isle of Wight and North Wales. What mattered was that they were allowed safe havens, where they could plan their return to power, and assembled on several occasions the minimum numbers needed to penetrate any coastal defences. Never did France or Scotland commit enough resources to determine the outcome. It was useful to Louis XI in particular to destabilize the English realm in 1467–9, when Edward IV intended invading France.

There are several reasons why Lancastrian resistance failed. All governments always had an advantage, both in the short term until the insurgents built up strength – foreign backers never supplied whole armies – and in the longer term, when they could deploy the whole residue of loyal subjects. Whilst some traitors were executed, fined and/or dispossessed, and suspects were imprisoned or placed under sureties, yet Edward recognized that he could not depend forever on his victorious faction and sought to win over the majority or, at least, to make his regime acceptable to all. He was only too willing to receive into his allegiance numerous former opponents, such as Lords Rivers, Scales and Grey of Codnor who had actually fought on the Lancastrian side in 1460–1. Even Sir William Plumpton, who was involved in killing the king's father, was forgiven. Those attainted were spared, allowed to 'work themselves back', were partially and even completely restored, or even recruited to the Yorkist establishment. If Edward's trust was sometimes and signally misplaced, generally it worked. Often enough erstwhile Lancastrians were successfully detached from his foes.[28]

Because irreconcilable noblemen were driven abroad, none remained with large connections around which to construct an army. However legitimate he was, Henry VI was no general. Edward did his best to deny the exiles access to money or manpower at home. Lancastrian wives and widows were allowed their jointures and inheritances, but were placed in the custody of trusted Yorkists or consigned temporarily to nunneries to ensure that they could not communicate, subsidize, or otherwise assist their recalcitrant menfolk. Whenever Lancastrian plots were uncovered, the usual suspects were swept up. Margaret, Lady Hungerford complained that she was arrested three times, once by the sheriff of Wiltshire, once confined to Amesbury Abbey, and once placed in the custody of the uncongenial young Duchess of Norfolk, whence she secured a transfer, at a price, to Syon Abbey.[29] Lancastrianism, it seems, did not enjoy popular support until 1469–70. Discontent and disillusion with the regime took time to develop. And although the Lancastrians in different areas were able to communicate, they failed to coordinate adequately. Messages were intercepted and the correspondents of Queen Margaret were scotched. Another issue, always a problem with underground movements, relates to numbers: were there ever enough Lancastrians?

Making Yorkist rule effective everywhere took all the 1460s. Many of those committed to Henry VI and his queen, including their households, had been killed at Blore Heath, Northampton, Second St Albans, Ferrybridge and especially at Towton. The Duke of Buckingham, earls of Devon, Northumberland, Shrewsbury and Wiltshire, Viscount Beaumont, Lords Clifford, Dacre, Egremont, Neville [of Raby], Rougemont-Grey and Welles had perished. Altogether 114 Lancastrians were attainted in 1461 and their property was forfeited in a ruthless purge of the Lancastrian establishment. To London and the Home Counties, which the Yorkists already occupied, the victory at

Towton added control of the West Country, the Midlands, and most of Wales and the North. By May 1462 all Wales was pacified except Harlech Castle in the north-west.[30]

Harlech is one instance of how the Lancastrians were confined to the periphery of the realm. Furthermore, Queen Margaret invited the French into Calais, where they failed to take possession, and the Channel Isles, where they succeeded. To the North, the Scots had occupied Roxburgh in Scotland and, at the queen's invitation, Berwick, and now invaded the northern marches, where the Cliffords, Dacres and Percies were at their strongest. The marches towards Scotland were a region of powerful castles, a multiplicity of fortified pele towers and bastle-houses, extensive liberties and militarized inhabitants, who lived by war and reiving (raiding), and where refuge and relief were readily available in Scotland and sometimes from the sea. It was there that Lancastrian royalty had retreated after Towton in 1461 with a rump of committed noblemen – Somerset, Roos and Hungerford – who are probably to be counted as individuals rather than retinues. It was those northerners with local connections who mattered most: Sir Ralph and Sir Richard Percy, Sir Ralph Grey of Chillingham (Northum.), Sir Humphrey Neville of Brancepeth (Durh.) and William Tailbois as lord of Tynedale.

However, the Yorkists brought thither from the South vastly superior armies, including former Lancastrians out to prove their fidelity, together with shipping and powerful ordnance. Lancastrian opposition in the West March was quickly quelled. However, resistance in Northumberland was more difficult to put down and had to be undertaken several times. Warwick and his brother John, Lord Montagu, were able to deploy overwhelming force and several times to capture the great castles of Alnwick, Bamburgh, Dunstanburgh and Warkworth, which were never supplied sufficiently to hold out for long against either side. The countryside remained hostile. Lancastrian leaders could retreat to Scotland and return later, and 800 French troops under Pierre de Brézé and supplies arrived by sea in 1462 to assist the Lancastrian cause. Reconciliation with the Yorkists in the winter of 1462–3 of Somerset, Sir Ralph Percy and Grey, and even the re-appointment of the two latter to constableships, failed to pacify the region, as each former Lancastrian deserted when opportunity offered. A golden opportunity to defeat Warwick at Alnwick was missed by the Scottish Earl of Angus in January 1463. Once again in control of the coastal castles and indeed the whole shire as far south as the Lower Tyne and emboldened, the Lancastrians twice engaged with Montagu's forces in Northumberland, at Hedgeley Moor (25 April 1464) and catastrophically at Hexham (15 May). The castles fell for the last time. And all the Lancastrian leaders – Somerset, Hungerford, Roos, both Percies, Grey and Tailbois – were killed or executed. Henry VI himself escaped so hurriedly that his coronet was left at Bywell Castle. Montagu, now created Earl of Northumberland, controlled Northumberland and the East and Middle Marches for the rest of the 1460s.[31]

Although the Lancastrians who fought on were the exception, they were unfortunately only a tiny minority of Edward's potential foes. All adults had been loyal Lancastrians at some time and many had served King Henry more directly, in his household, central or local government, on his estates, or even in battle. Many remained within the realm, often having lost preferments, many under surety or repaying fines, including a few who had been attainted. They had good personal grounds for dissent. Although immeasurable, it also appears that there were many retainers, officers and tenants of wholly dispossessed families, such as the Beauforts and Courtenays in the West Country and the Percies in the North, who wanted their masters restored and were prepared under the right circumstances to back them. The task of watching over all the potential suspects was well beyond the capacity of the government. The Lancastrian court strove to keep its cause alive, both by correspondence and by propaganda. Their chancellor-in-exile, the ex-chief justice Sir John Fortescue, wrote a string of screeds and larger works refuting the Yorkist title that circulated in England and apparently fell into the hands even of such pillars of the new regime as Alderman Sir Thomas Cook.[32] As long as a Lancastrian alternative survived abroad, was exempt from English reprisals, and had the means to communicate with its supporters in England, the Lancastrian cause could not be wholly scotched and remained a nagging concern to the new regime.

Even after the conquest of Northumberland, Harlech Castle in North Wales held out. Almost impregnable on a rocky outcrop, it could be supplied from the sea and proved beyond a succession of Yorkist commanders to reduce. Supposedly, a further Lancastrian uprising in Wales launched from the sea by Henry VI's half-brother Jasper Tudor, Earl of Pembroke, was planned in 1464, but it came to nothing. In 1466 Sir Richard Tunstall sallied forth, advanced to Wrexham, where he plotted with the men of Chester, took Holt Castle, and threatened Shrewsbury. Around midsummer 1468 it was with reinforcements from France that Pembroke with three ships and 50 Frenchmen invaded Wales through Harlech. He reached as far east as Denbigh, which he burnt, raising 2,000 men before he was routed by Lord Herbert. Twenty of Pembroke's men were executed.[33] It was a tiny garrison that capitulated in August 1468. Mont

Orgueil on Jersey having just fallen, this was the last Lancastrian possession in the kingdom.

King Henry had only narrowly escaped capture in Northumberland in 1464, yet he remained at liberty in northern England until 1465, when he was arrested in Lancashire. He was paraded humiliatingly through London and then imprisoned in the Tower, yet he was not executed. To kill him was merely to exchange a rival in one's power for one outside it – his son Prince Edward of Lancaster – and was not therefore to Edward IV's advantage. Queen Margaret and Prince Edward remained out of reach. Margaret's father King René – actually Duke of Anjou in France and Bar, Marquis of Provence, and titular King of Naples and Sicily – was used to nurturing and harbouring claims to lost realms. From September 1463 René had assigned to Margaret his castle of Koeur at Saint-Mihiel in Bar, now in France, but then within the Holy Roman Empire. Margaret was therefore located beyond French power, although King Louis could – if he wished – pressurize René, his subject for Anjou. King René also paid Margaret a pension of 6,000 crowns a year, to which Louis XI of France added 4,000–5,000 francs.

These pensions allowed Margaret to maintain a shadowy and impoverished court. Fortescue was her chancellor and principal propagandist. There at various times were Edmund Beaufort, titular Duke of Somerset, Henry, Duke of Exeter, John Courtenay, from 1469 titular Earl of Devon, the Earl of Wiltshire's youngest brother John, eventually Earl of Ormond, and Henry VI's half-brother Jasper Tudor, Earl of Pembroke, blood royal of France through his mother, Queen Katherine consort of Henry V. The churchmen included William Bird, Bishop of St Asaph, Dr John Morton the future cardinal, and Dr Ralph Mackerel. Often they were absent on diplomatic or military missions. 'The main purpose of this court in exile was to achieve the restoration of the Lancastrian monarchy in England.'[34] This court in exile maintained contacts with Lancastrians in England by letter and envoy, and sought to send supplies and reinforcements to Harlech and possibly also, if the ancient indictments are to be believed, to launch multi-pronged invasions of England. Risings on the south coast and in London were supposedly timed to coincide with Jasper Tudor's landing in Wales at midsummer 1468.

Much miscellaneous information is available in continental sources, often dependent on Lancastrian information and disinformation, and in English trial records. Lancastrians tried to conceal their activities, exaggerate their importance, mislead as well as inform. The Yorkists may have made too much of very little. After Hexham there was a trickle of small-scale trials of Lancastrians. Two related to Hampshire and the Isle of Wight, both obvious landfalls for invaders. The abbot of Quarr was among 17 plotters mainly at Newport and Newtown, Isle of Wight, who on 12 November 1465 invited Queen Margaret to return. On 6 March 1467 a shipload of Lancastrians landed at 'le Hurst' – presumably the site of the future Hurst Castle: their objective was allegedly Carisbrooke Castle. Seizure of Carisbrooke was also supposedly an objective in 1468, when several groups of conspirators emerged.[35] Allegedly, the London plotters knew both of the abortive *coup de main* at Carisbrooke and of the landing at Harlech before it happened. In response King Edward requisitioned every ship in the realm. Another Lancastrian expedition under preparation at Harfleur in October 1468 did not set sail.[36]

At the heart of all this was the so-called Cook conspiracy. This was un-covered when John Cornelius was arrested at Queenborough in Kent. He was a servant of Sir Robert Whittingham, a long-standing Lancastrian attainted in 1461. Formerly an usher of King Henry's chamber, keeper of the queen's wardrobe, receiver-general to Prince Edward and now again wardrober to Queen Margaret, Whittingham had been at the queen's court in Bar and in August 1468 he was at Harlech Castle. Cornelius revealed the names of those to whom he had brought letters. Among those he accused were John Hawkins, servant of the royal councillor, diplomat and Warwick's lieutenant at Calais, John, Lord Wenlock. In direct consequence 21 men were indicted, others co-incidentally, and many others were accused, arrested and bound on sureties. John Hawkins and John Norris were hanged at Tyburn.[37]

What the government found most alarming was the London connection and the ramifications. The London group was wholly unsuspected. Among the implicated were three aldermen – the draper and former mayor Sir Thomas Cook, the grocer Sir John Plummer, alias Leynham, and the goldsmith Humphrey Hayford. Of lesser rank were the drapers John Shuckburgh and William Brit; the mercers Piers Alfrey and John Fisher (another future alderman); the merchant John Bishop and the yeoman Robert Hunt; the widow Alice Paslow; and the skinner Richard Steres, a notable real-tennis player and past servant of the Lancastrian Duke of Exeter.

Whilst most of the others had London addresses too, they included ex-sheriffs of Wiltshire (Pakenham), Surrey and Sussex (Hous/Husy), Bedford and Buckingham, residents of the counties of Berkshire, Buckingham, Gloucester and Kent. They also included Sir Gervase Clifton, formerly treasurer of Henry VI's chamber, husband to the great heiress Maud Lady Willoughby. John Norris was son of another keeper of Queen Margaret's chamber and Hugh Mull was the brother of the attainted Sir William Mull. Clifton, Hous and Mull were excluded from the 1468 general pardon together with other Lancastrians who included the Warwickshire knight and author of the *Morte D'Arthur*, Sir Thomas Malory of Newbold Revel. Another pair tried and executed separately were Sussex squires and retainers of the Duke of Norfolk, Poynes, alias Poynings, and Alfrey, alias Alford, who was obviously a relative of Piers Alfrey, who had communicated with the Lancastrians when accompanying Princess Margaret to her marriage with Duke Charles of Burgundy. In October 1468 Henry Courtenay of Breamore (Hants.), next heir to the earldom of Devon, and Sir Thomas Hungerford, next heir to the baronies of Botreaux, Hungerford and Moleyns, were arrested: in January 1469 they were executed at Salisbury.

Another group of Lancastrians was supposedly plotting at Somerleytown in Suffolk on 12 February 1469. It included an attainted former exile at Koeur, Dr Ralph Makerell, and Richard Makerell clerk, perhaps a nephew: Ralph was in custody by 8 April. It was also reported that those accused included John, 13th Earl of Oxford, Sir John Marny of Layer Marney (Essex), Sir Robert Ughtred of Ughtred (Yorks.), Sir Edmund Hungerford of Down Ampney (Gloucs.), and the restored Sir Thomas Tresham, potentially involving East Anglia, the North and parts of the Midlands. Although those named were apparently 'sent for', nothing more is known and no further action was taken against any of them. Most probably the conspiracy report was unreliable therefore, but it indicates just how great a scare the Cook plot was, to government and observers alike.

There were two northern rebellions with Lancastrian overtones in 1469, a pro-Percy uprising in the East Riding of Yorkshire by Robin of Holderness early in the spring and another, presumably in County Durham, led by Sir Humphrey Neville of Brancepeth an attainted connection of Ralph, Earl of Westmorland.[38] Many of the survivors, such as Clifton, Cook, Makerell, Plummer and Tresham supported the *Readeption* of Henry VI, in 1470–1, and several were then killed at or executed after the Battle of Tewkesbury in 1471. Morton, Pembroke, Sir Richard Tunstall, William Tyler and William Brit survived to prosper under Henry VII.

It was not just the individuals, of course, who were alarming to the Yorkist regime, but their excellent and extensive affiliations. They had lots of other connections in London, where Cook's brother-in-law was yet another alderman, Sir Ralph Josselin. The indictments reveal Alfrey and Plummer as linking the Welsh, London and East Anglian conspirators. Plummer had a country estate at Horsenden in Buckinghamshire, near where other suspected plotters resided. His wife Margaret was daughter of Chief Baron Fray and his widow Agnes Danvers, the daughter of John Danvers of Colthope and Prescote (Oxon). Agnes had at least five brothers, including a clerk, two judges, and a recorder of London. One of these was Thomas Danvers of Adderbury in Oxfordshire, a former Lancastrian, who was arrested in 1468 on the discovery in Cornelius's possession of a letter to him from Whittingham. Although not apparently tried, Danvers made fine for Edward's favour. In 1465 he had courted and wanted to marry Dame Margaret Lucy, the widow of Sir William Lucy slain at the Battle of Northampton and the sister of the restored Lancastrian Sir Henry Lewis. Thomas's brother Richard Danvers was one of the first to avail himself of the general pardon on 18 July 1468. Both had close ties with Plummer, acting as his sureties and feoffees until his death, and Plummer appears to have assisted them in commercial ventures and their management of the customs.

Meanwhile, Sir Thomas Malory had a nephew George Burnaby, who was the son-in-law of Agnes's brother Sir Robert Danvers, brother of Thomas and Richard, and whose executor was Lord Wenlock. Thomas and Richard Danvers alike served William Waynflete, Bishop of Winchester, the former chancellor of Henry VI, to whom Thomas was the more important, four times being returned for his pocket borough in Dorset. They had joined in Bishop Waynflete's conveyances to Magdalen College, Oxford, not only with Plummer, but also with Hugh Pakenham, another servant of the bishop, King Henry and Queen Margaret who was also indicted in 1468. Waynflete's intimate relations with Henry VI were illustrated when he personally fetched Henry VI out of the Tower in the *Readeption*. In 1468 he protected himself with not just one but two pardons, separated by a few months. John Hawkins was described around 1465 by Pakenham as *his* servant in whom he reposed his trust and in 1468 as a servant of Lord Wenlock, who had just remarried Agnes Fray (née Danvers), mother-in-law of Plummer and sister of the Danvers brothers. Some years earlier Wenlock had been guardian of Agnes's nieces, the daughters of her brother Robert. He had formerly been custodian of Anne, Dowager-Lady Moleyns, and her daughter-in-law Eleanor, wife of the irreconcilable Lancastrian Robert, Lord Hungerford and Moleyns. Anne Moleyns herself was remarried to Sir Edmund Hampden, one attainted Lancastrian and a kinsman of Hugh Mull's wife, and Eleanor to yet another Lancastrian in Sir Oliver Manningham, who was in trouble again in 1469. It was Eleanor's son Sir Thomas Hungerford who was executed in 1469. It appears credible, to say the least, that Wenlock himself was suborned by his wards or new wife or that his original Lancastrian contacts took precedence over his later Yorkist ones.

And a case could be made for embroiling in a conspiracy even the Earl of Warwick, the patron of Wenlock. Thomas Porthaleyn and Sir Thomas Malory had both been Warwick retainers. A captured Lancastrian spy fingered Warwick 'because he had heard overseas suspicious words that the same earl might favour the part of Queen Margaret' – but that was proved frivolous, reports the chronicler pseudo-Worcester. It is best understood as a Lancastrian attempt to undermine Warwick rather than a real indication of the earl's loyalties. A heated row about Warwick between Louis XI (his friend) and Queen Margaret's brother John, Duke of Calabria (his foe), resulted early in 1467 in the duke's throw-away line that the earl and queen should combine against their common enemy Edward IV. The idea was repeated the following May. Fortescue may even have formally proposed a Lancastrian alliance with Warwick on the basis that one's enemy's enemy is one's friend.[39] At this stage, however, Warwick had no need of the Lancastrians.

The alarm of Edward IV in 1468–9 is understandable. There appeared to be a network of prominent old Lancastrians that linked the City, central administration and county establishments. In August 1468 Edward commandeered all the ships in the kingdom to repel a foreign invasion. The proposed invasion of France was postponed: indeed agreements between Burgundy and Brittany with France made it impractical. In 1468, Herbert was rewarded with the earldom of Pembroke for repelling Jasper Tudor and for capturing Harlech at last. Humphrey, Lord Stafford of Southwick, was created Earl of Devon. The trial of Sir Thomas Cook was especially high profile: when he was acquitted of the principal charge of treason but convicted of misprision (concealment), he was both heavily fined (£8,000) and, vindictively, queen's gold of 800 marks was also sought from him, unsuccessfully. The usual suspects, attainted and restored Lancastrians and their women, were rounded up, bound over, imprisoned, placed in irons, perhaps even tortured on the rack called the Duke of Exeter's Daughter.[40] Lancastrian conspiracy had reached a crescendo, extended ever wider across the English shires, and even into the London court of aldermen. In most cases, however, nothing is known against them. There are no indictments, and they had numerous other connections – kinsfolk, neighbours, colleagues, trading partners and contacts, co-witnesses, co-feoffees, co-executors, co-sureties – about whom there were no other grounds for suspicion. Whatever the wishful thinking of the Lancastrian court – and even, perhaps, whatever deliberate fomentation of division amongst Yorkists – any pro-Lancastrian conspiracy by Warwick before 1470 is highly improbable. His plots had quite different aims and resulted in coups, rebellions and even an attempted usurpation that was decidedly un-Lancastrian.

The problem is what these bewildering Lancastrian plotters, plots and networks actually mean. Obviously, the number of Lancastrian supporters fell when Henry VI was dethroned, declined further when the outcrops of resistance were mopped up, and most probably diminished steadily thereafter. Such sentiments could endure for a long time before finally disappearing on the evidence of the White Rose of York, royalism in the mid seventeenth century, and especially Jacobitism in the eighteenth century: the '45 was formidable more than half a century after the Glorious Revolution of 1688. Were the few dozen known names the sum total of all the Lancastrians there were? In which case, they amounted to irritants, not threats. Or were they the tip of an iceberg, the few amongst many who had come to light, the evidence of a much larger movement? The present author thinks they were probably individuals. Mass sympathy for Lancastrianism leading to mass rebellion demanded a confidence that was lacking in the late 1460s and a commitment that was confined to very few individuals. Among these few dozen conspirators, there are not many unfamiliar names. Many had prior Lancastrian connections and some, like Cook, were not actually traitors, but guilty merely of misprision – of concealing what they knew. On the other hand, more concrete hereditary attachments to the Percies in the North-East and Courtenays in the far west outlived Edward's *First Reign*. Lancastrian sympathies and discontent with the new regime may have been widespread, but in time they would ebb away as happened eventually with Yorkism after 1485. For them to explode into renewed civil war, let alone victory, they required opportunities or a catalyst, a real challenge to the regime, to be effective. That catalyst was the Earl of Warwick's rebellions.

CHAPTER 11

THE SECOND WAR 1469–71

What made the *Second War* possible was that the victorious Yorkists warred against themselves. Lancastrian plots were common enough, but even the financially feeble Edward IV crushed them with relative ease. 1461, however, had witnessed the defeat of traditional obligations of allegiance and obedience, and the victory of the right of subjects to reject royal decisions, to coerce, reform and even depose a legitimate sovereign. Such winning arguments could be recycled against the new monarch. A much more formidable threat was posed by Warwick the Kingmaker – an overmighty subject with resources greater than those of Richard, Duke of York a decade earlier and who proved able to reconstitute the foreign support, popular appeal and rival ideology that had prevailed in 1461. He had no aspirations for the Crown for himself: he had for his daughters – and so indeed did their two husbands, George, Duke of Clarence (d. 1478) and Prince Edward of Lancaster (d. 1471).

THE QUARREL WITH WARWICK

The root problem lies in the concentration of power that Warwick and his Neville family enjoyed early in Edward IV's reign. Anne Beauchamp's inheritance had made Warwick a magnate of the front rank, with concentrations of property particularly in South Wales and the West Midlands. By 1463 he had accrued his parents' earldom of Salisbury and Neville inheritance, comprising both lands in central southern England and lordships in Richmondshire in north Yorkshire, south Durham and Penrith (Cumb.). The king gave him the lordship of Cockermouth in Cumberland and the Percy lands in Craven (Yorks.). Already warden of the West March towards Scotland, Warwick became lieutenant of the North, and his brother John, Earl of Northumberland, warden of the East and Middle Marches. Warwick was chief steward of the north parts of the duchy of Lancaster and chief forester north of the River Trent. Already captain of Calais and keeper of the seas, Warwick now became warden of the Cinque Ports. Already premier earl, Warwick now became great chamberlain of England. As steward of England, it had been he who presided over Edward's coronation and pronounced sentence on the ex-king Henry VI. Warwick was also the kingdom's leading diplomat – the public face of the realm to outsiders. Warwick's uncle William, Lord Fauconberg, Earl of Kent 1461–3, and his brother Northumberland, deputized for him in the North. His other brother George, Bishop of Exeter, from 1464 Archbishop of York, was Lord Chancellor until 1467. If disappointed not to be a duke or Lord Admiral and although ineligible to become king himself, Warwick aspired to such advancement for his heirs. The teenage king was content in his early years to leave much to the Nevilles, asserting his authority infrequently. It is only a slight exaggeration to label the years 1461–7 'The Rule of the Nevilles'.[1]

Of course, it could not last. Indolent and self-indulgent though he was, King Edward was a vigorous and capable young man well able to do his own ruling and was bound in due course to do so, at which point the Nevilles had to accept a lesser role. It had besides to be Edward's policy to rule with and on behalf of everyone rather than for a faction, in which case the Nevilles had accrued too many posts. A key factor in the rupture of king and earl was Edward's ill-considered marriage in 1464 to Elizabeth Grey (née Wydeville), daughter of Richard, Lord Rivers, and Jacquetta of Luxemberg, dowager-duchess of Bedford. Elizabeth was a widow of limited means from a Lancastrian family, was burdened with two sons, and had few worthwhile connections. She was not the international match that politics demanded. However disapproving of such an improvident union,[2] everybody had of course to accept the new reality and Warwick did so in particular, escorting the new queen formally into Reading Abbey in September 1464, standing godfather to Princess Elizabeth, and apparently also presiding over the queen's first churching in 1466.[3]

Whether or not this marriage was a particular snub to the earl as diplomat, it brought the king a large number of down-at-heel in-laws. The queen's father Richard was created Earl Rivers. The king matched her sisters and her eldest son to the most eligible noble heirs and endowed them with royal grants. Supposedly the Wydevilles were unpopular. Directly or indirectly, Warwick is our main source and perhaps also the cause for any unpopularity, but these matches reveal that such major figures as the earls of Arundel (Warwick's brother-in-law) and Essex were happy to ally with them. The most immediately important match was to William, Lord Herbert of Raglan, who had constructed in southern and western Wales an estate and a hegemony worthy of a great magnate. Some of these matches were particularly offensive to Warwick. A child-bride was snatched from his little nephew George Neville, and he himself was denied eligible bridegrooms for his daughters, themselves great heiresses. Edward also forbade the wedding of Warwick's elder daughter Isabel Neville to his next brother George, Duke of Clarence, whom he reserved for a diplomatic match. Not just Warwick, but Clarence too was alienated by this. These were legitimate aspirations for Warwick that were being frustrated.[4]

There were also differences between Edward's new favourites and the Nevilles over policy. The Wydevilles were related to Pierre de Luxemberg, Count of St Pol. In urging a Burgundian alliance against France, the Wydevilles were probably reinforcing Edward's own inclinations, but this alignment was in fundamental opposition to Warwick's preference for a rapprochement with France. In recognizing the impossibility of reconquering France, it may have been that Warwick was more realistic, but a Burgundian foreign policy was a more popular option and was bound to prevail because, in the end, the king insisted on it. Warwick's popularity would surely have suffered had his Francophile sentiments been generally known. Instead an alliance matrimonial and offensive with Burgundy against France was concluded late in 1467.[5]

There were plenty of ominous signs ahead of the formal break in June 1467, when the king took advantage of Warwick's absence abroad on a diplomatic mission to dismiss his brother George as Lord Chancellor. In the longer term Warwick had surely to relinquish some of his constellation of offices and responsibilities, spheres of influence and even forfeited estates. What was resumed in 1467 from him and Archbishop Neville was a mere fraction of what they had been granted, not serious in itself. A ceiling was placed on the gains of George, Duke of Clarence. These mild reminders of the king's overriding authority merely warned what might be, but they were just as offensive to the losers. It was an unfunny jape when Edward forwarded to Neville the papal letter appointing Archbishop Bourchier as cardinal rather than himself and indeed cruel, malicious and exacerbating.[6] Such details indicate how embittered relations between the Nevilles and the king had become. In the longer term, in retrospect, Warwick came to insist on a larger and indeed conclusive say in royal decision-making, whilst Edward refused him a special role, probably excluded him and his brothers from his inner circle, and allowed them no more say than other leading peers. There was no way to reconcile a power behind the throne with a strong king who knew how to rule and what he wanted to do. Constitutionally, the king was bound to win. Not only, however, did Warwick not defer, but with all his experiences in the 1450s and especially in 1460–1 he was prepared to force on Edward a change of mind.

The development of the breakdown can be only dimly perceived. There are not even the summonses to or the agendas of the great council for 1467–9 that enable York's relations with King Henry fitfully to be traced in the previous decade. The laconic annals of the chronicler pseudo-Worcester shed only a little light. Although obviously aware of differences of opinion and arguments to be won, Warwick returned to England with a deal with France so good that he was sure the king could be persuaded to agree. It was an unexpected shock to find his brother dismissed and the French ambassadors that he brought with him disregarded and slighted. The earl absented himself to his northern estates. There was a great council at Kingston-on-Thames in Surrey early in October 1467, at which Edward's sister Margaret accepted the Burgundian match and the king's objections to Clarence's marriage to Isabel became known. Warwick refused the king's summons and was in the North, where he had to refute a charge of Lancastrianism. Evidently other unknown differences brought the earl very quickly near the brink of rebellion. When the king progressed to Coventry Cathedral priory for Christmas 1467, he took with him a bodyguard of 200 – perhaps in anticipation of a *coup de main* by the earl like that of 1459? He did pay £1,573 of Warwick's expenses.[7] Warwick was not present and rejected another summons in January 1468. He would not come to court whilst his enemies were there. Some sort of deal was brokered that January at Nottingham by Archbishop Neville and Earl Rivers, out of which there came a formal reconciliation between Warwick and Lords Herbert, Stafford of Southwick and Audley, but not yet Rivers and Scales. No source specifies what was at issue, but the same names occur in Warwick's manifesto next year, when these royal favourites were identified as evil councillors. Even Warwick could not accuse the king directly. Edward had to negotiate with Warwick like a separate potentate, just as had Henry VI with the Duke of York a decade earlier, and Thomas of Lancaster under Edward II. Like Henry VI, Edward IV treated differences between magnates as private matters to be sorted out at a lower level.

Quite what was resolved is unclear. Warwick reappears in London and at court. However, he continued to favour the pro-French foreign policy that the king had rejected. In 1468 it was the queen's brother Anthony Lord Scales who was granted the Channel Isles, which had belonged to Warwick's predecessor Henry Duke of Warwick (d. 1446), and who became keeper of the seas. The dangerous Herbert Earl of Pembroke, was matching his daughters to proscribed Lancastrians, Henry Tudor and Henry Percy, heirs to the earldoms respectively of Richmond and Northumberland, potentially to the loss of Warwick, his brother Northumberland and Clarence, who held those lands that would have been restored. With the archbishop's help, Warwick and Clarence continued to seek the papal dispensation necessary for Clarence's marriage, which was secured on 14 March 1469. A splendid wedding was celebrated out of King Edward's reach at Calais by Archbishop Neville on 11 July 1469.[8] Warwick's first *coup d'état* followed.

WARWICK'S FIRST COUP 1469

It certainly was not the case that the situation had become critical for Warwick, Clarence or Archbishop Neville, or that they had no choice but to rebel. Edward IV was quite unprepared and did not recognize what he was facing. Warwick did not pretend either in 1469 or in 1470 to be able to carry the peerage with him. Indeed, he seems to have been quite contemptuous of majority opinion among his fellow lords. Apart from the royal family, now much expanded by the king's in-laws, and Edward's own servants, many now elevated to the baronage, all peers owed allegiance and obedience to King Edward and few were inclined to join Warwick. The earl did not persuade any from outside his own family or affinity of the inadequacy of the government or his own qualifications as substitute. There is no indication that any of them bought the notion that his uprisings were loyal protestations to reform the realm on the model of those of York. Though he was the king's first cousin via Joan Beaufort, Warwick was not over-endowed with royal blood nor was he heir presumptive as York had claimed to be, but of course his ally and now son-in-law Clarence was. It was difficult early in 1470 to mobilize the retainers and tenants either of himself or Clarence in the Midlands or Yorkshire even with the authority of royal commissions of array. Potential recruits refused to breach their allegiance or to join a force that they suspected would be misdirected into treason.[9] Apart from Clarence, the most peers that Warwick could deploy – and then not all at once – were the four earls of Warwick, Northumberland, Oxford and Shrewsbury, a powerful subgroup amongst the highest nobility, and Barons FitzHugh, Latimer, Scrope of Bolton, Stanley and Welles. Warwick's military power derived from three sources: the bastard feudal connections of himself and his immediate allies, especially in Richmondshire in north Yorkshire; the Calais garrison, his shipmen and their Kentish allies; and the populace of the

South-East. Also important to his initial success was surprise, skilful coordination and disinformation. But Warwick could not withstand the combined
resources of the king and his loyal subjects. Nobody ever could.

Warwick's insurrection involved levying war against the king and constituted
treason by the 1352 Statute. He recycled York's arguments of 1459.[9] They were,
after all, the winning arguments. Warwick's justification for rebellion was again
the good of the common weal and a reform programme designed to deliver
good and self-sufficient governance in lieu of the misgovernment of Edward IV.
Warwick's invocation of the common good apparently did appeal to the discon-
tented populace, who were prepared to accept his self-appointed status as their
saviour. Once again what was needed, he said, was good counsel by 'great lords
of their blood', in particular Warwick and Clarence, who had been estranged
from the king's presence. Once again Warwick presumed that armed petitioning
to coerce the king in the name of the common good was not treasonable, but
indeed justifiable and praiseworthy. Although not labelled traitors, evil councillors interested only 'in their singular lucre and enriching of themselves' were to
be removed and punished, to wit Earl Rivers (the king's own father-in-law), his
wife and sons, the Earl of Pembroke, Humphrey Stafford of Southwick, Earl
of Devon, John, Lord Audley, Sir John Fogge 'and others of their mischievous
assent'. If their excessive and undeserved grants were resumed, then the king
would have no need to raise money from the people – the second instalment of
the 1468 taxes had fallen due on 25 March 1469 – and he could live of his own,
the laws could be enforced impartially, and subjects would be protected from the
depredations of the king's favourites. It may be that Warwick was obscurely
alluding to Cook's case and the execution of Henry Courtenay, which had obviously benefited the new Earl of Devon and may have been engineered by him.[10]
Although supposedly emanating from a northern popular insurrection, this
manifesto was actually the work of Warwick and was aimed at the same Kentish
audience that had risen upon very similar grounds in 1450, 1459 and 1460. Both
Fogge and the Wydevilles were Kentish and unpopular. It appears to have
appealed to its target audience, both penny-pinched and disappointed that
things had not improved.

Warwick, Clarence and the archbishop passed in force and unobstructed
through Kent and the City. Edward treated the northerners as rebels and sought
to defeat them militarily. Reading between the lines, he thought them to be naked
commons and hence summoned against them only his most trusted supporters
Pembroke and Devon, not all the loyal peers and subjects that he required for a
full-scale trial of strength. It was surprise that enabled the coup to proceed.

Warwick's military strategy also built on his experiences in 1459–60. The rebels did not flinch from using violence against the king or his favourites, who were to be eliminated, nor indeed from deposition. Even the initial manifesto drew ominous parallels between Edward IV and the misgovernment of other tyrannical kings who had been deposed. At least two forces were to be deployed against the king, from the North and from Calais. Probably there was also a West Midlands component. The northern insurrection was really a noble revolt in popular disguise. The leader was Robin of Redesdale, a pseudonym like Bluebeard, Jack Mortimer and Robin of Holderness that concealed and protected the real individual, who in this case was an aristocrat: most probably William Conyers of Marske (Yorks.).[11] The revolt centred on Warwick's Richmondshire connection, certainly including his cousin Sir Henry Neville, heir to the barony of Latimer, and Sir John Conyers, steward of Middleham. This gave them the necessary steel and leadership to outmanoeuvre and scatter Pembroke's Welshmen – Devon having withdrawn in a huff – in the Battle of Edgecote near Banbury in north Oxfordshire on 24 July 1469. *Warkworth's Chronicle* talks of large numbers – 20,000 versus 18,000 – but surely this was actually a small-scale engagement, yet decisive nevertheless. Pembroke's Welsh affinity was destroyed – as many as 2,000 Welshmen were slain – and played no further part in the fighting of the next three years. The victors also suffered serious losses, notably Henry Neville himself and his brother-in-law Oliver Dudley, both of whom were interred in the Beauchamp Chapel at Warwick. Secondly, but actually unnecessarily, Warwick, Clarence and Archbishop Neville advanced from Calais, presumably with a mixture of garrison, shipmen, commons and retainers, but did not have to fight. It was the archbishop who arrested King Edward at Olney (Bucks.). Unfortunately, the key figures survived the Battle of Edgecote, but Warwick was as ruthless as in 1455 and 1460. Earl Rivers, his son Sir John Wydeville, Pembroke and his brother Sir Richard Herbert were rounded up and executed at Northampton, and Thomas Herbert at Bristol. As for Devon, earl 'but half a year', he was lynched by the commons of Somerset at Bridgwater.[12]

Whatever the manifesto had claimed, Warwick's first objective was to seize control of the government, substitute himself, Archbishop Neville and Clarence for the king's evil councillors, and to rule in the king's name. Since Edward was much more effective than Henry VI and indeed highly dangerous, he could not be left so accessible and was therefore safely confined, first at Warwick and then at Middleham in Yorkshire. The government in London was led by Archbishop Neville as chancellor and Sir John Langstrother, the

Hospitaller prior of St John, as Lord Treasurer. They acted on directions from the Earl of Warwick from afar. Warwick himself took the offices in South Wales that he had hankered after in 1461 and that the king had bestowed on William Herbert. The earl appears also to have hoped for support from William, Lord Hastings, husband of his sister Katherine. A Parliament was summoned to York for 22 September 1469. Although cancelled, some sort of assembly was held there instead, perhaps a great council.[13] This Parliament was intended to consolidate the new regime, to give it legitimacy, and perhaps also to implement a reform programme. Much more may have been intended. Charges of sorcery levied against the queen's mother Duchess Jacquetta of Luxemberg were probably intended to discredit Edward's marriage and perhaps to bastardize his daughters. Rumours circulating that Edward himself was illegitimate recalled the allegations of bastardy against Prince Edward of Lancaster.[14] The king's next heir and certainly heir male, whether to be Lord Protector or if usurpation was intended, was Edward's second brother Clarence, now Warwick's son-in-law. Warwick's first coup thus began where York had taken a decade to arrive. Moreover, the Yorkist usurpation in 1460-1 had made a further dynastic revolution conceivable.

But Warwick's victory unravelled alarmingly. Nobody tried to reverse the coup by force, but it failed to command the obedience achieved in 1455 and 1460. That the commands of the new regime self-evidently were not those of the distant and incarcerated king was clearly one consideration. The collapse of civil government, as in 1450, was an opportunity for self-help. 'The kingdom proved rapidly to be ungovernable.'[15] It shows how well Edward had maintained order during his *First Reign*. There were six major outbreaks of violence in late 1469 and early 1470. Rioting resumed in London. Uncowed by the indictment of his retainers in June, John, Duke of Norfolk, now laid siege to the Pastons' castle of Caister in Norfolk. Attempts were made to restrain him by the council, Archbishop Neville and Clarence, unavailingly. 'He will not spare to do what is proposed for no duke in England.' A full-scale siege followed and some loss of life. All the central intervention achieved was the safe withdrawal on 27 September 1469 of the garrison, whom however Norfolk then sued for their offences against *him*.[16] Newly of age, Thomas Talbot, Viscount Lisle, resumed the Great Berkeley lawsuit. He challenged his distant cousin William, Lord Berkeley, to settle the issue by force of arms. Lisle it was who perished at the ensuing Battle of Nibley Green.[17] In Lincolnshire, moreover, somewhat obscurely, there were disturbances by November 1469 and a quarrel between the ex-Lancastrian Richard, Lord Welles and Willoughby and the king's favourite Sir Thomas Burgh, heir of the Percies of Atholl, which resulted probably after 2 February 1470 in the sack and destruction of Burgh's seat at Gainsborough. Apparently, Welles attracted mass backing.[18] Devon's death removed restraints in the West Country, where there was a violent quarrel between the Courtenays of Powderham and Bocannoc. On 16 March 1469 Edward IV had ordered Lords Dynham and FitzWarin to impose order and take sureties there. Instead, Sir Hugh of Bocannoc besieged the two peers at Exeter from 22 March to 10 April, a siege that was relieved only by the arrival of Warwick and Clarence.[19]

Most nationally important advantage of this power vacuum was taken by the unreconciled and attainted Lancastrian Sir Humphrey Neville of Brancepeth (Durh.), a cadet of the Nevilles of Raby, who rose in rebellion in the North presumably in County Durham. Alarmingly, even in Warwick's home territory, Sir Humphrey could not be repressed, as Warwick's own retainers and tenants declined to fight without explicit royal authorization. Summonses in the king's name did not suffice. Parliament was cancelled. If only more was known about the actual situation, Warwick's options and the reasons for his conduct! The course of action that he selected was to display the king in public, thus entitling himself to the royal authority with which he made short shrift of Sir Humphrey and his brother Charles, whom he executed at York in the king's presence.[20] No longer confined, King Edward took back his throne. A host of other lords rallied to him and escorted him into London on 10 October 1469. His mother-in-law Jacquetta of Luxemberg was acquitted of sorcery. Order was restored. Although Berkeley and Norfolk were left in possession of their winnings, the king planned a personal judicial progress to Lincolnshire in the New Year. The archbishop and prior were replaced as chancellor and treasurer and a great council was summoned to Westminster for November 1469, to which Warwick, Clarence and the archbishop, no longer in power, were invited on an appointed day (6 November). By that time, Edward had reconstituted his regime.

Apparently Edward had intended to use the great council, as his household wished, to punish those who had rebelled against him, but by the time the duke and earl arrived he had resolved against escalation, against further conflict. Edward did not want a permanent breach with his next brother and male heir, Clarence. There was mediation, negotiation, to-ing and fro-ing of go-betweens, until reconciliation was agreed and past offences were pardoned. Edward had received Warwick and Clarence cordially and a general pardon was issued in February 1470, forgiving offences committed rather later than the king had wished. No concessions were made by King Edward on their demands to be chief councillors, on the issue of reform, or on foreign policy. They were not to be allowed any fruits of their summer escapades and must limit themselves to their proper roles as loyal peers subject to their sovereign. It was not Warwick, but Edward's youngest brother Gloucester, as custodian of the Herbert interest, who deputized in Wales. Bishop Stillington again replaced Archbishop Neville as chancellor. Henry Percy was restored to the earldom of Northumberland and the wardenship of the East and Middle Marches towards Scotland to counterbalance the hegemony of the Nevilles: Clarence, Warwick and Warwick's brother John Neville lost their Percy grants, and John also lost his earldom. Although he was still under age, the restoration also of Henry Tudor as Earl of Richmond was contemplated. Since John Neville had been loyal in 1469 and Edward wished to retain his services, he was created Marquis Montagu and was awarded in compensation Courtenay lands of equivalent value in the West Country. Moreover – and presumably Edward saw it as a masterstroke – John's four-year-old heir George Neville, also Warwick's heir male, was betrothed to the king's heiress Princess Elizabeth of York and was created Duke of Bedford. Though not in the way Warwick had intended, a duchy and a crown were being offered to the Nevilles: incentive enough for Warwick to keep the peace, perhaps, as a counterbalance to Clarence and an attractive alternative to his brothers. As a marquis, Montagu now outranked his elder brother Warwick, a mere earl. Finally, perhaps to replace the Earl of Devon, the Duke of Buckingham's youngest uncle became Earl of Wiltshire. In a few deft moves, Edward had reconstituted his regime and firmly rebuffed those seeking to rule for him.

Warwick should have been able to live with this reshuffle, but certainly it was not 'agreeable' to him.[21] Although the earl was offered the uncertain prospect that his nephew George Neville might eventually reign, he must resign forever the dominant position in government and international respect that he demanded and accept the defeat of his pro-French foreign policy. His dominance of the North was also terminated and so too were his aspirations in South Wales: his rivals Henry Percy, Earl of Northumberland, and William Herbert, Earl of Pembroke, were formidable opponents. Clearly Warwick's position became much worse than that to which he had so forcibly objected the previous summer.

Yet clearly Edward had miscalculated. He did nothing to address the economic woes of his people and indeed worsened them by collecting the next instalments of the fifteenths,[22] no doubt of necessity. The proffer of the crown to George Neville presumed that the queen should produce no son herself and could bear no political fruits for a decade or more. It proved an insufficient bond. Montagu's border earldom and marcher wardenship had fulfilled his heart's desire. What he now gained in the West Country against what he had lost he disparaged as a (mag)pie's nest.[23] Perhaps Edward's forgiveness was false – or adjudged to be false – and his vengeance for the summer coup in due course was to be anticipated. Certainly, as in 1458, the victims of the coup – the new earls of Pembroke, Rivers, and their widows – went uncompensated. Apparently Edward took the submission and reconciliation of Warwick and Clarence to be genuine and underestimated their determination still to have their own way. However, they resolved to override the wishes of both king and Lords, to seize power and to complete the purge of the previous year, almost certainly also to substitute Clarence for Edward IV as king. They may well have resolved on this course of action even when making their peace with the king. Their attendance at the king's Christmas and Epiphany celebrations was a cover for their real intentions.

Regrettably, the origins and causes of the troubles in Lincolnshire in March 1470 are obscure. Nothing survives of the objectives, propaganda or messages to reveal how locally specific the rebellion and how similar it was to that of Robin of Redesdale. *The Chronicle of the Lincolnshire Rebellion* is a hostile official account that draws on confessions – one of which survives – which may well have been framed by the government. Wherever possible, however, this version has been checked against records and confirmed.[24] The insurrection again offered a stalking horse like Robin of Redesdale in the 'great captain of the commons of Lincolnshire' that Warwick and Clarence could exploit without revealing their own complicity. The immediate preliminary had been the attack on Sir Thomas Burgh's house at Gainsborough. Was he viewed as an evil councillor or were there local issues? Supposedly there was a reissue of Redesdale's manifesto of the previous year, with its appeal to popular and especially economic discontent. The third instalment of the 1468 tax fell due on 11 November 1469 and the fourth deadline was 25 March 1470. Evidently this was a genuinely popular uprising of 'poor and wretched commons', supposedly 30,000 strong, who trusted however in the leadership of Warwick and Clarence. It was skilfully fomented by reports – certainly true, if somewhat exaggerated – that the king was coming 'with great power into Lincolnshire' to 'hang and draw great number' of the offenders of the Gainsborough outrage, and it was directed by pulpit oratory coordinated by Lord Welles's son Sir Robert as the great captain.[25] There are no copies of his publicity to indicate how closely his message resembled Redesdale's manifesto. There does not seem to have been much stiffening of the rebels' ranks with bastard feudal retainers.

This time Edward did not underestimate what he faced. It was with a formidable force that he left London on 6 March 1470, even though he was as yet unaware of any ulterior motive on the part of his foes. Naively he commissioned Warwick and Clarence to array the West and North Midlands in his support. Men also assembled in Richmondshire. The rebel plan was for another pincer movement on the king, in which some of those who had been arrayed on Edward's authority would in fact be deployed against him. However, the Lincolnshiremen engaged too soon and proved militarily inept. The Midlanders proved to be more sceptical than the king about Warwick and Clarence's intentions and refused to join them in sufficient numbers. The Lincolnshire commons were more numerous – it was because victory was not assured that Edward had Lord Welles executed before the battle – but they proved not to be such good fighters. The battle was fought at Empingham near Stamford on 12 March 1470 and is also called Losecote Field. Apparently their battle cries were 'À Warwick! À Warwick! À Clarence! À Clarence'. Supposedly, correspondence was found on the battlefield that did incriminate the duke and earl. Certainly the confessions of the captured captains did, all of whom were to be executed.[26]

On 17 March the king summoned Warwick and Clarence to answer the charges against them 'as befitteth a liege man to come to his sovereign lord in humble wise' and modestly accompanied according to their rank. Further assemblies, he warned, would be treasonable and would carry the penalties of treason. Yet again he preferred reconciliation to further conflict and promised Warwick and Clarence equitable and favourable treatment, with due consideration for their closeness of blood. Warwick and Clarence did at least consider the offer, but they distrusted it. They would comply only with safe conducts for themselves and pardons for them and their associates to be secured by Edward's solemn oath, at which point they would renew their oaths of allegiance to him. Such conditions were unacceptable to Edward and his lords, since they forgave the earl and duke their heinous breaches of faith and treason, and treated them as equals to himself. They must submit by 27 March. Still recalling their blood, past affections, and loath to have lost them, Edward promised them clemency in return for their submission and on sureties for good behaviour. They declined. Supposing themselves to have sufficient support elsewhere to confront the king on equal terms, they recruited first in Richmondshire, then in Lancashire, and probably afterwards among Clarence's western clients such as the Courtenays of Powderham. Enough men could not be enlisted to a losing cause led by traitors against whom all loyal subjects were rallying. The strategic retreat of Warwick and Clarence via Richmondshire and the North-West became a flight the length of England as far as Exeter in the South-West and then, on 9 April, abroad.[27]

This was an emphatic victory for Edward, who had crushed both a popular and a noble revolt. His authority had been reasserted. However, that was not the end of the story. It was only the Lincolnshire commons who had been defeated. As Edward realized only too well, Warwick was as well able now as in 1459–60 to turn his flight into a springboard for future success, this time overtly with a change of king in mind. Edward had offered all he could. Just as in 1459 with Henry VI, it was the king's opponents who were not prepared to compromise. The struggle for the right to rule became a full-scale civil war involving both the masses and rival foreign states.

Warwick's Alliance with Queen Margaret

In retrospect, the stakes were raised decisively in the altercation after Losecote Field, which is reminiscent of the debate of 1459 in the *Somnium Vigilantis*. At this point reconciliation was still possible. Warwick and Clarence could have returned to their allegiance at the price of short-term humiliation, sureties for good behaviour, some loss of offices and grants, acceptance that their hege-mony was definitely over, and that their permanent role was as subjects, albeit amongst the greatest and most influential. However, they chose not to do so. Distrust was clearly a factor. They were unwilling to place themselves at Edward's mercy or to concede so much. Whilst they did not insist on all the gains of victory like their counterparts in 1459, they nevertheless set down conditions – life, liberty and property – that were unacceptable to the king. Edward stood on his dignity and on his prerogative as king. He insisted on utter submission, denounced them as traitors, and was henceforth unwilling to negotiate, even when they transformed themselves once again into dangerous rivals. Here was the ideological impasse that escalated in the autumn of 1470 into full-scale civil and indeed international warfare. Warwick and Clarence could only retrieve what they had lost by force, by conquest, a change of dynasty and a change of king. Warwick must have been very certain of supporters as yet untapped that the king could not match. Yet restoration was unattainable without attracting allies with very different objectives that hence-forth took priority. Never wholly reduced to the refugee status of some of the Lancastrians in the 1460s, it was nevertheless extraordinary that the exiles achieved such a revolution and in so short a time.

Warwick, as in 1459, made for Calais as his base, but Edward, who had been involved on the earlier occasion, had it shut against him. Warwick sought to reconstitute his fleet, but was again anticipated. Anthony Wydeville, now the new Earl Rivers and Warwick's victim at Sandwich in 1461, had the pleasure of reversing the advantage. He reached Southampton first, seized Warwick's splendid new ship *Trinity*, repelled the earl himself and captured a score of his men, whom Lord Constable Worcester, in another escalation, condemned and executed as traitors.[28]

In Warwick's favour were the ships that he still had and their battle-hardened crews, his favour with Louis XI, and the antipathy of France and Burgundy, which he deliberately inflamed by his attacks on Burgundian shipping. Louis XI was obliged to provide material support, unwillingly and in breach of the treaty of Péronne, ultimately on the scale and on the terms that Warwick wanted. Louis was the honest broker in reconciling those two bitter enemies – Warwick and the Lancastrians – against their common Yorkist enemy Edward IV. Margaret had perceived at once the opportunity for Lancaster that Yorkist divisions offered. Warwick seems to have proposed it as soon as he arrived in the River Seine, before 12 May, and Margaret promptly accepted. A ceremonial pantomime of exculpation and regret from Warwick, ritual humiliation and royal clemency from Margaret, was needed to satisfy both groups of supporters, abroad and in England alike. The Lancastrians had to see themselves in charge, their wrongs righted, and Warwick re-admitted only as an apologetic suppliant. Similarly, Warwick's supporters had to be persuaded that the deal was of Warwick's making and was to their advantage: his propaganda tract *The Manner and Guiding of the Earl of Warwick at Angers* achieved that. The treaty of Angers made Henry VI king, Prince Edward heir and Clarence first reserve. Henry (still held in the Tower of London) would reign rather than rule, which was to be undertaken by the teenaged prince obviously with advice, ideally – to Sir John Fortescue's mind – as figurehead of a conciliar government. Proscribed Lancastrians would be restored and would recover the lands they had forfeited. Prince Edward himself was married to Warwick's younger daughter Anne, thus securing the crown that Warwick still sought for his heir,[29] but no longer for his elder daughter Isabel. Clarence had good reason for wondering why he wanted that. Clarence had no obvious interest in replacing his elder brother King Edward with King Henry, but also, at this stage, no alternative. Once a victory was achieved, the rancour of Lancastrians remained, with serious consequences. From Louis XI's angle, this was another episode in the contest of France and Burgundy. Making it a reality – and even harbouring the exiles – made a dangerous enemy of Burgundy. Even as the successful coalition was forged, therefore, the roots of future failure rested in the contradictions that were apparent at the start.

Success came first. Four factors combined. First of all, the allies had a legitimate cause and a powerful case to argue. The Yorkists had not conclusively won the dynastic argument. Many aristocrats still preferred the heir male to the heir general. Henry VI had been king to most Englishmen and was still an anointed king. There were resolute Lancastrians and others who had abandoned King Henry only because they had no choice. For westcountrymen and indeed many northerners, the dispossessed Lancastrian peers were 'old inheritors of that country' scarcely distinguishable from the house of Lancaster itself.[30] Henry VI's half-brother Jasper Tudor, Earl of Pembroke, still had a personal following in Wales. The proclamation on behalf of King Henry was in the name of Pembroke as well as Warwick, Clarence and Oxford.[31] Moreover, Edward IV had failed to deliver what he had promised. He had not lived of his own nor delivered a programme of reform. He had not relieved economic discontent, surely now at its worst, and had indeed made it worse by his various exactions. He, too, was perceived as having evil councillors and he had estranged in Warwick someone who still identified himself with the reforming ideals of 1450–61. Secondly, therefore, Warwick had mass popular support. To the commons, all these were highly effective arguments. They turned out in overwhelming numbers for King Henry, whilst scarcely any mustered for King Edward. Amongst the political elite, it was mainly well-known Lancastrians and the retainers of Warwick and Clarence who rebelled. The rest of the lords, who appreciated the realities of the economy, the royal finances and Warwick's ambitions, were not to be persuaded. Thirdly, of course, it was from the immunity of French territory in the Côtentin peninsula that the expeditionary force was prepared with French funding and that supporters at home were coordinated.

The fourth factor was the sheer weakness of Edward IV. The new coalition was extremely difficult to defend against. At least Edward had a Burgundian fleet to prevent the invaders getting through, yet Warwick managed to evade it. Almost all Englishmen had been brought up under Henry VI and potentially there were enemies everywhere. During the past decade, Lancastrian plots had been exposed in North Wales, the Isle of Wight, East Anglia, the East Midlands and the North-East. Warwick and Clarence were strong in South Wales, the West and North Midlands, Yorkshire and Cumbria, Lincolnshire and the Home Counties. The Beauforts, Courtenays, Hollands and indeed Clarence and Prince Edward were great landholders in the West Country. There were indeed to be disturbances in 1470 in Wales, the West Country, West Midlands, Richmondshire and Kent. Which was the main attack and which the feint? When Lord FitzHugh raised Richmondshire prematurely, Edward was quick to suppress it,[32] but was therefore far adrift when the main landing came in the far south-west. There were no effective defences. Once ashore, at Plymouth and Dartmouth in Devon on 13 September 1470, Warwick appears to have attracted recruits too numerous to withstand. The Earl of Shrewsbury and Lord Stanley met the invaders at Bristol, where Warwick picked up the ordnance he had left there in the spring. According to one surely incredible account, they led 60,000 men. Edward, in contrast, seems to have been almost unsupported. Moreover Montagu turned the northerners raised on Edward's behalf against him. It had been Edward's botched regrouping of the previous year that turned the marquis from a friend into a foe. This time, however, Edward was not so easily arrested and fled abroad, towards the Low Countries.[33]

THE *READEPTION* OF HENRY VI, 1470-1

It was Bishop Waynflete and Lord Sudeley, two trusted Lancastrians, who fetched Henry VI from the Tower on 6 October 1470 to ascend his throne once more. This was his *Second Reign*, or *Readeption*. In the absence of the queen and prince, who were not to arrive from France until April 1471, and of the dukes of Exeter and Somerset, who cannot have returned before January, it was Warwick who took the lead. He was the king's lieutenant. His brother Archbishop Neville and Prior Langstrother were again chancellor and treasurer. A Parliament was held that confirmed the change of dynasty, restored to the Crown both the duchy of Lancaster and the possessions of the prince of Wales, and restorated in blood the Lancastrians. A treaty was concluded with France and hostilities against Burgundy were actually launched from Calais. Unfortunately, the parliament roll and original acts are lost. Perhaps there were some attainders of Yorkists: only the Earl of Worcester is known to have been actually executed. If there was no reform programme, perhaps as in 1455 and 1460 it was scheduled for the second session which, in this case, was overtaken by the return of Edward IV.

Restoration of property was contentious. Probably all Lancastrian attainders were reversed. If Warwick had most to lose from restorations, he gained most in other ways. However, Clarence is known to have refused to give up the honour of Richmond, which had been resumed in 1461, to the king's young nephew Henry Tudor, yet was regranted it only for life. How could the contradictory claims of Devon, Northumberland and Montagu to the Percy and Courtenay inheritances be reconciled? If Clarence was to be the next heir, however unlikely a situation, this was to the loss of the extended Lancastrian royal family, especially the dukes of Exeter and Somerset. Some Lancastrians, at least, were jealous of their new allies.[34] Clearly, Warwick's followers also lost out. Such problems did not divide them when faced by their common enemy, but may have impeded cooperation when Edward returned.

How was this possible?

Edward's exit had been abject. Moreover, he only just outpaced Hanseatic pursuers before his landfall at Flushing in the Low Countries. This was part of the possessions of his brother-in-law Charles the Bold, not necessarily a reliable ally. Charles wanted to avoid war with France and England. Despite his marriage to Edward's sister, Margaret of York, Charles favoured the Lancastrians – he had allowed Exeter and Somerset to return home – and he was disinclined to provoke conflict by backing Edward. He may even have considered handing him over.

That Warwick and Louis XI attacked Burgundy even before the new English regime drove Charles into supporting Edward and gave Edward some of the same advantages that Warwick had enjoyed the previous autumn. With Burgundian assistance, a small expeditionary force was prepared. Edward had been accompanied or followed into exile by some key figures: his brother Richard, Duke of Gloucester, brother-in-law Earl Rivers, Lord Hastings, lord chamberlain of his household, and Lords Dudley, Say and Duras.[35] Since there had been no battle, many other potential supporters remained in England, at liberty like his brother-in-law Suffolk, or in sanctuary at Westminster, St Martin's-le-Grand and Colchester.[36] So, too, was his queen and two of his sisters, who contrived to win over their brother Clarence once more. Always second best to Clarence, the *Readeption* had already brought financial loss and resentment of what he still retained. It also gave him political leverage and made him worth cultivating. Defeat, moreover, forced Edward to adopt a more conciliatory stance. It required him to abandon his intransigent insistence on submission and obedience. He now offered Clarence a fresh start without penalties and recriminations. At Clarence's request, he was even to offer terms to Warwick that the earl declined. Meantime most of his peerage remained convinced Yorkists and continued to support him rather than Warwick and the Lancastrians. Henry Percy, fourth Earl of Northumberland, was the son, grandson and three-times nephew of Lancastrians slain by the Yorkists, yet he had been restored by King Edward: which way would he jump? If Warwick's grip could be broken and all these resources could be concentrated, an army capable of competing could be assembled.

Once again invaders were able to destabilize the regime. Although Henry VI's total resources still exceeded those of King Edward, it was not possible to bring them together or to make them count. The leadership of Edward himself was essential. The *Readeption* regime had summoned and incarcerated Norfolk and others in whose loyalty they doubted. The regime's coastal defences were effective. With 2,000 men Edward tried first to land at Cromer in Norfolk on 12 March 1471, but had to re-embark. Landing again near Ravenspur in Yorkshire, coastal defenders were too powerful again. Even without noble backing, the local gentleman Martin of the Sea and the priest John Westerdale brought out the commons of Holderness 6,000-strong. At this point deceit and perjury gave Edward an advantage. He swore that he was only seeking his duchy, to which his right could not be denied, and his gullible adversaries allowed him to traverse the initial obstacles. He then passed into the Percy East Riding, which memories of the defeat at Towton made extremely hostile territory. Unable to carry his men into the Yorkist camp, the new Percy, Earl of Northumberland, was nevertheless able to neutralize them, so they 'sat still', and thus enabled Edward to thread himself through the defences to the relative security of the East Midlands. There Hastings's men and other diehard Yorkists totalling 3,000 men rallied to him and gave him an army. Even so, he still had a smaller force than Warwick both at Coventry and at the Battle of Barnet. Apparently Edward had not attracted popular backing, nor could he array county or town levies through commissioners: that was the prerogative of the government. He therefore bypassed Warwick, leaving him to his rear, and took the strategic initiative by striking at London. Warwick, however, still had 'many more than the king' at the Battle of Barnet (14 April 1471). Luck favoured his more aggressive opponent and victory went to King Edward.

In theory, the *Readeption* regime should have been much the stronger. Warwick himself had bastard feudal strength in the North and West Midlands, both of which he was able to mobilize, with Jasper Tudor in Wales, and in the South-East – in the City, Kent, Calais, and in his shipmen. He had supporters in the East Midlands and the East Anglia led by Exeter and Oxford – although rebuffed by King Edward near Newark, these were at Barnet – and in the West Country, where Prince Edward as Duke of Cornwall, the Beauforts, Hollands and Courtenays were the 'old inheritors'. Genuinely popular, this time he spoke with King Henry's authority and could command subjects to array. In combination these gave him enormous advantages, but they could not be combined.

Warwick was a logistics man, a thinking soldier, who did not wish to fight until he could bring all his resources to bear, but this did not happen – he was not altogether in control – and he was up against a bolder strategist and a superior tactician. The mass support that was so useful when dislodging a regime was not so readily arrayed, kept in being, and deployed in defence.

What exposed Warwick's weakness were the rifts within the *Readeption* coalition. Warwick deferred battle when Edward appeared before Coventry, expecting to be even stronger when Clarence arrived. Instead the duke carried his westcountrymen into Edward's camp. It was a blow, but hardly fatal. Much more serious was the loss of London. When allowing Edward to bypass him, Warwick had counted on holding the City, the seat of government and of the king, a source of popular support, and an essential route for his supporters in Kent, Calais, and his fleet. He planned to corner King Edward between his army and the City or alternatively to bring all his forces to bear on him. He expected a decisive advantage in numbers. He counted on the Lancastrian Duke of Somerset, Marquis of Dorset and Earl of Devon holding it for King Henry, yet in this crisis their priority was to receive Queen Margaret and Prince Edward on their landing at Weymouth in Dorset. On their departure, they left London almost undefended – Archbishop Neville and the aged Sudeley could not hold it – and Edward entered, imprisoned King Henry again, and thus cut Warwick off from the men of Calais, Kent and the fleet. The battles of the Wars of the Roses were highly unpredictable, Barnet being no exception. It was fought in thick fog, the armies were not precisely aligned, and Montagu's men fought Oxford's on the same side in error. Warwick's army was the larger and apparently better equipped, but it was Edward who attacked and Edward who won. The *Readeption* army was destroyed. Warwick and Montagu were killed. Exeter and Oxford escaped.

Now in control of the government and able to issue commissions of array, Edward was no more popular than before and was confronted by a still powerful but geographically dispersed enemy, which however he was able to defeat in detail. Many of those defeated at Barnet escaped the battle alive. There were still Neville supporters in Richmondshire and the West March, who rose again in May 1471. From late April, Warwick's cousin Thomas Neville, the Bastard of Fauconberg, mustered the earl's shipmen, supporters in Kent and perhaps in Calais to attack London. Jasper Tudor was raising the Welsh Lancastrians. There was support in Lancashire and Cheshire. And Queen Margaret, Prince Edward, Somerset and Devon were in the West Country, where they raised an army apparently from their hereditary family supporters. That it was weaker than the overwhelming force of the previous year was partly because Clarence had already recruited in the region, partly because they never reached Warwick's heartland in the West Midlands, and perhaps also because they were shorn of his own supporters and popular appeal. How far popular appeal depended on Warwick himself we cannot tell. Edward focused first on the south-western Lancastrians and struck at them, meantime abandoning London to the Bastard of Fauconberg. It was the right choice. Fewer in numbers, the Lancastrians were not able to meet up with Jasper Tudor in Wales or their other allies and were forced to fight on 4 May at Tewkesbury, where their army and indeed Lancastrianism were destroyed. Amongst those slain at or after the battle were Prince Edward, Edmund and John Beaufort – the future of the Lancastrian line – Devon, Wenlock, Langstrother, Hampden, Whittingham and other diehard Lancastrians of the previous decade. Queen Margaret was captured. King Henry, already a prisoner, could now be eliminated. What was there left to fight over? Again Jasper Tudor, Earl of Pembroke, fled abroad to Brittany, this time with his nephew the young Henry Tudor. By 14 May the Richmondshire rebels were pacified and the Bastard of Fauconberg's assault on London was repelled. Although too late, he appears to have raised Kent as a whole, including Mayor Nicholas Faunt of Canterbury, who was executed, and town councillors of the Cinque Ports, 200 artisans and tradesmen of London, and men from 60 different administrative districts fined for and presumably mustered as in 1450 by their constables. The bastard submitted on 26 May.[37]

The *Second War* was won and with it, surely, the Wars of the Roses as a whole. Although Edward's victory was against the odds, in the face of the popular will, in the depths of the slump, and indeed almost miraculous,[38] it was much more complete than had been that of 1461. Most of the diehard Lancastrians had been slaughtered at Tewkesbury and there were only 13 new attainders. The Kentishmen were 'hanged by the purse': that is, they were allowed to purchase pardons. So too, it appears, did many aristocratic offenders. Sir John Marny of Layer Marney (Essex), who had fought on the losing side at Barnet, was fined £800, placed under sureties with conditions, and was obliged to convey his lands to trustees nominated by the king.[39] Even Edward's brother-in-law, the Lancastrian Henry Holland, Duke of Exeter, was spared for the moment. There were only three significant exceptions to this amnesty: Jasper Tudor, Earl of Pembroke, who bore his nephew Henry off to Brittany with him, and John de Vere, Earl of Oxford. No longer was there a Lancastrian cause, leader, or anybody left to fight. Almost every opponent still living was eligible for forgiveness. The twice-perjured Clarence received back his precedence, possessions and even the Warwick inheritance of his duchess. Ex-Chief Justice Fortescue and Dr John Morton were welcomed into the king's council. The rift in Yorkism was healed and the future of the dynasty assured with the birth of Edward's son, the future Edward V. Thereafter, the royal finances were reconstructed, the economy recovered somewhat, and hence popular discontent dispelled. Problems in Wales were tackled by devolving central government to a council on the spot under Prince Edward at Ludlow (Salop.). There was continuous domestic peace from 1471 to 1483. It was an enormous achievement for a usurper created by a faction to die peacefully in his bed (9 April 1483) and transmit his crown without debate to his son.

CHAPTER 12

THE THIRD WAR: FIRST PHASE 1483–5

The Wars of the Roses resumed in 1483: the *Third War*. This *Third War* began with the death of Edward IV, the succession of his son Edward V (the elder of the Princes in the Tower), and the latter's deposition by his uncle Richard, Duke of Gloucester, King Richard III (1483–5). What began as a contest for power amongst loyal subjects now moved on to a different plane. Richard's accession was not accepted peacefully. His usurpation stimulated a variegated coalition amongst those whom it outraged. Later in 1483 he had to contend with an uprising throughout southern England called Buckingham's Rebellion and thereafter with plots organized abroad in favour of Henry Tudor, who in 1485 invaded, defeated and killed Richard at Bosworth, and made himself King Henry VII (1485–1509). Henry also enjoyed less than general support. Over the next 40 years both he and his son Henry VIII (1509–47) had to contend with a series of rivals: the most important being the rebels of 1486 and 1487, especially Lambert Simnel and the prolonged Perkin Warbeck conspiracy, which certainly had the potential to reverse the verdict of Bosworth.

All this was unexpected. Edward IV's victory in 1471 had seemed to mark the end of the Wars of the Roses. It ushered in the twelve peaceful years of his *Second Reign* (1471–83). All outstanding dynastic issues were settled. Indeed, with the death in 1471 of all the Lancastrian male lines, in the persons of Henry VI, his son Prince Edward and the Beaufort brothers, the House of York became the male line of Edward III, and Edward IV his heir male as well as heir general. Only obscure female permutations and the residual claims of the Duke of Clarence,[1] acceptable to neither Lancaster nor York, offered alternatives that nobody, surely, thought were practical. There should not have been a *Third War*. It owed little to what had gone before – to changing political attitudes in particular – and resulted primarily from new causes.

Successive governments remained extremely weak and susceptible to overthrow. Moreover, the prime mover Richard, Duke of Gloucester, had much in common with his father Richard, Duke of York, and his father-in-law Warwick the Kingmaker. Like them, he proved an overmighty subject. Remembering their successful blueprint which he had experienced at first hand, he consciously applied some of the lessons he had learnt and parotted some of the same ideals in his coups and his usurpation. Naturally, he had to justify his actions – after all, he hoped to persuade the political elite at least to accept himself and his fait accompli and to forestall any counterattack. In recent years Richard has been extraordinarily fortunate to find hordes of modern partisans who have bestowed credibility on his case, which four centuries of historians found unworthy of serious consideration. Yet actually Richard was different. His arguments were too far-fetched and were designed to conceal his own ambitions. He did realize that a purely dynastic revolution, changing one king for another, was not disinterested but selfish, not obviously beneficial to the commonweal, and was not worth anybody else fighting over or dying for. Richard therefore consciously modelled his coups on earlier demands for good governance, but he had to inflate the ills that he claimed to remedy. Really his principal objective was the Crown. Yet like York and Warwick, he started a process that he could not control. Moral outrage at his usurpation brought the Yorkist establishment of southern England to arms in 1483. Additional scandals, real or imagined, were exposed by Tudor propaganda, notably the fate of the Princes in the Tower, denied him the allegiance normally due to an anointed king and strengthened the case for rejecting him for a dynastic alternative. Richard's unavoidable countermeasures, the rule of the South by trusted northerners that southerners equated with tyranny and his forced revenue raising, fuelled claims of bad governance without noticeably enhancing aristocratic support.

Unintentionally, Richard unleashed a new set of conflicts that outlasted his own life and reign. Between 1483 and 1497 there were to be four kings, two usurpations, four battles, six rebellions, three *coups d'état*, two assassination plots, numerous conspiracies, and six invasions, two of them successful. This *Third War* became purely dynastic. An important theme was North versus South. Richard III was a northern king resisted by the southerners, Henry VII the king of the South who was resented in the North. Smaller in scale, this *Third War* attracted fewer English participants, noble or otherwise, had no popular component, and became dependent on foreign intervention, both to maintain rivals to the Crown and for the manpower of successive invasions.

What happened in the years 1471–83 was not, as the Tudor historians claimed, the reason for what followed, which had more immediate causes. However, Richard III presented it as such. The usurpation of 1483 and subsequent reactions to it actually broke the trend of historical development and reversed the expectations of contemporaries. It 'interrupted the process of recovery'.[2] Richard III's accession on 26 June 1483 was not predicted or even contemplated a few months before it befell, perhaps for most people not even a few weeks or a few days earlier, for instance on 16 June when he was perceived as the best hope for peace.[3] When he usurped the throne, it came as a great surprise and outrage. What happened has nevertheless to be set in an English context. The English background and factors that were entirely English contributed to a cycle of unforeseen events. This context is, however, essential and is discussed here.

There are hints of occasional riots and plots after 1471, but none that was significant. Indeed, all that threatened the stability of Edward's *Second Reign* was his foreign policy. Still a young king, still anxious for military honour, still apparently serious in his ambition to recover his kingdom of France, Edward was also disinclined to forgive the French king who had helped to dethrone him. Just as Warwick had embarked on war with Burgundy on Louis' behalf, so Edward saw war with France as the continuation not only of the alliance that he had agreed originally with Burgundy in 1467–8, but as the completion of the campaign of 1471. It was his intention to resume the Hundred Years War and recover his kingdom of France, he told Parliament in 1472. For the next three years he was reconstructing alliances with Burgundy and Brittany, neutralizing the threat of Scotland, raising money through parliamentary taxation and preparing a splendid army, which embarked in 1475 for what turned out to be a campaign of only a few weeks.[4]

King Louis, of course, did not know that Edward could be bought off so easily. Understandably, he feared a united attack by all his foes. One reaction, as in 1470, was to destabilize England by supporting English dissidents. There remained some supporters of the *Readeption* who had not been reconciled and who would cooperate. The Earl of Oxford sent King Louis twenty-four seals of dissident lords, including one duke. Louis thought them counterfeit, forged to secure his backing, and it does seem unlikely that any secret plotter would dare put his intentions on record.[5] If true, the duke was less likely to be Clarence, now back in the bosom of his family and wealthier than ever before, than Exeter, the last scion of Lancaster now all the male lines were deceased and a prisoner in the Tower. Archbishop Neville spoke foolishly of Edward's deposition and was imprisoned and despoiled in consequence.[6] Oxford, his brothers and a handful of others were willing to fight on and were supplied with shipping by King Louis. They were not a serious threat and took only five months to crush. When a landing in the earl's home country of Essex at St Osyth's was beaten off, he seized instead the impregnable St Michael's Mount in Cornwall on 30 September 1473. He was starved out on 15 February 1474.[7] Oxford spent the rest of the reign in prison at Calais. Exeter died in 1475 and Archbishop Neville in 1476. Jasper Tudor lived on in exile, but made no further attempts to inspire Welsh uprisings.

There remained only the Tudors, Jasper, Earl of Pembroke, and his nephew Henry, rightfully Earl of Richmond. If Jasper still had influence in Wales, no use was made of it, and Edward IV appears to have offered him nothing. Young Henry's hereditary claim, although slight, gave him some diplomatic value. He had done nothing wrong. He had still been a minor when taken from England by his uncle and he was not a free agent in Brittany, where he was in protective custody as a useful pawn for Duke Francis II in his dealings with both England and France, who both at various points wanted him. Legally, Henry may still have been an earl. His estates on the side of his father Edmund Tudor had been resumed in 1461, not forfeited, and after 1478 were back in the king's hands. Henry Tudor was also a significant heir as son to his mother Margaret Beaufort. Now remarried to the steward of the king's household Thomas, Lord Stanley, Lady Margaret was well placed in court circles. She planned for her son's return, in 1482 with the approval of King Edward, who had tried to negotiate Henry's handover on several occasions.[8] Why should all parties not agree? There was no longer a Lancastrian cause to fear.

It has often been claimed, on no concrete evidence at all, that Edward's brothers Clarence and Gloucester were conspiring for the throne.[9] Since the king was still relatively young, had two sons and numerous daughters, any such pretensions were highly imaginative. More credibly, the king and/or queen may have seen in the elder brother Clarence another overmighty subject who might attempt to seize power. Crowland reports that Clarence was popular and silver-tongued.[10] The 1470 treaty of Angers, apparently ratified by the *Readeption* Parliament, had made Clarence residual heir to the house of Lancaster, but any such claim was unacceptable to Lancastrians and Yorkists alike. Although restored in full in 1471 and allowed the inheritance of his duchess, Isabel Neville, he had thereafter suffered what could be regarded as a succession of highly expensive slights over the settlement of the Warwick inheritance, the resumption of his honour of Tutbury, and the frustration surrounding his proposed second marriage, to Mary of Burgundy in 1477. Relations between king and duke became very sour, as their private railings were apparently relayed to the other. Clarence also engaged in one of the classic abuses of power – the judicial murder of Ankarette Twynho – that under Henry VI would have resulted in a brief incarceration and under Edward, witness the siege of Caister, perhaps nothing. Yet when his retainer Thomas Burdet was executed, Clarence did not stage a coup, but protested to the king's council, thereby operating within, not outside, the political conventions. There is no evidence that he had any fellow dissidents and nobody else was charged with anything. Edward then took extreme action against his brother, trying him in Parliament and executing him on 18 February 1478, a shocking act of fratricide that no primary narrator thought to be justified.[11] It was not politically very important. As for the Duke of Gloucester, no historian before Sir Thomas More in 1516 attributed to him long-term ambitions for the throne.[12]

Edward's munificence to his supporters was not unqualified. Recipients of forfeited property were always liable to lose their gains to restored Lancastrians, and all recipients of royal bounty had regularly to justify their offices and other grants too if they were not to be resumed. This was adminis-tered in person by an imposing king who remembered everyone's face and circumstances, and whose signet office maintained comprehensive records of his patronage. Service had to be continued if grants in perpetuity or for life were to endure. Edward took his oversight of his leading subjects seriously and certainly manipulated their inheritances to the advantage of his kin and favourites. From 1478, however, Crowland discerns more assertiveness. King Edward, he reports, was so much more powerful that he could confront his greatest subjects with their offences to their faces, which historians have failed to confirm. This may well be because the fines and sureties that Edward exacted were lodged in the signet office, whose records are lost, and not yet systematically on the chancery close rolls that survive. The chancery files increasingly allow erratic glimpses of recognizances exacted for good behav-iour, to appear before the royal council, or to keep the peace, one on pain of forfeiting £26,000 and all threatening those bound over with potential ruin. Indentures between the king and marcher lords directed how the latter exercised their local power and made them responsible for the behaviour of their men. Sureties were again used to halt feuds, notably those of the Harringtons against the Stanleys, the next Berkeley–Lisle contestants, and the Herberts versus the Vaughans in Wales. Edward managed to lever the Welsh William Herbert out of Wales and indeed also out of his Welsh titles and estates, which he wished to retain, in exchange for the earldom of Huntingdon and less valuable and much less valued property in the West Country. Edward's signature signals his knowledge and approval of some key private transactions. He did not, however, flex his muscle in every case. Thus he allowed his youngest brother Gloucester not only to despoil the aged and blameless Countess of Oxford, but to retain his ill-gotten gains.[13]

Yet Edward ruled like his predecessors and left much to the routine opera-tions of government. Parliament and great council were consulted infrequently. Decisions were made in consultation with his ministers; with his chamberlain William, Lord Hastings, his elder stepson Thomas Grey, Marquis of Dorset, and his youngest brother-in-law Sir Edward Wydeville, all boon companions; and with the staff of his upper household, who were also rulers of the southern counties. Much land, authority and offices were delegated in Wales to Edward, Prince of Wales, who was managed by the queen's elder brother Earl Rivers and her younger stepson Lord Richard Grey, and in the North to the king's youngest brother Gloucester.

The queen's family, collectively known as the Wydevilles, were favoured but not excessively. Her brother Earl Rivers, for instance, was not a wealthy earl, nor even premier earl, neither of his many brothers nor the king's younger stepson Richard Grey became peers, and the king's own nuclear family was preferred to his Wydeville and Grey in-laws. The Wydevilles did not corner royal patronage. What they undoubtedly did do was use the resources of the queen and two princes Edward and Richard – and their prospects in reversion on the king's death – to construct an extensive connection of loyal Yorkists committed in particular to themselves. To some extent Edward IV provided for his brother, sons and stepsons at the expense of the legitimate claims of others.[14]

Although Edward spread office and patronage quite widely, there were factional jealousies at court and bitter distrust between the chamberlain Hastings and the household on the one hand and the queen's kin, which on occasion flared into dirty tricks.[15] Like his grandson Henry VIII, King Edward could be manipulated but never ignored. He was definitely in control right up to his death in 1483.

It was a triumph of financial management for Edward IV to progress from virtual bankruptcy to solvency. Most of the accumulated debts of Henry VI and Richard, Duke of York, were repaid, although the dowry of Edward's sister Margaret of York to Charles the Bold was never paid in full. Edward was able to 'live of his own' and indeed financed a war with Scotland from 1479 to 1483 without resort to parliamentary taxation. Much financial business was conducted in the treasury of his chamber, for which records do not survive, not the exchequer. Edward scrutinized his grants, checked that they still offered value for money, and on occasion resumed them. He did keep some Crown estate in hand towards his expenses, did allocate revenues to his household, and ensured it operated economically. He managed to live as a king was expected to live, with a magnificent court that aped the ceremony and etiquette so admired in contemporary Burgundy. He built on a princely scale, assembled a splendid library and patronized the Church. The re-interment that he arranged for his father at Fotheringhay in 1476 and the wedding of his second son in 1478 were especially impressive. Edward IV was reputed to have accumulated an immense treasure by his death.[16]

Yet all was not quite what it seemed. Some recovery in trade gave Edward significantly more customs revenue. His estate-management system involved very few estates, principally Clarence's own from 1478, and there is little evidence that more revenue was wrung out of them.[17] Political management, through patronage and provision for his son in Wales, took priority. To Chester and the principality were added the earldom of March, duchy of Lancaster and Herbert lordships in Wales, and the earldom of Pembroke.[18] Probably King Edward ended up in credit when the costs of the French war were deducted from the taxes raised for it.[19] From 1475 until 1482, moreover, there was a French pension of £10,000, a relatively small sum which was absolutely essential to achieve total revenues of about £70,000:[20] more than in Henry VI's last years, but little more than half of what Richard II had enjoyed and a mere drop in the ocean of Louis XI. By Edward's death, however, any treasure had been spent on the Scottish war. Edward left insufficient cash to pay for his funeral and his bequests exceeded whatever else he had to leave. By 1483 he needed taxes and his officers were struggling to match income to expenses on a weekly basis.[21] They were not, however, defaulting or unable to borrow, as Henry VI had been. Edward's credit remained good.

Edward's apparent wealth impressed others, made him more secure, and deterred any potential rebels, but it did not make him popular. The maximization of feudal revenues, with which he was credited but which modern historians have not confirmed, was held against him. The £118,625 in taxes required for 13,000 archers for his French war were voted reluctantly, transferred as far as possible from the normal taxpayers by a 10 per cent income tax which was appropriated solely to the war, and were made conditional on the king going to France – a signal of the distrust arising from his previous failure. Moreover, they were not to be a precedent. Not all the revenues could be collected and the final instalments were remitted when peace was agreed. Popular anger at home was anticipated that so much had been spent for so little, and special measures were taken to keep order.[22] The most favourable gloss was placed on the ensuing treaty – the king's title to the realm of France was not renounced, but was to be arbitrated. Edward's daughter Elizabeth, betrothed to the Dauphin Charles, was titled dauphiness. Probably anticipating that they would be held to account at a future Parliament (as in 1450), the negotiators of the treaty had exemplified (certified) the minute of the council that instructed them.[23]

Actually, no Parliament was held for more than two years and no further tax was sought then. In 1480, however, following the outbreak of war with Scotland, the balance of the taxation previously voted and remitted was collected, although not in the North. A benevolence or forced gift, was levied in 1481. Following the recapture of Berwick on the North-East border, which was portrayed as a great victory, the Parliament of 1483 voted a fifteenth and tenth and a poll tax on aliens. The clergy granted a clerical tenth, which Crowland (a cleric) railed against. That the benevolence was also unpopular is revealed by the act of Parliament abolishing benevolences in 1484.[24] Not only did hostility persist at taxation and Edward's perceived misappropriation of funds, but the burden in Edward's last years was unusually heavy. Avarice was charged against him. One of his own men lamented:

> I stored my coffers and also my chests
> With taxes taken of the communalty;
> I took their treasure but of their prayers [I] missed . . .
> I had enough, but was not content.[25]

By then, the worst of the *Great Slump* was over. Professor Hatcher reports: 'The rally in overseas trade from the 1470s, which drew support from a general revival of European transcontinental trade, was both strong and widely based, and some branches positively boomed: by 1479–82 annual imports and exports of merchandise paying *ad valorem* duties were valued at almost three times the level they had fallen to between 1456 and 1471. . . . The trough of the slump in the rural economy had also passed by the 1480s.' All the indices capable of measurement signal an economic recovery: exports of wool and cloth, imports of wine and other products, the prices of wool and cloth, wheat and barley, and cows. Tin and lead production increased.[26] If not yet back to the beginnings of the depression in the 1440s, still less to earlier prosperity, there were fewer grounds for economic discontent and still less the impoverishment that had made the populace so ready to engage in politics. If not the result of royal policy, the government benefited from a more contented populace. Even Richard III could not persuade them otherwise.

Yet all was not well when Edward died in 1483, and difficulties lay ahead. His foreign policy had collapsed, his French pension had ceased, and all his daughters were unmarried. He was embroiled in a war with Scotland without obvious objectives and which he could not bring to an end. Slighted by King Louis, Edward was tempted to wage another war against him without allies, which he was unlikely to win and could not afford. His treasury was empty and he was obliged to resort to unpopular taxation.[27] There were difficult decisions to be made. Yet this was very far from a crisis. Parliament approved of the recapture of Berwick. The economic misery, misgovernment, evil counsel, lack of access and lack of remedy for grievances that were preconditions to the first two Wars were noticeably absent, although the Duke of Gloucester was shortly to claim that they had recurred. There was no popular outrage, no foreign threat, and no alternative contender for the Crown. Barring a short minority, there was nothing to impede a peaceful transition from Edward IV's successful reign to that of his son Edward V.

The Usurpation of Richard III, 1483

Just over four years, only 50 months, separated the death of King Edward IV on 9 April 1483 from the defeat of Lambert Simnel by Henry VII at the Battle of Stoke on 16 June 1487. These years should be grouped together.[28] Whilst King Edward may have allowed some things to drift and certainly tolerated court intrigues, he maintained his authority and grip to the end. His death and the minority of his son Edward V promised both a relaxation of royal authority and an opportunity for one of these factions to take power. Faction fighting within the Yorkist establishment enabled the late king's brother Richard, Duke of Gloucester, first to seize control of the government and then to usurp the throne. This result was achieved by the temporary application of military force which did not last, not by a consensus. Resistance by those who disagreed and were disaffected with the new regime failed in 1483 (Buckingham's Rebellion), but, reinforced by substantial foreign support, succeeded in 1485.

What opened the door for the *Third War* was the death of Edward IV. Civil war did not look at all likely when his eldest son and heir Prince Edward was acknowledged next day, 10 April 1483, as King Edward V by the royal council. There was no debate. Everybody of political significance – the new king's mother Queen Elizabeth, her family (the Wydevilles) and dependants, the late king's brother Richard, Duke of Gloucester, William, Lord Hastings and Edward IV's own servants, the king's ministers, the royal council and indeed the Lords – had sworn allegiance to him already, many both in 1472 and in 1477.[29] New oaths to the new king were now sworn at Westminster, at York, and doubtless elsewhere.[30]

If who was to reign was not in doubt, who was to rule was. Aged only twelve, Edward V was too young even by medieval standards actually to govern in person. Others must rule on his behalf. Some changes were inevitable. The incorporation of his own servants and household as prince into that of the king must inevitably displace some of the incumbent officers. Lord Hastings and Edward IV's household may have wished only to retain their positions. Apparently they feared some sort of vengeance from their Wydeville rivals.[31] Whether that was indeed intended and what form reprisals might have taken remains unknown. Wydeville intentions need not have been malign. Hastings expected to be dismissed, but violence towards him was probably not in their minds. For the new king's maternal kindred and connections, King Edward V's accession was the opportunity for their own advancement in power, careers and offices. Here, therefore, were frictions to be resolved by agreement first among the Lords and then in parliament.

Apart from formally reconciling Hastings and Dorset on his deathbed,[32] Edward IV surely sought to regulate the government of his son – most probably by nominating his sole remaining brother Gloucester to be Lord Protector. Such kingly decisions inevitably died with their maker. The reconciliation was immediately discounted. Gloucester was far away, just as John, Duke of Bedford, had been in 1422. Gloucester was not heir presumptive and hence not automatically entitled to power. There was also a queen mother of English extraction and mature years, who was entitled to the utmost respect, determined to involve herself in her son's affairs, and who was backed moreover by a powerful faction that was set on power and had indeed been preparing for it.

Instead of waiting for Gloucester, therefore, and deferring decisions to the Lords in Parliament, Elizabeth and her eldest son Dorset exploited the opportunity that had opened for them and seized the initiative. They persuaded the council to crown Edward immediately, on 4 May. Since this was known at Ludlow on 14 April, the decision had therefore been made in the opening days – perhaps on the opening day – of the new reign.[33] On the precedent of 1429, when Henry VI was only seven years old, coronation would bring forward Edward's majority and his adult rule and remove the need for a minority council or protectorate. So young a king would need advice and assistance that Elizabeth and Dorset themselves were best placed to provide. Their existing guidance and direction of the prince could continue now that he was king. It made good sense to them.

Nevertheless, this was a Wydeville *coup d'état*. It overrode the rights of the Lords and of Parliament to participate and to decide. It rejected consent as irrelevant. It was not a personal rejection of Gloucester himself. Record evidence shows his relations with Elizabeth and Rivers to be cordial.[34] The coup carried no threat to him. It did relegate him to a secondary role. Although intended to decide the issue, impose order and ensure firm Wydeville government for the next few years, it was this Wydeville coup that brought instability. It provoked a desperate search amongst the Wydevilles' enemies for allies, not all as loyal or as disinterested as Hastings, and could only be resisted by force. Force was what followed. It was the application of force that enabled the quarrel to get out of control, in due course, of all parties. In the face of universal support for Edward V, it is hard without this coup to see how Gloucester could have usurped the throne. It appeared to expose as malign the intentions of the Wydevilles. It revealed them not as a source of continuity and not as the authentic voice of the Yorkist establishment, but as a self-interested and power-hungry clique. It united all the politically responsible against them. Far down the line of succession, Gloucester cannot have seriously hoped for the Crown before his brother's death. It was the Wydeville coup that made it all conceivable.

Almost at once, it appears, Gloucester decided to seize power. Private reasons may have made control of royal patronage essential. The death of the Marquis Montagu's son George Neville on 4 May, which may have been foreseen, undermined Gloucester's power base in the North and demanded revisions in the Warwick inheritance that were only attainable when Gloucester was politically ascendant.[35] When precisely Gloucester first aspired to the throne is unknown and probably unknowable.

The coronation of Edward V would consolidate Wydeville power. To achieve it, to remove Hastings and other unwanted officers, and to set the new government on the intended course was best achieved if backed by force: if the king brought an army from Wales and the entourages of all other peers were limited. Whether or not this was intended, this was what Hastings feared. He insisted successfully on limiting the king's escort to what seems a large number – 2,000 – but which he was confident that Buckingham and Gloucester would match. Hastings kept Gloucester informed about developments.[36] Earl Rivers timed his journey to coincide with the dukes and unwittingly placed himself and the young king in their hands. On 1 May 1483 at Stony Stratford, Northamptonshire, the two dukes seized the king, asserting their loyalty in the humblest manner, and denounced Rivers and Richard Grey as traitors. Of course, Edward protested but, a mere lad, he was disregarded. His most trusted mentors – Rivers, Grey and Vaughan – were imprisoned and his household was disbanded.[37] It was a complete surprise, a bloodless *coup d'état*: Gloucester's *First Coup*. 'Richard's behaviour lay outside their terms of reference'[38] – beyond the normal parameters of political debate. The date set for Edward V's coronation was allowed to pass.

Control of the young king was crucial. Henceforth, Gloucester and Buckingham could advise him. They could issue letters in his name under his signet. Converting control of his person into actual rule was more difficult. A counter-coup was predicted. The queen mother tried to orchestrate resistance in London, but quickly found Gloucester's actions approved. She took sanctuary at Westminster Abbey with her younger son Richard and daughters because she was suspicious that Gloucester really intended usurpation.[39] Given how many princes and princesses there were with better rights than the duke, such fears were fanciful and scoffed by almost everybody. Approaches made to her were rebuffed: by 9 June she was thought to be wholly unreasonable.[40]

Gloucester himself wrote skilfully to the royal council and the City corporation, protesting his loyalty and modestly advancing his reasonable claims to be Protector as the late king's brother and most loyal subject. These were open letters that were broadcast to the populace.[41] Opposition was thereby disarmed and the new king's joyous entry into London was applauded. King Edward V was housed in the City, where he was visible, could be visited, and was obviously coming to no harm. Gloucester made everybody significant swear allegiance to Edward and took the oath himself, for at least the third time – the fifth if 1472 and 1477 are included. With the support of Buckingham and Hastings, he was able to dominate the council, which by 8 May had appointed him as Lord Protector. Parliament was summoned for 22 June, and 24 June was set for the coronation, when the king would come of age and the protectorate cease. That the new protectorate would last for only seven weeks reassured everyone.[42]

Ostensibly, therefore, Gloucester's *First Coup* was a purely temporary measure. However, it did not assure him of future rule or security and promised a contest in Parliament. It left him vulnerable to the recovery of the Wydevilles, who now rightly viewed him as an enemy and had revenge in mind. It did not rule out Wydeville ascendancy over a young king regnant. There was some plan to enable Gloucester to retain power beyond the coronation,[43] presumably as chief councillor like Duke Humphrey of Gloucester from 1431, yet even if successful that was only a temporary expedient. The Lords were unlikely wholly to sideline the king's maternal kin, who were bound to have places on any appointed council, and they would certainly not countenance any executions. Neither indeed did the protectorate council. Whatever Rivers, Grey and Vaughan may have contemplated, it was not treasonable to oppose Gloucester before he became protector. The duke had to give way – he could not have them executed[44] – but he did not release them.

Even after his *First Coup* and his appointment as protector, therefore, Gloucester lacked the consent for his accession or indeed the prospect of consent. Eight weeks later he was king. Appointment as protector gave him control of Edward V, from 16 June also his next heir Prince Richard, and control of the machinery of government and the right legitimately to exercise royal authority. With Buckingham and Hastings as allies, the Lord Protector could dominate the royal council and household and direct affairs. Gloucester was able to neutralize the only considerable force in the hands of his enemies – the fleet commanded by Sir Edward Wydeville, who had to retire to France. The duke managed to remove opposition in the council. Three new ministers were appointed. On 13 June he staged his *Second Coup*. Supposedly this was a pre-emptive strike that anticipated a plot between Hastings and the queen:[45] a highly unlikely scenario, given Hastings's ascendancy, and one substantiated only by letters from Gloucester himself. Hastings was executed, a decisive if obviously illegal neutralization, and other potential critics/ loyalists in the royal household, chancery and council were imprisoned: Lord Stanley, steward of the household; Archbishop Rotherham, the ex-chancellor; Bishop Morton, master of the rolls; and John Forster, chancellor of the duchy of Lancaster. Though momentarily impotent, they and the whole of Edward IV's entourage were most probably alienated, with dangerous long-term repercussions.

That the Hastings plot was initially believed was what enabled Gloucester three days later, on 16 June, to wrest Prince Richard from sanctuary in Westminster Abbey. In the atmosphere of crisis, both coronation and Parliament were postponed and the protectorate thereby prolonged.[46] Throughout, moreover, the duke had a monopoly of military force. The king's Welshmen had been dismissed. Gloucester and Buckingham alone had substantial retinues. Other lords were directed to come minimally accompanied. Gloucester appealed directly to Londoners, courted popularity, and assembled them in large numbers on several occasions. 'Putting on purple raiment he often rode through the capital surrounded by a thousand attendants. He publicly showed himself so as to receive the attention and applause of the people as yet under the name of protector; but each day he entertained to dinner in his private dwelling an increasingly large number of men'. So indeed had Warwick behaved in the 1460s. To this, Gloucester added a northern army summoned as early as 10–11 June several thousand strong. Its arrival was long anticipated and it camped from late June at Finsbury Fields, just outside the City. In the absence of any counterweight, this army gave Gloucester the brute force to overawe the council, recognition procedures and his own coronation.

And of course Gloucester now presented a claim to succeed legitimately. Whilst never substantiated, although Gloucester affirmed it could be, this was designed to disarm potential hostility. Just like his father York in 1460, he claimed that Edward V had never been king and that the oaths of allegiance to him were based on a misunderstanding – that he was born in wedlock – and were therefore invalid.

Consent was necessary for Gloucester to keep the throne once he had usurped it. Consent may not have been essential for him to secure the throne, although a successful counter-measure by his opponents – such as the seizure of the king, or a wrong move by the duke that drove loyalists into direct opposition – were possibilities that could have frustrated his plans even at this stage.

Securing consent was therefore an important preoccupation. Gloucester claimed to continue the rule of his brother Edward IV: no change. His rule was necessary for public order and good governance and was legitimate. Evidently, he presented himself as the means to better governance and the solution to the rising disorder in London that the three coups had generated. Gloucester sought support from the political nation in council, the City corporation and in Parliament. He appealed directly to the people, who could bring decisive pressure to bear on the council, on Parliament, and on the unconstitutional assembly that was not a parliament which 'elected' him as king. The people in this context appear in the first place to have been Londoners and then his northern supporters. There is no evidence that he sought or gained popular backing more widely. The government of Edward V and later Richard's own regime portrayed themselves as legitimate successors of Edward IV, a rightful king, but depicted the conditions they had inherited as deplorable. Edward IV had not practised good governance. Supposedly his regime fell far short of the ideals of good rule, the pursuit of the common good, impartial justice and good order, victories abroad, and economic prosperity, commercial health and adequate livings for the poor. Instead, so Gloucester reported, there had been impoverishment and bad governance. The laws of man and God had been confounded. Instead of public-spirited, God-fearing, virtuous and prudent councillors like himself, who had been distanced and indeed excluded from affairs, Edward IV's advisers had been insolent parvenus, vicious and avaricious: the classic evil councillors. In the absence of concrete evidence of bad government, Gloucester denounced the immorality and sensuality of his brother's regime – an area in which both the late king and his intimates had offended against contemporary sexual morality. The Wydevilles and their clients, flattering courtiers, in Mancini's words had come to 'manage the public and private businesses of the crown, surround the king, give or sell offices, and finally rule the very king himself'. Gloucester even charged them with embezzling the king's treasure. As proof of their attempts to maintain their ascendancy by force, he displayed the cartloads of weapons that he claimed to have captured at Stony Stratford on 1 May and that justified his pre-emptive strike.[47] Richard made 'character assassination an instrument of policy'.[48] Most of his propaganda misrepresented the truth – he had been absent from court rather than excluded – or untrue. For instance, he invented the story about embezzlement of treasure, which he knew to be unfounded. However, it served very well to confirm public opinion against the Wydevilles.[49]

Gloucester's *Second Coup* of 13 June had placed a narrow faction in control. Securing Prince Richard on the 16th had removed the obvious alternative figurehead to Edward V. Postponing Parliament and the coronation revealed Gloucester's determination at least to remain in power. All these actions most probably signify the intent to usurp, but this was not yet realized generally and it was still possible for the duke to pull back. Richard's claim to the throne was first aired by Dr Ralph Shaa in a public sermon at St Paul's Cross on Sunday 22 June. By the 25th it had been fully written up as a formal petition to him to take the Crown, known as *Titulus Regius*.[50] The work of several days at least, it can be presumed, the petition was indeed more likely the result of sustained discussion and debate. It had to be based on the exclusion of other claimants to the throne rather than order of birth, since if primogeniture applied – and surely it should apply as the original justification of the Yorkist dynasty – then Edward IV's two sons and five daughters and Clarence's two children took precedence, Richard being only tenth in line. If Richard claimed as heir male (and, after all, all the male Lancastrian lines had expired), then he still came fourth in line to the throne, after Edward V, the king's younger brother Richard, Duke of York, and Clarence's son Edward, Earl of Warwick.

Several possibilities occurred and were deployed as supplementary arguments, some making it onto *Titulus Regius* and others apparently being discarded. One notion was to discount both elder brothers and their offspring as foreign and unable to inherit. A 1351 act that made denizens of sons of a king who were born abroad (thus Lionel of Antwerp and John of Gaunt) may not technically have been applicable since, when born at Rouen and Dublin respectively, Edward IV and Clarence had not been sons of a king, only of a rightful but unacknowledged heir. Richard himself was born safely in England, at Fotheringhay in Northamptonshire. Sorcery involving Queen Elizabeth was another possibility. If black magic was behind her match with Edward IV, as had apparently been argued in 1469, perhaps the marriage could be discounted and Edward's children bastardized. Her wedding was certainly clandestine, without banns and in a private place. In 1469 the rumour had circulated – and in 1483 it was attributed to Richard – that Edward IV himself was a bastard.[51] Bastardizing Edward after his death, in defiance of English common law, would have left York and hence his son Gloucester in line, but it had serious disadvantages. It disparaged Gloucester's own mother the Duchess Cecily and meant that he was not the successor to a rightful king. This charge was not included in *Titulus Regius*.

Evidently it was decided to argue instead that Edward IV's marriage was invalidated by a previous binding contract to Lady Eleanor Butler. This was not unlikely. A romantic tale of Queen Elizabeth's virtue recites how King Edward could not get her to bed except by first marrying her. Something very similar was later alleged about another mistress, Margaret Lucy. And Eleanor Butler, yet another young widow needing royal favour, had much in common both with Elizabeth and Margaret.[52] The precontract story bastardized and disinherited Edward V and all his siblings. Next in line were Clarence's children, who could be disqualified because their father was attainted.[53] This was a weak argument, since both Edward IV in 1461 and Henry VI in 1470 had been attainted before becoming kings, and so indeed was Henry VII to be. More significant, surely, Clarence's son was even younger than the princes and just as powerless. Matrimonial law, of course, was a matter for the Church, which was unlikely to rule so harshly against a union generally accepted as valid or to bastardize children like Edward V who were born after Eleanor

Butler's death in 1468. Since the English never did accept the canon law of illegitimacy, Parliament was within its rights to bastardize Edward's offspring. Although apparently unsubstantiated, the pre-contract story was a shocking tale that offended contemporary morality. The disinheritance of the progeny of an invalid marriage conformed to the common law rule sometimes pleaded in the courts that bastardy was a bar to inheritance.

In the short-run the pre-contract story justified the succession of Richard – who, like the speaker of the Commons and all popes, formally protested his incapacity, but allowed himself to be persuaded. His inauguration on 26 June 1483 was modelled on that of Edward IV in 1461, which in turn aped that of Henry IV in 1399. Richard was crowned on 6 July. His son and heir Prince Edward was invested as Prince of Wales at York on 8 September: a signal both that this was a dynasty that had come to stay and that (as Warwick had planned) the junior house of Neville had reached the throne in the person of Warwick's daughter Queen Anne and his grandson. *Titulus Regius* was enacted as law in 1484.[54] No evidence for the pre-contract story ever seems to have been produced and no church court ever did invalidate Edward's Wydeville marriage.

ANTI-RICARDIANISM

King Richard took immediate action to forestall resistance at Calais and in Brittany. At home he secured his rule by posing and acting as a good ruler, impartially administering justice, and refusing opportunities to exact monies as Edward IV had allegedly done. He proceeded immediately on a lengthy progress to win over those with whom he had no previous ties and to reward and to confirm the loyalty of the North.[55] Always important to him, the northerners came to bulk much larger in his regime than he had originally intended, and indeed were to become a disincentive for support from anyone south of the Humber.[56] Richard had allowed John, Lord Howard, and his son Thomas to succeed to the duchy of Norfolk and earldom of Surrey from which Edward IV had unjustly debarred them. In due course Richard was to allow William Herbert, Earl of Huntingdon, to resume the dominance of Wales that his father Pembroke had formerly exercised. Ricardians draw attention to the plaudits that Richard attracted.[57] Richard was en route to establish the sort of theoretical inevitability to his kingship that had been created for the Lancastrians and Edward IV – a Ricardian myth to match the Lancastrian and Yorkist myths that had preceded it. It took time, however, to embed a new regime – a decade as Edward IV had found – and Richard's claim to continue the established Yorkist regime seems never to have been generally accepted. It had been Richard's momentary concentration of overwhelming force that had compelled the Lords and the Yorkist establishment generally to share in his coronation, and naturally that dominance could not be maintained indefinitely.

The root problem was fivefold. Whatever his Wydeville associations, Edward V himself was untarnished and still enjoyed support – as his father's son, heir of the house of York, son of Edward IV the last king, and king himself, to whom everybody of significance had sworn allegiance. Secondly, Queen Elizabeth, her remaining son Dorset, her other kinsmen and dependants remained opposed. They were also immune from Richard's countermeasures, either because in sanctuary – whence Richard dared not wrest them – or overseas, like Sir Edward Wydeville. Thirdly, Brittany and then France were prepared to commit substantial resources to Henry Tudor to unseat Richard. Fourthly, the pre-contract story was not generally accepted and the bastardizing of Edward V and his siblings was not universally believed. Within a month of Richard's accession there was a plot in London in favour of the princes, and soon after Richard found it necessary to blockade Westminster Abbey to prevent the escape of the queen-dowager's daughters.[58] Princes and princesses alike were dangerous rivals – figureheads for and justifications of rebellion. Rebels against Richard included numerous members of the households of King Edward IV, Queen Elizabeth and Prince Edward, many of them substantial landholders and office-holders in the southern counties and collectively the Yorkist establishment. Those attainted in 1484 included 33 justices of the peace.[59] They included Richard's own brother-in-law Sir Thomas St Leger, second husband of his late sister Anne, Duchess of Exeter, and Sir John Fogge of Ashford in Kent, who had been on Warwick's hit list in 1469.

Fifthly and evidently crucial, there was hostility to Richard in his own right. Whether true or false, the whole cycle of events from his *First Coup* onwards was retrospectively reinterpreted at once by Mancini, Crowland, presumably other contemporaries and by centuries of later historians as part of a deliberate plot to usurp the Crown, and thus dyed Richard indelibly as faithless, treacherous, murderous and hypocritical. 'The degree to which opposition came from within the establishment suggests that Yorkist sensibilities had been outraged by the circumstances of Richard's accession. . . . Although in June he moved too quickly for his coup to meet overt resistance, a significant element in the political community acquiesced only for as long as it took to concert opposition.'[60]

Even when the princes were supposedly dead, many of their chief supporters declined to submit and make their peace with King Richard, instead transferring their support to Henry Tudor, Earl of Richmond, who was not Yorkist at all. Since Crowland states that the original objective was to restore Edward V, Tudor historians from André, Vergil and More onwards were engaged in retrospective rationalization in presenting Henry Tudor as always the intended beneficiary. He *may* have become the favoured claimant by 3 November 1483.[61] A sixth aspect that cannot adequately be explained is the desertion from Richard's side of Henry, Duke of Buckingham. It was certainly not because he objected to the usurpation that he actually orchestrated, nor because he felt the constellation of offices in Wales and lands that he received to be inadequate recompense. It was surely not because he hoped to make a reality of his own distant title to the throne, and improbably, in spite of Tudor propaganda, because he favoured Tudor's even more vestigial claims – although, almost uniquely, he had known Tudor as a child.[62] What was not a factor at this stage was the bad governance that had been so important in the *First* and *Second Wars*. The tyranny of Richard III was the result of Buckingham's Rebellion, but offered nevertheless a further justification for Richard's removal in 1485. Buckingham's Rebellion had dynastic objectives: to get rid of Richard and restore Edward V.

All these factors came together in the rebellion of the South in the autumn of 1483. It was quite a complex multi-pronged insurrection. There were plotters, musters and assemblies in every county south of the Thames, Gloucestershire, Oxfordshire and Buckinghamshire – the thirteen historic counties of southern England. Buckingham was to erupt from Brecon Castle in mid Wales into Gloucestershire. Duke Francis II of Brittany put up the money for seven ships and 515 men under the command of his own admiral in support of the two Tudors, Jasper, Earl of Pembroke, and Henry, Earl of Richmond.[63] This compared favourably with the tiny expeditions of Jasper Tudor in the 1460s and of the Earl of Oxford in 1473. The Marquis of Dorset, Lord FitzWarin, the Wydevilles, Fogge and St Leger, Courtenay of Bocannoc and Hungerford of Heytesbury featured prominently in the rebellion. No more than a handful of names is known for each county, but they were uniformly members of county elites with strong court affiliations. Buckingham's Rebellion was the revolt of the Yorkist establishment.

Yet it was a complete failure. Apparently it was purely aristocratic. Although Richard did refer to those 'blinded' into revolt,[64] any popular element seems to have been limited. There was no harvest of heads, no mass fining, no mass pardons. The countryside was not mobilized. The South declined to rise. Although none of the rebel propaganda has survived, Buckingham's Rebellion appears a conservative rising that sought to return to the status quo of 10 April

1483 and almost certainly promised neither reform nor the remedy of any popular grievances. Coordination was attempted, but without success. The Kentishmen rose up prematurely, by 10 October, and Buckingham by the 11th. Bad weather barred the crossing of the Severn to Buckingham, who was also attacked from the rear. His unpopularity in Wales is not surprising, since he had superseded all those who had ruled the province for Prince Edward. Contrary winds held up Henry Tudor, who was still at Paimpol on 30 October and arrived at Plymouth only in early November, when defeat was already assured. The Westcountrymen rose late. The Cornishmen mustered on 3 November.[65] Contingents from the various counties did not unite. Anyway, there were insufficient recruits to make a field army capable of confronting Richard.

Although taken by surprise, the premature Kentish rising gave Richard time. He acted energetically and decisively. Rumours that the princes were dead, perhaps spread at his instance, removed the principal objective of the insurrection and surely discouraged recruits. Any late substitute – whoever he was – lacked the same public recognition and appeal. Richard's attacks on the sexual morality of the Wydeville leaders may also have been a disincentive to potential supporters of the rebellion. Buckingham, St Leger and Thomas Rameney were executed at Salisbury, Sir George Browne, Sir Roger Clifford, and seven others in London.[66] Most of the other known leaders fled abroad: 500 joined Henry Tudor in Brittany.

There are parallels here with the equally extensive, but militarily more formidable, debacles at Ludford (1459) and Empingham (1470). In all cases, the victory was diminished by the escape and continued opposition of the rebel leaders who, secure abroad, were able to plot their future return. Not everyone fled in 1483. Some dissidents did submit and make their peace with Richard, saved their skins and their property, and avoided attainder, but relatively little is known about them. Did those who fled have any choice? Did Richard tender them any terms? Or did he merely, as his proclamations state, threaten them and set prices on their heads? Was it a considered decision, perhaps born of mistrust, not to submit to him?

Richard's Parliament early in 1484 attainted 95 offenders. Some of these were able subsequently to make their peace – 14 within five months of Parliament and 28 by the end of the reign. Usually they were bound over for their good behaviour on their own bonds and on sureties that threatened heavy financial penalties if the conditions were not fulfilled. Certainly some accepted other restrictions on their movements and liberty. Only six had been completely restored by the end of the reign, a mere twenty months away. There was insufficient time for the rest of them, indeed also for Richard. If Richard's policy resembles that of Edward IV in his *First Reign*, Richard was allowed too little time for offenders to prove their reliability and to work their way back.[67] It was a major boon for him that on 1 March 1484 ex-Queen Elizabeth reached agreement with Richard on behalf of herself, her daughters, and her son Dorset.[68] It signified her acceptance that her sons and their cause were dead, and that Richard had won. If Richard could have married Edward IV's eldest daughter Elizabeth of York, which was considered,[69] his title would have been much bolstered amongst those who denied his own right, and that of Henry Tudor would have been decisively weakened. The only English support for Tudor was from the Yorkist establishment. For them, Tudor was a stalking horse: the counterpart, perhaps, of Robin of Redesdale before him and Lambert Simnel and Perkin Warbeck afterwards. If Tudor had failed, there were other Yorkist princes and princesses to take his place.

If the two Princes in the Tower were not dead when it was first rumoured in October 1483, they died soon after and were henceforth accepted as politically dead. Although not stated explicitly in any document, their deaths were implied on Christmas Day 1483 at Rennes Cathedral when the new Yorkist exiles acknowledged as king Henry Tudor, who undertook to marry the next heir to the princes, their eldest sister Elizabeth of York. Soon after he secured a papal dispensation for the match,[70] most probably without Elizabeth's knowledge or consent. Yorkist support depended on a Yorkist candidate and Elizabeth, being female, could neither fight nor rule. Again this was an alliance based on mutual hostility to a common enemy. It was more important to remove Richard than who was to replace him. Henry Tudor was obscure, scarcely known in England which he had left when still a child, and inexperienced. How could people object to someone they scarcely knew? Particularly if – as they no doubt hoped, mistakenly – they were to manage him. Certainly it was not Henry who directed in the field.

Henry was not ineligible. He was an English aristocrat, titular earl of Richmond with modest hereditary expectations on his mother's side, and had a noble, even royal, lineage and good connections. He was a great-grandson and second cousin of kings of France, the son of Henry VI's half-brother Edmund, grandson of a royal duke, great-great-great-grandson of Edward III and great-great-nephew of Henry IV of the blood royal of England, son of Margaret Beaufort and stepson of Thomas, Lord Stanley, steward of Edward IV's household. Of course, Henry was also a quarter Welsh, the product on one side of an unlicensed match between Dowager-Queen Katherine of France and Owen

Tudor and on another from John of Gaunt's eldest legitimated bastard – 'Henry Tydder son of Edmund Tydder son of Owen Tydder', as Richard III put it, bastard on both sides. Henry's mother, however, for her part in Buckingham's Rebellion, did forfeit her own and her mother's estates, and Henry himself was attainted too.[71] It required a subtle genealogist indeed to make him into the head of the House of Lancaster, as he was to claim. The French, however, were persuaded he was the son of Henry VI!

Besides his uncle Jasper Tudor, the last vestige of a surely dead Lancastrian cause, and the Yorkist exiles, who included the queen's son Dorset, her three brothers and two bishops, the coalition was joined by John de Vere, Earl of Oxford, lately escaped from imprisonment at Hammes by Calais, his custodian James Blount, and a trickle of other defectors.[72] In theory, all these English exiles offered Henry pools of support in southern and eastern England, of which however he declined militarily to avail himself. The people did not turn out for him and apparently were not invited to do so.

The value of the English exiles was not so much military as political. They gave Henry credibility in England and, far more important, in Brittany and France, where he appeared to be a serious candidate for the English Crown and therefore worthy of investment. It was Duke Francis II of Brittany who funded him and his adherents, who assembled the two flotillas of 1483 and 1484, and it was to be French support that enabled Henry to launch his invasion in 1485 and to win the English throne. Yet such backing might not have been forthcoming. It depended on the cross-currents of French, Breton and even Burgundian politics. The minority government of the French King Charles VIII was menacing Brittany. Brittany's autonomy would have been protected had Archduke Maximilian, the ruler of Burgundy, been able to persuade Richard to ally with him against France. Richard did indeed provide troops to Brittany, in return for which Pierre Landais, minister to Duke Francis II, agreed in mid 1484 to hand over Tudor to him.

Tudor, however, escaped from Brittany to France, where he was welcomed in October 1484 by the minority government dominated by Charles VIII's elder sister Anne of Beaujeu. She had a serious rival in Louis, Duke of Orléans, who early in 1485 attempted a *coup d'état* and who was pro-Breton, pro-Burgundian, pro-Richard and therefore anti-Tudor. Maximilian meantime was conducting hostilities from Burgundy against France. However, the Beaujeu regime wrongly interpreted Richard's defensive countermeasures as a threat to France itself that he surely never contemplated. If Henry VII was sent instead to invade England, so the French regime apparently calculated, 'that would preoccupy Richard III, deprive Francis II and Landais of their foremost ally, and undermine the Orléans plots against Anne of Beaujeu'.[73] If one domino fell, so might the others, but actually distraction and destabilization would suffice. The failure of the Orléans coup against the Beaujeu regime offered a momentary pause that allowed Henry the opportunity and also the money to hire a substantial force of French and Scottish veterans equipped and trained to the much higher standards of continental war. It was more substantial military support than Louis XI or Charles VII had ever extended to Queen Margaret, Edward IV, Warwick or Oxford between 1461 and 1473. The court poets and historians of France were clear afterwards that it was French help that had made Henry king.[74]

Richard had won in 1483. In 1484 he secured parliamentary approval of the titles both of himself and his heir presumptive and the proscription of his foes. The political death of the Princes in the Tower and Richard's accord with the ex-queen should have disarmed much potential opposition. He had accrued a mass of forfeitures, both moveable wealth and lands, which could fund his defence measures and which could be used to reward and win over supporters. He still had his northern affinity, whose loyalty was reinforced by the more lucrative rewards attached to him as king.

Nevertheless, Richard had serious problems that in time became acute. Like Henry VI in 1460 and Edward IV in 1470, he had a rival out of his reach against whom he had to defend. He tried but failed to have his opponent extra-dited. Henry Tudor, meanwhile, could land anywhere. Some plotters allegedly invited him in mid 1484 to land at Poole in Dorset. The story that Richard expected Henry to land at Milford in Hampshire rather than Milford in Pembrokeshire, even if apocryphal, illustrates the problem.[75] The most likely landfalls were in areas that had recently rebelled, where invaders might expect to find support and where Richard himself was short of adherents.

With Buckingham's defection, the faction that had made Richard king had contracted rather than expanded. Richard had no choice but to redeploy into the South committed supporters from the North, who may have been fewer in number than was once thought but who aroused at least some resentment. He also had no choice but to raise money through the forced gifts and forced loans that had been so unpopular under Edward IV. These involuntary reactions offended southerners, who regarded them in themselves as tyrannical. In his letters from abroad to his supporters, Henry Tudor alluded to Richard as that 'homicide and unnatural tyrant' and 'odious tyrant'.[76] The king's supporters were also overstretched: Sir James Tyrell, for instance, had responsibilities both in Glamorgan and Cornwall. Richard had to rely unduly on men of lesser rank, such as Francis Lovell (at least a viscount), William Catesby and Sir Richard Ratcliffe, the eldest and second son of county gentry. A famous couplet harks both on their dominance and unsuitability:

> The Cat, the Rat, and Lovell the Dog
> Rule all England under the Hog.

Moreover, Richard's son and heir Edward died in the spring of 1484, then his queen, Anne, on 16 March 1485, leaving him the sole representative of the dynasty he was defending. Potentially, he alone could benefit from a civil war that was bound to bring bloodshed and to harm the common weal. Richard may have recognized as heir presumptive his sister's son John de la Pole, Earl of Lincoln. He even found a use for his bastard John of Pontefract,[77] but what he desperately needed was a legitimate son and heir of his own.

In April 1484 Brittany had provided Henry with a further flotilla of six ships and 890 men.[78] Nothing came of it, but precautionary defence measures were nevertheless necessary. The anticipated invasion was to come 16 months later in August 1485, by when King Richard's funds were exhausted and he had been driven to raise the hated benevolences that he himself had abolished.

It was of course damaging to Henry – as Richard stressed – that he was allied to 'our ancient enemy of France'. Henry Tudor wrote from abroad to known and potential supporters. Tudor propagandists blamed Richard for the death of the princes – he was guilty of regicide, infanticide and (like King Herod) of the murder of innocents – and he was tarred with the brush of incest with his niece (Elizabeth of York). Moreover, Henry actually asserted that he was already king. He started calling himself such and signed his documents in royal style and, apparently for French consumption, claimed to be the younger son of King Henry VI: a claim that Richard easily ridiculed in England![79] Apart from the garrison of Hammes, it seems unlikely that such propaganda won Henry much support in England. Although groups of plotters in London, the East Midlands and West Country, and at Calais were uncovered in 1484–5,[80] there seem to have been no uprisings in 1485 to coincide with the Bosworth campaign and there was certainly no upsurge of popular support for Tudor or revulsion against Richard. Tudor propaganda may, however, have deterred people from rallying to Richard.

Henry and his band of unruly exiles lived in and near Vannes in western Brittany, where their support was a considerable burden to Duke Francis. He paid them 3,100 livres in June 1484 alone. Others gave or lent money too.[81] King Charles in person urged the estates of Normandy to vote money, contributed 40,000 livres tournois of his own, and lent them a further sum on security. In the summer of 1485 Henry hired ships and a force of French veterans from the disbanded garrison of Pont l'Arche commanded by the Savoyard Philibert de Chandée and some Scotsmen probably led by Sir Alexander Bruce, who with his own Englishmen gave him an expeditionary force variously estimated at 5,000 men (Vergil), 4,000 (Griffiths), 3,600 (Molinet), 3,000 (Commines), or a mere 1,000 (Jones) – surely too few. They were conveyed overseas by the French vice admiral Guillaume de Casenove.[82] Strangely, Henry chose not to land in the South or South-West, where his Yorkist allies might have counted for something, but on 7 August 1485 his force landed at Milford Haven in Pembrokeshire, Jasper Tudor's home territory, conveniently close to where his correspondents Rhys ap Thomas and Walter Herbert resided,[83] and better placed for joining up with the forces that really did count of his Stanley stepfather from Cheshire and Lancashire. Henry's force marched across mid Wales to Shrewsbury, then east-wards past Coventry (Warw.) towards Leicester. The Battle of Bosworth was fought on 22 August 1485 between Coventry and Leicester, perhaps – as suggested by recent archaeological investigations – over four square miles around the villages of Dadlington, Shenton, Stoke Golding and Upton.[84]

The French and Scottish contingents were the heart of Henry's army at Bosworth, where their superior weaponry, training and experience may have been what was decisive. Although Rhys ap Thomas and others understandably maximized their contribution to the story once Henry was king, it seems unlikely that recruitment was particularly successful either in Wales or England. 'It is clear that he was actively supported by only a relatively small number of Englishmen.'[85] It was a polyglot army. Neither did Richard recruit well. Only six peers are *known* to have joined him: 'Richard was almost as wholly deserted in 1485 as Richard II had been in 1399'[86] One reason was lack of time. Some supporters were still en route when the battle was fought, or like Huntingdon and Tyrell were otherwise engaged in defence elsewhere. Richard chose to fight before all his partisans arrived. He may have felt bound to stop Henry bypassing him en route to London and perhaps accruing further support. This had been Warwick's mistake in 1471, which Richard had witnessed. A king regnant in his own kingdom could not refuse battle to a rebel! Richard's hold on Stanley's heir George Lord Strange did not force his father to declare his hand. Richard could not apparently rely on his troops. It may be that his own northerners were in the Earl of Northumberland's division, which did not engage. Had they done so, Richard should have won,[87] but clearly there were reasons (destined to be forever uncertain) why he did not deploy them.

Actually, the way that Richard chose to fight – a headlong attack by his centre and reserves – made many of his troops unnecessary. He took the boldest course. It seems likely that French and Scottish professionals equipped and trained to superior continental standards (and particularly with sixteen-foot pikes) defeated English amateurs peddling bygone weaponry and tactics.[88] When Richard was irretrievably committed, Sir William Stanley decisively intervened. Once King Richard was slain, the wings of his army had nothing to fight for. It was the scenario that Richard had planned for King Henry. Richard was the last English king to perish on the battlefield. It is difficult to imagine a more decisive result than this destruction both of the king and of his dynasty.

CHAPTER 13

THE THIRD WAR 1485–1525

The Battle of Bosworth on 22 August 1485 is the traditional end of the Wars of the Roses, a notion very much to the advantage of the Tudors, but actually it is now recognized that this is incorrect. Bosworth falls in the middle of the *Third War*, although admittedly it was the last occasion that a reigning king and dynasty were ousted by force. All governments thereafter in this period remained weak and susceptible to overthrow. Another forty years of strife lay in the future. Yet the Wars do change their character in this third phase.

After 1485 the Wars became purely dynastic. Evil governance and reform apparently featured only in Perkin Warbeck's invasions in 1496–7. The superior blood alleged for Lambert Simnel, Perkin Warbeck and the de la Poles seems to have secured public support from only very few citizens of substance. Alarming though such conspiracies were, each proved a passing episode.

The rebels against Henry VII were few in number, but the king's armies were also small. The two battles of Bosworth (1485) and Stoke (1487) were lesser affairs than Second St Albans (1461), Towton (1461), or Barnet (1471). It was the decline in the numbers of combatants that made the paltry complements of rebels so threatening. The three geographically more limited uprisings in 1486–7 were exclusively aristocratic affairs that engaged only a minority of peers, most of whom were killed. Despite their chivalric image, peers were not generally professional soldiers but noblemen who may well, like Lord Mountjoy, have found the risks too high.[1]

There was no large-scale involvement of the people in the *Third War*, although Richard had hoped for it in 1483, as Perkin Warbeck did in 1497, and Henry VII in 1489 feared that it had at last arrived. Richard had sought popular backing for his seizure of power, but actually the people did not

Pedigree 5 Title to the Crown 1485–1525

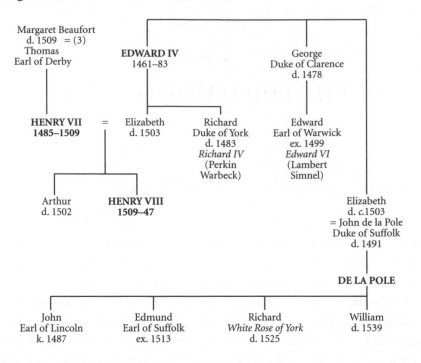

Margaret Beaufort
d. 1509 = (3)
Thomas
Earl of Derby

EDWARD IV
1461–83

George
Duke of Clarence
d. 1478

HENRY VII
1485–1509

=

Elizabeth
d. 1503

Richard
Duke of York
d. 1483
Richard IV
(Perkin
Warbeck)

Edward
Earl of Warwick
ex. 1499
Edward VI
(Lambert
Simnel)

Arthur
d. 1502

HENRY VIII
1509–47

Elizabeth
d. *c.*1503
= John de la Pole
Duke of Suffolk
d. 1491

DE LA POLE

John
Earl of Lincoln
k. 1487

Edmund
Earl of Suffolk
ex. 1513

Richard
White Rose of York
d. 1525

William
d. 1539

involve themselves in significant numbers. By the 1480s they had fewer grounds for economic discontent. Neither dynastic legitimacy nor even moral outrage propelled them back into power politics. If Richard knew how to appeal to the populace in 1483, before his narrow selfishness was exposed, no other demagogues found out how to draw them into action. Allegedly, southerners resented the rule of Richard's northerners and perhaps northerners resented Henry VII's southern regime, but neither South nor North was successfully mobilized on any occasion. Apparently, dynastic legitimacy left the commons unmoved. Fewer and fewer Englishmen of any rank turned out to fight. One factor may have been the effectiveness of Henry VII's counter-espionage and repression, but such a deduction is highly speculative.

The *Third War*, therefore, depended much more on foreign backing, not just the secure refuges needed for future planning, but even more for the military manpower: the modest quantities of ships and manpower needed to carry invaders safely past local defences to their welcoming supporters no longer sufficed because English support was lacking. Were foreign rulers foisting their choices on an apathetic majority? Certainly, substantial companies of professional soldiers trained and equipped to continental standards became major components of the invading armies both at Bosworth and at Stoke. Their presence, of course, was due to factors current on the continent, not primarily in response to internal English considerations. It may be that in 1485 these foreign forces were what was decisive. Had Simnel in 1487, Warbeck in 1497, or one of the de la Poles triumphed, it would also have been due principally to foreign support.

SECURING TUDOR RULE

Richard III was repudiated by subjects outraged by a king who was at once a usurper, tyrant, regicide, a slayer of children and incestuous. The inevitability of his rejection and the righteousness and permanence of his supplanter were certainly the messages that Henry VII's propagandists broadcast from the moment that Bosworth was won. Even Crowland, who had witnessed everything since 1459, subscribed within three months to this Tudor spin. He reports that King Richard had bad dreams the night before Bosworth and neither breakfast nor Mass that morning. Apart from William Catesby, who deserved to die, and the two Brechers, nobody was executed. Crowland praises Henry's clemency. The Wars apparently were over. It was because Crowland perceived Bosworth as the end of the distinct era that began in 1459 at Ludford that he took up his quill.

This deliberate sense of a new beginning was set by King Henry VII's first Parliament, which met at Westminster from 7 November 1485. The new king had already been crowned, on 29 September. His title derived from inheritance – hardly convincing, especially since his mother Lady Margaret Beaufort was still living – by election and by conquest, as confirmed by God's verdict in battle. Wisely, the royal justices found that the fact of his accession superseded his attainder or any other impediment. His title was enacted by Parliament.[2] Henry was credited with ending Ricardian horrors and the Wars of the Roses, but he was not committed to any particular programme of good governance. That was not what the victory of Bosworth was about. Dynastic legitimacy was.

There were reversals of attainders of many who had been attainted by Richard III in 1484, of Jasper Tudor and other Lancastrians or their heirs attainted since 1461. Their estates were restored. An act of resumption revoked all royal patronage since 1455, including grants not only of the Yorkists but of Henry VII himself.[3] The main losers were Richard's northerners, although there was also some manipulation to ensure that supporters of the new regime prospered – Edward Courtenay of Bocannoc becoming Earl of Devon, for instance, the nephews of the last earl being excluded. It was not until 18 November, in fulfilment of his promise at Rennes Cathedral, that Henry VII declared his intent to marry Elizabeth of York, thus unifying the two houses of York and Lancaster. Even though her title appeared conclusive[4] and the marriage was politically essential to refute any Yorkist rivals, Henry did not wish to tie his monarchy so tightly to Elizabeth that, in the event of her death with or without progeny, he would lose his Crown. Their wedding and her coronation were set for 18 January 1486. A sour note was, however, introduced, on 9 December and right at the end of the session of Parliament, by a bill to attaint 28 of those at Bosworth in accordance with their duty to King Richard: the new king was not merciful after all. Henry had declared himself king and adopted the royal style whilst abroad, and he had dated his reign from the day before Bosworth. If those who rallied to a king now suffered the penalties of treason, then what support could any king expect? 'Oh God!' lamented Crowland:

Oh God! What assurance will our kings have, henceforth, that on the day of battle they will not be deprived of the presence of their subjects who, summoned by the dreaded command of the king, are well aware that, if the royal cause should happen to decline, as has often been known, they will lose life, goods and inheritance complete?

'Howbeit there was many gentlemen against it, but it would not be, for it was the king's pleasure.'[5] Crowland was prophetic: it was to reassure the king's subjects that Henry found the *De Facto Act* of 1495 necessary. It is also indicative of divisions that had not yet been papered over that immediately after the second session of Parliament the king proceeded on progress to the northern shires. By April 1486, when Crowland again took up his pen, it was apparent that the Wars were not yet over and further conflict was to ensue. But official propaganda continued to preach that the Tudor victory and end of the Wars were permanent, and indeed developed into the Tudor Myth that eventually became the orthodoxy that was almost universally accepted.

Yet Bosworth by itself was not conclusive and efforts were made to reverse it. There were rebellions in 1486 and assassination plots both in 1486 and 1487.[6] An international coalition brought Henry once again to the field of battle at Stoke by Newark, in Nottinghamshire, in June 1487, from which Henry again emerged as victor. A decade later, in June 1497, he won once more at Blackheath, on the very outskirts of his capital, and another rival took flight. Lesser conspirators dogged the rest of his reign. It suited the Tudor victors to belittle these rivals as pretenders – Lambert Simnel and Perkin Warbeck – and to overlook the real titles of Clarence's son Edward, Earl of Warwick, and the de la Poles. These are traditionally portrayed as mere distractions that never seriously threatened to overturn the verdict of Bosworth. That, however, is not the case. Lambert Simnel's Stoke campaign in 1487 came close to success and nearly relegated the Tudors to a footnote in history. Instead of 'the inauguration of a new era of peace and prosperity . . . the debut of Henry Tudor [appears] a hastily contrived interlude, marking time for a further interlude of tension and uncertainty'. 'It is clear . . . that the dynastic threat facing Henry VII had not disappeared by 1500.'[7] The Perkin Warbeck conspiracy also was a serious threat – indeed a whole series of genuine threats – that caused King Henry much concern ahead of its defeat in 1497. Even the executions of Warbeck and Warwick in 1499 left credible contenders in the de la Poles to concern the first two Tudor kings.

Traditionally, the high politics of these years are explained by issues of dynastic legitimacy. This was where Henry personally was weakest. His lack of credible lineage may be why his body (like that of the usurping Henry IV) was not respected as sacral – neither Henry VI nor Edward IV, so far as we know, faced assassination as he did – and why there were traitors even within his household (and amongst the great officers of his household) who owed to kings the absolute obedience of sons to fathers. Hence his immediate decision in 1485 to recruit 200 yeomen of the guard – modelled undoubtedly on the French kings' Scottish guard, but not required by previous English monarchs.[8] It suited King Henry to present the Wars as a dynastic struggle that had been ended by his marriage and the Union of the Roses. It suited him that his most irreconcilable opponents fought on the most narrow of fronts – quibbles about the niceties of hereditary rights – rather than upon the broader interests of the common weal and its good governance that had justified dissent, coercion and the violent overthrow of earlier regimes, and which had proved to have such popular appeal. Inevitably, Henry took time to build up a track record of bad governance that could be condemned and become a rallying call. Perhaps one such reputation might have been manufactured, as Richard himself had done in 1483, but this did not happen until 1496. None of the leading rebels against King Henry was then old enough to remember how effectively York and Warwick had mobilized the people in the *First* and *Second Wars*. None of them now touched the right note – the sufferings of the common weal – to bring the commons in force back into politics. By 1496 Henry had recreated the necessary underlying grievances amongst the commons and by 1509 amongst the elite, but no rival exploited the opportunity. Dynasticism appeared narrow sectionalism that had little to offer the public or indeed the aristocracy at large. Culling alternative blood lines or keeping them safely confined was an easier strategy.

RICARDIANISM REVIVED 1486-7

Henry realized that some sort of counter-revolution was to be anticipated and expected it to come from the North, where Richard had been so strong. Henry's opponents agreed, staging northern uprisings in 1486, 1487 and (so it was thought at the time) 1489. The king identified the most dangerous dynastic threat as Clarence's son Edward, Earl of Warwick – the male heir of the house of York – and was quick to place him securely in the Tower. Fortunately, Warwick was only ten years old, the figurehead for plotting rather than the prime mover himself. King Henry made his peace with Richard's other potential heir – his nephew John de la Pole, Earl of Lincoln – and evidently thought that he had neutralized him. Resistance to the new regime did not occur on the basis of anything that Richard III stood for – a programme of political reform, for instance – or that his supporters wished to continue. If Richard was popular in the North, the popularity of a dead king did not translate automatically into successful revolution. Richard's northern retainers, who had passed over to the retinue of the Earl of Northumberland, failed in 1489 to protect the earl against the over-taxed commons. However closely these northerners had been associated with King Richard, whatever patronage they had lost with his demise, and whatever regrets they had suffered, such factors were insufficient to bring them out against King Henry in April 1486. This was a pivotal moment when, instead of joining Francis, Viscount Lovell, Richard's childhood friend, cousin and chief butler, the northerners helped Northumberland keep the new king on his throne.[9]

That Richard was dead removed one of the principal justifications for Henry VII. Amongst Henry's variegated coalition, there can have been very few who were convinced by his hereditary title to the Crown or who were primarily his men. Against him there stood potential rivals for his Crown. Ralph, Earl of Westmorland, the Holland heir, and other Lancastrian claimants remained silent. That Warwick also sported a Lancastrian claim via his father Clarence from the *Readeption* settlement was probably remembered by nobody. For most Yorkists, Elizabeth of York was the undisputed heiress, but not for all. She was after all a woman. There were those (including Henry himself) who thought women could transmit title to the Crown, but could not reign. His own mother Lady Margaret Beaufort was one such. The male heir to Edward IV and his sons was Warwick, whom both Richard III and Henry VII recognized as a potential rival. Richard had died without legitimate issue, but probably recognized as next heir his nephew Lincoln, son of his sister Elizabeth, Duchess of Suffolk.[10] Lincoln or Warwick may have been favoured by those in Richard's army at Bosworth who did not fight and suffered no penalty, and also amongst those who escaped to fight another day, most notably Viscount Lovell. Margaret, Dowager-Duchess of Burgundy, the other surviving sister of Edward IV and Richard III, preferred Warwick and/or Lincoln to the new Queen Elizabeth and King Henry. Margaret's backing for these males against her niece Elizabeth, eldest daughter of her eldest brother, may appear incomprehensible,[11] but we must remember that after 1471 – and arguably from Good Duke Humphrey's death in 1447! – the house of York were heirs of Edward III through the legitimate male as well as female lines and that many aristocrats, women included, preferred the precedence of male lines. (If any still believed the pre-contract story surrounding Edward IV, then not just Queen Elizabeth, but her young brother Richard, Duke of York, alias Perkin Warbeck, were bastards.) Margaret provided refuge to pretenders, and substantial resources. It was nostalgia for past lieutenants, Richard, Duke of York, and his son George, Duke of Clarence, that caused Irishmen to back Clarence's son Warwick and later the younger of the two princes, the boy Richard, Duke of York.

Clearly Henry's attainders, reversals of attainders and resumption were not without victims, some of whom had inherited lands awarded for good service by their fathers twenty years ago. Losers included Edward IV's stepson the Marquis of Dorset, whose acquisition of Holland lands was not confirmed, and Warwick and Richard Neville, Lord Latimer, both still minors, who were rightful heirs to lands held by Richard III for life in right of his consort Queen Anne Neville that Henry chose to confiscate.[12] They were the heirs to the Neville connection, to the Richmondshire connection in north Yorkshire, of the Earl of Salisbury, Warwick the Kingmaker and the Duke of Gloucester himself. Perhaps such men who had helped Richard become king and who had benefited greatly from his patronage should have expected to lose what they had been given by him, but lose they definitely had. Although Richard III's power and following in the North had originally been founded on his wife Anne Neville's inheritance, he had extended his sway far beyond this, even into Percy territory in Northumberland. Richard had made himself genuinely popular and he does not seem to have forfeited his northern supporters on Anne's death as Sir Richard Ratcliffe and William Catesby allegedly prophesied.[13] His fall and the consequent diminution of northern power and influence were regretted in the north, and it was certainly there that Henry anticipated his most dangerous opponents. Hence Henry's immediate arrest of the two earls of Northumberland and Westmorland, his rapid defence of the northern border, his judicial progress to the North in February 1486, the bonds that he imposed on those he feared, and his countermeasures against each northern uprising.[14] Although Richard's northerners were at Bosworth, it seems unlikely that they were engaged in the fighting. 'Richard's northern retine was undefeated on the battlefield and consequently many leading Ricardians remained at liberty.'[15] Some of them appear to have objected to the new regime throughout the 1480s. There may also have been a popular element in northern discontent, symbolized by obscure leaders with such reso-nant nicknames as Master Amend-All, Jack Straw and Robin of Redesdale. In 1487 the two Lords Scrope claimed to have been constrained into rebellion by their tenants: their excuses were believed, their lives spared, and yet they were excluded from the North on financial penalties.[16] Popular and dynastic risings were not synchronized. The resentment of the Richmondshire tenants at the loss of their traditional lords was to recur during the Pilgrimage of Grace (1536). Certainly it was in Richmondshire and in the Earl of Warwick's West Midlands that opposition to the new regime first reared its head.

Here was a potentially formidable alliance against the new regime with likely support in many parts of the kingdom. Numerous tiny groups of traitors are revealed by new attainders and indictments in many different places, such as the Thames Valley, many of whom were executed.[17] Those whom Henry suspected are revealed by the recognizances under which he systematically bound them, and those with guilty consciences feature among the thousands of pardons. Even slight misdemeanours threatened those so bound with finan-cial ruin: 'the king's purpose', wrote Edmund Dudley, 'was to have as many persons in his danger at his pleasure', to place them 'in terror'.[18] Yorkist dissent was dispersed and hard to identify, then or now. Surely service in Richard's army at Bosworth did not necessitate treasonable intentions after his death? Most such men and indeed almost everybody acquiesced in the new regime. The economic discontent of the past forty years was much reduced. Such disparate dissidence also posed all the problems of coordination that the Lancastrians in the 1460s and the Yorkists in 1483 had encountered. What unified these dissidents was nostalgia for Richard's past glories, loyalty to their traditional lord and hopes for rewards to be restored. These were no substitute for a cause that justified treason and the penalties of treason and the lack also of a figurehead capable of inspirational leadership. Obviously Warwick, a mere child, offered neither. When or if there was ever an agreed claimant is unclear. Recalcitrant Yorkists were to support four contenders – Warwick (Simnel), Prince Richard (Warbeck), John and Edmund de la Pole – from three different branches of the royal family. If Henry VII had few personal partisans, he was not objectionable in the way that King Richard had been. That the penalties of defeat were so high, that the obvious claimants were in Henry's hands, and that the prime-movers had no desire to be prematurely exposed may explain why (as in 1469 and 1470) the risings were headed by pseudonyms and pretenders.

The North was a major problem for Henry because his supporters were overwhelmingly from the South. Unless he was prepared for a 'southern tyranny' along the lines that Richard had practised in the South, he had to rely on the northern establishment that had served Richard and whose political inclinations were highly uncertain. Many northerners transferred seamlessly to Henry's service. Others rejected him, taking another Robin of Redesdale as one of their captains. Sir Robert and Sir James Harrington, Sir Thomas Broughton and Sir Thomas Pilkington were recalcitrant in the Furness peninsula in north Lancashire on 11 October 1485, when they were excluded from a general pardon.[19] The first active counterattack in spring 1486 was apparently orchestrated by Viscount Lovell and Sir Humphrey Stafford of Grafton, father-in-law of the Neville heir Richard, Lord Latimer, who had been in sanctuary together at Colchester. They evidently planned simultaneous uprisings in the North and West Midlands, most probably with the young Earl of Warwick as their candidate for the Crown. Certainly they sought to exploit the Warwick/Neville connection and Warwick's name. Despite Henry's conciliatory attempts to rule through Richard, Lord FitzHugh of Ravensworth in Richmondshire – the Kingmaker's nephew and Richard III's retainer – and through existing officers, it is possible that some redistribution of offices in Richmondshire had caused some offence.[20] Lovell knew the area well. He had resided for at least some time at Middleham when ward to the Kingmaker and had married a FitzHugh of Ravensworth. Apparently, Lovell raised a significant number of men around Middleham and Richmond, but not, evidently, enough.[21] Those later bound on surety are those whom Henry suspected or feared, not necessarily those who rebelled on this occasion.[22]

Of course, the men of Richmondshire were only one element, albeit the dominant one, in the North. Richard's death had dismantled his wider connection, allowing other peers greater independence. The Earl of Northumberland had been incarcerated for several months after Bosworth and was released on bonds. His defection at this point could have been decisive. Instead, he joined King

Henry at Doncaster in South Yorkshire in mid April with 33 knights, who included such key supporters of Richard III in Richmondshire as Sir James Strangways and Sir John Conyers. The latter, the longtime steward of Middleham, was a particularly significant figure. They might at this moment have ousted the new king – but they did not. It was a momentous decision that has been under-appreciated. Northumberland also thwarted an attempted assassination of the king at York.[23] The anonymous insurgents dispersed, without a fight and also undefeated, by 30 April 1486. Most of those of rank submitted in August. Initial resistance in the North had therefore ceased. Simultaneously Stafford sought to raise the West Midlands: Warwick's name was the talisman and bear-and-ragged-staff badges were distributed. Here even less seems to have been achieved. Indictments reveal only a handful of names.[24] From York, Henry marched to Worcester on 3 May, at which point the rising collapsed. Sir Humphrey and Thomas Stafford took sanctuary at Culham (Oxon.), whence they were wrested and executed. Viscount Lovell escaped.[25]

Fomenting rebellion from scratch seldom raised forces large enough to confront a king who could call on the residual loyalty of everyone else. Even so new a king regnant always had an advantage, both at the start of a campaign and however long it lasted. What Henry no longer possessed however was what had been decisive at Bosworth: a force of foreign veterans superior in military capability to any English counterparts whenever and wherever they were. That military superiority, choice of timing and terrain now passed to his foes. 'The conspiracies against Henry VII drew their sustenance from abroad rather than domestic discord.'[26] Richard III's northern connection, especially the men of Furness and Richmondshire, were unquelled and an important potential element in a larger conspiracy. That was why Simnel's invasion in 1487 took this route. In retrospect, this put all the eggs into just one basket and made it easier for Henry VII to defend his kingdom.

What made the campaign of 1487 more formidable than in 1486 was the participation of a recognized leader, John de la Pole, Earl of Lincoln, and the foreign support supplied by Margaret of Burgundy, who was to nurture a series of threats up to her death in 1503. The situation in Burgundy was compli-cated during these years. Charles the Bold (d. 1477) had been succeeded by Mary of Burgundy, who had married the Archduke Maximilian of Habsburg (d. 1519). Following Mary's death in 1482, their son Archduke Philip the Fair was heir, but he only came of age in 1493, and so Mary's husband and Philip's father Maximilian of Habsburg ruled – as indeed he was to do again for his grandson after Philip's death in 1506. In 1493 also, Maximilian succeeded his father Emperor Frederick III as Holy Roman Emperor, to the kingdom of Bohemia and to Austria. Meanwhile Margaret was not a head of state, but she held territory (notably Malines in the Low Countries), enjoyed large revenues, and (with Maximilian's and Philip's permissions) harboured English exiles. In the later 1480s Maximilan and his son the Archduke Philip needed to prevent their threatening neighbour France from absorbing Brittany or from deploying England, just conquered with French support, against them. They allied with Henry, whom Margaret could therefore not oppose. For Charles VIII of France such an alliance was motive enough to destabilize England, which the Yorkist dissidents could do for him, or even dethrone Henry. Actually, Henry was to prove nobody's tool. Despite the French support that had made him king, Henry was to interpret English interests as an independent Brittany, which he supported by force. In 1492 he invaded France. He may even have been serious about prosecuting the English claim to the kingdom of France.[27]

The pretenders Lambert Simnel and indeed Perkin Warbeck were figureheads around whom resistance could be orchestrated. It is not at all clear that either would have become king had they been victorious, rather than some genuine princeling for whom they were stalking horses. Probably their English backers always realized this. To attract significant support, whether amongst the populace or amongst foreign potentates who valued legitimacy, a strong case needed to be made that they were genuine. When Henry revealed that he still had the real Earl of Warwick in prison, this did not discourage Lincoln or Lovell or the Scropes, but it may well have stilled the Richmondshiremen and the populace who did not understand the game that was being played. This presumably was what the rumour of the death of the Princes in the Tower had been intended to achieve during Buckingham's Rebellion. When Warbeck claimed to be the younger prince in the Tower (Richard, Duke of York), King Henry could not prove the prince was dead.

Parts of the story remain unclear. Lambert Simnel himself was likely the son of Thomas Simnel of Oxford, 'a carpenter by trade who built organs', probably of Flemish extraction. There were disturbances and rumour in Ireland and England before the names of Warwick, Simnel or Lincoln occur in the records. The real Warwick was the son of Edward IV's brother Clarence and was safely imprisoned in the Tower. Yet in 1486 a 'Warwick' was recorded in the Channel Isles, a 'son of Clarence' (possibly a bastard?) was recorded at Malines on 1 July, and then a 'Warwick' in Ireland.[28] Such data imply that the plotters had already agreed that Warwick's name carried more appeal than Lincoln, and that an obscure boy probably called Lambert Simnel would impersonate him and seek support in Ireland. It seems a strange ploy, since Henry VII predictably displayed Warwick in the City,[29] but it may be that such protestations could be dismissed in Ireland as Tudor propaganda. Exposure as an imposter probably mattered more in England.

On 17 February 1487 the priest Richard Simonds confessed that it was he who had taken Simnel from Oxford to Ireland, then proceded himself to Furness in north Lancashire, and thence to London: a timescale that surely carries events back into 1486.[30] It seems implausible that Simnel then commuted to and from the Low Countries. It was not apparently until Christmas 1486 that John de la Pole, Earl of Lincoln, nephew of Edward IV and Richard III and supposedly Richard III's heir presumptive, defected to the Duchess Margaret in the Low Countries. Lovell and others joined him. From then onwards Lincoln took the lead. So successful was Simnel in Ireland that he gained the support of the Earl of Kildare, Lord Deputy, and was crowned King Edward VI in Dublin Cathedral. Although surely not originally intended, this surprising result forced the Yorkists to persist with Simnel and offered hope of substantial Irish support, for what that was worth. Meantime Duchess Margaret had hired the feared but unemployed captain Martin Schwarz and perhaps as many as 2,000 *Landsknechte* from Upper Germany and Switzerland. In April 1487 they were waiting in the Low Countries, perhaps at Middelburg in Brabant.

History was repeating itself. Like Richard III before him, Henry was obliged to guard the whole coastline, from Berwick on the North-East border to Dover to Plymouth in Devon, and hence expensively to disperse his forces. Evidently he thought East Anglia most at risk, where the de la Poles were important, since he visited Norwich for Easter, on 10 April 1487. Thence he proceeded to Coventry by the 22nd, where he could coordinate defences of the west coast against an Irish invasion. He was therefore relieved to know by 4 May that Margaret's Dutch expedition had sailed for Ireland, thus much reducing the threats he had to guard against.[31] Predictably, the combined force of Germans, Irish and some English landed at Furness and crossed the Pennines to Yorkshire. They did not recruit well[32] – indeed they did not give themselves enough time to do so. Their speedy passage prevented Henry from recruiting to the full, which was evidently more important than maximizing their own forces. From Masham in Richmondshire the Lords Scrope of Bolton and Masham attacked the city of York, a diversion that did deflect the Earl of Northumberland from joining King Henry in battle. The army that Simnel took to the field at Stoke by Newark (Notts.) on 16 June 1487, only twelve days after landing, was apparently only 8,000 strong, comprising principally a professional German core, a smattering of miscellaneous Englishmen, and many ill-trained and equipped Irishmen. King Henry was well prepared. He led a significantly larger number of men, including at least 16 peers. Skilful manoeuvring – including an unexpected crossing of the Trent – negated some of his advantage and enabled the rebels to surprise the Earl of Oxford's division. Unable to complete the task before the rest of Henry's army arrived, the rebels were defeated. Lincoln and Schwarz were killed and Simnel was captured.[33] Lovell probably escaped once more, but disappeared: he was not recorded again. It may have been his body that centuries later was discovered in a secret chamber in his residence at Minster Lovell in Oxfordshire.

THE PERKIN WARBECK CONSPIRACIES 1491-7

Henry VII continued to fear Ricardian insurgency in the North and treated the Yorkshire Rebellion of 1489 as such, wrongly as we now know, but the defeat of Ricardianism did not terminate the challenges to his throne. The Battle of Stoke was not the end. There remained alternative candidates for the Crown. There were to be further conspiracies, rebellions and even invasions. Margaret of Burgundy sheltered more dissidents, funded their plots and invasions, and so indeed did the Scots. There were to be two major popular revolts, in Yorkshire in 1489 and in the West Country in 1497. These destabilizing elements did not interact and were not to remove Henry VII from the throne. Yet the threats were real for another fifteen years at least. What links the most serious from 1491 to 1497 was Perkin Warbeck.

Like Simnel, Warbeck was a youth of modest stock. Most probably he was a son of Jehan and Nicaise de Werbecque, a prosperous mercantile family of Tournai in northern France, who embarked early on an appenticeship in trade in Burgundy and courtly service in Portugal, whence he was plucked in Ireland as a suitable impostor for the younger of Edward IV's sons and Prince in the Tower, Richard, Duke of York. In time he styled himself King Richard. Warbeck had the noble demeanour, manner and manners required of a prince and courtier. He was literate and must also have been a brilliant linguist, fluent in French, Flemish, English, perhaps also Portuguese and Latin. His imposture convinced many with no desire to be convinced as well as those, like his supposed aunt Margaret, who were looking for a credible Yorkist claimant. He was admitted to the courts of the Empire, Burgundy and Scotland, and treated with much more honour than most pretenders. Warbeck even married in Lady Katherine Gordon a noble lady connected to the Scottish Crown. Yet he was an impostor. Nothing suggests either political competence or military capacity, whether in generalship, prowess, or courage. Presumably he did not have the conventional aristocratic education at arms and was indeed 'a prince for chambers and gardens'.[34]

Yet Warbeck did have about him men who knew Edward IV's court, current English affairs, and much else of relevance. Indeed, at times his court in exile in Burgundy and Scotland was several hundred strong and comparable perhaps to that of Henry Tudor in 1484–5. Like Margaret of Anjou before him, Warbeck was an important pawn on the international scene, who was harboured by all the principal powers in turn, received military aid for invasions of Kent from Burgundy in 1495 and of northern England from Scotland in 1496, and sought to combine this activity with internal conspiracies. Much more is now known both of the international dimension[35] and of those prosecuted in England. It remains uncertain whether the defendants were all the plotters there were or just the most important. 'The names of the plotters are thus in no sense random, but closely associated with the royal court and its children.' They failed because Henry's 'network of spies was superb' and because Henry broke Warbeck's English support.[36] Yorkist dissidents in England are now credited with better prospects that were never realized. Amongst those implicated of treason were some prominent individuals – a prior of St John, a dean of St Paul's Cathedral, an abbot of Abingdon and several knights, even the chamberlain and steward of the king's household, but nobody of the front rank. There is actually no evidence of any substantial noble support, nor indeed popular support before 1497.

'Due to the Anglo-Burgundian entente, which lasted with minor interruptions from 1488 to 1492, there was no support from Burgundy for Yorkist pretenders.'[37] Some plotting nevertheless continued. Formerly a Clarence retainer, the obscure John Taylor backed the Yorkist claims of the Earl of Warwick until November 1491 at Cork in Ireland, whence he launched Warbeck on his imposture and whence he took him to France, which needed Yorkist dissension to withstand Henry's threatened invasion. Charles VIII called Warbeck cousin and Duke of York. The invasion of France ended in 1492 with the treaty of Étaples on 3 November. On 12 December Warbeck arrived at Malines, the court of Margaret of Burgundy, who acknowledged him as her nephew and called him the White Rose. She pensioned him and the circle of supporters that he assembled. Henry then frantically prepared for an invasion from Burgundy to link up with the numerous pockets of dissidence in England, but managed instead to come to terms on 14 August 1493 with Archduke Philip, now of age, who promised not to harbour Warbeck. Since this clause did not bind either Dowager-Duchess Margaret or Maximilian,

Henry imposed a trade embargo on Burgundy. It did not, however, secure Warbeck's extradition. Now Holy Roman Emperor, Maximilian even took Warbeck to the funeral of his father Frederick III in Vienna on 6 December.

It was not until 1495 that Warbeck was able to launch his invasion of England. He promised to pay off Margaret's dowry, to repay her expenses for both himself and Simnel, grant her Hunsdon (Herts.) and Scarborough (Yorks.), and he made Maximilian and Philip his heirs to England, France, Wales and Ireland if he had no children of his own.[38] Warbeck's intention was to land within striking distance of the capital and to combine with supporters within England. The force he brought from Flushing – 14 ships, a core of professional *Landsknechte* led by the respected Rodrigue de Lalaing, and no fewer than 6,000 men – was by far the largest of all the expeditionary forces launched from the continent during the Wars of the Roses, larger especially than those in 1485 and 1487. King Henry feared and had to guard against simultaneous uprisings elsewhere, but none materialized, perhaps because of the immediate failure of Warbeck's main assault. Arriving in error at Deal in Kent on 3 July 1495, the 150-strong advance guard that was put ashore was destroyed before Warbeck's very eyes by local levies. Those not killed, eight captains and 40 rank-and-file, were executed.[39] It may have been strategically mistaken not to retaliate with Warbeck's main party. It was certainly an error not to move on, like Edward IV in 1471, northwards to East Anglia or Norfolk, but instead to sail to Ireland – now strongly held by Henry and far from where Warbeck's force could wreak any harm. Repulsed with heavy losses at Waterford in southern Ireland, his army then sailed to Scotland.

On his arrival at Stirling on 20 November 1495, Warbeck was welcomed by King James IV, pensioned, and married on 13 January 1496 to Katherine Gordon. In return for an indemnity to be paid over five years, the surrender of Berwick, and other concessions, King James attacked Northumberland, albeit very late in the campaigning season (21 September). He invaded only a few miles (the Raid of Ellem), and withdrew after a mere two days in the face of an English force only a modest 4,000 strong. Disappointing though this was, incursions from Scotland into the well-defended English borders 250 miles from the capital were never likely to overthrow the government any more than in the 1460s. James was not prepared to focus west of the Pennines, where Warbeck apparently had most support, nor to risk enough to give Warbeck a reasonable chance of success. Actually, Warbeck posed no threat to England, but Henry in retaliation planned for 1497 a massive assault by land and sea against Scotland. Many of his own supporters were conveyed to the Scottish borders just when the Cornish rejected the excessive exactions that his Scottish ambitions had provoked. 'There were no soldiers between Taunton and Guildford to oppose them.' Although convenient, the Cornish uprising in June 1497 was not actually timed to coincide with events in the Scottish borders. It originated as a popular uprising against taxation in Cornwall (and ultimately the whole south-west). Some gentry and every other class in Cornwall, Devon and Somerset featured in the uprising, which enjoyed the passive and some-times overt support of the West Country elite. 4,541 individuals from Dorset, Hampshire, Somerset and Wiltshire were fined, and many more from Devon and Cornwall. Indeed it was, writes Arthurson, a revolt of 'the entire commu-nity' or 'political nation of the west', against which 'the showing made by Tudor loyalists was pathetic'. Led by James, Lord Audley, the insurgents reached Blackheath before they were dispersed, on 17 June.[40]

If only this popular insurrection had been stiffened by noble retinues and led by a prince bidding for the throne! What might have happened then? Distance and chronology suggest that Warbeck knew nothing of the Cornish uprising when he left Scotland on 6 July for Ireland. The insurrection had already been suppressed when he reached Cornwall on 7 September. He succeeded in raising another substantial rebellion and besieging Exeter. The opportunity had passed, however, and substantial forces had been recalled from the North, none of whom chose to desert to the rebels. So on 19 September at Taunton, Warbeck abandoned his followers.[41] However, he was unable to find a ship to take him abroad and hence keep his cause alive. He took sanctuary at Beaulieu Abbey in the New Forest. Soon after he was in custody and the greatest threat to Henry VII had passed.

Undoubtedly, Queen Elizabeth of York had a better title by primogeniture than Lincoln and the de la Poles and one superior also to Warwick unless the male line took priority, but there was no argument or ambiguity that her brother Richard – 'King Richard IV' as Warbeck called himself – had a better claim than herself or her husband Henry VII, separate or combined. If Warbeck was actually the son of Edward IV, he was rightfully king. Legitimacy was desirable, but it is doubtful whether many thought it worth the risk of ruin. What else Warbeck offered, if anything, is obscure, because none of the letters he wrote to Englishmen in or any manifestos he issued exist before the one of 1496 issued to coincide with his invasion from Scotland.[42] This surviving mani-festo reveals a good appreciation of the defects of Henry VII's rule.

Warbeck promised a nostalgic return to the days of good rule, proper order and prosperity of Edward IV in place of the bloodthirsty tyranny of Henry VII.

Henry was a tyrant both because he attained the throne unjustly and also because he ruled not in the interests of his people – the common weal of the commonwealth – but against them. Warbeck had a point. The foreign backing that made Warbeck into a constant threat required of Henry heightened awareness, defensive vigilance and continuous expense. Like Richard III, merely to keep his throne, Henry was driven into unpopular measures. Henry had to be ruthless. He did not spare traitors real, potential, or, in some cases, perhaps imaginary: the convicted traitor Sir William Stanley may not even have committed himself to Warbeck's cause.[43] Undoubtedly, Henry's system of bonds that threatened poor behaviour with ruin – 'ransoms' Warbeck's manifesto calls them – was oppressive and unjust. The manifesto presumes that the aristocracy felt under-appreciated and disparaged. Warbeck was able to list proper respect for the rank as one of his objectives.

Henry's bond system was also a source of income. Like Edward IV, even this early in his reign, Henry was accused of avarice, of building up treasure – indeed even of salting it away ready for retirement in exile like some modern dictator! – and of exactions of all kinds. Here Henry was as vulnerable as Warbeck's manifesto emphasized. From 1488 to 1492 he and Burgundy had sought expensively to keep Brittany independent, first in staving off collapse and then launching a full-scale invasion of France in 1492, all at great cost. But Henry had failed. All the money and effort of taxpayers and the aristocracy were wasted. The treaty of Étaples in 1492, like Picquigny in 1475, bought the king off with a pension. France, 'our mortal enemy', the manifesto declares, 'hath trodden under foot the honour of our nation, selling our best confederated friends for money' in 'feigned wars' that served 'only to enrich his coffers'. Henry was exposed to the same complaint as Edward IV, as set out in Warwick's manifesto of 1469 and in *Warkworth's Chronicle*, and as was feared again after Picquigny, namely, of exacting taxes for wars that were not waged. Yet this war – and defence against all Warbeck's external threats, most of them abortive – demanded taxation, always unpopular. Henry sought to increase the tax-take and to extend those liable. He taxed northerners hitherto exempt, which provoked the Yorkshire uprising of 1489.[44] In 1496–7 the fiscal burden was unprecedented in weight and novelty and, to a Cornish audience, for an irrelevant war in distant Scotland. Henry levied the equivalent of four fifteenths and tenths totalling £120,000 in one year without the traditional exemptions, a forced loan of £51,000; and for the clergy a loan, a normal tenth and a special clerical tax.[45] Because these years are less well documented than the 1460s, little is known of popular feeling, though the two tax rebellions indicate acute discontent. The Milanese ambassador deplored the king's avarice: 'The king is very powerful in money, but if fortune allowed some lord of the royal blood to rise and he had to take the field, he would fare badly because of his avarice. The people would abandon him.'[46] This amounted, said Warbeck, to a 'daily pill[ag]ing of the people to the likely destruction and desolation of the whole realm'. Mark Horowitz has demonstrated how unbridled the king's rapacity was to become.[47]

It was, moreover, a most serious miscalculation in 1493 by Henry to put pressure on Burgundy by suspending English cloth exports and banning Burgundian imports. Whilst undoubtedly this did cause unemployment and poverty in the Low Countries, the impact was even more serious in England. Labour was instantly laid off, English wool-producers and cloth-makers lost their markets and livelihoods, and there was an immediate riot against the Hanseatic merchants in London. Burgundy seized the goods of English merchants and banned trade with England on 8 April 1494. The embargo lasted for three years and primarily hurt England, for the Burgundians quickly established other sources of wool, notably via the Hanse.[48] That there was economic distress was principally because Henry recreated the *Great Slump* that in and after 1450 had generated such popular unrest. This time it could be blamed on him, not on aliens or international trading conditions.

Warbeck promised that as king he would manage international trade 'more to the common weal and prosperity of our subjects'. He would spend his revenues properly and seek no taxation other than that customarily voted by 'subjects and true liegemen [for] aid, succour and help' of the government in genuine necessity. He would also purge Henry's low-born and self-interested evil councillors, 'the principal finders, occasioners, and counsellors of the misrule and mischief now reigning in England', now identified as Belknap, Bray, Dudley, Empson, Heron, Lovel, Lucas, Mordaunt, Smith, Southwell and Wyatt.[49] Warbeck would rule with 'the help and assistance of the great lords of our blood'. This echo of the earlier appeals of Jack Cade, Richard, Duke of York, and Warwick the Kingmaker reveals a good knowledge of and skilful slant on English conditions compatible with the south-western grievances next year. Whether people elsewhere felt this way is not recorded.

In particular, we cannot know whether northerners, to whom Warbeck's manifesto was directed, felt like this. Henry had learnt from the Yorkshire Rebellion not to tax them, and the military threat was very specifically their own affair – an attack on themselves by the Scots against whom they apparently united, rather than join Warbeck in alliance with their traditional enemy.

Yet Warbeck does seem to have tailored his appeal to a northern audience. Richard III had been popular in the North. Whilst not able to deny that 'desire of rule did blind' his 'unnatural uncle', who had tried to kill him after all, Warbeck recognized Richard to have sought the honour of his realm and the contentment of his nobles and people. Similarly, Warbeck's denunciation of Henry's breaches of liberties and sanctuaries had particular appeal in the North. The Scottish army behaved like any other raiders, killing and pillaging, which Warbeck recognized to be counterproductive, and then quickly withdrew, putting Scottish interests before his own. Warbeck, therefore, never reached those northerners whom he was targeting.

THE DE LA POLES

Even the defeat and capture of Perkin Warbeck did not put a stop to Yorkist dissidence. Ralph Wilford, the son of a London cordwainer (shoemaker), impersonated Warwick in 1499. Both the real Warwick and Warbeck were implicated. Although the plot may have been engineered by the king, all three were tried, condemned and executed in November 1499.[50] Even that did not suffice, as it returned to the forefront the claims of Edmund, Richard and William de la Pole, the three younger sons of Edward IV's sister Elizabeth, Duchess of Suffolk and younger brothers of Richard III's supposed heir John, Earl of Lincoln, slain at Stoke in 1487.

After the death of Duke William in 1450, the de la Poles were never in the front rank of either wealth or local power amongst English magnates, and indeed they struggled to support the estate of duke. They had modest estates in Oxfordshire and East Anglia. The Earl of Lincoln's treason in 1487 entailed the forfeiture of the family lands that had been settled on him, which meant that his younger brother Edmund inherited only a small proportion on his father's death in 1492. His mother held much of the rest of their estates. The king agreed with Edmund to allow him some of the forfeited lands in return for reverting from the dukedom to a mere earldom, but charged him £5,000 for the privilege, to be repaid in annual instalments of £200 during his mother's lifetime, which may well have comprised half his income, and £400 thereafter that certainly did. This was harsh treatment for a young nobleman who seems to have been a model of chivalry, an adornment at court and conspicuously loyal. Edmund, Earl of Suffolk, had firmly refused involvement in Yorkist plots and in particular resisted the opportunity to join Warbeck's Cornish incursion in 1497. All this was recognized by King Henry, who had him elected knight of the Garter in 1495, yet the suspicious and over-autocratic king also put him under such pressure that he precipitated his flight abroad in July 1499. Henry had succeeded in making a dynastic rival of Suffolk.[51] International conditions, however, were not propitious for support from Burgundy. Suffolk was extradited by Archduke Philip and was permitted by Henry to submit and recover his possessions. The conditions, however, were so harsh, the monitoring so close, and his everyday affairs so impeded, that in August 1501 he fled abroad again, this time with the overt intention of making his title to the Crown good. Henry had succeeded in making an enemy of a friend and a rival out of a mere relative.

Edmund also planned to combine an invasion sponsored by Emperor Maximilian with local uprisings in East Anglia. Although Maximilian harboured him at Aachen in Germany and elsewhere, it was not in the interests either of himself or Archduke Philip to confront Henry, who was able massively to subsidize their continental machinations. Henry knew who Suffolk's East Anglian supporters were and was able to embroil them all in bonds. In 1506, therefore, Suffolk returned to imprisonment in the Tower. His younger brother Richard de la Pole remained abroad, pensioned first by the King of Hungary and then from 1512 by the French kings Louis XII and then Francis I, who recognized him as a useful pawn in international politics and a means of destabilizing Henry VIII's generally hostile regime. Suffolk was executed in 1513 following Richard's declaration of his own title.[52] The French planned to support his invasion of England in 1514, 1516 and 1522 – that of 1514 was aborted only by the peace treaty – but nothing came of these plans. There were hopes of support from Scotland and in East Anglia, yet surely the number of those committed to the de la Poles and House of York dwindled with time. Richard meantime served Kings Louis and Francis militarily and was slain on the French side at the Battle of Pavia in Italy in 1525. Thus ended the threat posed by the White Rose, celebrated King Henry VIII.[53]

PART IV
WHY THE WARS ENDED

CHAPTER 14

THE END OF THE WARS

The Battle of Bosworth in 1485 was not the end of the Wars of the Roses. The Stoke campaign of 1487 showed that. The reign of Henry VII was the end, argued Sir Francis Bacon in 1622, and has been followed by almost all historians since. Bacon highlighted Henry's own political management, in particular his curbing of the nobility and rooting out of the livery and maintenance (bastard feudalism) that had given them excessive military power. 'Few would disagree that 1509 did not look the same as 1485.'[1]

MANAGING DISSIDENCE

That Henry had been brought up and politically educated abroad may have contributed to his success in keeping his throne. As an outsider, the English may have appeared to him (like Commynes) as an insubordinate race much inclined to overthrow and kill their kings. He guarded himself more carefully. His creation of the yeomen of the guard made his assassination or seizure more difficult. He was ruthless in striking at his foes and normally exacted the death penalty on traitors, even those whose offences seem rather technical or minor. He or his parliaments sought to still popular dissidence with the first Tudor poor laws and to safeguard the Isle of Wight by preventing depopulation.[2] Moreover, he realized that English dissidence was more easily uncovered abroad than at home. His agents seem to have infiltrated the Yorkist courts in exile and relayed the names of their correspondents, who were destroyed or otherwise curbed. A surprising number of trials convicted circles of conspirators who had not actually committed anything.

Henry VII's rule contrasted sharply with that of the usurpers Henry IV, Edward IV and Richard III, who had been bountiful to those who made them kings and thus gave them even more cause to back their title. These usurpers had created vested interests in the continuance of their regimes. Edward IV even admitted former Lancastrians to his Yorkist establishment. Henry VII was not a liberal patron and was much more sparing in his patronage. Although attainders against his supporters were reversed and lands restored, although offices had to be filled and were staffed with his supporters, he created very few titles and granted away relatively few estates, or indeed lands at all, from the substantial quantities in his hands. Patronage did not buy Henry the support of his subjects. Denying himself the carrot, Henry resorted to the big stick: to coercion.

Traitors suffered forfeiture of all their possessions under the acts of attainder that were passed in all Henry's parliaments. Altogether 131 traitors suffered, the numbers escalating as the reign progressed. Henry was much less inclined than his predecessors to reverse such sentences to contrite offenders or their heirs.[3] Appalling though the penalties of treason had become, they nevertheless failed to deter Lovell and Lincoln, Fitzwalter and Stanley, Warwick, Suffolk and Audley. From the first months of his reign, like Henry VI and Edward IV, Henry VII bound offenders or suspects – for their good behaviour ('good a bearing') – under bonds or recognizances for debt which conceded that they owed the king large sums to be payable only if the conditions were breached. Offenders might be confined to the king's household or required to report any rumours of disloyalty immediately. Conspiracy or mere disobedience threatened them with financial ruin comparable to attainder itself. This developed into the system of 'bonds, coercion and fear' in which Henry enmeshed not just traitors and suspects, not even just his aristocracy, but all those with property. It was normal practice also for royal officers, especially those handling royal revenues, voluntarily to make out bonds, to offer fines for wardships or other favours secured on bonds, and to act as sureties for all kinds of associates. Literally thousands of subjects of all ranks, politically important or not, featured as principals and sureties, often several times over. Similarly, those guilty of offences, often poaching or other trivia, were heavily fined and bound to pay on pain of larger penalties.

Since all parties meant to meet the conditions, they did not expect ever to have to pay the penalties. Former kings had generally allowed defaulters to compound for the penalties or to pay by easy instalments. Henry, however, treated these recognizances as debts and enforced the penalties, to the financial loss of sureties who had committed no offences themselves. Alternatively, he used them to force those involved into submission and absolute obedience, often in matters unrelated to the original bond. Those who had made out bonds were subjected to unexpected arbitrary pressures. Henry operated a far more comprehensive system than his predecessors: it resembled the blank charters that Richard II extorted in his last years and that were one of the articles of tyranny against him at his deposition in 1399. Those so bound so feared the financial penalties named in their recognizances that they were not only deterred from rebelling, but from actions that could be construed as dissidence or even misbehaviour.[4] Henry amassed evidence for all such bonds, including ancient obligations that had been fulfilled, was casual about cancelling all enrolments when conditions were met, not infrequently exacted penalties that should have been revoked, and sometimes imposed massive losses on inadequate grounds. He and his councillors collectively and individually determined whether the conditions had been achieved. Even the king's notorious agent Edmund Dudley admitted oppression. Dudley's petition lists an appalling 84 injustices that he knew of that cried out for remedy.[5] From about 1500 such bonds were additionally enrolled on the chancery close rolls. Fulfilment of conditions and cancellation of bonds were recorded far less systematically. Such bonds included even those on whom Henry relied for national security. Henry was able to demand fuller obedience, better service, better enforcement of royal policies in the localities, and better supervision of retainers. Even to hear of sedition and not report it was potentially ruinous, let alone to plot. To comply could be ruinous too, as payments were levied nevertheless. These bonds were

> arbitrary measures of financial strangulation that crippled the nobility, emptied the purses of the mercantile classes and stifled the social advancement of the gentry. Bonds delivered all the devious traps and restrictions that a suspicious and vulnerable monarch could have hoped for. By linking the continuation of personal influence to financial solvency within the ruling elites, Henry came to control how the authority of the Crown's chief supporters was employed.

Modern historians credit the system with 'success . . . in keeping King Henry on the throne during his deepest crises' and helping 'to quell potential revolts under the first Tudor by making them literally costly and by hindering any local aristocratic intentions against the monarch not only through their obligations but also those of their affinities and would-be followers'.[6]

Such judgements of what might otherwise have been can only be specula-
tion. Perhaps many individuals were deterred – if indeed they were ever
tempted to act in these ways. Not many of those bound seem to have ignored
such restraints and rebelled. Of course, many suspects, like the sixty connections of Edmund de la Pole placed under bond, may have had no such
intentions. Obviously such a policy was of no avail against those who were
determined to rebel – those who were prepared to risk the much greater penalties attendant on treason such as death, forfeiture, disinheritance and corruption of blood were unlikely to be put off by mere financial ruin. However, on
the evidence, there were not many of these. Raising up straw men, the
pretenders Simnel and Warbeck, was surely intended to shield any real
claimants from exposure and danger until their movement had taken off
and had a reasonable hope of success. But such bullying could be counterproductive. Victims could justifiably be paranoid and think themselves victim-
ized, and even be driven to extremes that they had never intended. That
possibly is what befell Edmund de la Pole, whom Henry's cackhanded management made into an enemy and hence more dangerous than he needed to be.

Henry suffered some confusion of motives and sought too many contradictory objectives at once. It is not likely that sureties were reconciled to massive
financial losses just because they were accustomed to recognizances that did
not produce such results, which they had never intended.[7] To turn such bonds
into money-raising devices muddled the original objectives. Very large sums
may have raised perhaps hundreds of thousands of pounds in the king's last
years, much more than could be raised by taxation.[8] Henry applied such penalties to take control of estates, to threaten the families of those involved in loss,
and to exploit, for instance, the financial fecklessness of Richard, Earl of Kent.
Forcing sureties and principals to pay the penalties regardless made a fearsome
threat into a reality, actually ruined those involved, and removed the deterrent
element. It certainly created the large pool of the aggrieved who felt unjustly
treated that Warbeck identified in 1496. Henry breached the convention that
government was a partnership of mutual advantage in which the nobility and
gentry governed themselves on the king's behalf without pay in return for local
authority and standing. This was 'a comprehensive misunderstanding of the
nature of medieval kingship'. If Henry does not seem to have discouraged
service, there are indications that he alienated some loyal noblemen.[9] Perhaps
they were too frightened to plot, but should a landing actually take place,
might they not join up or, as in 1497, decline to resist? Would then de la Pole's
East Anglian affinity remain quiescent?[10] The bond regime may have made

conspiracy less likely, but it made any insurrection once launched more likely to succeed. Fortunately, only in 1497 did popular outrage and a credible dynastic alternative coincide.

Moreover, it may have been in well-founded expectation of public outrage that Henry held no further parliaments after 1504, which he could well afford not to do. The very personal autocracy that he had operated depended ultimately on bluff, since even Henry VII could not have stood against all the nobility had he enraged them enough. Henry's death could have unleashed the anger of the political nation and endangered the succession. Such discontent was much more soundly based than the misgovernment that Warwick in 1469–70 and Gloucester in 1483 had attributed to Edward IV. Henry's bond regime resembles the tyrannies of Edward II (1322–6) and Richard II (1397–9), which generated such hostility that both kings were swept away. Wisely, however, Henry's son Henry VIII refused to defend his father's legacy. Although he dared not explicitly concede his father's tyranny, 'tarnishing the image of the ruler who was often the prime mover behind such policies', nor even denounce Empson and Dudley as evil councillors, he did manufacture a treasonable conspiracy that enabled him to eliminate them just the same.[11] The public's notions of treason were more drastic than those proscribed by law and certainly encompassed the oppressions of the two royal agents. Jack Cade's rebels would have applauded their show trial, the blood vengeance that was wreaked on them, the repudiation of the late king's policy and the drastic reduction in its money-raising potential, the cancellation of at least some bonds, and the righting of some of the worst injustices.[12] Any potential storm was defused. What was different when Henry VIII came to the throne in 1509, therefore, was that a new king who was not a usurper disowned the evil councillors and evil counsel that he had inherited. In 1525 that same Henry VIII bowed to rather than withstood the storm and revoked his levy of a forced gift (the Amicable Grant).[13] How sharp is the contrast to Henry VI's obdurate resistance to York and defence of Somerset in 1450–5!

The crisis that was averted in 1509 and continuing de la Pole issues show that Henry VII did not completely terminate the Wars of the Roses. Bosworth in 1485 was not as conclusive as the battles of Towton in 1461 and Tewkesbury in 1471 had been: Henry VII was to be faced by further battles for twelve years after Bosworth. He had rivals for the rest of his reign and indeed passed on the last de la Poles as unresolved business to his son Henry VIII. That Henry VII successfully saw off all his rivals was certainly necessary if any resumption of the Wars of the Roses was to be averted, but by themselves his short-term achievements were not decisive. It may be indeed that he prolonged the dynastic debate and made his rivals more likely to succeed. The longer the Tudors reigned, of course, and especially Henry VIII who embodied the Union of the Roses, the less relevant dynastic issues and loyalties became until eventually they disappeared altogether. Undoubtedly, the Wars of the Roses did come to an end. At some point during the first two Tudor reigns – we cannot be sure when, but it was well after 1485 and probably after 1509 too – a further dynastic revolution of the old type ceased to be possible. This chapter looks next at these deeper reasons why the Wars ended: the reasons that messily marked the termination of this distinct era of civil war.

OTHER FACTORS

Henry did not build a new Tudor dynasty, it has recently been pointed out, but an offshoot of the Plantagenets,[14] and his descendants were to be few indeed and too many of them disadvantageously female. Two of his three sons were dead by 1502 and so too in 1503, aged only 37, was his queen Elizabeth of York, whose Yorkist title counted for so much more than his own. Henry had recognized this contingency from the start and guarded against it, declaring that his offspring by a subsequent queen could succeed him.[15] Although Henry considered remarrying after 1503 and could hope thereby further to secure the succession (having only one living son), his negotiations came to nothing and might not have increased his security much anyway, as any such babies by another queen could not have inherited Elizabeth's Yorkist title. It was about 1503, when the king himself lay sick at Wanstead near London, that members of the Calais garrison – informed, weighty, militarily equipped, and whose loyalty the king had done his utmost to assure – were looking elsewhere to the succession, to Edward Stafford, Duke of Buckingham, or Edmund de la Pole, Earl of Suffolk. 'But none of them spake of my lord prince' [the future Henry VIII].[16] If Henry VII had indeed died in 1503, leaving as heir a boy, Prince Henry, even younger than Edward V, might another 1483 have ensued? And if Prince Henry had perished, what then? Actually, King Henry VII did die relatively young. He was still only 52 in 1509, yet he had managed to survive six years beyond the Calais debate and to outlive his wife Elizabeth by six years also – long enough for his last remaining son Henry VIII, aged 17 in 1509, to succeed as an adult if very inexperienced king. Son of the last king and grandson of King Edward IV, Henry VIII had a superior Yorkist title to any conceivable rival and never faced a serious dynastic threat.

Ruling and survival had become much easier. It was a key factor that the old nobility had been destroyed. 'Time hath his revolutions', Lord Chief Justice Crewe famously observed:

> There must be a period and an end to all things temporal, – *finis rerum* – an end of names and dignities, and whatever is terrene. For where is Bohun? where is Mowbray? where is Mortimer? nay, which is more and most of all, where is Plantagenet? They are entombed in the urns and sepulchres of mortality.[17]

A combination of multiple executions, premature deaths and a natural failure to reproduce had together removed half the high nobility of the 1450s from the political scene.[18] Only Buckingham of the greatest noble houses remained intact. The duchies of Lancaster and of York were merged with the Crown. Henry VII himself disinherited the heirs of the estates of Warwick the Kingmaker and his sons-in-law Clarence and Gloucester: Edward, Earl of Warwick, he continuously confined and then judicially murdered.[19] The Mowbray duchy of Norfolk had been divided and the Howard half forfeited: it took Thomas Howard almost thirty years to rebuild his half share by diligent royal service.[20] The Stafford dukedom of Buckingham and the Percy earldom of Northumberland were in minority until 1498. For Henry's first fifteen years, therefore, there existed no overmighty subjects to mobilize these great regional connections, though others tried in 1486 and 1487.

It was not that Henry necessarily wished to dispense with the great nobility. He relied on Jasper Tudor in Wales, the Earl of Oxford to rule East Anglia, and others to manage the North on his behalf. The nobility featured prominently on all his campaigns. Apparently he intended to establish noble estates for his sons Henry, Duke of York, and Edmund, Duke of Somerset, that instead remained in Crown hands. It was not entirely a matter of his own choice, therefore, to rule the localities through the lesser men denounced by Warbeck, perhaps less effectively, nor the preferred option of his rivals to raise local conspiracies through churchmen and mere gentry rather than through exploiting large-scale hereditary connections. Whatever was planned, none of his rivals ever succeeded in raising their retainers in rebellion, and there were to be no uprisings timed simultaneously with external invasions like those of 1459–71. Dynastic rivals still planned for rebellions within England and Henry himself continued to guard against them, but the forces that were brought from abroad mattered much more during this phase of the Wars of the Roses.

Moreover, the conditions had now ceased that had made civil war so easy to start and so likely to succeed, and that had placed remaining on the throne beyond the capacity of even the ablest kings. The four key factors that were conducive to such upheavals no longer applied. If what defines the Wars of the Roses as a separate era and made them possible was the combination of collapse of the economy, the invasion of English politics both by an angry populace and foreign powers, and the sheer helplessness of successive regimes, the disappearance of all these factors and the apparent expiry also of the willingness to rebel amongst the political elite are powerful explanations why the Wars ended and never resumed. After 1485, the 'credit crunch' and the *Great Slump* passed, and a modest economic recovery occurred. The impoverishment passed away that predisposed ordinary people to rebellion and that propelled them into national politics. The people were no longer in politics except when infuriated by Henry's taxation and trade embargo. The government became solvent, credit-worthy, even modestly prosperous, and hence able to confront any overmighty subject and to deploy the resources necessary for any contingency. It was not that the dynastic rivalry was over, but rather that the political elite were no longer inclined to wage civil war in favour of any candidate. Whereas hitherto kings had struggled to defend themselves, now the most superhuman effort was needed for any dynastic contender to raise up a rebellion, create a sufficiently substantial party, or to overthrow the monarch in possession. No charismatic leader was to materialize. Time passed, the regime became accepted fact, until there were no potential leaders at all.

ECONOMIC RECOVERY AND THE END OF POPULAR INSURGENCY

There is little evidence of economic recovery from the aftermath of the Black Death until the second decade of the sixteenth century. Book I of Thomas More's *Utopia* in 1516 catalogues growing unemployment and poverty, depopulation and a shortage of peasant land-holdings, and rising grain prices, which he (and other contemporaries into the 1540s) wrongly thought was due to enclosure of arable land as pasture for sheep.[21] Actually, these were the first signs that population was now growing modestly, hence straining both available land-holdings and the supply of food, generating surplus labour that was underemployed, and creating the new Tudor problems of poverty and vagrancy. Although potential criminals, it was never the destitute that threatened revolutions, but respectable community leaders who were aggrieved. Economic conditions now favoured them. Rents ceased to fall on many estates by the 1480s and 'the prospects for rentiers and agricultural producers improved thereafter'. They could now afford consumer durables. The recovery was not at first recognized: not fully perhaps until well into Henry VIII's reign. Retreat from the much more acute *Great Slump* was a great deal quicker and was apparent in some sectors almost immediately. In 1479–82 'a general revival of transcontinental European trade' restored the levels of wool and cloth exports, wine imports, and the prices of wool, cloth and wheat abruptly to the levels of the late 1430s, to the benefit especially of those areas of cloth production that had suffered most around 1450. Although we must 'be wary against setting too early a date' for this recovery and remember how persistently low were the prices of many products, how many towns were still stagnating or declining, and note that Cornish tin production did not recover until the sixteenth century, yet the dismal gloom had thinned or even often been dispelled.[22] Through no credit of their own, the early Tudors were fortunate to be spared the acute economic distress that had been blamed on their predecessors and which had been so conducive to political disaffection and popular insurrection. There was a 'feel-good' factor from which they benefited.

Economic recovery mitigated the worst causes of popular discontent – unemployment, low sales and low prices, and the absence of coin and credit. The forty-year credit crunch was over. Henceforth acute and worsening economic conditions were no longer a chronic grievance at every juncture to be held against the government or an impetus for violent political insurgency. Popular grievances did not end. Strikes, grain and enclosure riots occur from the thirteenth to the eighteenth centuries, the villains – and therefore sometimes the victims – being the rebels' landlords. Tax revolts were a characteristically Tudor form of popular protest.[23] However, these are not political in the same sense. The objective in every case was forcibly to attract the attention of those able to alleviate the grievance and thus to negotiate it away. Such rioters and rebels were convinced of the legitimacy of their case and sought to make the system work rather than to overthrow it.[24] Such attitudes were also conspicuous in the two major regional revolts, in Yorkshire in 1489 and in Cornwall in 1497, which, however, frightened Henry VII and his government very much. Although willing and indeed obliged to accept mass petitioning, Tudor governments found the assemblies threatening, illegitimate and sometimes themselves treasonous. The first, in Yorkshire and south Durham in April–May 1489, may have attracted up to 20,000 insurgents and the leadership of an aristocrat in Sir John Egremont. The people lynched the Earl of Northumberland, the government's representative in the North, and took the northern capital York with the assistance of an alderman and the citizens. It looked like the Ricardian raising of the North most feared by the king, who led a massive force against it, but it dispersed as he approached.[25] Such revolts needed aristocratic leadership, like Egremont and in 1497 Audley and Warbeck, to convert them from protests with a limited time expectancy into genuine threats to regimes and kings. In both cases, what triggered the uprising was government action – the taxation in 1489 of areas, communities and individuals normally exempt – and in 1497 of the far west for a war on the northern borders. What the insurgents wanted was removal of their griev-ances. These were not insurrections with deep-seated causes such as the fundamental disaffection with the regime of 1450, but were rather injuries self-inflicted by the government and thus easily, if rather ignobly, allayed. Henry VII, Henry VIII and their successors learnt at first hand of the English reluctance to pay taxes, whatever the necessity, that Henry VI and Edward IV had already encountered.

Probably therefore the commons – and especially the key commons of Jack Cade's Home Counties and the Earl of Warwick's Richmondshire – were no longer permanent pools of discontent to be aroused and directed into national politics by skilful demagogues. This was a real change that may have occurred as early as the *Third War* of 1483–5. Richard, Duke of Gloucester did seek to enlist Londoners on his side and thus put pressure on the City corporation and his political opponents.[26] Thereafter, however, the populace turned out in force for nobody, although they were grateful on occasion for the leadership of aris-tocrats, who had better notions of political realities, how to provide direction and discipline, and how to make their numbers count. They prided themselves on remaining the king's loyal liegemen. The major popular uprisings of the Tudors and early Stuarts, from the Pilgrimage of Grace in 1536 and Robert Kett's Rebellion in 1549 to the Midland Revolt of 1607, were therefore limited demonstrations that sought the remedy of grievances by the auth-orities. The Pilgrimage of Grace was such a formidable regional revolt that Henry VIII could not confront it on equal terms. The Pilgrims moreover pursued their objectives by peacefully negotiating them away rather than by dethroning the king.[27] The populace had to re-learn how to exercise direct political power in the Civil War of the mid seventeenth century.

This new-found popular prosperity was not universal or permanent. In particular, the Tudor population explosion created mass unemployment and massive poverty that forced governments to develop the Tudor system of poor relief. They feared that the populace would again be driven to rebel. Rural distress was initially and officially attributed to aggressive landlords, especially those who enclosed open fields and commons, converted arable to pasture, and depopulated villages. Class hostility towards such social superiors became an element in popular protest. However, the principal losers, the paupers, were not generally those peasants of standing who were the popular insurgents during the Wars of the Roses and who were subsequently the leaders in the major Tudor uprisings. More important, there was a substantial gap in time, more than a generation long, between the 'political' intervention of the commons during the Wars of the Roses and the more limited insurgency of the Pilgrimage of Grace and of 1549.

Warwick the Kingmaker had shown how popular insurgents could be directed to political ends, but he had no successors. Neither Buckingham and the Wydevilles in 1483, Henry VII in 1485, the rebels of 1486, nor Simnel nor Warbeck discovered the trigger to launch the populace back into violent politics. Only Warbeck indeed sought to revive popular grievances like those invoked by Jack Cade in 1450 and Warwick in 1459–60 and 1469–70.

THE RECOVERY OF ROYAL FINANCES

Economic recovery also removed the financial distress of the Crown, making it more effective both politically and militarily, and removing the necessity for unbridled dependence on purveyance that had so exacerbated poverty and aggravated the people in 1450. The government shared in national growth through the painless medium of the customs levied on trade abroad.

Henry VII and Henry VIII both benefited from the repair of the royal finances by the Yorkist kings. From the most appalling abyss of debt, Edward IV emerged modestly solvent by his death and may indeed have been somewhat better off a few years earlier. Edward retained significant forfeitures in his own hands, notably those of his brother Clarence, and his modest French pension made a real difference. The debts that Henry VII brought with him were relatively small and easily repaid. From 1492 Henry also was pensioned by the French and he too enhanced the Crown lands: he was fortunate, of course, to have no family to provide for. He appropriated particular estates to finance the defences of Berwick, Carlisle and the northern borders. Much more important was the recovery of trade and hence of the customs, which brought a steady enhancement of his income. By his death he enjoyed at least £104,863 a year – much more than the Yorkists or Henry VI and comparable to the income of Richard II – but this left little margin beyond ordinary charges. He secured relatively little in taxes. Henry VII could finance his administration, his house-hold and court, maintain more garrisons, and build (at Richmond and Westminster Abbey!) as kings were expected to do without undue recourse to borrowing or to oppressive purveyance. Yet he was to do much more than this. He disbursed subsidies of at least £260,000 to his allies in his last years and thus raised his profile abroad. Almost certainly he left on death a substantial treasure, presumably as the fruits of the bond policy: £600,000, Horowitz spec-ulates, perhaps even £1 million. Dudley alone may have exacted every year as much as half of Henry's ordinary revenues.[28] After 1500, therefore, Henry could finance emergency actions against any potential threat in contrast to his unfor-tunate predecessors, for whom such a luxury had been almost unthinkable.

DIPLOMATIC REVOLUTION

If dynastic rivals could no longer invoke popular support, then foreign backing came to matter more. Foreign shipping was always necessary if any invasion was to reach the British Isles, but beyond that York, Warwick and Edward IV had needed only sufficient manpower to thwart the coastal defences and to enable them to reach their own supporters. During this final phase of the Wars, however, it was the supporters within England who were supplementary and the foreign manpower that was essential. Neither Henry Tudor himself, nor any subsequent contender, enjoyed such substantial connections of their own or sufficient popular backing to overthrow the regime. In 1485, in 1487 and 1495 the core of the invading armies consisted of foreign mercenaries. No such forces were actually forthcoming in 1493, as Henry VII found, nor were they on any of the other occasions when the de la Poles apparently threatened the realm. The political initiative had passed decisively from the dynastic rivals, who sought the Crown for themselves, to foreign rulers, who now deter-mined the time and objective of the attack. However, the priorities of Valois and Habsburg had changed. Unlike Louis XI and Charles the Bold, they were not interested in changing the English king, even to attack thereby their conti-nental neighbour. Backing a contender became a diplomatic ploy. It was a threat that Henry VII and Henry VIII could remove by making concessions elsewhere. Contenders, in short, were no longer prime movers, but had become pawns in the schemes of their backers.

Warwick the Kingmaker repeatedly committed the Calais garrison to his domestic programmes. Changes in the organization of Calais by Edward IV had spread responsibility more widely, so that all power no longer rested with a single captain. This did not necessarily prevent the commanders of the principal military garrison from plotting as in 1503, but in practice they did not behave in this way. Ireland was exposed as Henry's weakest point by both Simnel and Warbeck, symbolized by Simnel's coronation at Dublin, but Simnel's Irish levies were defeated at Stoke in 1487 and no others actually fought on English soil. By backing the Earl of Kildare, Henry succeeded in closing Ireland to Warbeck. Support was also secured by Warbeck from the Scots, but James IV (like Angus in 1463) proved unwilling to risk enough to give him a fighting chance of success. However troublesome, the Scots and Irish were not the serious threats to Henry that France and Burgundy had been.

A diplomatic revolution occurred nevertheless, which meant that England's principal continental neighbours no longer wished to destabilize England, nor indeed had much to fear from Henry VII. The Hundred Years War had pitched Englishmen against Frenchmen from 1337 to 1453 and beyond. For much of the fifteenth century, there had been a north-west European diplomatic system of England, France and Burgundy, which after 1453 was primarily a context between France and Burgundy. Far from the English conquering France, it was the French and Burgundians in turn who had intervened in England to advantage themselves against the other. What had gradually evolved by 1519 was the consolidation of Europe into two great powers, Habsburg and Valois, with which lesser realms like England could neither compare nor effectively compete. In retrospect the treaty of Arras of 1482, which had defeated but not destroyed Burgundy, was a decisive moment. Henceforth Burgundy was ruled by Habsburg princes with wider European interests, in which England did not loom so large. French kings after Louis XI (d. 1483) were less alarmed by English threats and less concerned to interfere. From 1494, when King Charles VIII attacked Naples, successive French kings – and increasingly all other rulers too – prioritized the Italian Wars that lasted on and off until 1559. The titanic struggle of the two new superpowers – Francis I and Charles V – was fought out on Italian soil. The great powers looked southwards and cared little about what was happening over the Channel. The rivalries of France and Burgundy that had helped overthrow both Edward IV and Henry VI in 1470–1 almost ceased.

This new diplomatic system did not emerge all at once and was not initially recognized. The humiliation of 1453 was not easily accepted in England and almost a century passed before the loss of France was recognized as permanent. There was still English rhetoric about reconquering France, and English kings were to call themselves kings of France until George III. It remained possible for Englishmen to suppose that England could match its most powerful neighbour and for kings to persuade Parliament in 1467–8, 1475, 1492 and even in 1513 to fund invasions of France. Yet kings, ministers and the public too increasingly realized that England was a minnow in a Europe dominated by two superpowers, as it remained until the 1650s. Internationally, the English settled into a diminished role. France did not back Henry Tudor in 1485 to harm Burgundy, nor did Margaret of Burgundy aid Simnel in 1487 to strike at France. These invasions were not byproducts of continental conflicts, but were possible only because there was peace on the continent that freed resources which could be used in England.

The French no longer threatened England to compete with Burgundy, although French kings resurrected the de la Poles whenever the English appeared aggressive. No invasions resulted. In practice, French control of the whole coastline of the Channel towards England did not result in French aggression against England, nor even against English shipping. Italy had become the French priority. What happened in the Channel and even English invasions of France appear in retrospect rather frivolous distractions, not serious threats, and did not prompt the retaliatory action from France, systematic support for pretenders, nor invasions that the English feared. Memories of English prowess in the Hundred Years War seem indeed to have allowed Henry VII still a weight in international relations quite out of proportion to his actual might or his willingness to commit English manpower, for instance in constructing the anti-French Holy League.[29] The Emperor Maximilian, moreover, ranged himself with the multi-national coalitions designed to thwart French ambitions in Italy. However much he believed in the claims of Warbeck and Edmund de la Pole, Maximilian was not willing to commit significant resources to make them kings of England, nor indeed could Margaret of Burgundy. Neither Edmund nor Richard de la Pole could achieve anything effective without substantial foreign help.

Rebuilding Allegiance

The greatest strength of any monarch was the obligation of allegiance owed to him by everyone, and the greatest weakness that there were other alternative claimants to that allegiance. The Wars of the Roses took so long to get started at least in part because everyone recognized binding ties of allegiance to King Henry VI, which in 1450–61 the majority – and especially most of the nobility – scrupulously observed, often apparently despite being critical of his policies, actions or inactions. A minority – growing minorities in the first two

Wars – committed themselves to the opposition. *The Third* War, however, appears different. Neither side at Bosworth was strongly supported. Although the number of nobles who accompanied Henry VII to Stoke in 1487 and to Yorkshire in 1489 was impressive, King Henry himself was disappointed by the number of his supporters. A mere handful of noblemen was prepared to rebel at any time. The total numbers rebelling and total numbers attainted over the whole reign were more impressive. Apparently the nobility were no longer prepared to rebel or even to fight for the king any more.

It was not that the dynastic issue was dead. The first two Tudor kings were insufficiently fertile to create the new royal family needed to buttress the throne. The passage of time enabled the de la Poles to flourish, grandchildren of Clarence and children of Edward IV's younger daughters to be born, and – in a genealogically conscious age – the diluted but nevertheless royal blood of Staffords, Nevilles of Raby and others to proliferate. If John de la Pole died in 1487, his brothers Edmund in 1513, Richard in 1525 and William (still confined safely in the Tower) in 1539, female lines continued. Clarence's daughter Margaret, Countess of Salisbury, was executed only in 1541. Such claims were for connoisseurs, for persistent plotters of whom, by the 1530s, there were none. Perhaps dynastic difference had never been motive enough. The *First War*, remember, was fought about governance, good and bad, and only became dynastic when the stakes were raised. The *Second War*, also, started over governance and only became dynastic when Warwick's initial coup failed. Even Richard, Duke of Gloucester pretended that good governance was his objective, not self-advancement, and it was to remove a tyrant, not to make a dubious princeling king, that was the purpose of the victors in 1485. Blatant and unvarnished dynasticism appears after 1485. Dynasticism, on the evidence, had limited public appeal.

There were plenty of other reasons for aristocrats not to get involved in treason. They were primarily civilians rather than professional soldiers. The prospects of success were too poor. If what distinguishes the Wars of the Roses from other civil wars is how often governments were unseated – four times – it remains true that most of the coups, invasions and rebellions were defeated, often catastrophically. Civil war had simply become too dangerous. Most of the leaders of the Wars of the Roses perished in battle or were arrested afterwards. The male lines of Beaufort, Holland, Lancaster, junior Neville, and York had been exterminated. Henry Tudor further raised the risks and reduced the chances.

Far from being a matter of personal taste or honourable, participation in the Wars had become treasonable for all losers, whatever side they were on, and nothing had become more discreditable or destructive than treason. Those defeated were liable to forfeiture, their wives and children to relative penury, to the loss of rank and status, estates and wealth, to corruption of blood and dishonour. Warfare, of course, was always dangerous. No wonder that noblemen serving abroad extracted concessions for their families before departing or that the fourth Earl of Northumberland made his will before Bosworth. At least the chivalric code had minimized mortality among aristocrats serving abroad by making them valuable, by enabling them to surrender rather than be butchered when defeat was inevitable, to be imprisoned and cared for, and in due course to be ransomed and released. It had protected wives and children and regulated family losses. Often, indeed, honourable defeat had added lustre to ancestral renown.

During the Wars of the Roses, however, the nobility became targets. If not slain in battle, they were liable to wholesale execution afterwards. Even sanctuary no longer protected them. Henry's bond policy threatened everyone of significance with financial loss even for loose talk and concealments that fell well short of treason. The hazards were no longer confined to principals. Several of those fighting for Richard III had been executed immediately or attainted. No wonder, it may be deduced, that in 1495 aristocrats hesitated to fight for King Henry, fearing that they would suffer as traitors at the hands of his vanquisher. Even Sir William Stanley, a chief officer of his household, was ambivalent. Hence the *De Facto Act* of that year, which declared that those who fought for a de facto king were safe from attainder.[30] How many, one wonders, were convinced by an act so easily repealed or disregarded at the next dynastic revolution.

Just as important, however, was a change in ideology. It is highly unlikely that financial threats generated *loyalty* to the regime:[31] compliance, acquiescence, absolute obedience, far more probably. Moreover, it ceased to be possible for plotters to justify their actions in conscience to themselves or others as falling within their constitutional rights and in the public interest. Instead, it came to be accepted that order was paramount – the concept of order – and that opponents should submit to royal authority even if they disagreed with it. There was no right of resistance to royal authority and even tyrants must be tolerated.

THE CONCEPT OF ORDER AND DOCTRINE OF NON-RESISTANCE

This is a surprising change that owes much to the Wars of the Roses. It was of course generally accepted that government was created by God and that kings as God's representatives were entitled to obedience. 'The powers that be are ordained of God', wrote St Paul in Romans chapter 13 verse 1 – a much-quoted Tudor text. Moreover the best-known works of political theory stated that it was better to suffer tyrants rather than to dethrone them.[32] Yet this last bit seems not to have been applied in England, where several tyrants had been overthrown well before the Wars of the Roses. Such behaviour remained wrong.

Allegiance and the obligation of obedience was the normal language of kings and governments and was attributed to Henry VI, Edward IV, Richard III and Henry VII. However, 'in almost every reign, the "opposition" emphasised the paramountcy of the common weal while the "crown" insisted on an overriding duty of obedience'.[33] Indeed, the Wars of the Roses testifies repeatedly to the defeat of this royal doctrine of obedience. Back in 1459, Henry VI's case triumphed on paper in the *Somnium Vigilantis*, which ridiculed the Yorkist arguments. It was only through obedience 'to the king and his laws . . . that the common weal could be served'.[34] Yet it was their opponents who won the *First War*. A decade later when Warwick and Clarence took up York's arguments, Edward IV, now king, asserted his authority. He would only treat them as a sovereign should and made no allowances. Yet Warwick it was who won. And even in 1471 Edward claimed at first to be a loyal subject of Henry VI before waging war against him. Richard, Duke of Gloucester, broke his oaths of allegiance and obligation of obedience when he rebelled. His own proclamations and those of Henry VII demanded obedience too. In 1487 Archbishop Morton urged on Parliament 'the obedience and respect of subjects to the prince'.[35] Yet Buckingham in 1483, adherents of the Wydevilles both in 1483 and 1485, and Simnel's and Warbeck's English followers thereafter by their actions all rejected this case. The argument was not yet won.

The homily on obedience of 1547 shows how sixty years of Tudor rule had transformed the dominant ideology. The homily was one of twelve official sermons prescribed by both Church and State to be read in churches where there was no licensed preacher. Declaimed several times a year from almost every pulpit, it became a commonplace, echoed in the Puritan *Admonition* of 1572 and in Ulysses's famous speech in Shakespeare's *Troilus and Cressida*. It had been summarized matter-of-factly in the earlier *Gorboduc* (*c.*1561) and was fully integrated into Shakespeare's cycle of fifteenth-century history plays. God, stated the homily, had created everything in the most perfect order. To upset such order, whether by disobedience to the king or an employer or any other superior, was potentially disastrous and against God's will. In particular, kings were God's representatives who must be obeyed in 'all their godly proceedings, laws, statutes, proclamations and ordinances'. Should their actions not be godly, in the public interest, or indeed tyrannical, there was admittedly no obligation to obey, but also no right to resistance. Because of the potential for disorder from his overthrow, the tyrant must be tolerated and his tyranny suffered patiently by his victims, retribution being reserved to God alone after his death.[36] No rebel or potential rebel could draw any comfort here, although rebellions still happened.

Between Bosworth in 1485 and the homily in 1547, therefore, there was a complete transformation, in which the case for forceful coercion and even deposition of kings that had prevailed during the Wars of the Roses was decisively rejected, and was replaced as political orthodoxy by the concept of order and doctrine of non-resistance. The victory of such doctrines – and the eventual acceptance also of the Tudor Myth – cannot really be doubted, although there were always exceptions, and in the remote North these doctrines may not have prevailed until after the Northern Rebellion of 1569.[37]

There were earlier indications of this sea change, notably in William Tyndale's *Obedience of a Christian Man* (1528). Undoubtedly the change was fostered, stimulated and publicized after the era of this book, in particular during the 1530s under the aegis of Henry VIII's minister Thomas Cromwell and by such government propagandists as Richard Morison and Thomas Starkey. They, however, were building on what already existed. When did the decisive change occur? Was it early enough to assist the Tudors in deterring further aristocratic upheavals like those led by York, Warwick, Richard III and indeed Henry VII himself? It seems that it was.

The essential elements were already present at Henry's accession in 1485.

First of all, Henry's victory at Bosworth was undeniably God's verdict on the dynastic dispute. It had been prefigured by a whole series of signs. Henry's victory was like the sacrament of the mass. 'Out of this warfare came peace for the whole kingdom.' The new king was God's instrument to relieve the people of 'the evils which had hitherto afflicted them beyond measure'.[38]

Like his Lancastrian and Yorkist predecessors, Henry maximized the image and panoply of kingship to demonstrate the inevitability of his rule and that he had come to stay. He identified himself with the British legends, tracing his line back to the supposedly historical Brutus, Cadwallader and above all Arthur. It was no accident that the birth of his heir in 1486 was staged at Winchester, where King Arthur's table was displayed, not that the baby prince was named Arthur. A second King Arthur was thereby prefigured. Henry exploited all his more recent connections, showered his buildings, decorations and hangings with roses and other emblems, and cultivated the magnificence borrowed from Burgundy that his father-in-law Edward IV had begun. Like anything new, the creation and acceptance of the Tudor Myth took time, but unlike its Lancastrian and Yorkist predecessors the Tudor Myth was never overthrown and has endured.

From the moment of his accession King Henry set himself apart from other usurpers by differentiating between Richard III and other ousted kings. Richard himself had been a usurper and in his own lifetime he had been labelled a tyrant and a monster. The 1485 act of attainder declared Richard guilty of 'unnatural, mischievous and great perjuries, treasons, homicides, and murders, in shedding of infants' blood, with many other wrongs, odious offences and abominations against God and man'. Richard was a wicked king.[39] It was therefore legitimate to depose him. Henry asserted that he had the better title and was already king before Bosworth. He chose to regard his prior recognition at Rennes Cathedral as an election. It was therefore Richard who was the pretender. It was righteous for Henry to deprive Richard of his crown and just also to punish those who fought for him as traitors against himself. The chancellor's sermon that opened Parliament on 7 November 1485 described Henry as 'a second Joshua . . . who was snatched us from the depths of despair and will strike either to reform the wicked or to drive them out and reform them'.[40] Henry was not prepared to tolerate any hedging of bets where loyalty to himself was concerned.

Also from the start Henry claimed that his accession was a break not just with the immediate past, but with the whole period of the Wars of the Roses which, as an outsider viewing from abroad, he could perceive as a unity. His marriage to Elizabeth of York was intended 'to end the dissensions which have prevailed between their ancestors of their respective houses or families of Lancaster and York'.[41] Reference to Lancaster harks back of course to the 1450s and possibly to 1399. Even more explicit is his proclamation of 13 June 1486 that reported the Pope's confirmation of his title and the excommunication (and hence eternal damnation) that befell anybody who opposed it. The proclamation explained that his marriage terminated 'the variances, dissensions, and debates that had been in the realm of England between the houses of the Dukes of Lancaster on the one part and the house of the Duchy of York on the other'.[42] The first two parliaments of his reign opened with sermons from the Lord Chancellors urging the interests of the commonwealth and especially prosperity and peace.[43]

Henry also presented himself as heir to the House of Lancaster: on rather doubtful grounds, as we have seen. Early in 1486 Giovanni de Gigli and later that year Pietro Carmeliano wrote of his inheritance from the martyred Henry VI.[44] Supposedly, the royal martyr had prophesied Henry's future accession.[45] Yet it was Elizabeth's title that Henry asserted when seeking the dispensation from the Pope necessary to validate his marriage to her. Their union, he claimed, united the two warring houses, and would bring back peace. Not only did Pope Innocent VIII (1484–92) sanction the match, therefore, but he excommunicated anybody who opposed it.[46] No wonder Emperor Maximilian and Duchess Margaret assured Pope Alexander VI (1492–1503) that his predecessor had mistaken the situation and urged him to revoke his bull.[47] However, their case was not accepted. They remained de facto excommunicate and the Tudors retained their papal sanction, even securing the title Defender of the Faith, until Henry VIII himself broke with Rome in the early 1530s.

CHAPTER 15

EPILOGUE

When the last de la Pole brother, William, died naturally in 1539, he had been imprisoned in the Tower almost all his adult life and his passing was scarcely noticed. He and his cause had faded almost into forgetfulness. York versus Lancaster was a dead contest. The Wars of the Roses gradually petered out and were supplanted by other, newer and more relevant divisions.

The problem of succession remained very much alive, however, for two reasons. First of all, Henry VIII proved unable to breed sons of his own. Hence his divorce from Katherine of Aragon, his break with Rome, and the English Reformation, which 'introduced fundamental ideological divisions within the English polity'. Hence therefore a new 'threat of foreign invasion by Catholic powers dedicated to upholding papal authority and the Roman church' and, moreover, 'the danger that some of his subjects would consider him a heretic and therefore begin to question the nature of their allegiance and whether loyalty first to the king or their conscience'. 'When he rejected papal authority and divorced Catherine, Henry VIII opened new divisions between noble families and factions at court and in the country.'[1] Security considerations accelerated up Henry's list of priorities and a new round of executions followed, including amongst them Clarence's daughter Margaret, Countess of Salisbury, and Henry, Marquis of Exeter, grandson of Edward IV's daughter Princess Katherine. If Henry VII had disparaged his sisters-in-law by his choice of their partners, as Warbeck supposed in 1496,[2] allowing them to marry at all bred up new rivals to the Crown, in Henry VIII's eyes at least. Actually, the greatest threats to Tudor monarchs did not hark back to the Wars of the Roses, but were offshoots of the ruling dynasty itself.

Not only was their dynasty legitimate, so all Tudor regimes argued, but it was also necessary if peace and order were to be maintained. Dissent was permissible, but never rebellion nor resistance. The catalogue of Tudor rebellions, however, was very long. There were *coups d'état* in 1549 and 1553, attempted coups in 1553 and 1601, numerous plots, full-scale aristocratic revolts in 1554 and 1569, and major regional revolts in 1536 and 1549.[3] The necessity for order and the illegitimacy of forceful resistance were never completely ingrained. The lowest orders suffered great economic distress that the government perceived as dangerous and sought to alleviate. There came to be hundreds of principled Catholics and Protestants who accepted death for religious dissent that was also perilous politically. There were frequent foreign threats, including the Spanish Armada of 1588, which was much more formidable than any of the invasions of the Wars of the Roses. A second armada in 1596 actually achieved a landfall in Ireland. All the resources of the English Crown could not make England militarily the equal of either Habsburg or Valois. If the Tudors survived, it was as much because of their international insignificance as their strength. It was also in part because their foes seldom if ever united against them or were agreed on their aims. Never did aristocratic nor popular insurrections move from their regional beginnings to become truly national. The northern earls of 1569 proved to be less than overmighty. The Pilgrimage of Grace of 1536 might have decisively ended Henry VIII's reign and the Reformation almost at once. Too formidable to confront in the field, the Pilgrims had no desire to overthrow King Henry. They acknowledged the legitimacy of his government and sought instead to negotiate away their grievances just as Jack Cade's rebels had done in 1450. The stories of Kett's Rebellion in Norfolk and the Western Rebellion, both in 1549, are much the same. And it is more probable that in 1588 the persecuted Catholics would have rallied to Elizabeth rather than made common cause with the Spanish invader.

Political dissent did not end with the Wars of the Roses. Neither did the power of the aristocracy, bastard feudalism, popular insurrection, or external dabbling in dynastic issues. However, the political issues and the political process had changed decisively. It was not until the 1640s that memories of the Wars of the Roses had faded enough for civil war again to be a respectable way to resolve the most intractable political differences. Not until then did the people re-learn their potential for direct political action. Participants then and historians ever since have recognized the profound and modern constitutional issues then at stake whilst shrugging off the claims to serious consideration of the Wars of the Roses. Undoubtedly the Wars were anomalous and cannot be identified with constitutional progress, yet they were not mere faction-fighting, but rather a distinct era brought about by a combination of destabilizing factors that ceased when the original causes disappeared.

Abbreviations

Anglica Historica	*The Anglica Historica of Polydore Vergil AD 1485–1537*, Camden 3rd ser., lxiv (1950).
Annales	'William Wyrcester Annales Rerum Anglicarum', in *Letters and Papers illustrative of the Wars of the English in France*, ed. J. Stevenson, Rolls Series, ii.ii (1864).
Arrivall	*Historie of the Arrivall of Edward IV*, ed. J. Bruce, Camden Society i (1838).
Arthurson, *Warbeck*	Ian Arthurson, *The Perkin Warbeck Conspiracy 1491–99* (Stroud, 1994).
Benet's Chron.	'John Benet's Chronicle for the years 1400 to 1462', ed. G.L. and M.A. Harriss, *Camden Miscellany* xxiv (1972).
BIHR	*Bulletin of the Institute of Historical Research.*
Brut	*The Brut or the Chronicles of England*, ed. F.W.D. Brie, Early English Text Society 131, 136 (1908).
Carpenter, *Wars*	C. Carpenter, *The Wars of the Roses: Politics and the Constitution in England, c. 1437–1509* (Cambridge, 1997).
CChR	*Calendar of Charter Rolls.*
CCR	*Calendar of the Close Rolls.*
CPL	*Calendar of the Papal Registers.*
CPR	*Calendar of the Patent Rolls.*
Crowland	*The Crowland Chronicle Continuations 1459–86*, ed. N. Pronay and J. Cox (Gloucester, 1986).
CSPM	*Calendar of State Papers Milan.*
CW	W. Shakespeare, *The Complete Works*, ed. P. Ackroyd (2006).

Death & Dissent	*Death and Dissent: The Dethe of the Kynge of Scots and Warkworth's Chronicle*, ed. L.M. Matheson (Woodbridge, 1999).
EcHR	*Economic History Review.*
EETS	Early English Text Society.
EHR	*English Historical Review.*
Eng. Chron.	*An English Chronicle 1377–1461: A New Edition*, ed. W. Marx (Woodbridge, 2003).
Foedera	T. Rymer, *Foedera, Conventione, Literae et cujuscunque generis Acta Publica*, ed. J. Caley et al, 18 vols, Record Commission (1827).
Gregory	*Historical Collections of a Citizen of London*, ed. J. Gairdner, Camden Society, ns. xvii (1876).
Griffiths, *Henry VI*	R.A. Griffiths, *The Reign of King Henry VI: The Exercise of Royal Authority 1422–61* (London, 1981).
Griffiths, *King & Country*	R.A. Griffiths, *King and Country: England and Wales in the Fifteenth Century* (London, 1991).
Hall's Chronicle	*Hall's Chronicle*, ed. H. Ellis (London, 1809).
Harvey, *Cade*	I.M.W. Harvey, *Jack Cade's Rebellion of 1450* (Oxford, 1991).
Hatcher, 'Great Slump'	John Hatcher, 'The Great Slump of the Mid-Fifteenth Century', in *Progress and Problems in Medieval England: Essays in Honour of Edward Miller*, ed. Richard Britnell and John Hatcher (Cambridge, 1996).
Hicks, *Anne Neville*	Michael Hicks, *Anne Neville, Queen to Richard III* (Stroud, 2006).
Hicks, '*Brief Treatise*'	Michael Hicks, 'Edward IV's *Brief Treatise* and the Treaty of Picquigny of 1475', *Historical Research*, lxxxiii (2010).
Hicks, *Clarence*	Michael Hicks, *False, Fleeting, Perjur'd Clarence: George Duke of Clarence 1449–78* (Gloucester, 1980).
Hicks, *Edward IV*	Michael Hicks, *Edward IV* (London, 2004).
Hicks, *Edward V*	Michael Hicks, *Edward V* (Stroud, 2003).
Hicks, *Richard III*	Michael Hicks, *Richard III* (London, 2000).
Hicks, *Rivals*	Michael Hicks, *Richard III and his Rivals: Magnates and their Motives during the Wars of the Roses* (London, 1991).
Hicks, *Warwick*	Michael Hicks, *Warwick the Kingmaker* (Oxford, 1998).

Horowitz, *Henry VII*	*Who was Henry VII?*, ed. Mark Horowitz, *Historical Research* lxxxii (2009).
HR	*Historical Research.*
JMH	*Journal of Medieval History.*
John Vale's Bk	*The Politics of Fifteenth-Century England: John Vale's Book*, ed. M.L. Kekewich, C. Richmond, A.F. Sutton, L. Visser-Fuchs and J.L. Watts (Stroud, 1995).
Johnson, *York*	P.A. Johnson, *Duke Richard of York 1411–1460* (Oxford, 1986).
Lander, *Crown*	J.R. Lander, *Crown and Nobility 1450–1509* (1976).
Lay Taxes	*Lay Taxes in England and Wales 1188–1688*, ed. M. Jurkowski, C.L. Smith and D. Crook, Public Record Office Handbook 31 (1998).
McFarlane, *Wars*	K.B. McFarlane, 'The Wars of the Roses', in *England in the Fifteenth Century* (1981).
Mancini	D. Mancini, *The Usurpation of Richard III*, ed. C.A.J. Armstrong (2nd edn, Oxford, 1969).
NMS	Nottingham Medieval Studies.
Paston L & P	*Paston Letters and Papers of the Fifteenth Century*, ed. R. Beadle, N. Davis and C. Richmond, 3 vols, Early English Text Society supplementary series 20–2 (2004–5).
PL	*The Paston Letters 1422–1509*, ed. J. Gairdner, 6 vols (1904).
Plumpton L & P	*The Plumpton Letters and Papers*, ed. Joan Kirby, Camden 5th ser., viii (1996).
Pollard, *LM England*	A.J. Pollard, *Late Medieval England 1399–1509* (Harlow, 2000).
Pollard, *NE England*	A.J. Pollard, *North-Eastern England during the Wars of the Roses: Lay Society, War and Politics 1450–1500* (Oxford, 1990).
Pollard, *Wars*	A.J. Pollard, *Wars of the Roses* (Basingstoke, 2001).
Pollard, *Warwick*	A.J. Pollard, *Warwick the Kingmaker: Politics, Power and Fame* (London, 2007).
Pollard, *Worlds*	A.J. Pollard, *The Worlds of Richard III* (Stroud, 2001).
POPC	*Proceedings and Ordinances of the Privy Council*, ed. N.H. Nicolas (London, 1834).
PROME	*The Parliament Rolls of England 1275–1504*, ed. C. Given Wilson, 16 vols (Woodbridge, 2005).

Ross, *Edward IV*	C.D. Ross, *Edward IV* (1974).
Ross, *Richard III*	C.D. Ross, *Richard III* (1981).
Ross, *Wars*	C.D. Ross, *The Wars of the Roses: A Concise History* (1976).
Storey, *Lancaster*	R.L. Storey, *The End of the House of Lancaster* (1966).
TNA	The National Archives.
TRHS	*Transactions of the Royal Historical Society.*
Vergil	*Three Books of Polydore Vergil's English History*, ed. H. Ellis, Camden Society xxix (1844).
Virgoe, *East Anglian Society*	Roger Virgoe, *East Anglian Society and the Political Community of Late Medieval England*, ed. Caroline Barron, Carole Rawcliffe and Joel T. Rosenthal (Norwich, 1997).
Wars, ed. Pollard	*The Wars of the Roses*, ed. A.J. Pollard (Basingstoke, 1995).
Watts, *Henry VI*	J.L. Watts, *Henry VI and the Politics of Kingship* (Cambridge, 1996).
Wedgwood, *Biographies*	Wedgwood, J., *History of Parliament 1439–1509*, ii (1938).
Weightman, *Margaret*	Christine Weightman, *Margaret of York, Duchess of Burgundy 1446–1503* (Gloucester, 1989).
Wroe, *Perkin*	Ann Wroe, *Perkin: A Story of Deception* (2004).

NOTES

Chapter 1: What Were the Wars of the Roses?

1. Carpenter, *Wars*, abstract.
2. *Crowland*, 182–5.
3. Walter Scott, *Anne of Geierstein* (1901), 111.
4. *Vergil*, 84, 172.
5. *Brut*, 533.
6. *Crowland*, 123.
7. *Crowland*, 183.
8. *John Vale's Bk*, 178–9; *Death & Dissent*, 105–6.
9. *Crowland*, 182–5, 190–1.
10. Carpenter, *Wars*, abstract.
11. C. Richmond, 'Identity and Morality. Power and Politics during the Wars of the Roses', *Power and Identity in the Middle Ages*, ed. H. Pryce and J. Watts (Oxford, 2007), 226–41, esp. 229, 240.

Chapter 2: Why Did the Wars of the Roses Happen?

1. Storey, *Lancaster*, 6; K. Dockray, *Henry VI, Margaret of Anjou and the Wars of the Roses: A Sourcebook* (Stroud, 2000), ix; Ross, *Wars*, 13–15, 51–2, 106, 148; Ross, *Richard III*, pl.18.
2. *Crowland*, 182–3.
3. *York House Books 1461–90*, ed. L.C. Attreed, 2 vols (Stroud, 1991), 482; A.J. Pollard, *The Wars of the Roses* (Basingstoke, 2001) 6–8.
4. Ross, *Wars*, 14–15.
5. Pollard, *Wars*, 7; Scott, *Anne of Geierstein* (1901), 111; see also D. Hume, *The History of England from the Invasion of Julius Caesar to The Revolution in 1688* (Indianapolis, IN, 1983), ii, 456.
6. *PROME*, xii, 517, 521.
7. BL Add MS 10099 f. 142; K. Dockray, *William Shakespeare, the Wars of the Roses and Historians* (Stroud, 2002), 75.
8. Principally Warwick the Kingmaker, *PROME* xii, 57–9; see also M.A. Hicks, 'The Neville Earldom of Salisbury 1429–71', repr. in *Rivals*, 360; Hicks, *Warwick*, 226; *Eng. Chron.*, 70–100; *Brut*, 533.

9. M. Bennett, 'Edward III's Entail and the Succession to the Crown', *EHR* cxiii (1998), 582–94; M. Levine, *Tudor Dynastic Problems 1460–1571* (1973), 26.
10. W. Shakespeare, *Richard II*, Act III, scene III (*CW*, 499).
11. Dockray, *Shakespeare*, 22.
12. W. Shakespeare, *Henry V*, Act IV, scene II (*CW*, 613).
13. W. Shakespeare, *Henry VI Part 2*, Act I, scene I (*CW*, 668).
14. W. Shakespeare, *Henry VI Part 3*, Act IV, scene VII (*CW*, 733).
15. W. Shakespeare, *Richard III*, Act V, scene V (*CW*, 790).
16. W. Shakespeare, *Henry VI Part I*, Act II, scene III (*CW*, 640); Ross, *Wars*, 23.
17. W.C. Sellar and R.J. Yeatman, *1066 and All That* (1930), 55, 58–9.
18. Dockray, *Shakespeare*, 1.
19. Harvey, *Cade*, 188–90.
20. M.A. Hicks, 'Propaganda and the Battle of St Albans, 1455', *NMS* xliv (2000), 167–83, esp. 180.
21. *PROME* xii, 454–60.
22. *PROME*, xii, 516–17; xiii, 13–16, 42–51.
23. E.g. *Eng. Chron.*, 70–90; *Brut*, 533. I hope to demonstrate this elsewhere.
24. Hicks, *Edward IV* (2004), 58, 62–3; F.J. Levy, *Tudor Historical Thought* (San Marino, CA, 1967), 60; *Crowland*, 150–1; *Hall's Chronicle*, ed. H. Ellis (London, 1809), 219; F. Bacon, *History of the Reign of King Henry the Seventh*, ed. J. Weinberger (Ithaca, NY, 1996), 1.
25. *Vergil*, 71, 84, 119; *Hall's Chronicle*, 219; Shakespeare, *Richard III*, Act I, scenes II, III (*CW*, 748, 754–5); T. More, *History of King Richard III*, ed. R.S. Sylvester (New Haven, CT, 1963), 8–9.
26. J. Fortescue, *On the Laws and Governance of England*, ed. S. Lockwood (Cambridge, 1997), 92, 100–6; see also Harvey, *Cade*, 188–91.
27. See, e.g., M.L. Kekewich, ' "Though shalt be under the power of man": Sir John Fortescue and the Yorkist Succession', *NMS* xlii (1998), 188–230.
28. Hume, *History*, 316–22, 430–2, 470–2.
29. W. Stubbs, *Constitutional History of England in the Middle Ages*, 3 vols (Oxford, 1872–8), iii, esp. 2–3, 91.
30. C.H. Williams, 'The Yorkist Kings', *Cambridge Medieval History* viii (Cambridge, 1936), 421.
31. Carpenter, *Wars*, 16–25, esp. 17; see also K.B. McFarlane, 'The Lancastrian Kings', in *Cambridge Medieval History* viii (Cambridge, 1936).
32. Storey, *Lancaster*, ix, 5; Ross, *Wars*, 39–42; Carpenter, *Wars*, 20.
33. Storey, *Lancaster*, ix, 1–27.
34. Ross, *Wars*, 28–42; Carpenter, *Wars*, 93.
35. Harvey, *Cade*; C.F. Richmond, 'Fauconberg's Kentish Rising of May 1471', *EHR* lxxxxv (1970), 674–92; I. Arthurson, 'The Rising of 1497: A Revolt of the Peasantry?', *People, Politics and the Community in the Later Middle Ages*, ed. J. Rosenthal and C. Richmond (Gloucester, 1987).
36. Carpenter, *Wars*, 22–3.
37. Carpenter, *Wars*, cover, 17, 22–3.
38. L. Stone, *The Causes of the English Revolution 1529–1642* (1972).
39. Hicks, *Warwick*, 310.

Chapter 3: How the System Worked

1. This is understated by A.L. Brown, 'The Authorisation of Letters under the Great Seal', *BIHR* xxxviii (1964).
2. J.L. Watts, 'Ideals, Principles and Politics', in *Wars*, ed. Pollard, 110–11; Harvey, *Cade*, 191.

3. J.L. Watts, *Henry VI and the Politics of Kingship* (Cambridge, 1996), 165; Hicks, *Richard III*, 38, 48–9; Harvey, *Cade*, 187; For the system, see J.A. Tuck, 'Richard II's System of Patronage', in *The Reign of Richard II*, ed. F.R.H. Du Boulay and C.M. Barron (1971), 5, 15, 17–18.
4. Harvey, *Cade*, 189; S. Anglo, 'The Courtier', in *The Courts of Europe*, ed. A.G. Dickens (1977), 35.
5. Harvey, *Cade*, 189.
6. M.A. Hicks, *English Political Culture in the Fifteenth Century* (2002), 33–4; *PROME* xii, 306–7.
7. G. Dodd, *Justice and Grace* (Oxford, 2007).
8. M. Bennett, 'Edward III's Entail and the Succession to the Crown', *EHR* cxiii (1998), 582–94.
9. *Crowland*, 147.
10. M.A. Hicks, 'Out of Session: Edward Guildford of Halden, Justice of the Peace for Kent, 1436–43', *Southern History* 28 (2006), 24–35, esp. 36–8.
11. M.A. Hicks, *Bastard Feudalism* (Harlow, 1995), 119–24. This is the source of the next four paragraphs.
12. D. Youngs, *Humphrey Newton 1466–1536* (Woodbridge, 2008).
13. *The Herald's Memoir 1486–1490*, ed. E. Cavell (Donington, 2009), 72–3; *Paston L & P* ii, 195–9.
14. D.A.L. Morgan, 'The King's Affinity in the Polity of Yorkist England', *TRHS* 5th ser. xxiii (1973), 17.
15. Hicks, 'Dynastic Change and Northern Society: The Career of the Fourth Earl of Northumberland 1470–89', repr. in *Rivals*, 366–7; Hicks 'Bastard Feudalism: Society and Politics in the Fifteenth Century', *Rivals*, 38–9.
16. C.F. Richmond, 'Fauconberg's Kentish Rising of May 1471', *EHR* lxxxv (1970), 683.

Chapter 4: Problems with the System

1. Storey, *Lancaster*, 5, 21, 27.
2. *PROME* xii, 147.
3. *John Vale's Bk*, 208–9.
4. *PROME* xiii, 15; *Brut*, 511–12; *Death & Dissent*, 205; Hicks, 'Idealism in Late Medieval English Politics', repr. in *Rivals*, 57.
5. Storey, *Lancaster*, 8–27 at 17.
6. M.A. Hicks, 'Lawmakers and Lawbreakers', in *An Illustrated History of Late Medieval England*, ed. C. Given-Wilson (Manchester, 1996), 206–24.
7. H. Kleineke, 'Why the West was Wild: Law and Disorder in Fifteenth-Century Cornwall and Devon', in *Authority and Subversion*, ed. L. Clark, *The Fifteenth Century* iii (2003), 75–8, 84–8.
8. J.G. Bellamy, 'The Coterel Gang: An Anatomy of a Band of Fourteenth-Century Criminals', *EHR* lxxix (1964), 698–717; E.L.G. Stones, 'The Folvilles of Ashby-Folville, Leicestershire and their Associates in Crime, 1326–47', *TRHS*, 5th ser., vii (1957), 117–36. 19 serial offenders were condemned at the 1459 Parliament, *PROME* xii, 499–502; see also R.A. Griffiths, 'William Wawe and his Gang, 1427', *Proceedings of the Hampshire Field Club and Archaeological Society* xxxiii (1976), 89–93.
9. E.g. J.G. Bellamy, *Bastard Feudalism and the Law* (1989), ch.2; J. G. Bellamy, *Criminal Law and Society in Late Medieval and Tudor England* (1984), 70.
10. M.E. James, 'English Politics and the Concept of Honour, 1485–1642', in *Culture, Politics and Society* (Cambridge, 1986), esp. 314.
11. *The Armburgh Papers*, ed. C. Carpenter (Woodbridge, 1998), 6; *Plumpton L & P*, 8, 15n.
12. For the Warwick examples, see K.B. McFarlane, *The Nobility of Late Medieval England* (Oxford, 1973), 72–3; M.A. Hicks, 'Descent, Partition and Extinction: The "Warwick

Inheritance" ', *Rivals*, 324; Hicks, *Warwick*, 39; see also Hicks, 'Piety and Lineage during the Wars of the Roses: The Hungerford Experience', repr. in *Rivals*, 171.

13. Hence the celebrated Berkeley–Lisle dispute, see A. Sinclair, 'The Great Berkeley Lawsuit Revisited 1417–39', *Southern History* 9 (1987), 34–50.

14. T.B. Pugh and C.D. Ross, 'The English Baronage and the Income Tax of 1436', *BIHR* xxvi (1953), 7–8; Griffiths, 'The Hazards of Civil War: The Case of the Mountford Family', repr. in *King & Country*, 367–9.

15. Hicks, *Warwick*, 39; 'Between Majorities: The "Beauchamp Interregnum" 1439–49', *HR* lxxii (1999), 34–41.

16. C.F. Richmond, *The Paston Family in the Fifteenth Century: The First Phase* (Cambridge, 1990), 33, 48–53.

17. Hicks, 'Counting the Costs of War: The Moleyns Ransom and the Hungerford Land-Sales 1453–87', repr. in *Rivals*, 191–3; R. Virgoe, 'Inheritance and Litigation in the Fifteenth Century: The Buckenham Disputes', repr. in *East Anglian Society*, 136–41.

18. Hicks, 'Warwick Inheritance', 117, 125.

19. E.g. Hicks, 'Idealism', 48–50; P. Maddern, *Violence and the Social Order: East Anglia 1422–1442* (Oxford, 1992), 226.

20. McFarlane, *Wars*, 247–8; Griffiths, *Henry VI*, 570–2, 579, 587; Lander, 'Bonds, Coercion and Fear: Henry VII and the Peerage', repr. in *Crown*, 278–9; Pollard, *LM England*, 124–5; Pollard, *NE England*, 246–8; Storey, *Lancaster*, 87–8; Watts, *Henry VI*, 178, 233; B.P. Wolffe, *Henry VI* (1981), 40–4, 119–20.

21. E. Powell, *Kingship, Law and Society* (Oxford, 1989), 203–8, 272.

22. E.g. *PROME* xiv, 114–19, 274–96.

23. *PROME* xii, 102–4, 156; Harvey, *Cade*, 191; 'Some Ancient Indictments in the King's Bench referring to Kent, 1450–2', ed. R. Virgoe, *Kent Records* (Ashford, 1964), 226, 233–4.

24. *Paston L & P* i, 277, ii, 46–8, and passim; Virgoe, 'Ancient Indictments', 225, 243.

25. Pollard, *LM England*, 125.

26. Virgoe, 'Ancient Indictments', 216; see also M.A. Hicks, *English Political Culture in the Fifteenth Century* (2002), 137, 194–7.

27. Lander, *Crown*, 19.

28. C. Given-Wilson, 'Legitimation, Designation and Succession to the Throne in Fourteenth-Century England', in *Building Legitimacy: Political Discourses and Forms of Legitimacy in Medieval Societies*, ed. I. Alfonso, N. Kennedy and J. Escalonia (Leiden, 2004), 89–105.

29. F.M. Powicke, *Henry III and the Lord Edward* (Oxford, 1947), 733.

30. M. Bennett, 'Edward III's Entail and the Succession to the Crown', *EHR* cxiii (1998), 582–94; 'Henry IV, the Royal Succession and the Crisis of 1406', in *The Reign of Henry IV: Rebellion and Survival 1403–13*, ed. G. Dodd and D.Biggs (Woodbridge, 2008), 9–27, esp. 11n; *PROME* vii, 358–9.

31. M.V. Clarke, *Fourteenth-Century Studies*, ed. L.S. Sutherland and M. McKisack (Oxford, 1937), 91–4.

32. *PROME* vii, 344–7.

33. *PROME* xii, 520–1.

34. *PROME* xii, 517, 519; Hicks, '*Brief Treatise*', 6.

35. W. Dugdale, *Monasticon Anglicanum*, ed. J. Caley et al. (1846), vi (3), 1,600–2.

36. T.B. Pugh, 'Richard, Duke of York and the Rebellion of Henry, Duke of Exeter, in May 1454', *HR* lxiii (1990), 248.

37. Griffiths, 'The Sense of Dynasty in the Reign of Henry VI', repr. in *King & Country*, 89n. But was Henry IV's insertion in the confirmation known?

38. *PROME* xii, 95.

39. Griffiths, 'Sense of Dynasty', 89–92.

40. See below, page 80

41. *Annales*, 700–1 (if authentic – the source is very late).

42. Harvey, *Cade*, 32, 78, 189.
43. Hicks, 'Brief Treatise', 6.

Chapter 5: Preconditions: The Crisis of 1450

1. P. Nightingale, 'England and the European Depression of the Mid-Fifteenth Century', *Journal of European Economic History* xxvi (1997), 632, 634–5; J. Hatcher and R. Britnell, eds, 'The Great Slump of the Mid-Fifteenth Century', in *Progress and Problems in Medieval England* (Cambridge, 1996), 237–72, esp. 240–1; R.H. Britnell, 'The Economic Context', in *Wars*, ed. Pollard, 41–64.
2. McFarlane, *Wars*, 240; T.B. Pugh, 'The Estates, Finances and Regal Aspirations of Richard Plantagenet (1411–60), Duke of York', in *Revolution and Consumption in Late Medieval England*, ed. M.A. Hicks (Woodbridge, 2001), 76–7; J. Hare, 'Winchester College and the Angel Inn, Andover: A Fifteenth-Century Landlord and its Investments', *Proceedings of the Hampshire Field Club & Archaeological Society* lx (2005), 189–90.
3. McFarlane, *Wars*, 240.
4. Britnell, 'Economic Context', 43.
5. M. Mate, 'The Economic and Social Roots of Medieval Popular Rebellion: Sussex in 1450–1451', *EcHR* 2nd ser., xlv (1992), 661–2.
6. J.N. Hare, 'The Wiltshire Risings of 1450: Political and Economic Discontent in Mid-Fifteenth-Century England', *Southern History* iv (1982), 18; Britnell, 'Economic Context'; B.P. Wolffe, *Henry VI* (1981), 220.
7. Nightingale, 'European Depression', 635, 638; J.L. Bolton, 'The City and the Crown 1456–61', *London Journal* 12 (1986), 11–24.
8. P. Slack, ed., *Rebellion, Protest and the Social Order in Early Modern England* (Cambridge, 1984), 6–12; Bolton, 'City and Crown', 12–15; Hare, 'Wiltshire Risings', 25; Harvey, *Cade*, 186–7; Mate, 'Sussex', 663, 666–7.
9. *PROME* xii, 151–2.
10. T. More, *Utopia*, ed. P. Turner (1965), 43–53; W.R.D. Jones, *The Tudor Commonwealth 1529–59* (1970), 194–213. There were some precursors in the 1530s, see G.R. Elton, *Reform and Renewal* (Cambridge, 1973), ch. 5.
11. Britnell, 'Economic Context', 56.
12. Harvey, *Cade*, 57; Britnell, 'Economic Context', 45–6; Wolffe, *Henry VI*, 220; *PROME* xii, 60.
13. Hare, 'Wiltshire Risings', 20; Harvey, *Cade*, 189.
14. *PROME* xii, 148; Britnell, 'Economic Context', 46, 48, 56; Mate, 'Sussex', 667.
15. Griffiths, 'Local Rivalries and National Politics: The Percies, the Nevilles, and the Duke of Exeter, 1452–5', repr. in *King & Country*, 331.
16. Bolton, 'City and Crown', 11–24, esp. 15.
17. M. Bohna, 'Armed Force and Civic Legitimacy in Jack Cade's Revolt, 1450', *EHR* cxviii (2003), 563–82.
18. Harvey, *Cade*, 31nn, 32nn, 64–7; Johnson, *York*, 79–80; see also below pp. 68–71.
19. J.A. Doig, 'Propaganda, Public Opinion and the Siege of Calais in 1436', in *Crown, Government, and People in the Fifteenth Century*, ed. R.E. Archer (Stroud, 1995), 92–106.
20. C.T. Allmand, *Lancastrian Normandy 1415–50* (Oxford, 1983), 173–86, 235–8.
21. Ibid., 234.
22. M.K. Jones, 'John Beaufort, Duke of Somerset and the French Expedition of 1443', in *Patronage, The Crown and The Provinces in Later Medieval England*, ed. R.A. Griffiths (Gloucester, 1981), 85–97.
23. *Brut*, 511–12. This passage was written not before 1464. However, the story was current in 1458, *CSPM*, 18; T. Gascoigne, *Loci e Libro Veritatum*, ed. J.E.T. Rogers (Oxford, 1881), xxx.

24. Wolffe, *Henry VI*, 169–83, esp. 183.
25. M.K. Jones, 'Somerset, York and the Wars of the Roses', *EHR* civ (1989), 291–2; *PROME* xii, 34.
26. Johnson, *York*, 46.
27. Jones, 'Somerset', 297–8.
28. *PROME* xii, 55.
29. M.H. Keen and M.J. Daniel, 'English Diplomacy and the Sack of Fougères in 1449', *History* lix (1974), 388–91.
30. *PL* i, 105.
31. *PROME* xii, 67.
32. Wolffe, *Henry VI*, 210.
33. Jones, 'Somerset', 301–3.
34. Ibid., 293.
35. Ibid., 298; *PL* i, 104–5.
36. G.L. Harriss, 'The Struggle for Calais: An Aspect of the Rivalry between Lancaster and York', *EHR* lxxv (1960), 30–7.
37. Harvey, *Cade*, 189.
38. Harvey, *Cade*, 189.
39. Doig, 'Siege of Calais', 92–7; Jones, 'John Beaufort', 86.
40. Johnson, *York*, 40.
41. G.L. Harriss, 'Marmaduke Lumley and the Exchequer Crisis of 1446–9', in *Aspects of Late Medieval Government and Society*, ed. J.G. Rowe (Toronto, 1986), 148–9.
42. *Lay Taxes*, 90, 94.
43. Britnell, 'Economic Context', 62.
44. Wolffe, *Henry VI*, 229–31; R. Virgoe, 'The Parliamentary Subsidy of 1450', *BIHR* lv (1982), 125–37 at 128–30, 133.
45. Storey, *Lancaster*, 49.
46. B.P. Wolffe, *The Royal Demesne in English History* (1971), 114; Storey, *Lancaster*, 49.
47. Harriss, 'Marmaduke Lumley', 143–78.
48. J.L. Kirby, 'The Issues of the Lancastrian Exchequer and Lord Cromwell's Estimates of 1433', *BIHR* xxiv (1951), 121–52; G.L. Harriss, 'Budgeting at the Medieval Exchequer', in *War, Government, and the Aristocracy in the British Isles c.1150–1500*, ed. C. Given-Wilson, A. Kettle and L. Scales (Woodbridge, 2008), 194; Wolffe, *Royal Demesne*, 114–15.
49. Harvey, *Cade*, 189.
50. R. Somerville, *History of the Duchy of Lancaster*, 2 vols (1953–70), i, 206, 210–12.
51. B.P. Wolffe, 'Acts of Resumption in the Lancastrian Parliaments, 1399–1456', *EHR* lxxiii (1958), 601; Storey, *Lancaster*, 49.
52. Wolffe, *Royal Demesne*, 113, 135–6.
53. Britnell, 'Economic Context', 59, 62; Pollard, *Wars*, 50; Harriss, 'Marmaduke Lumley', 143–4.
54. Pollard, *LM England*, 126.
55. C. Nall, 'Perceptions of Financial Mismanagement and the English Diagnosis of Defeat', in *Conflict, Consequences and the Crown in the Later Middle Ages*, ed. L. Clark, *Fifteenth Century* vii (Woodbridge, 2007), 124, 126–7, 129–31.
56. Griffiths, *Henry VI*, 394.
57. *PROME* xii, 55.
58. Harvey, *Cade*, 189; *PROME* xii, 95–105, 107–8, 184–5.
59. Bolton, 'City and Crown', 15.
60. *Political Poems and Songs*, ed. T.Wright, Rolls Series (2 vols, 1859–61), ii, 221–50, at 229.
61. Griffiths, *Henry VI*, 678.
62. Griffiths, *Henry VI*, 679.

63. Wolffe, *Henry VI*, 225; J.H. Ramsay, *Lancaster and York*, 2 vols (Oxford, 1892), ii, 117.
64. *PROME* xii, 103.
65. Griffiths, *Henry VI*, 681.
66. R. Virgoe, 'William Tailboys and Lord Cromwell: Crime and Politics in Lancastrian England', *East Anglian Society*, 290–1.
67. *PROME* xii, 106.
68. Harvey, *Cade*, 102–11, 186–8, 192–9; Bohna, 'Cade's Revolt', 563–82.
69. Hare, 'Wiltshire Risings', 20.
70. *PROME* xii, 107, 149–50.
71. *Six Town Chronicles*, ed. R. Flenley (1911), 130–1; see also R.W. Hoyle, 'Petitioning as Popular Politics in Early Sixteenth-Century England', *HR* lxxv (2002), 365–89.
72. J. Watts, 'Ideas, Principles and Politics', in *Wars*, ed. Pollard, 110–11; for the next three paragraphs on Cade's Rebellion, see Griffiths, *Henry VI*, ch. 21.
73. Harvey, *Cade*, 186–91.
74. Harvey, *Cade*, 186.
75. Bohna, 'Cade's Revolt', 575–6; *Six Town Chronicles*, 104.
76. 'Some Ancient Indictments in the King's Bench referring to Kent, 1450–2', ed. R. Virgoe, *Kent Records* (Ashford, 1964), 240; *Six Town Chronicles*, 131.
77. M.A. Hicks, 'From Megaphone to Microscope: The Correspondence of Richard Duke of York with Henry VI in 1450 Revisited', *JMH* xxv (1999), 251–4.
78. Ibid., 255; *John Vale's Bk*, 187–8.
79. Hicks, *Warwick*, 73–5.
80. *PL* i, 107.
81. Harvey, *Cade*, 187; see also *John Vale's Bk*, 187–8.
82. *PROME* xii, 99; Harvey, *Cade*, 189, 191.

Chapter 6: Preconditions: Personalities and Issues

1. J.L. Watts, 'When Did Henry VI's Minority End?', in *Trade, Devotion and Governance: Papers in Later Medieval History*, ed. D.J. Clayton, R.G. Davies and P. McNiven (Stroud, 1994), 116–39; Watts, *Henry VI*, 122ff.; see also Carpenter, *Wars*, 92.
2. B.P. Wolffe, 'The Personal Rule of Henry VI', in *Fifteenth-century England 1399–1509*, ed. S.B. Chrimes, C.D. Ross and R.A. Griffiths (Manchester, 1972), 36–40; *PROME* xii, 248.
3. Griffiths, *Henry VI*, 698.
4. Wolffe, 'Personal Rule', 37–44.
5. So Robin Jeffs showed, at Sheffield in 1976. Sadly he died without publishing his evidence.
6. E.g. *PROME* xii, 386, 444, 532.
7. J. Blacman, *Henry VI*, ed. M.R. James (Cambridge, 1919), 17, 39.
8. McFarlane, *Wars*, (1981), 240.
9. R. Lovatt, 'A Collector of Apocryphal Anecdotes: John Blacman Revisited', in *Property and Politics*, ed. A.J. Pollard (Gloucester, 1984), 172–97 at 174.
10. Watts, *Henry VI*, esp. ch. 5; Carpenter, *Wars*, 93.
11. Carpenter, *Wars*, 74, 115, 119–20, 129–30, 137–43; Griffiths, *Henry VI*, *passim*; Pollard, *Wars*, 20–3.
12. Watts, *Henry VI*, 199, 235; Carpenter, *Wars*, 93.
13. E.g. 'iratus rex', *Benet's Chron.*, 205; Lovatt, 'Blacman', 182; Brown, 'Authorisation of Letters', 153; see below pp. 127–8.
14. Blacman, *Henry VI*, 9–12, 17, 31–3, 39; Wolffe, 'Personal Rule', 38; see also Lovatt, 'Blacman', 182.
15. See Lovatt, 'Blacman', 186–7.
16. *PROME* xii, 464, 532; Blacman, *Henry VI*, 17, 39.

17. *Paston L & P* ii, 164; Hicks, *Warwick*, 153n.
18. Watts, *Henry VI*, 129-32, 145-7; *John Vale's Bk*, 223; H. Summerson, '"Hardyng, John", chronicler and forger', *ODNB* http://www.oxforddnb.com/view/article/12296?docPos=2
19. Storey, *Lancaster*, 48.
20. T. Gascoigne, *Loci e Libro Veritatum*, ed. J.E.T. Rogers (Oxford, 1881), 191.
21. B.P. Wolffe, *Henry VI* (1981), 316.
22. *John Vale's Bk*, 223.
23. Wolffe, 'Personal Rule', 44; G.L. Harriss, *Shaping the Nation: England 1360-1461* (Oxford, 2005), 611.
24. I intend to discuss this topic fully elsewhere.
25. Harriss, *Shaping*, 610.
26. Ibid., 610-11; Watts, *Henry VI*, 103.
27. E.g. Johnson, *York*, 115n.
28. *John Vale's Bk*, 187-9; *PROME* xii, 275-6, 516-17, 520-1.
29. W. Dugdale, *Monasticon Anglicanum*, ed. J. Caley et al. (1846), vi, 344; vii, 1,600-2; C. Given-Wilson, 'Chronicles of the Mortimer Family, *c*.1250-1450', in *Family and Dynasty in Late Medieval England*, ed. R. Eales and S. Tyas (Donington, 2003), 67-77.
30. A. Goodman and D.A.L. Morgan, 'The Yorkist Claim to the Throne of Castile', *JMH* xii (1985), 61-9; T.B. Pugh, 'The Magnates, Knights and Gentry', in *Fifteenth-century England, 1399-1509*, ed. S.B. Chrimes, C.D. Ross and R.A. Griffiths (1972), 87-128 *passim*; T.B. Pugh, 'Richard Plantagenet (1411-60), Duke of York, as the King's Lieutenant in France and Ireland', in *Aspects of Late Medieval Government and Society*, ed. J.G. Rowe (Toronto, 1986), 110-23; see also T.B. Pugh, 'The Estates, Finances and Regal Aspirations of Richard Plantagenet (1411-60), Duke of York', *Revolution and Consumption in Late Medieval England*, ed. M.A. Hicks (Woodbridge, 2001), 71-88; Johnson, *York*.
31. *Annales*, 770.
32. Pugh, 'Richard Plantagenet', 113-14, 117, 126.
33. Ibid., 127-8; *POPC* vi, 199-206.
34. Pugh, 'The Estates', 79-81, 88.
35. Pugh, 'Richard Plantagenet', 112; Pugh, 'Magnates', 108, 118; Pugh, 'The Estates', 76-81; *PROME* xii, 446.
36. Pugh, 'Richard Plantagenet', 125-6.
37. Ibid., 125; M.A. Hicks, 'From Megaphone to Microscope: The Correspondence of Richard Duke of York with Henry VI in 1450 Revisited', *JMH* xxv (1999), 250.
38. Storey, *Lancaster*, 75.
39. G.L. Harriss, 'The Struggle for Calais: An Aspect of the Rivalry between Lancaster and York,' *EHR* lxxv (1960), 33.
40. *PROME* xii, 353-4.
41. Pugh, 'Richard Plantagenet', 127-8.
42. Ibid., 122, 127.
43. Harvey, *Cade*, 187, 191.
44. M.K. Jones, 'Somerset, York and the Wars of the Roses', *EHR* civ (1989), 304.
45. Griffiths, 'Duke Richard of York's Intentions in 1450 and the Origins of the Wars of the Roses', repr. in *King & Country*, 299-304; *John Vale's Bk*, 185-90. The next paragraphs are based on chapters 5 and 6 below, *passim*.
46. *John Vale's Bk*, 189.
47. *John Vale's Bk*, 190.
48. *John Vale's Bk*, 187-8.
49. *PROME* xii, 208-9.
50. Jones, 'Somerset', 287-8. I differ here from Pollard, *Warwick*, 158-9.
51. M.A. Hicks, *English Political Culture in the Fifteenth Century* (2002), 214-15; *PROME* xii, 309-11.
52. *PROME* xii, 275.

53. *PROME*, xii, 254–6. York may have felt justified since Thorpe was speaker in 1453 when his chamberlain Oldhall was attainted.
54. Jones, 'Somerset', 300.
55. *PROME* xii, 164, 329, 444.
56. *PROME* xii, 443; J.L. Bolton, 'The City and the Crown 1456–61', *London Journal* 12 (1986), 18–20.
57. *PROME* xii, 385–7.
58. Griffiths, *Henry VI*, 729, 750–2, 752n (at 770).
59. Jones, 'Somerset', 285–307; see below p. 105; see also TNA C 81/1472/66.
60. J.G. Bellamy, *The Law of Treason in England in the Later Middle Ages* (Cambridge, 1970), 117–20; Hicks, *English Political Culture*, 134–7.
61. *PROME* xii, 274–5, 343–5, 465–7.
62. W. Sellar and R.C. Yeatman, *1066 and All That* (1930), 34.
63. 'Some Ancient Indictments in the King's Bench referring to Kent, 1450–2', ed. R. Virgoe, *Kent Records* (Ashford, 1964), 257–60.
64. *John Vale's Bk*, 193–4.
65. *John Vale's Bk*.
66. Johnson, *York*, 112.
67. *PROME* xii, 520–1.
68. *PROME* xii, 275–6, 338–43, 516–17; *Eng. Chron.*, 78.
69. *GEC*, iv, 326; ix, 606; xi, 395–8; *RP* iv, 262–4; Lander, Marriage and Politics in the Fifteenth Century: The Nevilles and the Wydevilles', repr. in *Crown*, 96–8.
70. Griffiths, 'The Crown and the Royal Family in Later Medieval England', repr. in *King & Country*, 6.
71. *Paston L&P* i, 162; E. Gilson, 'A Defence of the Proscription of the Yorkists', *EHR* xxvi (1911), 514–25, as interpreted by Hicks, *English Political Culture*, 214. These are the source of this paragraph.
72. Gilson, 'Defence', 515.
73. *PL* iii, 204; Hicks, *English Political Culture*, 214.

Chapter 7: Preconditions: Recovery Aborted 1451–6

1. E.g. *Brut*, 511–12; *Death & Dissent*, 105; Hicks, 'Idealism in Late Medieval English Politics', repr. in *Rivals*, 57.
2. *John Vale's Bk*, 212.
3. Pollard, *Wars*, 21.
4. To write of 'a degree of economic recovery' is to exaggerate; see P. Nightingale, 'England and the European Depression of the Mid-Fifteenth Century', *Journal of European Economic History* xxvi (1997), 631–2.
5. B.P. Wolffe, *The Royal Demesne in English History* (1971), 133–5.
6. *Lay Taxes*, 104–8.
7. E.g. Pollard, *Wars*, 21; Pollard, *LM England*, 136.
8. Hicks, *Warwick*, 75.
9. Storey, *Lancaster*, 8, 17, 27 and *passim*; C. Carpenter, 'Sir Thomas Malory and Fifteenth-Century Local Politics', *Bulletin of the Institute of Historical Research* liii (1980), 31–43; H. Castor, ' "Walter Blount was gone to serve traytours": The Sack of Elvaston and the Politics of the North Midlands in 1454', *Midland History* xix (1994), 21–39; M. Cherry, 'The Struggle for Power in Mid-Fifteenth-Century Devonshire', in *Patronage, The Crown and The Provinces in Later Medieval England*, ed. R.A. Griffiths (Gloucester, 1981), 123–44; A. Herbert, 'Herefordshire, 1413–61: Some Aspects of Society and Public Order', in ibid., 103–22; Griffiths, 'Gruffydd ap Nicholas and the Fall of the House of Lancaster', repr. in *King & Country*, ch. 12; 'Local Rivalries and National Politics: The Percies, the Nevilles, and the Duke of Exeter, 1452–55', repr. in

King & Country, ch. 20; 'The Hazards of Civil War: The Mountford Family and the Wars of the Roses', repr. in *King & Country*, 21; Hicks, *Warwick*, chs 3, 4; S.J. Payling, 'The Ampthill Dispute: A Study in Aristocratic Lawlessness and the Breakdown of Lancastrian Government', *EHR* civ (1989), 881–907; Pollard, *NE England*, chs 10, 11; Pugh, 'Richard, Duke of York', *HR* lxiii, 248–62; Virgoe, 'William Tailboys and Lord Cromwell: Crime and Politics in Lancastrian England', *East Anglian Society*.

10. TNA E 28/82/71–2.
11. Pollard, *Warwick*, 102.
12. Hicks, *Warwick*, 89; Cherry, 'Struggle', 124–39.
13. T. Gascoigne, *Loci e Libro Veritatum*, ed. J.E.T. Rogers (Oxford, 1881), xxxix, 203.
14. Lander, 'Bonds, Coercion and Fear', repr. in *Crown*, 278–9.
15. Castor, 'Elvaston', 30.
16. *PROME* xii, 256, 260–1.
17. Virgoe, 'Tailboys', *East Anglian Society*, 291–2, 294.
18. Payling, 'Ampthill', 886, 889–90, 892–3.
19. Ibid., 881; Pollard, *LM England*, 136.
20. B.P. Wolffe, *Henry VI* (1981), 248, 251–2, 268–70; *PROME* xii, 248.
21. *PROME* xii, 275.
22. Griffiths, *Henry VI*, 579, 587; *Six Town Chronicles*, ed. Flenley, 123.
23. *Benet's Chron.*, 205.
24. Griffiths, *Henry VI*, 618; Griffiths, 'The King's Council and the First Protectorate of the Duke of York, 1453–1454', repr. in *King & Country*, 316; Storey, *Lancaster*, 101.
25. Cherry, 'Struggle', 132.
26. Payling, 'Ampthill', 893.
27. *PROME* xii, 211; Griffiths, *Henry VI*, 732; *POPC* vi, lvi, lxx; *CCR 1454–61*, 318.
28. E.g. Carpenter, *Wars*, 126–9, 139, 141; Griffiths, 'Local Rivalries and National Politics: The Percies, the Nevilles, and the Duke of Exeter, 452–5', *King & Country*, 320ff.; Watts, *Henry VI*, 300; Payling, 'Ampthill', 893; see also Storey, *Lancaster, passim*.
29. *PROME* xii, 248.
30. Griffiths, 'Percies', repr. in *King & Country*, 326; Hicks, *Warwick*, 85–90; Storey, *Lancaster*, 239–40.
31. *POPC* vi, 159–63; Pollard, *LM England*, 137.
32. Hicks, *Warwick*, 83.
33. Hicks, *Warwick*, 89.
34. See below, pp 156–7.
35. *PROME* xii, 105–6, 275, 339; *POPC* vi, 206–7.
36. *PROME* xii, 307–9, 445–6.
37. *PROME* xii, 275, 445, 514.
38. *PROME* xii, 307–9, 453–61; *Benet's Chron.*, 223.
39. Storey, *Lancaster*, 94–5; Cherry, 'Struggle', 131. Unless otherwise stated, the next two paragraphs are based on Storey, *Lancaster*, ch. 6; Griffiths, *Henry VI*, ch. 22.
40. *PL* i, 97–8.
41. As cited in Johnson, *York*, 112.
42. T.B. Pugh, 'Richard, Duke of York and the Rebellion of Henry, Duke of Exeter, in May 1454', *HR* lxiii (1990), 258; *Brut*, 520. However, the allegations also occur in indictments from as early as 16 May 1452, 'Some Ancient Indictments in the King's Bench referring to Kent, 1450–2', ed. R. Virgoe, *Kent Records* (Ashford, 1964), 259.
43. *PROME* xii, 306–9.
44. *John Vale's Bk*, 193–4.
45. Hicks, *Warwick*, 80.
46. Virgoe, 'Indictments', 257–60; Johnson, *York*, 17.
47. *PROME* xii, 306–9; TNA C 49/29/10–11.
48. *PROME* xii, 218.

49. Hicks, *Warwick*, 81.
50. Johnson, *York*, 120–1.
51. Johnson, *York*, 119.
52. C. Rawcliffe, 'Richard, Duke of York, the King's "Obeisant Liegeman": A New Source on the Protectorates of 1454 and 1455', *HR* lx (1987), 232, 237–8.
53. The fullest recent account is in Hicks, *Warwick*, 98–112.
54. Castor, 'Elvaston', 31.
55. Rawcliffe, ' "Obeisant Liegeman" ', 238–9.
56. *Benet's Chron.*, 217; but see Johnson, *York*, 177.
57. Griffiths, 'Percies', repr. in *King & Country*, *passim*, esp. 344, 350–1.
58. TNA KB 29/85.
59. Hicks, *Warwick*, 113.
60. *Foedera* xi, 361–4; *CPR 1452–61*, 226.
61. Storey, *Lancaster*, 147, 253–4; Pugh, 'Exeter', 256; J.L. Bolton, 'The City and the Crown 1456–61', *London Journal* 12 (1986), 13; *POPC* vi, 234, 245–6, 358–9; *CCR 1454–61*, 13, 109; *Foedera* xi, 362–5.
62. Johnson, *York*, 155; Storey, *Lancaster*, 159–61; Wolffe, *Henry VI*, 289–91; Watts, *Henry VI*, 314–16.
63. *Foedera* xi, 363–4; *POPC* vi, 358.
64. *CSPM*, 16.
65. TNA C 81/1474/8.
66. *PROME* xii, 340–1.
67. As suggested by Pollard, *Warwick*, 29.
68. C.A.J. Armstrong, 'Politics and the Battle of St Albans, 1455', *BIHR* xxxiii (1960); M.A. Hicks, 'Propaganda and the Battle of St Albans, 1455', *NMS* xliv (2000), 168–83 at 178.
69. Pollard, *Warwick*, 32.
70. *Paston L & P* iii, 156.
71. *Handbook of British Chronology*, ed. E.B. Fryde et al. (1986), 87, 106.
72. *POPC* vi, 244–5.
73. Hicks, 'Propaganda', 177–80.
74. *PROME* xii, 335–6, 338–9, 345; *Six Town Chronicles*, 109, 142. For Henry's sign manual, see TNA C 49/30/18.
75. *Paston L & P* iii, 158.
76. *PROME* xii, 348–50.
77. TNA E 28/87/19.
78. *PROME* xii, 351–4.
79. J.L. Watts, '*De Consulatu Stilicho*: Texts and Politics in the Reign of Henry VI', *JMH* xvi (1990), 83–96; see L. Visser-Fuchs, ' "Honour is the Reward of Virtue": The Clandian Translation made for Richard, Duke of York, in 1445', *Ricardian* xviii (2005), 66–82.
80. *PROME* xii, 443–6.
81. *PROME* xii, 445–6.
82. Storey, *Lancaster*, 148–50.
83. *CCR 1454–61*, 318; TNA KB 27/778 rex rot 3d.
84. Storey, *Lancaster*, 115, 166–72; *pace* Cherry, 'Struggle', 137–8. For the exchange of challenges, see Hicks, 'Idealism in Late Medieval English Politics', repr. in *Rivals*, 48–9.
85. *Benet's Chron.*, 216; *PROME* xii, 445–7; TNA E 28/87/7; *Paston L & P* iii, 162.
86. TNA KB 27/786 rex rot. 43; *CCR 1454–61*, 171; see also below, p. 131.
87. *PROME* xii, 336–8.
88. G.L. Harriss, 'The Struggle for Calais: An Aspect of the Rivalry between Lancaster and York', *EHR* lxxv (1960), 40–3.
89. Bolton, 'City and Crown', 16. Harriss antedates the dynastic rivalry to 1456 and earlier, 'Struggle for Calais', 30–53.
90. Bolton, 'City and Crown', 18.

91. *PROME* xii, 442–6.
92. Bolton, 'City and Crown', 17.
93. *PROME* xii, 443–6.
94. Wolffe, *Royal Demesne*, 139n; *PROME* xii, 443.
95. Pollard, *Warwick*, 31.
96. *Paston L & P* ii, 158.
97. *PROME* xii, 339, 444.
98. TNA C 49/30/8–17, 20–1; SC 8/109/5422; SC 115/5704; SC 28/1389. It is regrettable that *PROME* does not systematically record endorsements on original acts and provisos.
99. *Benet's Chron.*, 216; *Paston L & P* iii, 161. Pollard stresses, possibly correctly, that only Warwick backed York: Pollard, *Warwick*, 1.
100. TNA SC 8/28/1390; SC 8/97/4766A; *Benet's Chron.*, 216; *PROME* xii, 445–7.
101. *PROME* xii, 381–428; for the quotation, see Pollard, *Warwick*, 32.
102. *PROME* xii, 443–6.

Chapter 8: Preconditions: No Progress 1456–9

1. See below ch. 9.
2. *Eng. Chron.*, 78.
3. G.L. Harriss, 'The Struggle for Calais: An Aspect of the Rivalry between Lancaster and York', *EHR*, lxxv (1960), 40–3. The finances of Calais were settled by removing both the costs and appropriated customs revenues from the royal balance sheet.
4. Griffiths, *Henry VI*, 785.
5. Griffiths, *Henry VI*, 788; B.P. Wolffe, *Henry VI* (1981), 307n.
6. Griffiths, *Henry VI*, 305.
7. A. Gross, *The Dissolution of the Lancastrian Kingship: Sir John Fortescue and the Crisis of Monarchy in Fifteenth-Century England* (Stamford, 1990), 19–21.
8. *Eng. Chron.*, 78.
9. G.L. Harriss, 'Richard Duke of York and the Royal Household', in *Soldiers, Nobles and Gentlemen*, ed. P. Coss and C. Tyerman (Woodbridge, 2009), 333–4; Carpenter, *Wars*, 140–3; Griffiths, *Henry VI*, 776–7, 799, 807, 822; Gross, *Dissolution*, 46–58, at 46–7; Pollard, *Wars*, 21–2, 58–9; Pollard, *Warwick*, 34; Storey, *Lancaster*, 176; Watts, *Henry VI*, 335–40; Wolffe, *Henry VI*, 302–4; see also D. Dunn, 'The Queen at War: The Role of Margaret of Anjou in the Wars of the Roses', in *War and Society in Medieval and Early Modern Britain*, ed. D. Dunn (Liverpool, 2000), 149–51; H.E. Maurer, *Margaret of Anjou: Queenship and Power in Late Medieval England* (Woodbridge, 2003), 131.
10. Griffiths, *Henry VI*, 776.
11. Gross, *Dissolution*, 50–1.
12. Rawcliffe, 'Richard, Duke of York, the King's "Obeisant Liegeman"', *HR* lx (1987), 237–8; *PL*, ii, 297. The queen's title may have been aired in Parliament.
13. *Paston L & P*, iii, 162.
14. Gross, *Dissolution*, 49; Pollard, *Wars*, 22; *Warwick*, 31; Storey, *Lancaster*, 176; Watts, *Henry VI*, 333; Wolffe, *Henry VI*, 301; Harriss, 'Richard Duke of York', 333; see also Maurer, *Margaret*, 128–9.
15. Gross, *Dissolution*, 49; see above.
16. *Paston L & P*, iii, 161–2. This rumour becomes fact in Harriss, 'Richard Duke of York', 332.
17. TNA E 28/87/ 31, 36–44.
18. Hicks, *Warwick*, 138–9; C.F. Richmond, 'The Earl of Warwick's Domination of the Channel and the Naval Dimension to the Wars of the Roses 1456–60', *Southern History* 20/21 (1998–9), 3–8.
19. *Eng. Chron.*, 84.
20. *Benet's Chron.*, 216; TNA KB 29/86 Hillary rot. 12; *CSPM*, 27; *Eng. Chron.*, 78. Whethamstede's comments feature in a section written after 12 November 1457,

Registrum Abbathiae Johannis Whethamstede Abbatis Monasterii Sancti Albani, ed. H.T. Riley, i (1872), 247–68, at 247.

21. *Eng. Chron.*, 78; Wolffe, *Henry VI*, 317; *Benet's Chron.*, 224; *Gregory*, 204; *Political Poems and Songs*, ed. T. Wright, ii (1861), 251; *Historical Poems of the Fourteenth and Fifteenth Centuries*, ed. R.H. Robbins (New York, 1959), 138–9.
22. *Brut*, 511–12.
23. Griffiths, *Henry VI*, 776.
24. Gross, *Dissolution*, 46.
25. T. Gascoigne, *Loci e Libro Veritatum*, ed. J.E.T. Rogers (Oxford, 1881), *passim*, esp. 205.
26. *Benet's Chron.*, 217; *Brut*, 523; *GC*, 188.
27. *Six Town Chronicles*, ed. R. Flenley (1911), 110; *Paston L & P*, i, 164–5; *Paston L & P*, iii, 161–3. Gascoigne lived in Oxford.
28. Griffiths, *Henry VI*, 237–8.
29. *Brut*, 523.
30. *PL* iii, 103.
31. *Benet's Chron.*, 217.
32. *CPR 1452–61*, 357, 515; Griffiths, *Henry VI*, 782–3.
33. See the endorsements on TNA C 81.
34. TNA C 81/1371/47; TNA C 81/1468/21, 27. 'Undoubtedly . . . the king himself granted the bills' and 'wrote the endorsements', wrote Brown, 'Authorization of Letters', *BIHR* xxxvii (1964), 11.
35. TNA C 81/1371/3; TNA C 81/1467/4, TNA 1468/16.
36. TNA C 81/1466/12; TNA 1467/5; TNA 1468/16, 32; TNA 1471/32; TNA /14.
37. TNA C 81/1468/27, 29, 35, 36, 45; TNA C 81/1471/22.
38. TNA E 28/88/51.
39. *Pace* Wolffe, *Henry VI*, 316.
40. Whether they were initialled before, during, or after conciliar consideration is not apparent.
41. Wolffe, *Henry VI*, 307–11. Henry had not planned to stay a whole year away from Westminster.
42. E.g., Griffiths, *Henry VI*, 862; Storey, *Lancaster*, 180–1; Wolffe, *Henry VI*, 309.
43. *Benet's Chron.*, 217.
44. Johnson, *York*, 174, 177n; *Paston L & P*, ii, 164.
45. *Paston L & P*, ii, 164; *Benet's Chron.*, 217.
46. *POPC*, vi, 360: not London, as erroneously reported in Johnson, *York*, 177n.
47. Carpenter, *Wars*, 141; Pollard, *Warwick*, 38; see also Watts, *Henry VI*, 335.
48. *The Coventry Leet Book*, ed. M.D. Harris, EETS 134–5 (1907–13, 285–92).
49. *Eng. Chron.*, 78.
50. *Hardyng's Chronicle*, ed. H. Ellis (1812). Hardyng may well have been writing of the 1430s or 1440s.
51. Johnson, *York*, 175.
52. Griffiths, *Henry VI*, 800n, 841.
53. Griffiths, *Henry VI*, 802; Storey, *Lancaster*, 173–4; M. Cherry, 'The Struggle for Power in Mid-Fifteenth-Century Devonshire', in *Patronage, The Crown and The Provinces in Later Medieval England*, ed. R.A. Griffiths, (Gloucester, 1981), 138; *PROME* xii, 447; *Benet's Chron.*, 218.
54. Maurer, *Margaret*, 136–7.
55. TNA KB 27/786 rex m 43; KB 29/87 Mich. rot. 4; C237/44/134; Griffiths, *Henry VI*, 802n; Carpenter, *Wars*, 139.
56. J.L. Bolton, 'The City and the Crown 1456–61', *London Journal* 12 (1986),13–15.
57. *Benet's Chron.*, 217; but see Johnson, *York*, 177.
58. *Benet's Chron.*, 223.
59. Hicks, *Warwick*, 152–3; Pollard, *Warwick*, 38; *Eng. Chron*, 77; *John Vale's Bk*, 209.

60. *CCR 1454-61*, 350.
61. Griffiths, *Henry VI*, 799-800.
62. Griffiths, 'Gruffydd ap Nicholas and the Fall of the House of Lancaster', repr. in *King & Country*, 206-12.
63. *PROME* xii, 445.
64. A. Herbert, 'Herefordshire, 1413-61: Some Aspects of Society and Public Order', in *Patronage, The Crown and The Provinces in Later Medieval England*, ed. R.A. Griffiths (Gloucester, 1981); R.A. Griffiths and R.S. Thomas, *The Making of the Tudor Dynasty* (Gloucester, 1985), 44-7; *CCR 1454-61*, 174, 222-3; TNA KB 29/87 rot. 32d; Johnson, *York*, 179; Storey, *Lancaster*, 180-1; *Benet's Chron.*, 218. There is no concrete evidence that Richmond was acting for the queen, as suggested by Pollard, *Warwick*, 33.
65. TNA KB 9/35.
66. *CPR 1452-61*, 340; TNA C 81/1466/24.
67. Johnson, *York*, 178-9; Maurer, *Margaret*, 144-5; Pollard, *Warwick*, 204.
68. *PROME* xii, 456-7; *John Vale's Bk*, 193.
69. *Benet's Chron.*, 223. The present author prefers 1459: Hicks, *Warwick*, 156-8.
70. Pollard, *Warwick*, 34.
71. *Benet's Chron.*, 216.
72. *PROME* xii, 446.
73. TNA E 28/87.
74. Johnson, *York*, 175-83.
75. *Paston L & P* iii, 161-2.
76. Johnson, *York*, 175; TNA E 28/88/7; C 81/1472/18; Wolffe, *Henry VI*, 312; Griffiths, *Henry VI*, 813.
77. E.g., Griffiths, *Henry VI*, 805; Wolffe, *Henry VI*, 309-10, 315, 317.

Chapter 9: The First War 1459-61

1. E.g., *Great Chronicle of London*, ed. A.H. Thomas and I.D. Thornley (1938), 190.
2. Johnson, *York*, 180.
3. Hicks, *Warwick*, 136.
4. Lander, 'Bonds, Coercion and Fear', repr. in *Crown*, 280; *CCR 1454-61*, 292-3; *Paston L & P* ii, 533.
5. Hicks, *Warwick*, 135.
6. Griffiths, *Henry VI*, 804-5; Watts, *Henry VI*, 343.
7. British Library Cotton, ch. xvi, 71.
8. *CCR 1454-61*, 223; Pollard, *NE England*, 269.
9. BL Cotton, ch. xvi, 71; *CCR 1454-61*, 369.
10. Hicks, *Warwick*, 149.
11. B.P. Wolffe, *Henry VI*, (1981), 316-21; Griffiths, *Henry VI*, 818-25; Pollard, *Wars*, 58; Pollard, *LM England*, 154.
12. Pollard, *NE England*, 269-70.
13. Hicks, *Warwick*, 166.
14. Pollard, *NE England*, 278.
15. Hicks, *Warwick*, 149-51.
16. Pollard, *Warwick*, 34, 39, 206; see above.
17. *Benet's Chron.*, 223; Hicks, *Warwick*, 158-9.
18. *John Vale's Bk*, 208-10, at 209; *Eng. Chron.*, 79-80.
19. Hatcher, 'Great Slump', 241-2, 250.
20. Pollard, *Warwick*, 38.
21. Griffiths, *Henry VI*, 805; *Lay Taxes*, 106.
22. Hicks, *Warwick*, 161; Watts, *Henry VI*, 351-2.
23. *Eng. Chron.*, 84.

24. *John Vale's Bk*, 208–9.
25. Pollard, *Warwick*, 41.
26. *PROME* xii, 458.
27. Maurer, *Margaret*, 166.
28. Hicks, *Warwick*, 163.
29. Hicks, *Warwick*, 166; J. Blacman, *Henry VI*, ed. M.R. James (Cambridge 1919), 17, 39.
30. *Eng. Chron.*, 79–80.
31. *PROME* xii, 454–60.
32. As expected by Wolffe, *Henry VI*, 319.
33. *PROME* xii, 461–2, 464, 502–3.
34. *PROME* xii, 465–7; S.J. Payling, 'The Coventry Parliament of 1459: A Privy Seal Writ Concerning the Election of Knights of the Shire', *HR* lx (1987), 349–52.
35. M.L. Kekewich, 'The Attainder of the Yorkists in 1459: Two Contemporary Sources', *HR* lv (1982), 25–34.
36. *PROME* xii, 461.
37. *PROME* xii, 460.
38. Wolffe, *Henry VI*, 321.
39. C.L. Scofield, *Life and Reign of Edward the Fourth*, 2 vols (1923), i, 81–4.
40. Wolffe, *Henry VI*, 321.
41. Hicks, *Warwick*, 174.
42. Hatcher, 'Great Slump', 243–50; R.H. Britnell, 'The Economic Context', in *Wars*, ed. Pollard, 48–9.
43. Griffiths, *Henry VI*, 790–5; J.L. Bolton, 'The City and the Crown 1456–61', *London Journal* 12 (1986), 17, 21.
44. Hicks, *Warwick*, 146; C. Richmond, 'The Earl of Warwick's Domination of the Channel and the Naval Dimension of the Wars of the Roses 1456–60', *Southern History* 20/21, 2–8.
45. Pollard, *Warwick*, 38.
46. *John Vale's Bk*, 209.
47. Hatcher, 'Great Slump', 241; Pollard, *Warwick*, 155.
48. Griffiths, *Henry VI*, 827.
49. Wolffe, *Henry VI*, 309.
50. Pollard, *Warwick*, 158–60.
51. *John Vale's Bk*, 210–12; D. Grummitt, 'Deconstructing Cade's Rebellion: Discourse and Politics in the Mid Fifteenth Century', *Identity and Insurgency in the Later Middle Ages*, ed. L. Clark, *The Fifteenth Century* vi (2006), 118–21.
52. *Eng. Chron.*, 82–5.
53. TNA C 81/1475/2, 20, 34; 1476/7, 10, 16, 21.
54. *Six Town Chronicles*, ed. Flenley (1911), 149, 151.
55. C. Richmond, 'The Nobility and the Wars of the Roses 1459–61', *NMS* xxi (1977), 74.
56. *Registrum Abbathiae Johannis Whethamstede Abbatis Monasterii Sancti Albani*, ed. H.T. Riley, 2 vols, Rolls Series (1872), i, 374.
57. Hicks, *Warwick*, 180–1.
58. Hicks, *Warwick*, 182–6.
59. TNA C 81/1475/49.
60. W. Dugdale, *Monasticon Anglicanum*, 8 vols, London (1846), vi, 344; vii, 1,600–2; Given-Wilson, 'Chronicles of the Mortimer Family', *Family and Dynasty*, ed. Eales and Tyas, 67–77.
61. Griffiths, 'The Sense of Dynasty in the reign of Henry VI', repr. in *King & Country*, 98n.
62. *PROME* xii, 516; Hicks, '*Brief Treatise*'; F. Riddy, 'John Hardyng's Chronicle and the Wars of the Roses', *Arthurian Literature* 12 (1993), 100–1.
63. Pollard, *Warwick*, 43–5.
64. *Engl. Chron.*, 82; *John Vale's Bk*, 210.
65. Pollard, *Warwick*, 45.

66. Johnson, *York*, 211–12.
67. Griffiths, *Henry VI*, 867; Johnson, *York*, 214; McFarlane, *Wars*, 237–8.
68. Johnson, *York*, 212–17.
69. *PROME* xii, 523.
70. *PROME*, xii, 532, 535.
71. *Benet's Chron.*, 216.
72. Maurer, *Margaret*, 187.
73. Pollard, *NE England*, 279–81.
74. *Annales*, 774–5.
75. *PROME* xii, 524.
76. Pollard, *Warwick*, 116–17; *Eng. Chron.*, 97.
77. M.A. Hicks, 'A Minute of the Lancastrian Council at York, 20 January 1461', *Northern History* xxx (1999), 214–21.
78. *Eng. Chron.*, 214–21.
79. This was a commonplace in Yorkist chronicles, e.g. *Ingulph's Chronicle of the Abbey of Croyland*, ed. H.T. Riley (1859), 422.
80. E.g., *Brut*, 532; *PROME* xiii, 20.
81. Richmond, 'Nobility', 75; Hicks, 'Minute', 218.

Chapter 10: Wounds Unhealed 1461–9

1. Unless otherwise stated, this chapter summarizes C.L. Scofield, *The Life and Reign of Edward IV*, 2 vols (1923); Ross, *Edward IV*.
2. R.E. Horrox, *Richard III: A Study of Service* (Cambridge, 1989), 328.
3. *The Logge Register of Prerogative Court of Canterbury Wills, 1479–86*, ed. L. Boatwright, M. Habberjam and P. Hammond, 2 vols (Knaphill, 2008), ii, 448.
4. *Historical Poems of the Fourteenth and Fifteenth Centuries*, ed. R.H. Robbins (New York, 1959), 221–2.
5. *PROME* xiii, 12–15; Hicks, '*Brief Treatise*', 3.
6. Hicks, 'Idealism in Late Medieval English Politics', repr. in *Rivals*, 57–8.
7. R. Radulescu, 'Yorkist Propaganda and the Chronicle from Rollo to Edward IV', *Studies in Philology* 100 (2003), 401–24.
8. Ross, *Edward IV*, 91–6, 117; *PROME* xiii, 270; Hicks, 'The Changing Role of the Wydevilles in Yorkist Politics to 1483', repr. in *Rivals*, 214–17; M.A. Hicks, *False, Fleeting, Perjur'd Clarence: George Duke of Clarence 1449–78* (Gloucester, 1980), 34–8.
9. Hicks, '*Brief Treatise*'; A. Allan, 'Yorkist Propaganda: Pedigree, Prophecy and the "British History" in the Reign of Edward IV', in *Patronage, Pedigree and Power in Later Medieval England*, ed. C.D. Ross (Gloucester, 1979), 171–3.
10. Virgoe, 'Inheritance and Litigation in the Fifteenth Century', *East Anglian Society*, 141.
11. *Paston L & P* i, 544; M.A. Hicks, 'The 1468 Statute of Livery', *HR* lxiv (1991), 24.
12. Hicks, '*Brief Treatise*', 3–5.
13. *Annales*, 789.
14. Hatcher, 'The Great Slump', 241–3; Pollard, *Warwick*, 59–60.
15. *Plumpton L & P*, 7.
16. B.P. Wolffe, *The Royal Demesne in English History* (1971), 179.
17. Ibid., 189; *CPR 1461–7*, 107; *1476–85*, 341.
18. C.D. Ross, 'The Reign of Edward IV', in *Fifteenth-century England 1399–1509*, ed. S.B. Chrimes, C.D. Ross and R.A. Griffiths (Manchester, 1972), 55–6; Hicks, 'Attainder, Resumption and Coercion 1461–1529', repr. in *Rivals*, 72–4.
19. Lander, *Crown*, 307–8.
20. *CPR 1461–7*, 327; R. Somerville, *History of the Duchy of Lancaster*, 2 vols (1953–70), i, 233, 238.

21. *PROME* xiii, 257; *John Vale's Bk*, 215.
22. *John Vale's Bk*, 213–14; *Death and Dissent*, 96.
23. *Lay Taxes*, 109–11.
24. *John Vale's Bk*, 215.
25. *Death and Dissent*, 100.
26. Hicks, *Warwick*, 247.
27. M.L. Kekewich, ' "Though shalt be under the power of man": Sir John Fortescue and the Yorkist Succession', *NMS*, 42, 188–230.
28. Lander, 'Attainder and Forfeiture 1453–1509', repr. in *Crown*, 131–6; Hicks, 'Edward IV, the Duke of Somerset, and Lancastrian Loyalism in the North', repr. in *Rivals*, 149–55; see also ch. 11.
29. J.T. Rosenthal, 'Other Victims: Peeresses as War Widows, 1450–1500', *History* lxxii (1987), 222; Hicks, 'Counting the Costs of War: The Moleyns Ransom and the Hungerford Land–Sales 1453–87', repr. in *Rivals*, 190.
30. *PROME* xiii, 42–6; Lander, *Crown*, 133; R.A. Griffiths and R.S. Thomas, *The Making of the Tudor Dynasty* (Gloucester, 1985), 57.
31. Hicks, *Warwick*, 238–48.
32. E.g., Sir Thomas Cook, *John Vale's Bk*, 9.
33. Griffiths and Thomas, *Tudor Dynasty*, 62–6; Ross, *Edward IV*, 113n, 114n; *Annales*, 791; *CSPM*, 125.
34. M.L. Kekewich, 'The Lancastrian Court in Exile', in *The Lancastrian Court*, ed. J. Stratford (Donington, 2003), 95–108, at 98.
35. TNA KB 29/97 Mich. 6 Edward IV m. 19-d.
36. *Annales*, 792.
37. *Annales*, 790.
38. Hicks, 'The Case of Sir Thomas Cook, 1468', repr. in *Rivals*, 428–30, esp. 424nn; *PROME* xiii, 50; *Death and Dissent*, 97–8; K. Dockray, 'The Yorkshire Rebellion of 1469', *Ricardian* 83 (1983), 249–52; M. Kekewich, 'The Mysterious Dr Makerell: His General Pardon of 27 November 1469', *Much Heaving and Shoving*, ed. M. Aston and R. Horrox (Lavenham, 2005), 48–9; *Plumpton L & P*, 39–40; but see Pollard, *Warwick*, 63. Kirby's confirmatory evidence relates to 1462, Kirby, *Plumpton L & P*, 40n; *Chronicles of London*, ed. C.L. Kingsford (1905), 180; *Great Chronicle of London*, ed. A.H. Thomas and I.O. Thornley (1938), 204–6; P.J.C. Field, *The Life and Times of Sir Thomas Malory* (Woodbridge, 1993), 138; TNA KB 27/830 m. 170d; KB 27/837 m.64d; KB 29/99 m.31; see also P. Holand, 'Cook's Case in History and Myth', *HR* lxi (1988), 21–36.
39. *Annales*, 788, 790; *Plumpton L & P*, 35; Wedgwood, *Biographies*, 256–8, 506; Hicks, *Edward V*, 35–6; Hicks, 'Piety and Lineage in the Wars of the Roses: The Hungerford Experience', repr. in *Rivals*, 173–4; Field, *Malory*, 141; J.S. Roskell, 'John Lord Wenlock of Someries', *Parliament and Politics in Late Medieval England* (1981–3), ii, 232–3; *CSPM*, 117, 120.
40. Hicks, 'Sir Thomas Cook', repr. in *Rivals*, 424–32; TNA KB 29/98 m.1; *Great Chronicle*, 43.

Chapter 11: The Second War 1469–71

1. Hicks, *Warwick*, ch. 8.
2. The fullest recent discussion is in Hicks, *Edward V*, 37–48.
3. Hicks, *Warwick*, 258.
4. Lander, *Crown*, 121; Hicks, *Clarence*, 35, 38–9, 41; Hicks 'The Changing Role of the Wydevilles in Yorkist Politics to 1483', repr. in *Rivals*, 213–16.
5. Hicks, *Warwick*, 261–3, 268.
6. *Annales*, 787–9; Hicks, *Clarence*, 43; Hicks, *Warwick*, 263; *PROME* xiii, 270.
7. *PROME* xiii, 42–53, 122–7; *Death and Dissent*, 94, 96–7; *Chronicle of the First Thirteen Years of Edward IV*, ed. J.O. Halliwell, Camden Society x (1839), 38, 40.

8. Hicks, *Clarence*, 38–9, 41, 45.
9. 'Chronicle of the Rebellion in Lincolnshire, in 1470', ed. J.G. Nichols, *Camden Miscellany* i (1847), 11–12.
10. *John Vale's Bk*, 212–15; *Lay Taxes*, 111; *Death and Dissent*, 98.
11. Hicks, *Warwick*, 275; K. Dockray, 'The Yorkshire Rebellion of 1469', *Ricardian* 83 (1983), 252–9; Pollard, *NE England*, 304n, 305n.
12. *Death and Dissent*, 98–9.
13. *CPR 1467–77*, 165; *PROME* xiii, 391; Hicks, *Clarence*, 5.
14. *CPR 1467–77*, 190; Hicks, *Edward V*, 52.
15. See Pollard, *Warwick*, 66.
16. Hicks, *Clarence*, 51; C. Richmond, *The Paston Family in the Fifteenth Century: The First Phase* (Cambridge, 1990), 198–208.
17. P. Fleming and M. Wood, *Gloucestershire's Forgotten Battle of Nibley Green 1470* (Stroud, 2003).
18. *Death and Dissent*, 100; Hicks, *Clarence*, 66–7; see also R.L. Storey, 'Lincolnshire in the Wars of the Roses', *NMS* xiv (1970), 71–2. For the chronology, see also P. Holand, 'The Lincolnshire Rebellion of March 1470', *EHR* ciii (1988), 853–4.
19. Hicks, *Clarence*, 72; see also Holand, 'Lincolnshire Rebellion', 860–1, which seems, however, to confuse the two Courtenay families. The Harington–Stanley dispute is not discussed here.
20. *Death and Dissent*, 100.
21. Hicks, *Clarence*, 56–61. *Pace* Pollard, *LM England*, 283–4, all the key decisions antedate Warwick and Clarence's arrival.
22. *Lay Taxes*, 111.
23. *Death & Dissent*, 104.
24. Hicks, *Clarence*, 65–6; *pace* Holand, 'Lincolnshire Rebellion', 850, 862–3.
25. *John Vale's Bk*, 212; *Lay Taxes*, 111; *Chron. Lincs.*, 9, 22.
26. *Chron. Lincs.*, 10–11, 17–18, 21–3; *Death and Dissent*, 100–1.
27. *Chron. Lincs.*, 12–15.
28. Hicks, *Clarence*, 71–2.
29. Hicks, *Clarence*, 76–82; Hicks, *Warwick*, 296; Hicks, *Anne Neville*, 82–9; Pollard, *Warwick*, 69–70, predictably fails to reconcile *The Maner and Gwidinge* with the record evidence; see Hicks, *Clarence*, 79–81.
30. *Arrivall*, 23.
31. *John Vale's Bk*, 220.
32. Hicks, *Warwick*, 300.
33. A.J. Pollard, 'Lord FitzHugh's Rising in 1470', *BIHR* lii (1979), 170; idem, *NE England*, 311–12; P.W. Fleming, 'The Lovelace Dispute: Concepts of Property and Inheritance in Fifteenth-century Kent', *Southern History* xii (1990), 8; for the West Country, see above.
34. Hicks, *Warwick*, 300.
35. Hicks, *Clarence*, 99; *Arrivall*, 23.
36. *Arrivall*, 149; Ross, *Edward IV*, 153, 160.
37. H. Kleineke, 'Gerard von Wesel's Newsletter from England, 17 April 1471', *Ricardian* xvi (2006), 69. Unless otherwise stated, the next four paragraphs are based on *Arrivall*, *passim*.
38. Richmond, 'Fauconberg's Kentish Rising', *EHR* lxxxv, 676–89.
39. Ibid., 684–6; Lander, *Crown*, 136–7; Hicks, *Clarence*, 110–12; Kekewich, ' "Though shalt be under the power of man": Sir John Fortescue and the Yorkist Succession', *NMS* xlii, (1998) 188–230; TNA KB 9/41/28.

Chapter 12: The Third War: First Phase 1483–5

1. See above, ch. 11.
2. Pollard, *Wars*, 67.

3. *The Cely Letters 1472–88*, ed. A. Hanham, EETS 273 (1975), 185.
4. Lander, *Crown*, 226, 228; Ross, *Edward IV*, ch. 9.
5. Hicks, *Clarence*, 118.
6. Hicks, *Clarence*, 118–19; *Death & Dissent*, 120–1; Scofield, *Life and Reign of King Edward the Fourth* (1923), ii. 58.
7. *Death & Dissent*, 122–4.
8. M.K. Jones, 'Richard III and Lady Margaret Beaufort. A Re-assessment', in *Richard III: Loyalty, Lordship and Law*, ed. P.W. Hammond (1986), 29–30; M.K. Jones and M.G. Underwood, *The King's Mother: Lady Margaret Beaufort, Countess of Richmond and Derby* (Cambridge, 1992), 60–1; R.A. Griffiths and R.S. Thomas, *The Making of the Tudor Dynasty* (Gloucester, 1985), 83–5.
9. T. More, *History of King Richard III*, ed. R. Sylvester (New Haven, CT, 1963), 7–9; Hicks, *Clarence*, 118.
10. *Crowland*, 132–3.
11. Hicks, *Clarence*, ch. 4; Hicks, *Edward IV*, 191–200. For the final clause, see *Mancini*, 62–3; *Crowland*, 144–7; *Vergil*, 167–8; More, *Richard III*, 7.
12. More, *Richard III*, 8–9.
13. *Crowland*, 146–7; P.M. Barnes, 'Chancery *Corpus cum causa* files, 10–11 Edward IV', *Medieval Legal Records*, ed. R.F. Hunnisett and J. Post (1978), 430–45; Hicks, 'Attainder, Resumption and Coercion, 1461–1529', repr. in *Rivals*, 63–76; Hicks, 'The Last Days of Elizabeth, Countess of Oxford', repr. in *Rivals*, 309; Hicks, Piety and Lineage in the Wars of the Roses: The Hungerford Experience', repr. in *Rivals*, 176; Hicks, *Edward V*, 113–14; T.B. Pugh, 'Henry VII and the Tudor Nobility', in *The Tudor Nobility*, ed. G.W. Bernard (Manchester, 1992), 60; M.K. Jones, 'Richard III and Lady Margaret Beaufort: A Re-assessment', in *Richard III: Loyalty, Lordship and Law* (1986), ed. P.W. Hammond, 29.
14. Hicks, *Edward V*, 117–20, 126–34.
15. Hicks, *Richard III*, 51.
16. *Crowland*, 138–9; *Mancini*, 66–7, 70–1.
17. C.D. Ross, 'The Reign of Edward IV', in *Fifteenth-century England 1399–1509*, 57–60.
18. Hicks, *Edward V*, 113–15.
19. Hicks, *Edward IV*, 142.
20. Ross, *Edward IV*, 386.
21. 'Financial Memoranda of the Reign of Edward V', ed. R.E. Horrox, *Camden Miscellany* 29 (1987), esp. 209–10.
22. Ibid., 210–12; *Lay Taxes*, 118, 120; *Crowland*, 138–9.
23. Hicks, '*Brief Treatise*', 12; *CPR 1467 77*, 583; *Foedera*, xii, 14.
24. *Lay Taxes*, 118–20; *Crowland*, 150–1; *PROME* xv, 58–9.
25. Hicks, *Richard III*, 126; see also *Crowland*, 138–9, 150–1.
26. Hatcher, 'Great Slump', 241–3, 270–1.
27. Ross, *Edward IV*, 292–3; *John Vale's Bk*, 71.
28. P.M. Kendall, *Richard III* (1955), 373.
29. Hicks, *Clarence*, 57–8, 151; BL Add. MS 6113 f.74v.
30. *Crowland*, 154–7. Unless otherwise stated, the following account is based on Ross, *Richard III*, ch. 4.
31. *Mancini*, 72–3; *Crowland*, 154–5.
32. *Mancini*, 68–9.
33. M.A. Hicks, 'A Study of Failure: The Minority of Edward V', *Royal Minorities of Medieval and Early Medieval England*, ed. C. Beem (Basingstoke, 2008), 198–9.
34. C. Moreton, 'A Local Dispute and the Politics of 1483: Roger Townshend, Earl Rivers and the Duke of Gloucester', *Ricardian* 107 (1989), 305–6.
35. Hicks, 'Richard III as Duke of Gloucester: A Study in Character', repr. in *Rivals*, 276.
36. *Mancini*, 70–3; *Crowland*, 155–6.
37. *Mancini*, 74–9; *Crowland*, 154–9.

38. C.F. Richmond, '1485 and All That, or What Was Going On at the Battle of Bosworth', in *Richard III: Loyalty, Lordship and Law*, ed. P.W. Hammond (1986), 181.
39. *Crowland*, 156-7.
40. *Stonor Letters and Papers of the Fifteenth Century*, ed. C.L. Kingsford, Camden 3rd ser., xxx (1919), ii, 160.
41. *Mancini*, 80-3.
42. Hicks, *Richard III*, 112.
43. S.B. Chrimes, *English Constitutional Ideas in the Fifteenth Century* (Cambridge, 1934), 177.
44. *Mancini*, 84-5.
45. ed. P.W. Hammond and A.F. Sutton, *Richard III: The Road to Bosworth Field* (1985), 103.
46. Hicks, *Richard III*, 114; *Mancini*, 129.
47. *PROME* xv, 14-17; *Mancini*, 64-5, 82-3, 94-5, 131-3; Hicks, *Richard III*, 127.
48. C.D. Ross, 'Rumour, Propaganda, and Popular Opinion in the Wars of the Roses', *Patronage, The Crown and The Provinces in Later Medieval England*, ed. R.A. Griffiths (1979), 26.
49. Hicks, *Richard III*, 124-9.
50. *PROME* xv, 14-16.
51. More, *Richard III*, 218; *CPR 1467-77*, 190; *Mancini*, 60-3; *PROME* xv, 15.
52. Hicks, *Edward V*, 31-40.
53. *PROME* xv, 16.
54. *PROME* xiv, 14-16.
55. Hicks, *Richard III*, 144-53.
56. Pollard, *Worlds*, 27-30.
57. E.g., J. Potter, *Good King Richard?* (1985), 89.
58. R.E. Horrox, *Richard III: A Study of Service* (Cambridge, 1989), 149-50.
59. Ibid., 170.
60. *Crowland*, 158-9; Horrox, *Richard III*, 137, 171.
61. *Crowland*, 162-3; *Vergil*, 194; I. Arthurson and N. Kingwell, 'The Proclamation of Henry Tudor as King of England, 3 November 1483', *HR* lxiii (1990), 102.
62. *Vergil*, 194; Hicks, *Clarence*, 35.
63. Griffiths and Thomas, *Tudor Dynasty*, 102.
64. *PROME* xv, 123-9.
65. A.V. Antonovics, 'Henry VII, King of England, "By the Grace of Charles VIII of France"', in *Kings and Nobles in the Later Middle Ages*, ed. R.A. Griffiths and J.W. Sherborne (Gloucester, 1986), 171; Arthurson and Kingwell, 'Proclamation', 104. Vergil's 5,000 Bretons are incredible, *Vergil*, 200-4.
66. Griffiths and Thomas, *Tudor Dynasty*, 109.
67. Horrox, *Richard III*, 273-6; S. Cunningham, 'Henry VII and Rebellion in North-Eastern England, 1485-92: Bonds of Allegiance and the Establishment of Tudor Authority', *Northern History* xxxii (1996), 46.
68. Hammond and Sutton, ed., *Richard III*, 165-6.
69. Hicks, *Anne Neville*, 195-210.
70. Griffiths and Thomas, *Tudor Dynasty*, 108; P.D. Clarke, 'English Royal Marriages and the Papal Penitentiary in the Fifteenth Century', *EHR* cxx (2005), 1,025.
71. Hammond and Sutton, ed., *Richard III*, 209; *PROME* xv, 28-9, 36.
72. Griffiths and Thomas, *Tudor Dynasty*, 111.
73. Ibid., 118n, 119, 121.
74. M.K. Jones, *Bosworth 1485: Psychology of a Battle* (Stroud, 2002), 131-2; Antonovics, 'Henry VII', 169-77.
75. Griffiths and Thomas, *Tudor Dynasty*, 111,
76. *Crowland*, 170-1; R.E. Horrox, 'Henry Tudor's Letters to England during Richard's Reign', *Ricardian* 80 (1983), 155-6; Hicks, *Richard III*, 173.

77. Hicks, *Anne Neville*, 193; P. Morgan, 'Those were the days: A Yorkist Pedigree Roll', *Estrangement, Enterprise and Education in Fifteenth-Century England*, ed. S. Michalove and A. Compton Reeves (Stroud, 1998), 114–16.
78. Griffiths and Thomas, *Tudor Dynasty*, 104.
79. Horrox, 'Henry Tudor's Letters', 155–7; Hicks, *Richard III*, 173–82; Griffiths and Thomas, *Tudor Dynasty*, 125–6; Jones, *Bosworth*, 123.
80. Horrox, *Richard III*, 275–81.
81. Griffiths and Thomas, *Tudor Dynasty*, 106.
82. Ibid., 127, 129; Jones, *Bosworth*, 132; Antonovics, 'Henry VII', 176–7.
83. Griffiths and Thomas, *Tudor Dynasty*, 128–9, 131.
84. See http://www.bosworthbattlefield.com/battle/archaeology/battlefield.htm accessed 4 January 2010; G. Foard, 'Bosworth Uncovered', *BBC History Magazine* 11(3) (March 2010), 23–30.
85. D. Luckett, 'The Thames Valley Conspiracies against Henry VII', *HR* lxviii (1995), 165.
86. Richmond, '1485 and All That', 173; but see Pollard, *NE England*, 364–5; Pollard, *Wars*, 72.
87. Pollard, *Wars*, 72; Pollard, *LM England*, 347.
88. The discovery of twenty-two bullets and roundshot (possibly fired) on the battlefield confirms the presence of firearms, not that they were decisive: Molinet mentions the use of guns by Richard not Henry, http://www.bosworthbattlefield.com/battle/archaeology/battlefield/battlefield_bft.htm accessed 4 January 2010.

Chapter 13: The Third War: 1485–1525

1. *The Logge Register of Prerogative Court of Canterbury Wills, 1479-86*, eds L. Boatwright, M. Habberjam, and P. Hammond, 2 vols (Knaphill, 2008), 11, 448.
2. S.B. Chrimes, *English Constitutional Ideas in the Fifteenth Century* (Cambridge, 1936), 378–9.
3. *PROME* xv, 102–3, 113–37, 233.
4. *Crowland*, 194.
5. *Crowland*, 194–5; *Plumpton L & P*, 63; *Parliamentary Texts of the Later Middle Ages*, ed. N. Pronay and J. Taylor (Oxford, 1980), 188.
6. *PROME* xv, 89; *The Herald's Memoir 1486-1490: Court Ceremony, Royal Progress and Rebellion*, ed. E. Cavell (Stroud, 2010), 72–3; D. Grummitt, 'Household, Politics and Political Morality in the Reign of Henry VII', in M.R. Horowitz, *Who Was Henry VII, Historical Research* lxxxii (2009), 398.
7. M. Bennett, *Lambert Simnel and the Battle of Stoke* (Gloucester, 1987), 27–9; S. Cunningham, 'Loyalty and the Usurper: Recognizances, the Council and Allegiance under Henry VII', in M.R. Horowitz, *Who was Henry VII?* (2009), 461; for a contrary view, see T.B.Pugh, 'Henry VII and the Tudor Nobility', *The Tudor Nobility*, ed. G.W. Bernard (Manchester, 1992), 52.
8. S. Cunningham, *Henry VII*, (2007) 204.
9. Hicks, 'Dynastic Change and Northern Society: The Fourth Earl of Northumberland 1470-89', repr. in *Rivals*, 384–7; Cavell, ed., *Herald's Memoir* 72–3.
10. P. Morgan, 'Those were the days: A Yorkist Pedigree Roll', *Estrangement, Enterprise and Education in Fifteenth Century England*, eds S. Michalove and A. Compton Reeves (Stroad, 1998), 114–16.
11. C. Weightman, *Margaret of York, Duchess of Burgundy, 1446-1503* (Gloucester, 1989), 148.
12. Hicks, 'Descent, Partition and Extinction: The "Warwick Inheritance"', repr. in *Rivals*, 332–3; M.A. Hicks, 'Richard Lord Latimer, Richard III, and the Warwick Inheritance', *Ricardian* 154 (2001), 317–18.
13. *Crowland*, 174–5.

14. Pollard, *NE England*, 368-71.
15. S. Cunningham, 'Henry VII and Rebellion in North-Eastern England, 1485-92: Bonds of Allegiance and the Establishment of Tudor Authority', *Northern History* xxxii (1996), 44; K. Dockray, 'The Political Legacy of Richard III in Northern England', in *Kings and Nobles in the Later Middle Ages*, eds R.A. Griffiths and J.W. Sherborne (Gloucester, 1986), 206.
16. Cunningham, *Henry VII*, 58.
17. D. Luckett, 'The Thames Valley Conspiracies against Henry VII', *HR* lxviii (1995), 164.
18. C.J. Harrison, 'The Petition of Edmund Dudley', *EHR* lxxxvii (1972), 86.
19. Cunningham, 'Henry VII and Rebellion', 50; Dockray, 'Political Legacy', 212-14; see also Hicks, 'Latimer', 317-18.
20. Cunningham, 'Henry VII and Rebellion', 51-9.
21. Dockray, 'Political Legacy', 216-17.
22. Cunningham, 'Henry VII and Rebellion', 52-6.
23. Ibid., 54; see also Cavell, ed., *Herald's Memoir* 72-3; Bennett, *Simnel*, 37; Pollard, *NE England*, 372.
24. C.H. Williams, 'The Rebellion of Humphrey Stafford in 1486', *EHR* xliii (1928), 181-9; Hicks, 'Latimer', 317.
25. Bennett, *Simnel*, 38.
26. Pollard, *LM England*, 355.
27. J.M. Currin, 'Henry VII and the Treaty of Redon (1489): Plantagenet Ambitions and Early Tudor Foreign Policy', *History* lxxxi (1996), 354-8.
28. Bennett, *Simnel*, 39, 50, 120; Weightman, *Margaret*, 158; Williams, 'Stafford', 183.
29. *Anglica Historica*, 18-19.
30. Bennett, *Simnel*, 42-4, 120.
31. Ibid., 59-63.
32. Pollard, *NE England*, 375-7.
33. Bennett, *Simnel*, ch. 6; P.M. Kendall, *Richard III* (1955), 373-6.
34. Arthurson, *Warbeck*, chs. 5-10; M. Ballard and C.S.L. Davies, 'Etienne Fryon: Burgundian Royal Secretary and "Principal Counsellor" to Perkin Warbeck', *HR* lxii (1989), 245-59; Weightman, *Margaret*, ch. 6; A. Wroe, *Perkin: A Story of Deception* (2003).
35. Arthurson, *Warbeck*; Wroe, *Perkin*. In general, these are the source of the next four paragraphs.
36. Arthurson, *Warbeck*, 77, 91; Cunningham, *Henry VII*, 77-80; Wroe, *Perkin*, 172.
37. Weightman, *Margaret*, 165.
38. Arthurson, *Warbeck*, 101.
39. Wroe, *Perkin*, 208-12.
40. I. Arthurson, 'The Rising of 1497: A Revolt of the Peasantry', in *People, Politics and the Community in the Later Middle Ages*, eds J. Rosenthal and C. Richmond (Gloucester, 1987), 1-18, esp. 3-5.
41. Arthurson, *Warbeck*, 181-7.
42. Diana Kleyn, *Richard of England* (1990), 199-202. For the dating see Arthurson, *Warbeck*, 146-7, 163. This is the source of the next two paragraphs.
43. S.B. Chrimes, *Henry VII* (1970), 85.
44. Hicks, 'The Yorkshire Rebellion of 1489 Reconsidered', repr. in *Rivals*, 406-9.
45. M. Bush, 'Tax Reform and Rebellion in Early Tudor England', *History* lxxvi (1991), 387; Pugh, 'Henry VII', 54.
46. *CSPM*, 299.
47. M.R. Horowitz, *Who was Henry VII?* (2009), 575; Cunningham, 'Loyalty', 470.
48. Arthurson, *Warbeck*, 68, 73.
49. M.R. Horowitz, *Henry VII*, 425-9.
50. S. Gunn, 'Ralph Wilford c.1479-99', *Oxford Dictionary of National Biography* (*ODNB*) lviii (2004), 942.

51. S. Gunn, 'Edmund de la Pole, Eighth Earl of Suffolk (1472?–1513)', *ODNB* xliv (2004), 696–7; Pugh, 'Henry VII', 64–5 (whose assessment of Edmund is harsher).
52. Gunn, 'Edmund de la Pole', 697–8.
53. S. Cunningham, 'Richard de la Pole (d. 1525)', *ODNB* xliv (2004), 725–7.

Chapter 14: The End of the Wars

1. F. Bacon, *The History of the Reign of King Henry the Seventh*, ed. J. Weinberger (Ithaca, NY and London, 1996), esp. 185–6; M.R. Horowitz, *Who was Henry VII?* (2009), 376.
2. P.H. Ramsay, *Tudor Economic Problems* (1962), 37, 159.
3. Lander, 'Attainder and Forfeiture', repr. in *Crown*, 143–8.
4. Lander, 'Bonds, Coercion and Fear', repr. in *Crown*, 282–4, 287–8, 293.
5. Harrison, 'Edmund Dudley', *EHR* lxxxvii, 87–90.
6. S. Cunningham, 'Loyalty and the Usurper', in Horowitz, *Henry VII*, 459–81, esp. 459–60; Horowitz, 'Policy and Prosecution in the Reign of Henry VII', in *Henry VII*, 412–44, esp. 434.
7. As Cunningham suggests, 'Loyalty', 469.
8. Horowitz, 'Henry VII's Treasure', in *Henry VII*, 560–79, esp. 576–7.
9. Cunningham, 'Loyalty', 477; Carpenter, *Wars*, 240.
10. Cunningham, 'Loyalty', 475; Carpenter, *Wars*, 244.
11. M.R. Horowitz, 'Richard Empson, Minister of Henry VII', *BIHR* lv (1982), 45.
12. Horowitz, 'Policy and Prosecution', in *Henry VII*, 434, 450–1.
13. G.W. Bernard, *War, Taxation and Rebellion in Early Tudor England: Henry VII, Wolsey and the Amicable Grant of 1525* (Brighton, 1986), 71–2.
14. C.S.L. Davies, ' "The Tudors": A Challenge', *Times Literary Supplement*, 17 July 2009.
15. *CPL 1484–92*, 1; *PROME* xv, 97.
16. *Letters and Papers illustrative of the Reigns of Richard and Henry VII*, ed. J. Gairdner, 2 vols, Rolls Series (1861–3), i, 239; G.R. Elton, *The Tudor Constitution* (Cambridge, 1962), 5–6; S.B. Chrimes, *Henry VII* (1970), 308–9; see also Grummitt, 'Household, Politics', in Horowitz, *Henry VII*, 406–8.
17. T.K. Oliphant, 'Was the Old English Aristocracy Destroyed by the Wars of the Roses?' *TRHS* i (1875), 443.
18. M.A. Hicks, 'Richard III, the Great Landowners and the Results of the Wars of the Roses', in *Tant D'Emprises – So Many Undertakings*, ed. L. Visser-Fuchs (2003), 260–70; T.B. Pugh, 'Henry VII and the Tudor Nobility', *The Tudor Nobility*, ed. G.W. Bernard (Manchester, 1992).
19. Hicks, 'Descent', *Rivals*, 332.
20. Virgoe, 'The Recovery of the Howards in East Anglia, 1485 to 1529', *East Anglian Society*, 222–8.
21. T. More, *Utopia*, ed. P. Turner (Harmondsworth, 1965), 44–8.
22. Hatcher, 'Great Slump', 241–3, 270–2.
23. Hicks, *Richard III*, 170–1.
24. P. Slack, ed., *Rebellion, Protest and the Social Order in Early Modern England* (Cambridge, 1984), 1–15; E.P. Thompson, 'The Moral Economy of the English Crowd in the Eighteenth Century', *Past and Present* 50 (1971), 76–136.
25. M. Bennett, 'Henry VII and the Northern Rising of 1489', *EHR* cv (1990), 56–8; Hoyle, 'Petitioning as Popular Politics', *HR* lxxv, esp. 365–7.
26. *Mancini*, 94–5, 98–9.
27. A. Fletcher and D. McCulloch, *Tudor Rebellions* (4th edn, Harlow, 1997), 33–4, 131, 135–6.
28. B.P. Wolffe, *The Royal Demesne in English History*, 117, 123; Pugh, 'Henry VII', in *Tudor Nobility*, 65, 90; Horowitz, 'Henry VII's Treasure', in *Henry VII*, 564, 576.
29. J.M. Currin, 'Henry VII, France and the Holy League of Venice: the Diplomacy of Balance', in Horowitz, *Henry VII*, 526–46.

30. *PROME* xvi, 237-8; McFarlane, *Wars*, 246.
31. As argued by Cunningham, 'Loyalty', 472.
32. J. Watts, 'Ideas, Principles and Politics' in *Wars*, ed. Pollard, 122.
33. Ibid., 111.
34. 'Chronicle of the Rebellion in Lincolnshire', ed. J.G. Nichols, *Camden Miscellany*, i, (1847), 116
35. *PROME* xv, 337.
36. *Certain Sermons and Homilies*, ed. R.B. Bond (1987), 161-72.
37. M.E. James, 'The Concept of Order and the Northern Rising, 1569', in *Culture, Politics and Society in Early Modern England* (Oxford, 1986), 270.
38. *Crowland*, 190-1.
39. *PROME* xv, 107.
40. *PROME*, xv, 91.
41. *CPL 1484-92*, 1-2.
42. *Tudor Royal Proclamations*, ed. P.L. Hughes and J.F. Larkin, i (1964), 4.
43. *PROME* xv, 90, 337.
44. S. Anglo, *Spectacle, Pageantry and Early Tudor Policy* (Oxford, 1969), 41.
45. *Vergil*, 135.
46. *CPL 1484-92*, 1-2.
47. Wroe, *Perkin*, 186.

Chapter 15: Epilogue

1. K. Sharpe, *Selling the Tudor Monarchy: Authority and Image in Sixteenth-Century England* (2009), xvii, 68.
2. Kleyn, *Richard of England*, 200.
3. A. Fletcher and D. McCulloch, *Tudor Rebellions* (4th edn, Harlow, 1997).

BIBLIOGRAPHY

PRIMARY SOURCES

MANUSCRIPTS

The National Archives: Classes C 1, C 49, C 67, C 81, C 237; E 28, E 101, E 159, E 404; KB 9, KB 27, KB 29; PSO 1; SC 6, SC8.
British Library: Additional, Cottonian, Egerton, Harleian, Royal and Sloane MSS.

PRINTED BOOKS

The Anglica Historica of Polydore Vergil AD 1485–1537, ed. D. Hay, Camden 3rd ser. lxiv (1950).
The Armburgh Papers: The Brokholes Inheritance in Warwickshire, Hertfordshire and Essex c.1417–c.1453, ed. C. Carpenter (Woodbridge, 1998).
Bacon, F., *History of the Reign of King Henry the Seventh*, ed. J. Weinberger (Ithaca, NY, and London, 1996).
Basin, T., *Histoire de Charles VII*, ed. C. Samaran (Paris, 1933–4); *Louis XI* (Paris, 1963).
Baskerville, G., 'A London Chronicle of 1460', *English Historical Review* xxviii (1913).
Blacman, John, *Henry VI*, ed. M.R. James (Cambridge, 1919).
British Library Harleian Manuscript 433, ed. P.W. Hammond and R.E. Horrox, 4 vols (Gloucester, 1979–83).
The Brut or the Chronicles of England, ed. F.W.D. Brie, Early English Text Society 131, 136 (1908).
Calendar of Entries in the Papal Registers relating to Great Britain and Ireland, ed. W.H. Bliss, J.A. Twemlow et al. (1893–).
Calendar of the Charter Rolls, vi, 1427–1516 (1927).
Calendar of the Close Rolls, 1436–1509 (1933–53).
Calendar of the Fine Rolls, 1422–1509.
Calendar of the Patent Rolls 1436–1509 (1897–1910).
Calendar of State Papers and Manuscripts relating to English Affairs in the Archives and Collections of Milan, ed. A.B. Hinds (1913).
The Cely Letters 1472–88, ed. A. Hanham, Early English Text Society 273 (1975).
Chronicle of the First Thirteen Years of Edward IV, ed. J.O. Halliwell, Camden Society x (1839).

'Chronicle of the Rebellion in Lincolnshire, in 1470', ed. J.G. Nichols, *Camden Miscellany* i (1847).

Chronicles of London, ed. C.L. Kingsford (London, 1905).

Chronicles of the Revolution 1397–1400, ed. C. Given-Wilson (Manchester, 1993).

Commines, P. de, *Mémoires*, ed. J. Calmette and G. Durville, 3 vols (Paris, 1923–5).

The Coventry Leet Book and Mayor's Register, ed. M.D. Harris, Early English Text Society 134–5, 138, 146 (1907–13).

The Crowland Chronicle Continuations 1459–86, ed. N. Pronay and J. Cox (Gloucester, 1986).

Death and Dissent: The Dethe of the Kynge of Scots and Warkworth's Chronicle, ed. L.M. Matheson (Woodbridge, 1999).

'A Defence of the Proscription of the Yorkists', ed. E. Gilson, *English Historical Review* xxvi (1911).

Devon, F., *Issues of the Exchequer* (London, 1837).

Dudley, E., *The Tree of the Commonwealth*, ed. D.M. Brodie (Cambridge, 1948).

Dugdale, W., *Monasticon Anglicanum*, ed. J. Caley et al., 8 vols (1846).

An English Chronicle 1377–1461: A New Edition, ed. W. Marx (Woodbridge, 2003).

English Historical Documents, iv, *1327–1485*, ed. A.R. Myers (1969).

Excerpta Historica, ed. S. Bentley (1831).

'Financial Memoranda of the Reign of Edward V', ed. R.E. Horrox, *Camden Miscellany* 29 (1987).

Fortescue, J., *The Governance of England*, ed. C. Plummer (Oxford, 1885).

Fortescue, J., *On the Laws and Governance of England*, ed. S. Lockwood (Cambridge, 1997).

Gascoigne, T., *Loci e Libro Veritatum. Passages selected from Gascoigne's Theological Dictionary illustrating the condition of church and state*, ed. J.E.T. Rogers (Oxford, 1881).

Great Chronicle of London, ed. A.H. Thomas and I.D. Thornley (1938).

Hall's Chronicle, ed. H. Ellis (London, 1809).

Henry VI, Margaret of Anjou and the Wars of the Roses: A Sourcebook, ed. K. Dockray, (Stroud, 2000).

Henry the Sixth: A Reprint of John Blacman's Memoir, ed. M.R. James (Cambridge, 1919).

The Herald's Memoir 1486–1490: Court Ceremony, Royal Progress and Rebellion, ed. E. Cavell (Stroud, 2010).

Historical Collections of a Citizen of London, ed. J. Gairdner, Camden Society new series xvii (1876).

Historical Poems of the Fourteenth and Fifteenth Centuries, ed. R.H. Robbins (New York, 1959).

The Historie of the Arrivall of Edward IV and the Finall Recouerye of his Kingdomes from Henry VI, ed. J. Bruce, Camden Society, i (1838).

Ingulph's Chronicle of the Abbey of Croyland, ed. H.T. Riley (1859).

'John Benet's Chronicle for the years 1400 to 1462', ed. G.L. Harriss and M.A. Harriss, *Camden Miscellany* xxiv (1972).

Letters and Papers illustrative of the Reigns of Richard and Henry VII, ed. J. Gairdner, 2 vols, Rolls Series (1861–3).

Letters and Papers illustrative of the Wars of the English in France, ed. J. Stevenson, 3 vols in 2, Rolls Series (1864).

The Logge Register of Prerogative Court of Canterbury Wills, 1479–86, ed. L. Boatwright, M. Habberjam and P. Hammond, 2 vols (Knaphill, 2008).

Mancini, D., *The Usurpation of Richard III*, ed. C.A.J. Armstrong, (2nd edn, Oxford, 1969).

Memorials of Henry VII, ed. J. Gairdner, Rolls Series (1858).

More, T., *History of King Richard III*, ed. R.S. Sylvester (New Haven, CT, 1963).

The Parliament Rolls of England 1275–1504, ed. C. Given Wilson, 16 vols (Woodbridge, 2005).

Parliamentary Texts of the Later Middle Ages, ed. N. Pronay and J. Taylor (Oxford, 1980).

The Paston Letters, ed. J. Gairdner, 6 vols (1904).

Paston Letters and Papers of the Fifteenth Century, ed. R. Beadle, N. Davis and C. Richmond, 3 vols, Early English Text Society supplementary series 20-2 (2004-5).

The Plumpton Letters and Papers, ed. J. Kirby, Camden 5th ser., viii (1996).

Political Poems and Songs, ed. T. Wright, Rolls Series, 2 vols (1859-61).

The Politics of Fifteenth-Century England: John Vale's Book, ed. M.L. Kekewich, C. Richmond, A.F. Sutton, L. Visser-Fuchs and J.L. Watts (Stroud, 1995).

Proceedings and Ordinances of the Privy Council, ed. N.H. Nicolas (6 vols, 1834-7).

Registrum Abbathiae Johannis Whethamstede Abbatis Monasterii Sancti Albani, ed. H.T. Riley, 2 vols, Rolls Series (1872).

The Reign of Henry VII from Contemporary Sources, ed. A.F. Pollard (3 vols, 1913).

Richard III: The Road to Bosworth Field, ed. P.W. Hammond and A.F. Sutton (1985).

Rymer, T., *Foedera et cujuscunque Acta Publica*, ed. J. Caley et al., 18 vols, Record Commission (1827).

Shakespeare, W., *The Complete Works*, ed. P. Ackroyd (2006).

Six Town Chronicles, ed. R. Flenley (1911).

'Some Ancient Indictments in the King's Bench referring to Kent', ed. R. Virgoe, *Kent Records: Documents Illustrative of Medieval Kentish Society* (Ashford, 1964).

Stonor Letters and Papers of the Fifteenth Century, ed. C.L. Kingsford, 2 vols, Camden 3rd ser., xxix, xxx (1919); *Camden Miscellany* xiii (1924).

Three Books of Polydore Vergil's English History, ed. H. Ellis, Camden Society xxix (1844).

Three Fifteenth-Century Chronicles, ed. J. Gairdner, Camden Society, new series xxviii (1880).

The Tudor Constitution, ed. G.R. Elton (Cambridge, 1962).

Tudor Royal Proclamations, ed. P.L. Hughes and J.F. Larkin, i (1964).

Visser-Fuchs, L., 'Edward IV's *Mémoire* on Paper to Charles Duke of Burgundy: The so-called "Short Version of *The Arrivall*"', *Nottingham Medieval Studies* xxxvi (1992).

Waurin, J. de, *Recueil des Croniques et anciennes istoires de la Grant Bretaigne*, ed. W. and E.L.C.P. Hardy, Rolls Series, v (1891).

York House Books 1461-90, ed. L.C. Attreed, 2 vols, Stroud (1991).

SECONDARY SOURCES

Allan, A., 'Yorkist Propaganda: Pedigree, Prophecy and the "British History" in the Reign of Edward IV', in *Patronage, Pedigree and Power in Later Medieval England*, ed. C.D. Ross (Gloucester, 1979).

Allmand, C.T., *Lancastrian Normandy 1415-50* (Oxford, 1983).

Anglo, Sydney, *Spectacle, Pageantry and Early Tudor Policy* (Oxford, 1969).

Antonovics, A.V., 'Henry VII, King of England, "By the Grace of Charles VIII of France"', in *Kings and Nobles in the Later Middle Ages*, ed. R.A. Griffiths and J.W. Sherborne (Gloucester, 1986).

Archer, R.E., *Crown, Government and People in the Fifteenth Century* (Stroud, 1995).

Armstrong, C.A.J., *England, France and Burgundy in the Fifteenth Century* (1983).

—— 'The Inauguration Ceremonies of the Yorkist Kings and their Title to the Throne', *Transactions of the Royal Historical Society*, 4th ser., v (1948); repr. in *England, France and Burgundy*.

—— 'Politics and the Battle of St Albans', *Bulletin of the Institute of Historical Research* xxxiii (1960), 1-72; repr. in *England, France and Burgundy*.

Arthurson, I., 'The Rising of 1497: A Revolt of the Peasantry?', *People, Politics & the Community*, ed. C. Richmond and J. Rosenthal (Gloucester, 1987).

—— *The Perkin Warbeck Conspiracy 1491-1499* (Stroud, 1994).

—— and N. Kingwell, 'The Proclamation of Henry Tudor as King of England, 3 November 1483', *Historical Research* lxiii (1990).

Bacon, F., *History of the Reign of King Henry the Seventh*, ed. J. Weinberger (Ithaca, NY, 1996).

Ballard, M. and C.S.L. Davies, 'Etienne Fryon: Burgundian Agent, English Royal Secretary, and "Principal Counsellor" to Perkin Warbeck', *Historical Research* lxii (1989).

Barnes, P.M., 'Chancery *Corpus cum causa* files', *Medieval Legal Records*, ed. R.F. Hunnisett and J. Post (1978).

Bellamy, J.G., *Bastard Feudalism and the Law* (1989).

—— 'The Coterel Gang: An Anatomy of a Band of Fourteenth-century Criminals', *English Historical Review* lxxix (1964).

—— *Criminal Law and Society in Late Medieval and Tudor England* (1984).

—— *The Law of Treason in England in the Later Middle Ages* (Cambridge, 1970).

Bennett, M., *The Battle of Bosworth* (Gloucester, 1985).

—— 'Edward III's Entail and the Succession to the Crown', *English Historical Review* cxiii (1998).

—— 'Henry IV, the Royal Succession and the Crisis of 1406', in *The Reign of Henry IV: Rebellion and Survival 1403–13*, ed. G. Dodd and D. Biggs (Woodbridge, 2008).

—— 'Henry VII and the Northern Rising of 1489', *English Historical Review* cv (1990).

—— *Lambert Simnel and the Battle of Stoke* (Gloucester, 1987).

Bernard, G.W., *War, Taxation and Rebellion in Early Tudor England: Henry VII, Wolsey and the Amicable Grant of 1525* (Brighton, 1986).

Bohna, M., 'Armed Force and Civic Legitimacy in Jack Cade's Revolt, 1450', *English Historical Review* cxviii (2003).

Bolton, J.L., 'The City and the Crown 1456–61', *London Journal* 12 (1986).

Britnell, R.H., 'The Economic Context', in *Wars of the Roses*, ed. A.J. Pollard (Basingstoke, 1995).

Brown, A.L., 'The Authorisation of Letters under the Great Seal', *BIHR* xxxvii (1964).

Buck, G., *History of King Richard III*, ed. A.N. Kincaid (Gloucester, 1979).

Bush, M., 'Tax Reform and Rebellion in Early Tudor England', *History* lxxvi (1991).

Calmette, J. and G. Périnelle, *Louis XI et l'Angleterre 1461–83* (Paris, 1930).

Carpenter, C., *Locality and Polity: A Study of Warwickshire Landed Society 1401–99* (Cambridge, 1992).

—— 'Sir Thomas Malory and Fifteenth-Century Local Politics', *Bulletin of the Institute of Historical Research* liii (1980).

—— *The Wars of the Roses: Politics and the Constitution in England, c. 1437–1509* (Cambridge, 1997).

Castor, H., *The King, the Crown and the Duchy of Lancaster: Public Authority and Private Power 1399–1461* (Oxford, 2000).

—— ' "Walter Blount was gone to serve traytours": The Sack of Elvaston and the Politics of the North Midlands in 1454', *Midland History* xix (1994).

Cherry, M., 'The Struggle for Power in Mid-Fifteenth-Century Devonshire', in *Patronage, The Crown and The Provinces in Later Medieval England*, ed. R.A. Griffiths (Gloucester, 1981).

Chrimes, S.B, *English Constitutional Ideas in the Fifteenth Century* (Cambridge, 1936).

—— 'The Fifteenth Century', *History* xxiv (1963).

—— *Henry VII* (London, 1970).

—— *Lancastrians, Yorkists and Henry VII* (1964).

—— C.D. Ross and R.A. Griffiths, eds, *Fifteenth-century England, 1399–1609: Politics and Society* (Manchester, 1972).

Clarke, P.D., 'English Royal Marriages and the Papal Penitentiary in the Fifteenth Century', *English Historical Review* cxx (2005).

Crawford, A., *The Yorkists: The History of a Dynasty* (2007).

Cunningham, S., *Henry VII* (2007).

—— 'Henry VII and Rebellion in North-Eastern England, 1485–92: Bonds of Allegiance and the Establishment of Tudor Authority', *Northern History* xxxii (1996).

—— 'Loyalty and the Usurper: Recognizances, the Council and Allegiance under Henry VII', in M.R. Horowitz, ed., *Who Was Henry VII? Historical Research*, lxxxii (2009).

Currin, J.M., 'Henry VII and the Treaty of Redon (1489): Plantagenet Ambitions and Early Tudor Foreign Policy', *History* lxxxi (1996).

—— 'Henry VII, France and the Holy League of Venice: the Diplomacy of Balance', in M.R. Horowitz, ed., *Who Was Henry VII? Historical Research* lxxxii (2009).

Davies, C.S.L., 'John Morton, the Holy See, and the Accession of Henry VII', *English Historical Review* (1987).

—— ' "The Tudors": A Challenge', *Times Literary Supplement*, 17 July 2009.

Delany, S., *Impolitic Bodies: Poetry, Saints and Society in Fifteenth-Century England. The Work of Osbern Bokenham* (Oxford, 1998).

Denton, W., *England in the Fifteenth Century* (1888).

Dickens, A.G., *The Courts of Europe* (1977).

Dockray, K., *Henry VI, Margaret of Anjou and the Wars of the Roses: A Sourcebook* (Stroud, 2000).

—— 'The Political Legacy of Richard III in Northern England', in *Kings and Nobles in the later Middle Ages*, ed. R.A. Griffiths and J.W. Sherborne (Gloucester, 1986).

—— *William Shakespeare, the Wars of the Roses and Historians* (Stroud, 2002).

—— 'The Yorkshire Rebellion of 1469', *Ricardian* 83 (1983).

Dodd, G., *Justice and Grace: Private Petitioning and the English Parliament in the Late Middle Ages* (Oxford, 2007).

Doig, J.A., 'Propaganda, Public Opinion and the Siege of Calais in 1436', in *Crown, Government and People in the Fifteenth Century*, ed. R.E. Archer (Gloucester, 1995).

Dunn, D., 'Margaret of Anjou, Queen Consort of Henry VI: A Reassessment of her Role, 1445–53', in *Crown, Government and People in the Fifteenth Century*, ed. R.E. Archer (Stroud, 1995).

—— 'The Queen at War: The Role of Margaret of Anjou in the Wars of the Roses', in *War and Society in Medieval and Early Modern Britain*, ed. D. Dunn (Liverpool, 2000).

Elton, G.R., *The Tudor Constitution* (Cambridge 1962).

Field, P.J.C., *The Life and Times of Sir Thomas Malory* (Woodbridge, 1993).

Fleming, P.W, 'The Lovelace Dispute: Concepts of Property and Inheritance in Fifteenth-century Kent', *Southern History* xii (1990).

Fleming, P. and M. Wood, *Gloucestershire's Forgotten Battle of Nibley Green 1470* (Stroud, 2003).

Fryde, E.B., 'Popular Revolt after 1381', *Agrarian History of England and Wales*, iii, 1348–1500, ed. E. Miller (Cambridge, 1991), 800.

Gairdner, J., *History of Richard III* (1878).

Gill, L., *Richard III and Buckingham's Rebellion* (Stroud, 1999).

Gillingham, J., *The Wars of the Roses: Peace and Conflict in Fifteenth-Century England* (1981).

Given-Wilson, C., 'Chronicles of the Mortimer Family, c.1250–1450', in *Family and Dynasty in Late Medieval England*, ed. R. Eales and S. Tyas (Donington, 2003).

Goodman, A., *A History of England from Edward II to James I* (Harlow, 1977)

—— *The Wars of the Roses* (1981).

—— and D.A.L. Morgan, 'The Yorkist Claim to the Throne of Castile', *Journal of Medieval History* xii (1985).

Griffiths, R.A., 'The Crown and the Royal Family in Later Medieval England', in *Kings and Nobles in the Later Middle Ages*, ed. R.A. Griffiths and J. Sherborne (Gloucester, 1986); repr. in *King & Country*.

—— 'Duke Richard of York's Intentions in 1450 and the Origins of the Wars of the Roses', *Journal of Medieval History* i (1975); repr. in *King & Country*.

—— 'Gruffydd ap Nicholas and the Fall of the House of Lancaster', *Welsh History Review* 11 (1965); repr. in *King & Country*, ch. 12.

—— 'The Hazards of Civil War: The Mountford Family and the Wars of the Roses', *Midland History* v (1980); repr. in *King & Country*.

—— *King and Country: England and Wales in the Fifteenth Century* (1991).

—— 'The King's Council and the First Protectorate of the Duke of York, 1453–1454', *English Historical Review* xcix (1984); repr. in *King & Country*.

—— 'Local Rivalries and National Politics: The Percies, the Nevilles, and the Duke of Exeter, 1452–55', *Speculum* xliii (1968); repr. in *King & Country*.

—— ed., *Patronage, The Crown and The Provinces in Later Medieval England* (Gloucester, 1981).

—— *The Reign of King Henry VI: The Exercise of Royal Authority 1422–61* (1981).

—— 'The Sense of Dynasty in the Reign of Henry VI', in *Patronage, Pedigree and Power in Later Medieval England*, ed. C.D. Ross (1979); repr. in *King & Country*.

—— 'William Wawe and his Gang, 1427', *Proceedings of the Hampshire Field Club and Archaeological Society* xxxiii (1976), 89–93.

—— and Sherborne, J., eds, *Kings and Nobles in the Later Middle Ages* (Gloucester, 1986).

—— and R.S. Thomas, *The Making of the Tudor Dynasty* (Gloucester, 1985).

Gross, A., *The Dissolution of the Lancastrian Kingship: Sir John Fortescue and the Crisis of Monarchy in Fifteenth-Century England* (Stamford, 1996).

Grummitt, D., *The Calais Garrison: War and Military Service in England, 1436–1558* (Woodbridge, 2008).

—— 'Deconstructing Cade's Rebellion: Discourse and Politics in the Mid Fifteenth Century', in *Identity and Insurgency in the Later Middle Ages*, ed. L. Clark, *The Fifteenth Century* vi (2006).

—— 'Household, Politics and Political Morality in the Reign of Henry VII', in M.R. Horowitz, ed., *Who Was Henry VII? Historical Research* lxxxii (2009).

Habington, W., *Edward the Fourth* (1640).

Hammond, P.W., ed., *Richard III: Loyalty, Lordship and Law* (1986).

Hanham, A., *Richard III and his Earlier Historians 1483–1535* (Oxford, 1975).

Hare, J.N., 'The Wiltshire Risings of 1450: Political and Economic Discontent in Fifteenth-Century England', *Southern History* iv (1982).

Harrison, C.J., 'The Petition of Edmund Dudley', *English Historical Review* lxxxvii (1972).

Harriss, G.L., *Cardinal Beaufort: A Study of Lancastrian Ascendancy and Decline* (Oxford, 1988).

—— 'Marmaduke Lumley and the Exchequer Crisis of 1446–9', in *Aspects of Late Medieval Government and Society*, ed. J.G. Rowe (Buffalo, Canada, 1986).

—— 'Richard Duke of York and the Royal Household', in *Soldiers, Nobles and Gentlemen*, ed. P. Coss and C. Tyerman (Woodbridge, 2009).

—— *Shaping the Nation: England 1360–1461* (Oxford, 2005).

—— 'The Struggle for Calais: An Aspect of the Rivalry between Lancaster and York', *English Historical Review* lxxv (1960).

Harvey, I.M.W., *Jack Cade's Rebellion of 1450* (Oxford, 1991).

Hatcher, J., 'The Great Slump of the Mid-Fifteenth Century', in *Progress and Problems in Medieval England*, ed. J. Hatcher and R. Britnell (Cambridge, 1996).

Herbert, A., 'Herefordshire, 1413–61: Some Aspects of Society and Public Order', in *Patronage, The Crown and The Provinces in Later Medieval England*, ed. R.A. Griffiths (Gloucester 1981).

Hicks, M.A., 'The 1468 Statute of Livery', *Historical Research* lxiv (1991).

—— *Anne Neville, Queen to Richard III* (Stroud, 2006).

—— 'Attainder, Resumption and Coercion 1461–1529', *Parliamentary History* iii (1984); repr. in *Richard III and his Rivals*.

—— *Bastard Feudalism* (Harlow, 1995).

—— 'Between Majorities: The "Beauchamp Interregnum" 1439–49', *Historical Research* lxxii (1999).

—— 'The Case of Sir Thomas Cook, 1468', *English Historical Review* xc (1978) repr. in *Richard III and his Rivals*.

—— 'The Changing Role of the Wydevilles in Yorkist Politics to 1483', in *Patronage, Pedigree and Power*, ed. Ross (1979); repr. in *Richard III and his Rivals*.

—— 'Counting the Costs of War: The Moleyns Ransom and the Hungerford Land-Sales 1453–87', *Southern History* viii (1986); repr. in *Richard III and his Rivals*.

—— 'Descent, Partition and Extinction: The "Warwick Inheritance"', *Bulletin of the Institute of Historical Research* lii (1979); repr. in *Richard III and his Rivals*.

—— 'Dynastic Change and Northern Society: The Fourth Earl of Northumberland, 1470–89', *Northern History* xiv (1978); repr. in *Richard III and his Rivals*.

—— *Edward IV* (2004).

—— 'Edward IV's *Brief Treatise* and the Treaty of Picquigny of 1475', *Historical Research* lxxiii (2010).

—— 'Edward IV, the Duke of Somerset, and Lancastrian Loyalism in the North', *Northern History* xx (1984); repr. in *Richard III and his Rivals*.

—— *Edward V: The Prince in the Tower* (Stroud, 2003).

—— *English Political Culture in the Fifteenth Century* (2002).

—— *False, Fleeting, Perjur'd Clarence: George Duke of Clarence 1449–78* (Gloucester, 1980).

—— 'From Megaphone to Microscope: The Correspondence of Richard Duke of York with Henry VI in 1450 Revisited', *Journal of Medieval History* xxv (1999).

—— 'Henry IV's Yorkshire Perjuries of 1399 Revisited', *Northern History* (2009).

—— 'Idealism in Late Medieval English Politics', in *Richard III and his Rivals*.

—— 'Lawmakers and Lawbreakers', in *An Illustrated History of Late Medieval England*, ed. C. Given-Wilson (Manchester, 1996).

—— 'A Minute of the Lancastrian Council at York, 20 January 1461', *Northern History* xxx (1999).

—— 'Out of Session: Edward Guildford of Halden, Justice of the Peace for Kent, 1436–43', *Southern History* 28 (2006).

—— 'Piety and Lineage in the Wars of the Roses: The Hungerford Experience', in *Kings and Nobles in the Later Middle Ages*, ed. R.A. Griffiths and J. Sherborne (1986); repr. *Richard III and his Rivals*.

—— 'Propaganda and the Battle of St Albans, 1455', *Nottingham Medieval Studies* xliv (2000).

—— 'Richard Lord Latimer, Richard III, and the Warwick Inheritance', *Ricardian* 154 (2001).

—— *Richard III* (2000).

—— *Richard III and his Rivals: Magnates and their Motives during the Wars of the Roses* (1991).

—— 'Richard III, the Great Landowners and the Results of the Wars of the Roses', in *Tant D'Emprises – So Many Undertakings*, ed. L. Visser-Fuchs (2003).

—— 'A Study of Failure: The Minority of Edward V', in *Royal Minorities of Medieval and Early Medieval England*, ed. C. Beem (Basingstoke, 2008).

—— *The Wars of the Roses 1455–85*, Essential Histories (Oxford, 2003).

—— *Warwick the Kingmaker* (Oxford, 1998).

—— 'The Yorkshire Rebellion of 1489 Reconsidered', *Northern History* xxii (1986); repr. in *Richard III and his Rivals*.

Holand, P., 'Cook's Case in History and Myth', *Historical Research* lxi (1988).

—— 'The Lincolnshire Rebellion of March 1470', *English Historical Review* ciii (1988).

Horowitz, M.R., 'Henry Tudor's Treasure' in Horowitz, *Who Was Henry VII?* (2009).

—— 'Richard Empson, Minister of Henry VII', *BIHR* lv (1982).

—— ed., *Who Was Henry VII?*, *Historical Research* lxxxii (2009).

Horrox, R.E., 'Henry Tudor's Letters to England during Richard's Reign', *Ricardian* 80 (1983).

—— *Richard III: A Study of Service* (Cambridge, 1989).

Hoyle, R.W., 'Petitioning as Popular Politics in Early Sixteenth-Century England', *Historical Research* lxxv (2002).

Hughes, J., *Arthurian Myths and Alchemy: The Kingship of Edward IV* (Stroud, 2002).

Hume, D., *The History of England from the Invasion of Julius Caesar to the Revolution in 1688* (Indianapolis, IN, 1983).

James, M.E., 'The Concept of Order and the Northern Rising, 1569', *Past and Present* 60 (1973); repr. in James, *Culture, Politics and Society*.

—— *Culture, Politics and Society: Studies in Early Modern England* (Cambridge, 1986).

—— 'English Politics and the Concept of Honour, 1485–1642' (*Past & Present*, Supplement, 3, 1978); repr. in *Culture, Politics and Society* (Cambridge, 1986).

Johnson, P.A., *Duke Richard of York 1411–1460* (Oxford, 1986).

Jones, M.K., *Bosworth 1485: Psychology of a Battle* (Stroud, 2002).

——'John Beaufort, Duke of Somerset and the French Expedition of 1443', in *Patronage, the Crown and the Provinces in Later Medieval England*, ed. R.A. Griffiths (Gloucester, 1981).

—— 'Richard III and Lady Margaret Beaufort: A Re-assessment', in P.W. Hammond, ed., *Richard III: Loyalty, Lordship and Law* (1986).

—— 'Somerset, York and the Wars of the Roses', *English Historical Review* civ (1989).

—— and M.G. Underwood, *The King's Mother: Lady Margaret Beaufort, Countess of Richmond and Derby* (Cambridge, 1992).

Jurkowski, M., C.L. Smith and D. Crook, eds, *Lay Taxes in England and Wales 1188–1688* (1998).

Keen, M.H., and M.J. Daniel, 'English Diplomacy and the Sack of Fougères in 1449', *History* lix (1974).

Kekewich, M., 'The Attainder of the Yorkists in 1459: Two Contemporary Accounts', *Bulletin of the Institute of Historical Research* lv (1982).

—— 'The Lancastrian Court in Exile', in *The Lancastrian Court*, ed. J. Stratford, *Harlaxton Medieval Studies* xiii (Donington, 2003).

—— 'The Mysterious Dr Makerell: His General Pardon of 27 November 1469', in *Much Heaving and Shoving*, ed. M. Aston and R. Horrox (Lavenham, 2005).

—— ' "Though shalt be under the power of man": Sir John Fortescue and the Yorkist Succession', *Nottingham Medieval Studies* xlii (1998).

Kendall, P.M., *Richard III* (1955).

Kingsford, C.L., *English Historical Literature of the Fifteenth Century* (1913).

Kirby, J.L., 'The Issues of the Lancastrian Exchequer and Lord Cromwell's Estimates of 1433', *Bulletin of the Institute of Historical Research* xxiv (1951).

Kleineke, H., *Edward IV* (2009).

—— 'Gerard von Wesel's Newsletter from England, 17 April 1471', *Ricardian* xvi (2006).

—— 'Why the West was Wild: Law and Disorder in Fifteenth-Century Cornwall and Devon', in *Authority and Subversion*, ed. L. Clark, *The Fifteenth Century* iii (2003).

Kleyn, Diana, *Richard of England* (1990).

Lander, J.R., 'Attainder and Forfeiture 1453–1509', *Historical Journal* iv (1961); repr. in *Crown and Nobility*.

—— 'Bonds, Coercion and Fear: Henry VII and the Peerage', in *Florilegium Historiale*, ed. J.G. Rowe and W.H. Stockdale (Toronto, 1971); repr. in *Crown*.

—— *Conflict and Stability in Fifteenth-Century England* (1969).

—— *Crown and Nobility 1450–1509* (1976).

—— *Government and Community: England 1450–1509* (1980).

—— 'Henry VI and the Duke of York's Second Protectorate, 1455–6', *Bulletin of John Rylands Library* xliii (1960); repr. in *Crown*.

—— 'Marriage and Politics in the Fifteenth Century: The Nevilles and the Wydevilles', *Bulletin of the Institute of Historical Research* xxxvi (1963), 120–2; repr. in *Crown*.

—— *Wars of the Roses* (1965).

Laynesmith, J.L., *The Last Medieval Queens* (Oxford, 2004).

Levine, M., *Tudor Dynastic Problems 1460–1571* (1973).

Levy, F.J., *Tudor Historical Thought* (San Marino, CA, 1967).

Lovatt, R., 'A Collector of Apocryphal Anecdotes: John Blacman Revisited', in *Property and Politics*, ed. A.J. Pollard (Gloucester, 1984).

Luckett, D., 'The Thames Valley Conspiracies against Henry VII', *Historical Research* lxviii (1995).

McFarlane, K.B., *England in the Fifteenth Century* (1981).

—— 'The Lancastrian Kings', *Cambridge Medieval History*, viii (1936).

—— *The Nobility of Later Medieval England* (Oxford, 1973).

—— 'The Wars of the Roses', *England in the Fifteenth Century* (1981).

Maddern, P., *Violence and the Social Order: East Anglia 1422–1442* (Oxford, 1992).

Mate, M., 'The Economic and Social Roots of Medieval Popular Rebellion: Sussex in 1450–1451', *Economic History Review*, 2nd ser., xlv (1992).

Maurer, H. E., *Margaret of Anjou: Queenship and Power in Late Medieval England* (Woodbridge, 2003).

Moreton, C., 'A Local Dispute and the Politics of 1483: Roger Townshend, Earl Rivers and the Duke of Gloucester', *Ricardian* 107 (1989).

Morgan, D.A.L., 'The King's Affinity in the Polity of Yorkist England', *Transactions of the Royal Historical Society*, 5th ser. xxiii (1973).

Morgan, P., 'Those were the days: A Yorkist Pedigree Roll', in *Estrangement, Enterprise and Education in Fifteenth-Century England*, ed. S. Michalove and A. Compton Reeves (Stroud, 1998).

Mortimer, I., 'Richard II and the Succession to the Crown', *History* xci (2006).

Nall, C., 'Perceptions of Financial Mismanagement and the English Diagnosis of Defeat', *Conflict, Consequences and the Crown in the Later Middle Ages*, ed. L. Clark, *Fifteenth Century England* vii (Woodbridge, 2007).

Nightingale, P., 'England and the European Depression of the Mid-Fifteenth Century', *Journal of European Economic History* xxvi (1997).

Payling, S.J., 'The Ampthill Dispute: A Study in Aristocratic Lawlessness and the Breakdown of Lancastrian Government', *English Historical Review* civ (1989).

—— 'The Coventry Parliament of 1459: A Privy Seal Writ Concerning the Election of Knights of the Shire', *Historical Research* lx (1987).

Pollard, A.J., *Late Medieval England 1399–1509* (Harlow, 2000).

—— 'Lord FitzHugh's Rising in 1470', *Bulletin of the Institute of Historical Research* lii (1979).

—— *North-Eastern England during the Wars of the Roses: Lay Society, War and Politics 1450–1500* (Oxford, 1990).

—— ed., *Property and Politics: Essays in Later Medieval English History* (Gloucester, 1984).

—— *Richard III and the Princes in the Tower* (Stroud, 1991).

—— 'The Richmondshire Community of Gentry during the Wars of the Roses', in *Patronage, Pedigree and Power in Later Medieval England*, ed. C. Ross (Gloucester, 1979); repr. in Pollard, *Worlds*.

—— 'St Cuthbert and the Hog: Richard III and the County Palatine of Durham, 1471–85', in *Kings and Nobles in the Later Middle Ages*, ed. R.A. Griffiths, and J. Sherborne (Gloucester, 1986); repr. in Pollard, *Worlds*.

—— 'The Tyranny of Richard III', *Journal of Medieval History* 3 (1977); repr. in Pollard, *Worlds*.

—— *The Wars of the Roses* (Basingstoke, 2001).

—— ed., *The Wars of the Roses* (Basingstoke, 1995).

—— *Warwick the Kingmaker: Politics, Power and Fame* (2007).

—— *The Worlds of Richard III* (Stroud, 2001).

Potter, J., *Good King Richard?* (1985).

Powell, E., *Kingship, Law and Society: Criminal Justice in the Reign of Henry V* (Oxford, 1989).

Pugh, T.B., 'The Estates, Finances and Regal Aspirations of Richard Plantagenet (1411–60), Duke of York', in *Revolution and Consumption in Late Medieval England*, ed. M.A. Hicks (Woodbridge, 2001).

—— 'Henry VII and the Tudor Nobility', in *The Tudor Nobility*, ed. G.W. Bernard (Manchester, 1992).

—— 'The Magnates, Knights and Gentry', in *Fifteenth-Century England*, ed. S.B. Chrimes, C.D. Ross and R.A. Griffiths (Manchester, 1972).

—— 'Richard, Duke of York and the Rebellion of Henry Holand, Duke of Exeter, in May 1454', *Historical Research* lxiii (1990).

—— 'Richard Plantagenet (1411–60), Duke of York, as the King's Lieutenant in France and Ireland', in *Aspects of Late Medieval Government and Society*, ed. J.G. Rowe (Buffalo, Canada, 1986).

Radulescu, R., 'Yorkist Propaganda and the Chronicle from Rollo to Edward IV', *Studies in Philology* 100 (2003).

Ramsay, J.H., *Lancaster and York*, 2 vols (Oxford, 1892).

—— *Tudor Economic, Problems* (1962).

Rawcliffe, C., 'Richard, Duke of York, the King's "Obeisant Liegeman": A New Source on the Protectorates of 1454 and 1455', *Historical Research* lx (1987).

Richmond, C.F., '1485 And All That, or What Was Going On at the Battle of Bosworth?' in *Richard III: Loyalty, Lordship and Law*, ed. P.W. Hammond (1986).

—— 'The Earl of Warwick's Domination of the Channel and the Naval Dimension to the Wars of the Roses 1456–60', *Southern History* 20/21 (1998–9).

—— 'Fauconberg's Kentish Rising of May 1471', *English Historical Review* lxxxxv (1970).

—— 'Identity and Morality: Power and Politics during the Wars of the Roses', in *Power and Identity in the Middle Ages*, ed. H. Pryce and J. Watts (Oxford, 2007).

—— 'The Nobility and the Wars of the Roses 1459–61', *Nottingham Medieval Studies* xxi (1977).

—— *The Paston Family in the Fifteenth Century: The First Phase* (Cambridge, 1990).

Riddy, F., 'John Hardyng's Chronicle and the Wars of the Roses', *Arthurian Literature* 12 (1993).

Rosenthal, J.T., 'Other Victims: Peeresses as War Widows 1450–1500', *History* lxxii (1987).

Rosenthal, J., and C. Richmond, eds, *People, Politics and the Community in the Later Middle Ages* (Gloucester, 1987).

Roskell, J.S., 'John Lord Wenlock of Someries', *Publications of the Bedfordshire Historical Record Society* xxxviii (1958), 12–48; repr. Roskell, *Parliament and Politics in Late Medieval England*.

—— 'The Office and Dignity of the Protector of England', *English Historical Review* lviii (1953); repr. in Roskell, *Parliament and Politics*, i.

—— *Parliament and Politics in Late Medieval England*, 3 vols (1981–3).

—— 'Sir William Oldhall', *Nottingham Medieval Studies* v (1961), 87–112; repr. Roskell, J.S., *Parliament and Politics in Late Medieval England*, ii (London, 1981).

Ross, C.D., *Edward IV* (1974).

—— ed., *Patronage, Pedigree and Power in Later Medieval England* (Gloucester, 1979).

—— 'The Reign of Edward IV', in *Fifteenth-century England 1399–1509*, ed. S.B. Chrimes, C.D. Ross and R.A. Griffiths (Manchester, 1972).

—— *Richard III* (1981).

—— 'Rumour, Propaganda and Popular Opinion in the Wars of the Roses', *Patronage, The Crown and The Provinces in Later Medieval England*, ed. R.A. Griffiths (1979).

—— *The Wars of the Roses: A Concise History* (1976).

Scofield, C.L., *Life and Reign of King Edward the Fourth*, 2 vols (1923).

Sellar, W.C., and Yeatman, R.J., *1066 and All That* (1930).

Sharpe, K., *Selling the Tudor Monarchy: Authority and Image in Sixteenth-Century England* (2009).

Sinclair, A., 'The Great Berkeley Lawsuit Revisited 1417–39', *Southern History* 9 (1987).

Slack, P., ed., *Rebellion, Protest and the Social Order in Early Modern England* (Cambridge, 1984).

Somerville, R., *History of the Duchy of Lancaster*, 2 vols (1953–70).

Stone, L., *The Causes of the English Revolution 1529–1642* (1972).

Stones, E.L.G., 'The Folvilles of Ashby-Folville, Leicestershire and their Associates in Crime, 1326–47', *Transactions of the Royal Historical Society*, 5th ser., 7 (1957).

Storey, R.L., *The End of the House of Lancaster* (1966).

—— 'Lincolnshire in the Wars of the Roses', *Nottingham Medieval Studies* xiv (1970).

Stubbs, W., *Constitutional History of England in the Middle Ages*, 3 vols (Oxford, 1872–8).

Sutton, A.F., ' "A Curious Searcher for our Weal Public": Richard III, Piety, Chivalry and the Concept of the "Good Prince" ', in *Richard III: Loyalty, Lordship and Law*, ed. P.W. Hammond (Gloucester, 1986).

Thompson, B., ed., *The Reign of Henry VII* (Stamford, 1995).

Thomson, J.A.F., *Transformation of Medieval England 1370–1529* (Harlow, 1983).

Tillyard, E.M.W., *The Elizabethan World Picture* (Harmondsworth, 1966).

Tuck, J.A., 'Richard II's System of Patronage', in *The Reign of Richard II*, ed. F.R.H. Du Bouley and C.M. Barron (1971).

Virgoe, R., 'The Death of William de la Pole, Duke of Suffolk'; repr. in *East Anglian Society*.

—— *East Anglian Society and the Political Community of Late Medieval England*, ed. C. Barron, C. Rawcliffe and J.T. Rosenthal (Norwich, 1997).

—— 'Inheritance and Litigation in the Fifteenth Century: The Buckenham Disputes', *Journal of Legal History* 15 (1994); repr. in *East Anglian Society*.

—— 'The Parliamentary Subsidy of 1450', *Bulletin of the Institute of Historical Research* lv (1982).

—— 'The Recovery of the Howards in East Anglia, 1485 to 1529', in *Wealth and Power in Tudor England*, ed. E.W. Ives, R.J. Knecht and J.J. Scarisbrick (1978); repr. in *East Anglian Society*.

—— 'William Tailboys and Lord Cromwell: Crime and Politics in Lancastrian England', *Bulletin of the John Rylands Library* lv (1973), 459–82; repr. in *East Anglian Society*.

Watts, J.L., '*De Consulatu Stilicho*: Texts and Politics in the Reign of Henry VI', *Journal of Medieval History* xvi (1990).

—— *Henry VI and the Politics of Kingship* (Cambridge, 1996).

—— 'The Pressure of the Public in Late Medieval Politics', in *Political Culture in Late Medieval Britain*, ed. L. Clark and C. Carpenter (Woodbridge, 2004).

—— 'When Did Henry VI's Minority End?', in *Trade, Devotion and Governance: Papers in Later Medieval History*, ed. D.J. Clayton, R.G. Davies and P. McNiven (Stroud, 1994).

Wedgwood, J., *History of Parliament 1439–1509*, 2 vols (1936–8).

Weightman, C., *Margaret of York, Duchess of Burgundy 1446–1503* (Gloucester, 1989).

Williams, C.H., 'The Rebellion of Humphrey Stafford in 1486', *English Historical Review* xliii (1928).

—— 'The Yorkist Kings', *Cambridge Medieval History* viii (Cambridge, 1936).

Wolffe, B.P., 'Acts of Resumption in the Lancastrian Parliaments, 1399–1456', *English Historical Review* lxxiii (1958).

—— *Henry VI* (1981).

—— 'The Personal Rule of Henry VI', in *Fifteenth-century England, 1399–1509*, ed. S.B. Chrimes, C.D. Ross and R.A. Griffiths (Manchester, 1972).

—— *The Royal Demesne in English History* (1971).

Wroe, A., *Perkin: A Story of Deception* (2003).

Youngs, D., *Humphrey Newton 1466–1536* (Woodbridge, 2008).

INDEX